W9-BZU-554

Greg Perry
Dean Miller

Sams **Teach Yourself**

Beginning Programming

in **24 Hours**

Third Edition

SAMS 800 East 96th Street, Indianapolis, Indiana, 46240 USA

MAI 855 7250

Sams Teach Yourself Beginning Programming in 24 Hours, Third Edition

ISBN-10: 0-672-33700-2

ISBN-13: 978-0-672-33700-0

Library of Congress Catalog Card Number: 2013951919

Printed in the United States of America

First Printing: December 2013

Trademarks

All terms mentioned in this book that are known to be trademarks or service marks have been appropriately capitalized. Sams Publishing cannot attest to the accuracy of this information. Use of a term in this book should not be regarded as affecting the validity of any trademark or service mark.

Warning and Disclaimer

Every effort has been made to make this book as complete and as accurate as possible, but no warranty or fitness is implied. The information provided is on an "as is" basis. The authors and the publisher shall have neither liability nor responsibility to any person or entity with respect to any loss or damages arising from the information contained in this book.

Special Sales

For information about buying this title in bulk quantities, or for special sales opportunities (which may include electronic versions; custom cover designs; and content particular to your business, training goals, marketing focus, or branding interests), please contact our corporate sales department at corpsales@pearsoned.com or (800) 382-3419.

For government sales inquiries, please contact governmentsales@pearsoned.com.

For questions about sales outside the U.S., please contact international@pearsoned.com.

Acquisitions Editor
Mark Taber

Managing Editor
Kristy Hart

Project Editor
Elaine Wiley

Indexer
Brad Herriman

Proofreader
Anne Goebel

Technical Editor
Siddhartha Singh

Publishing Coordinator
Vanessa Evans

Cover Designer
Mark Shirar

Compositor
Nonie Ratcliff

Contents at a Glance

Table of Contents

Part II: Programming Fundamentals

About the Authors

Greg Perry is a speaker and writer in both the programming and applications sides of computing. He is known for bringing programming topics down to the beginner's level. Perry has been a programmer and trainer for two decades. He received his first degree in computer science and then earned a Master's degree in corporate finance. Besides writing, he consults and lectures across the country, including at the acclaimed Software Development programming conferences. Perry is the author of more than 75 other computer books. In his spare time, he gives lectures on traveling in Italy, his second-favorite place to be.

Dean Miller is a writer and editor with more than 20 years of experience in both the publishing and licensed consumer products businesses. Over the years, he has created or helped shape a number of bestselling books and series, including *Sams Teach Yourself in 21 Days*, *Sams Teach Yourself in 24 Hours*, and the *Unleashed* series, all from Sams Publishing. He has written books on C programming and professional wrestling, and is still looking for a way to combine the two into one strange amalgam.

Dedication

*To my wife and best friend, Fran Hatton, who's always supported
my dreams and was an incredible rock during the most
challenging year of my professional career.*
—Dean

Acknowledgments

Greg: My thanks go to all my friends at Pearson. Most writers would refer to them as editors; to me, they are friends. I want all my readers to understand this: The people at Pearson care about you most of all. The things they do result from their concern for your knowledge and enjoyment. On a more personal note, my beautiful bride, Jayne; my mother Bettye Perry; and my friends, who wonder how I find the time to write, all deserve credit for supporting my need to write.

Dean: Thanks to Mark Taber for considering me for this project. I started my professional life in computer book publishing, and it is so gratifying to return after a 10-year hiatus. I'd like to thank Greg Perry for creating outstanding first and second editions upon which this version of the book is based. It was an honor working with him as his editor for the first two editions and a greater honor to co-author this edition. I can only hope I did it justice. I appreciate the amazing work the editorial team of Elaine Wiley, Anne Goebel, and the production team at Pearson put into this book. On a personal level, I have to thank my three children, John, Alice, and Maggie and my wife Fran for their unending patience and support.

We Want to Hear from You!

As the reader of this book, you are our most important critic and commentator. We value your opinion and want to know what we're doing right, what we could do better, what areas you'd like to see us publish in, and any other words of wisdom you're willing to pass our way.

You can email or write to let us know what you did or didn't like about this book—as well as what we can do to make our books stronger.

Please note that we cannot help you with technical problems related to the topic of this book, and that due to the high volume of mail we receive, we might not be able to reply to every message.

When you write, please be sure to include this book's title, edition number, and authors, as well as your name and contact information.

Email: feedback@samspublishing.com

Mail: Sams Publishing
         ATTN: Reader Feedback
         800 E. 96th Street
         Indianapolis, IN 46240
         USA

Reader Services

Visit our website and register this book at **informit.com/register** for convenient access to any updates, downloads, or errata that might be available for this book.

Introduction

Learning how to program computers is easier than you might think. If you approach computers with hesitation, if you cannot even spell *PC*, if you have tried your best to avoid the subject altogether but can do so no longer, the book you now hold contains support that you can depend on in troubled computing times.

This 24-hour tutorial does more than explain programming. This tutorial does more than describe the difference between JavaScript, C++, and Java. This tutorial does more than teach you what programming is all about. This tutorial is a *training tool* that you can use to develop proper programming skills. The aim of this text is to introduce you to programming using professionally recognized principles, while keeping things simple at the same time. It is not this text's singular goal to teach you a programming language (although you will be writing programs before you finish it). This text's goal is to give you the foundation to become the best programmer you can be.

These 24 one-hour lessons delve into proper program design principles. You'll not only learn how to program, but also how to *prepare* for programming. This tutorial also teaches you how companies program and explains what you have to do to become a needed resource in a programming position. You'll learn about various programming job titles and what to expect if you want to write programs for others. You'll explore many issues related to online computing and learn how to address the needs of the online programming community.

Who Should Use This Book?

The title of this book says it all. If you have never programmed a computer, if you don't even like them at all, or if updating the operating system of your phone throws you into fits, take three sighs of relief! This text was written for *you* so that, within 24 hours, you will understand the nature of computer programs and you will have written programs.

This book is aimed at three different groups of people:

> ▶ Individuals who know nothing about programming but who want to know what programming is all about.

▶ Companies that want to train nonprogramming computer users for programming careers.

▶ Schools—both for introductory language classes and for systems analysis and design classes—that want to promote good coding design and style and that want to offer an overview of the life of a programmer.

Readers who seem tired of the plethora of quick-fix computer titles cluttering today's shelves will find a welcome reprieve here. The book you now hold talks to newcomers about programming without talking down to them.

What This Book Will Do for You

In the next 24 hours, you will learn something about almost every aspect of programming. The following topics are discussed in depth throughout this 24-hour tutorial:

▶ The hardware and software related to programming

▶ The history of programming

▶ Programming languages

▶ The business of programming

▶ Programming jobs

▶ Program design

▶ Internet programming

▶ The future of programming

Can This Book Really Teach Programming in 24 Hours?

In a word, yes. You can master each chapter in one hour or less. (By the way, chapters are referred to as "hours" or "lessons" in the rest of this book.) The material is balanced with mountains of shortcuts and methods that will make your hours productive and hone your programming skills more and more with each hour. Although some chapters are longer than others, many of the shorter chapters cover more detailed or more difficult issues than the shorter ones. A true attempt was made to make each hour learnable in an hour. Exercises at the end of each hour will provide feedback about the skills you learned.

Conventions Used in This Book

This book uses several common conventions to help teach programming topics. Here is a summary of those typographical conventions:

- ▶ Commands and computer output appear in a special `monospaced` computer font. Sometimes a line of code will be too long to fit on one line in this book. The code continuation symbol (➡) indicates that the line continues.

- ▶ Words you type also appear in the `monospaced` computer font.

- ▶ If a task requires you to select from a menu, the book separates menu commands with a comma. Therefore, this book uses File, Save As to select the Save As option from the File menu.

In addition to typographical conventions, the following special elements are included to set off different types of information to make it easily recognizable.

TRY IT YOURSELF ▼

The best way to learn how to program is to jump right in and start programming. These Try it Yourself sections will teach you a simple concept or method to accomplish a goal programmatically. The listing will be easy to follow and then the programs' output will be displayed along with coverage of key points in the program. To really get some practice, try altering bits of the code in each of these sections in order to see what your tweaks accomplish.

NOTE

Special notes augment the material you read in each hour. These notes clarify concepts and procedures.

TIP

You'll find numerous tips that offer shortcuts and solutions to common problems.

CAUTION

The cautions warn you about pitfalls. Reading them will save you time and trouble.

Hands-On Programming

You have this book because you want to go farther than the typical computer user. You don't just want to use computers; you want to write programs for them. You want the skills necessary to make computers do exactly what you want.

This 24-hour tutorial shows that you don't have to be a wizard to become a proficient (or even an expert) programmer. By the time you finish this one-hour lesson, you will have entered your first computer program, run it, and looked at the results. This chapter springboards you into programming so you can get a feel for programming right away. Once you've had this hands-on experience, subsequent hours will explain more of the background you need to understand how to design and write programs.

The highlights of this hour include:

► Learning what a program does

► Understanding the truth behind common programming myths

► Mastering source code concepts

► Entering and running your first program

Get Ready to Program

You'll find this hour divided into these two areas:

► An introduction to the nature of programming

► A hands-on practice with your first programming language

Most new programmers want to start programming right away. Yet, some background is necessary as well. This hour attempts to take care of both demands by offering an introductory background look at programming and then quickly jumping head-first into hands-on programming. If you went straight into a new programming language with absolutely no background first, you might miss the entire point of programming in the first place. So, the next few pages bring all readers up to a level playing field so that everyone who takes this 24-hour course can begin to write programs right away.

What a Computer Program Does

Most people today have some understanding of a computer's purpose. For example, a computer can help people balance their books or track their inventory. If you want to begin programming, chances are you have probably been using a computer for some time. Nevertheless, as a future programmer, you should review some fundamental computing concepts before mastering the ins and outs of a new computer language.

At its simplest level, a computer *processes data*. Figure 1.1 shows this as the primary goal of all computer programs. Many businesses call their computer programming departments *data processing departments* because computers process data into meaningful information. You may not have considered the difference between the words *data* and *information* before, but there is a tremendous difference to a computer professional. Raw data consists of facts and figures, such as hundreds of days of stock prices. A program might process that data into meaningful information, such as a line chart that shows the overall trend of the stock prices over time. It is the computer *program* that tells the computer what to do. Sometimes, a program might simply process data from another program without showing any output for the user. The processed data is still information because the program's output, stored on the disk, is changed in some way. For example, a program that closes monthly account balances may collect data from various accounting systems in a company and combine, balance, and close that data, resetting the data for the following month.

FIGURE 1.1
Programs convert raw data into meaningful information.

A *program* is a list of detailed instructions that the computer carries out. The program is the driving force behind any job that a computer does. The computer cannot do anything without a program. It is the job of the programmer to design and write programs that direct the computer to take raw data and transform that data into meaningful information for the end-user. The *end-user* (usually just called the *user*) of the computer is generally the nontechnical, nonprogramming person who needs the results (the information) that the program provides.

You, as the programmer, are responsible for guiding the computer with the programs you write. Learning to program computers takes a while, but it is certainly rewarding. Computer programming offers the advantage of instant feedback, unlike a lot of other jobs you can train for.

Common Programming Misconceptions

This text aims directly at the heart of the matter: Computers are easy to use and easy to program. A computer is nothing more than a dumb machine that "knows" absolutely nothing. You must supply the program that tells the computer what to do. A computer is like a robot that waits on your every command and acts out your instructions exactly as you give them. Sometimes your program instructions are incorrect. If they are, the computer goes right ahead and attempts them anyway.

CAUTION

Don't fear computer programming. Computers are tools to help you get your job done. You can learn to program.

Many misconceptions about computers exist and stem from a lack of understanding about how computers work and what computers are physically capable of doing. This book wants to shoot down the myths and improve your understanding of these machines. You'll be programming computers in no time. The computer is nothing more than a tool that helps you do certain types of work. The computer itself is not bad or good. A hammer is a tool you can use for good (to build houses) or for bad (to break things). A computer in the wrong hands can be used for bad purposes, but that isn't the computer's fault any more than it is the hammer's fault if someone misuses it.

The next three sections attack the three most popular computer myths. Have you heard any of them? Did you think some were true?

Myth 1: Only Math Experts Can Program Computers

Thank goodness this is a myth and not reality—thousands of people would be out of work (including most computer book authors!). Computers would be elitist machines used by only the best engineers and scientists; the casual user could not master them. Computers would still be beneficial in some areas but they would not provide the benefits that so many people can enjoy.

Not only can you be poor at math—you don't even have to like math or have the desire to learn math to be a good computer programmer. The computer does all the math for you; that's one of its jobs. There are countless expert computer programmers in the world who cannot tell you the area of a circle or the square root of 64. Relax if you thought this myth was reality.

Programming can provide beneficial side effects. It turns out that, as you become a better programmer, you may find your math skills improving. Developing programming skills tends to improve your overall capability for logical thinking, which underlies many skills in math as well. Therefore, being better in math might be a result of programming but it's not a prerequisite.

TIP

People who favor logic puzzles, crosswords, anagrams, and word-search games seem to adapt well to programming, but again, liking these gaming activities is not a programming prerequisite. You will find that you can learn to program computers, and actually become extremely good at it, without liking math, being good at math, or having any flair at all for puzzles or word games.

Myth 2: Computers Make Mistakes

You might have heard the adage, "To err is human, but to *really* foul things up takes a computer!" This might be accurate, but only in that a computer is so very fast that it duplicates a person's mistakes rapidly.

Computers do not make mistakes—people make mistakes. If you have heard a bank teller tell you that $24 was incorrectly deleted from your savings account because "the computer program made an error," the teller probably has no idea what really happened. People program computers, people run them, and people enter the data that the computer processes.

The odds of a computer randomly fouling up a customer's bank balance are minute. Computers simply do not make random mistakes unless they are programmed incorrectly. Computers are finite machines; when given the same input, they always produce the same output. That is, computers always do the same things under the same conditions. Your job, as you learn to program, will be to reduce the chance of computer mistakes.

When a computer malfunctions, it does not make a simple mistake, rather, it really messes things up. When a computer fails, it typically breaks down completely, or a storage device breaks down, or the power goes out. Whatever happens, computers go all out when they have a problem and it is usually very obvious when they have a problem. The good news is that computers rarely have problems.

Before people invented computers, banks kept all their records on ledger cards. When a teller found a mistake (possibly one that the teller had made), do you think the teller said, "The ledger card made a mistake"? Absolutely not. Computers can have mechanical problems, but the likelihood of small mistakes, such as an incorrect balance once in a while, is just too small to consider. Such mistakes are made by the people entering the data or by (gulp) the programmers.

Myth 3: Computers Are Difficult to Program

Computers are getting easier to use, and to program, every day. If you used a microwave, drove a car, or used an iPod recently, then chances are good that you used a computer when you did. Yet, did you know you were using a computer? Probably not. The makers of computers have found ways to integrate computers into your everyday life to monitor and correct problems that might otherwise occur without them.

Of course, if you are reading this book, you want to learn enough about computers to write your own programs. Writing computer programs does take more work than using a microwave oven's computerized timer functions. The work, however, primarily involves getting down to the computer's level and learning what it expects.

Not only are computers getting easier to program every day, but you have more opportunities to learn about them than ever before. Cable television channels are loaded with educational shows about using and programming computers. Books and videos on the subject are all around you. The Internet itself contains scores of classes on all aspects of computers and other topics. There is probably a computer programming class now in session somewhere within 15 minutes of your house as you read this.

Many Programs Already Exist

Although there are many programs already written for you to use, sometimes you need a program that fills a specific need and you cannot find one that does exactly what you want. When you are done with this book, you will know exactly what you need to design and write your own programs.

Programmers Are in Demand

Look at help-wanted websites. You'll find that there is a shortage of computer programmers. Amidst the requests for Java programmers, C++ programmers, Ruby on Rails programmers, mobile app developers, systems analysts, senior systems analysts, object-oriented programmers, systems programmers, HTML coders, and application programmers, you may find yourself lost in a sea of uncertainty and *TLAs* (three-letter acronyms) that might, at first, seem hopeless. Do not fret; this book will help direct you toward areas of programming that might be right for you.

Hour 22's lesson, "How Companies Program," explores the chain of computer jobs and describes what each type of programming job is all about. If you are just starting out, you probably won't be able to go to work as the most senior-level programmer, but you will be surprised at the salary your programming skills can bring you.

The Real Value of Programs

Although individual computer programs are going down in price, companies and individual computer owners invest more and more in programs every year. Not only do people purchase new programs as they come out, but they update the older versions of programs they already have.

Businesses and individuals must factor in the cost of programs when making computer decisions. Whereas an individual usually buys a computer—called *hardware* because the machine isn't changed often or easily—and is done with the hardware purchasing for a while, the purchasing of programs—the *software*—never seems to end, because software changes rapidly. As a future programmer, this is welcome news because you have a secure career. For the uninformed computer purchaser, the cost of software can be staggering.

A business must also factor in the on-staff and contract programmers and the time needed to write the programs it uses. More information on the programming and support staff appears in the next section.

Users Generally Don't Own Programs

When a company purchases software, it most often purchases a *software license*. If a company wants to buy a word-processing program for 100 employees, legally it must purchase 100 copies of the program, or at least buy a *site license* that allows the company to use the software on more than one machine. When a company buys a program, it does not own the program. When you buy a record, you do not own the music; you have only purchased the rights to listen to the music. You cannot legally alter the music, record it, give away recordings of it, and most importantly, you cannot sell recordings that you make of it. The same is true for software that you buy. The license for individual software grants you permission to use the software on one computer at any one time.

Giving Computers Programs

Figure 1.2 shows the code for a simple program that creates a web page with an interactive button, all created by a computer programmer. As a matter of fact, that computer programmer is about to be you after you create the code using JavaScript. JavaScript is a programming language that enables you to improve websites by letting you customize the look and feel of your site's presentation, increasing interaction with your website users, and validating any data they enter. You may think JavaScript is specifically for web masters and site designers, but it's a simple language and learning its basics can help you learn basic programming concepts.

Another advantage to JavaScript is that most programming languages need you to install an interpreter or compiler on your computer in order to execute your code. With JavaScript (and HTML), you only need a text editor. You type in your code, save it with an .html extension, and then open the saved file with your web browser.

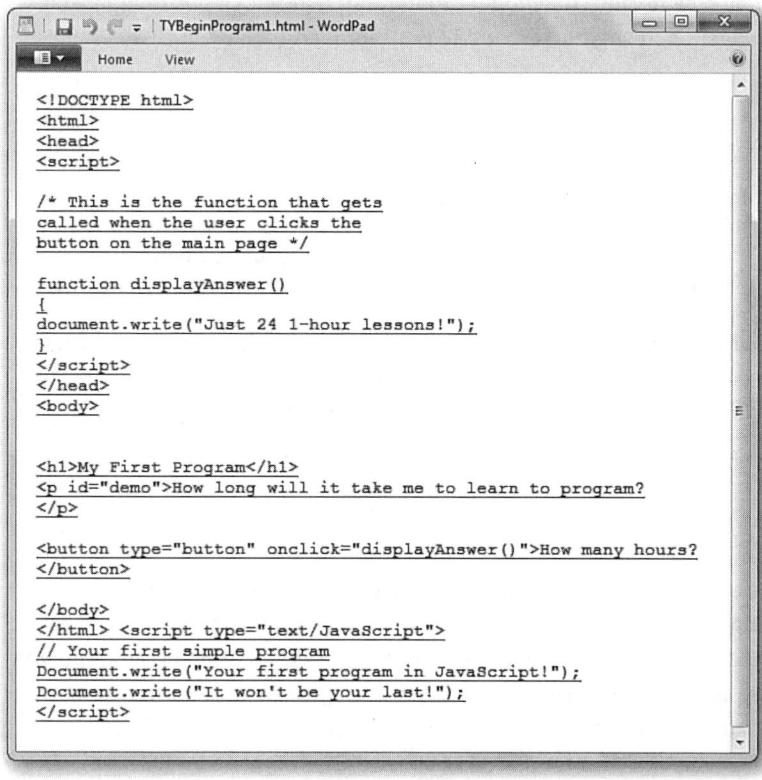

```
TYBeginProgram1.html - WordPad

  Home     View

<!DOCTYPE html>
<html>
<head>
<script>

/* This is the function that gets
called when the user clicks the
button on the main page */

function displayAnswer()
{
document.write("Just 24 1-hour lessons!");
}
</script>
</head>
<body>


<h1>My First Program</h1>
<p id="demo">How long will it take me to learn to program?
</p>

<button type="button" onclick="displayAnswer()">How many hours?
</button>

</body>
</html> <script type="text/JavaScript">
// Your first simple program
Document.write("Your first program in JavaScript!");
Document.write("It won't be your last!");
</script>
```

FIGURE 1.2
A program's instructions are somewhat cryptic, but readable by people.

A computer is only a machine. To give a machine instructions, your instructions might be fairly readable, as Figure 1.2's are, but the *code* (another name for a program's instructions) must be fairly rigid and conform to a predefined set of rules and regulations according to the programming language you use. Therefore, to write a program in the JavaScript programming language, you must conform to JavaScript's rules of proper command spelling and placement. This programming language grammar is called *syntax*. (And you thought syntax was just a levy placed on cigarettes and liquor!)

Despite its name, JavaScript is not tied to the Java programming language (which is covered in Part III, "Object-Oriented Programming with Java," of this book). In fact, the name has caused some confusion as computer fans thought that JavaScript was either an extension or spin-off of Java, but it got the name because Java was a hot new language at the time, and some thought the connection of the scripting language to the web development language would benefit the adoption and growth of JavaScript. Misleading name aside, the more you learn JavaScript, the more easily you will be able to learn additional programming languages. Although computer languages have different goals, syntaxes, and reasons for being, they are often similar in structure.

NOTE

It is important to understand that the first section of this book is teaching you the basics of computer programming using the JavaScript language, and is not a complete JavaScript tutorial. This may seem like the same thing, but it is not. The aim of the book is to teach you basic computer programming techniques (with examples in JavaScript code) in the first half of the book and introduce you to a variety of programming languages and jobs in the second half. There are scores of excellent books, including *Teach Yourself JavaScript in 24 Hours*, also by Sams Publishing, that can take you through every in and out of the JavaScript language. That book will take you far more in-depth into the language than this book. Now that we've properly calibrated your expectations, let's get back to beginning programming!

Source Code

Even after you make the effort to learn a computer language such as JavaScript, and after you go to the trouble of typing a well-formed and syntactically accurate program such as the one in Figure 1.2, your computer still will not be able to understand the program! The program you write is called *source code*. It is the source code that you write, manipulate, and correct. Your computer, on the other hand, can understand only *machine language*, a compact series of computer-readable instructions that make no sense to people. They make sense to some advanced computer gurus, but my general assertion stands that they don't make sense to people.

Listing 1.1 shows machine language. Can you decipher any of it? Your computer can. Your computer loves machine language. Actually, it's the only language your computer understands. And different computers understand their own version of a machine language so what works on one type of computer will not necessarily work on another. It's best to stay away from machine language and let products such as JavaScript convert your higher-level language into machine language's cryptic 1's and 0's. To convert source code such as your JavaScript program to machine language, you need an interpreter (or for other languages, a *compiler*).

LISTING 1.1   Machine language is extremely difficult for people to decipher.

```
01100100
10111101
10010011
10010100
00001111
01010101
11111110
```

All programs you run on your computer, phone, or tablet, including Microsoft Word, Internet Explorer, and programming languages, are already converted into machine language. That's why you can click a program's icon and the program begins immediately. No interpretation or compilation is required. By providing you with the machine language only, software vendors serve two purposes:

1. They give you programs that execute quickly without the intervening compiling step.

2. They ensure that you don't change the source code, thereby protecting their intellectual property.

Your First Program

The first program that you write will be simple. You may not understand much of it, and that's fine. The goal here is not to explain the program details, but to walk you through the entire process of the steps that are typical of computer programming:

1. Type a program's source code and save it.

2. Load the code document, which is now an HTML document saved to your hard drive, with your web browser and see what happens.

3. If the page is not doing what you want and has errors, called *bugs*, you'll need to fix those bugs in your source code and repeat these steps. Hour 7, "Debugging Tools," explains how to locate and fix common bugs. You may need to do some bug hunting earlier than Hour 7 if you experience problems with your programs in these first few hours. If a program does not work as described, you will need to compare your source code very carefully to the code in the book and fix any discrepancies before saving it again.

Starting with JavaScript

You can write your JavaScript code in either your text editor or a word processor. If you choose the latter, you must make sure to save your files as text only. Save your programs with an .html extension, and then when you double click on the file, it should automatically open with your default web browser.

NOTE

Unlike word processors, your editor will not wrap the end of a line down to the subsequent line. It's important that programming instructions (called *statements*) remain separate and stay on their own lines in many cases. Even if a programming language allows multiple program statements per line, you'll find that your programs are more readable and easier to debug if you keep your statements one per line. Sometimes, a single statement can get lengthy and you may span long statements over two or three lines, but rarely would you want multiple statements to appear on the same line.

Clarifying Comments

The program presented in Figure 1.2 not only has program statements, but also some lines that do not do anything when the program is run by the interpreter, but have great value to anyone reading your code. These lines start with either a slash and asterisk (/*) or two consecutive slashes (//) and are known as *comments*.

You may be asking if there's any difference between the slash and asterisk comment and the double-slash comments. Taking the second type first, the double-slash comment is known as a single-line comment. JavaScript will ignore all text to the right of the two slashes. As soon as you hit return, JavaScript will start paying attention to your code again. So if you want to keep commenting, you will need to start the next line with a fresh pair of slashes.

```
// The next five lines ask web visitors for their favorite
// color and Steinbeck novel
```

In the previous example, if you left off the two slashes, JavaScript would assume you were either typing color or calling a function named color and you might not get the results you were expecting.

When JavaScript encounters a comment that begins with the slash and asterisk, it will treat everything that follows as a comment until it sees a closing asterisk and slash (*/). This can be on the same line:

```
/* Next, the code calculates the area of the circle. */
```

Or it can go on for several lines:

```
/* This section is used to enter a contact
The user can enter a name, physical address,
up to 5 email addresses, home, work, and cell
phone numbers, and any additional comments
to help remember how they know the person. */
```

All languages support comments, which are also called *remarks*, although some languages use an apostrophe instead of the slashes. Although you'll find many comments in programs, and you should put many comments in the programs you write, comments are not for the interpreter or for the computer. Comments are for people. In JavaScript, for example, the interpreter ignores all text to the right of the slashes or slash/asterisk. The computer knows that comments are for you and not for it.

Reasons for Comments

Comments help produce more understandable program listings. The programming industry considers the inclusion of comments to be one of the most important good programming habits you can develop. Here are common reasons programmers put comments in their programs:

► Comments can identify programmers—If you develop programs with others or write programs for a company, you should put your name and contact information in comments at the top of your programs. Later, if someone has a question about the program or wants you to change the program, they'll know that you wrote the program and they can locate you.

► Before a section of tricky code, you can use comments to include your explanation of the code's purpose. Later, if you or someone else needs to change the program, the change will be easier; reading the comments is much simpler than trying to figure out the goals of the tricky code from uncommented code.

Placement of Comments

When you use the double slashes (//), a comment can appear on the same line as code. The following code shows comments to the right of lines of other program instructions. Notice that double slashes precede the text. These comments explain what each line of code does.

```
if hours > 12            // Test the hour for AM/PM indicator
   hours = hours - 12    // Convert 24-hour time to 12-hour
   amOrPm$ = " PM"       // Set indicator that will print
```

TIP

Most programming languages are *free-form*, meaning that you can indent lines and add as many spaces and blank lines as you like. Doing so makes a program more readable. In Hour 7, you'll learn how to use this *whitespace* (extra spaces and lines in code) to improve your programs' readability by separating one program section from another and, thereby, making it easier for programmers to understand your code.

Sure, as a programmer, you will often understand code without the need to put a remark to the right of each line. But at the time you write a program, the program is clearest to you. When you later go back to edit a program, what may have been clear before is no longer clear because time has passed. A few comments will go a long way toward reminding you of your original intent.

However, do not overdo comments. Some comments are redundant, as the following shows:

```
document.write("Martha");   // Prints the word Martha
```

Such a comment is not helpful and serves only to cloud an already-understandable instruction. Don't overuse comments, but use them generously when needed to clarify your code.

Entering Your Own Program

You're now ready to type and run your own program from scratch. The program will be simple. The goal here is to get you used to using the editor.

Follow these steps to create your own program:

1. In your text editor, select File and then New File to create a brand-new document.

2. Type the program in Listing 1.2 into the editor. Be careful that you type the program exactly as you see it in the listing. If you make a typing mistake, you will not be able to run the program. The program is a little bit complicated, but if you type it as is, you should have a working program. Notice that both styles of comments are used in the program.

LISTING 1.2 Type your first program into the editor.

```
<!DOCTYPE html>
<html>
<head>
<script>

/* This is the function that gets
called when the user clicks the
button on the main page */

function displayAnswer()
{
document.write("Just 24 1-hour lessons!");
}
</script>
</head>
<body>


<h1>My First Program</h1>
<p id="demo">How long will it take for me to learn to program?.</p>

<button type="button" onclick="displayAnswer()">How many hours?</button>

</body>
</html>
```

3. Save the program as text only, and give it a name with an .html ending. I named mine TYBeginProgram1.html. After you save the program, either double click the file's icon in your explorer or open the file in your web browser. You should see the web page shown in Figure 1.3 to start and in Figure 1.4 when you click the button.

NOTE

The page you load into your web browser should have an .html extension (.htm works as well). Eventually, you will want to separate your JavaScript code into its own files, using .js files. For now, you can embed all your code into .html files.

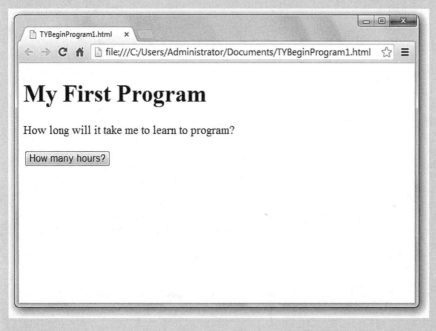

FIGURE 1.3
With less than two dozen lines of code, you've created a simple web page, complete with a button for the visitor to click.

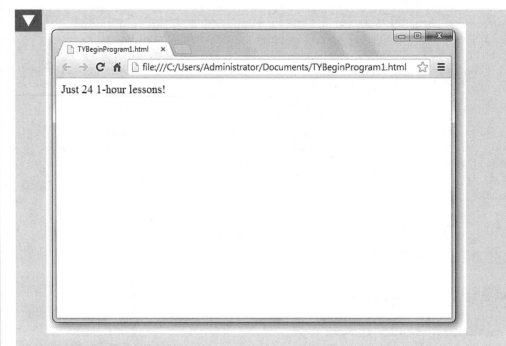

FIGURE 1.4
Once you click the button on your web page, you get a new page with more information. Awesome interactivity, right?

If your program contained an error, the page would not show up like the ones in Figures 1.3 and 1.4. You would have to work through your version line-by-line to see where the error might be.

TIP

In addition to checking for errors, it is also a smart idea to check your created pages in different browsers when possible to see the subtle difference in presentation from browser to browser.

Summary

Now that you know a bit more about the computer industry as a whole, you have a better idea of where programmers fit into the picture. Computers can do nothing without programs and programmers are responsible for providing those programs.

You already got a taste of programming this hour by typing your first JavaScript program and opening the resulting document in your browser. As you saw by typing your own program into an editor, entering and running a code is not painful at all. As a matter of fact, the quick feed-back that programming offers is a rewarding experience. Programmers often like their profession very much because they can see the results of their work quickly.

Q&A

Q. Once I write a program, is my job finished?

A. It is said that a program is written once and modified many times. Throughout this 24-hour tutorial, you will learn the importance of maintaining a program after it is written. As businesses change and computing environments improve, the programs that people use must improve as well. Companies provide upgrades to software as new features are needed. The programs that you write today will have to change in the future to keep up with the competition as well as with new features that your users require.

Q. Can I enter other programming language listings in my editor as well?

A. You can write programs in other programming language, such as C, C++, and Java, in your text editor. However, you would need a compiler or interpreter (depending on the language) to convert the programming language's code to machine language. A machine language program is your program's instructions compiled to a language your computer can understand.

Workshop

The quiz questions are provided for your further understanding.

Quiz

1. What is the difference between data and information?
2. What is a program?
3. What is a programming language?
4. True or false: Computers never make mistakes.
5. Why should people not fear the computer replacing their jobs?
6. What do programmers use editors for?
7. True or false: Java and JavaScript are related to each other.
8. What filename extension should you use when you create a JavaScript program?
9. True or False: There's no problem writing your programs in your typical word-processing program.
10. Tweak the program in Listing 1.2 so the dialog box asks, "Who wrote this program?" and the answer the user gets upon clicking the button is your name.

Answers

1. Data consists of raw facts and figures, and information is processed data that has more meaning.
2. A program is a set of detailed instructions that tells the computer what to do.

3. A programming language is a set of commands and grammar rules with which you write programs that give computers instructions.

4. False. A computer might make a mistake, but it's rare that it does so. In the vast majority of cases where a computer is blamed, a person entered bad data or typed a bad program.

5. Computers increase jobs, not replace them. The information industry is one of the reasons for the past two decades of economic growth.

6. Programmers use editors to type programs into the computer.

7. False. JavaScript and Java only share a name; JavaScript was a scripting language that was developed at the same time Java was hot, so it was named in a way to take advantage of Java's popularity.

8. If your code is going to stay in your HTML document, you can use .html or .htm, but when you create separate JavaScript files, use .js.

9. False. The default method of saving files in word processors will add formatting codes that will generate errors when you try to run your program. You can still use a word processor, but you must always remember to save your files as plain text.

10. Here is one possible solution:

```
<!DOCTYPE html>
<html>
<head>
<script>

/* This is the function that gets
called when the user clicks the
button on the main page */

function displayProgrammer()
{
document.write("Dean Miller did!");
}
</script>
</head>
<body>


<h1>My First Program</h1>
<p id="demo">Who wrote this program?.</p>

<button type="button" onclick="displayProgrammer()">And the answer is...</button>

</body>
</html>
```

HOUR 2
Process and Techniques

The words *program* and *programmer* are mentioned throughout each of these 24 lessons and you've undoubtedly heard them before you picked up this book. Before going back into specifics of JavaScript and other programming languages, this hour explains what a program really is. A firm grasp of this hour's material is a prerequisite for moving on to the more advanced programming concepts that appear throughout this book.

As you read this hour's lesson, keep in mind that programming is rewarding, not only financially, but also mentally and emotionally. Programmers often feel the same sense of creative rush that artists and skilled craftspeople feel while honing their projects. Writing a program, however, can be tedious. It is often a detailed task and ample frustration comes with the territory. The computer's quick feedback on your mistakes and results, however, often provides a sense of accomplishment that keeps you programming until you get it right.

The highlights of this hour include

- ▶ Directing the computer with programs
- ▶ Detailing programs enough so that a computer can follow the instructions
- ▶ Executing programs in memory rather than from the hard drive
- ▶ Looking at whether programming is an art or science
- ▶ Learning why computers cannot yet understand a human language

Understanding the Need for Programs

When individuals and companies need a program or app, they can obtain it in one of three ways:

- ▶ Buy a program that's already written
- ▶ Buy a program and modify it so that the customized version does exactly what they need
- ▶ Write their own program

There are advantages and disadvantages to each option (see Table 2.1). The first two options are much quicker than the third and also are much less expensive.

TABLE 2.1 Advantages and disadvantages of obtaining programs

Option	Advantages	Disadvantages
Buy	The program can be obtained quickly and inexpensively.	The program may not be exactly what is needed.
Buy and customize	A usable program that does what is needed can be obtained fairly quickly. Also, the program is relatively inexpensive, depending on the changes needed.	It isn't always possible to modify the program.
Write	The program (after proper design and testing) does exactly what you want it to do.	This option can be very expensive and takes a lot longer than the other options.

Most computer users (of PCs, Macs, tablets, and smartphones) choose the first option because the programs are fairly inexpensive given their power. Because companies such as Apple, Microsoft, and Adobe sell so many of the same programs, they can do so at reasonable prices. Individual computer users simply don't have the resources that companies have to write the many programs they need.

Companies, on the other hand, do not always choose the first option, although you may question why. The reason is that companies spend many years developing products and services to distinguish themselves from other companies, and they learn to keep records in specific ways so that they can manage those services effectively. When a company computerizes any of its record keeping, it is vital that new programs reflect exactly what the company already does. The company should not have to change the way it does business just so it can use programs found in stores or in mail-order software outlets. On the other hand, programs that can be purchased off the shelf have to be generic so that the producers of the programs can sell them to more than one customer.

The second option—buy a program and customize it—might seem like the smartest option, but it is chosen least often. If companies could buy a program that is already written, they would have a framework in which to quickly adapt the program to their specific needs. The problem is that software is rarely sold, as you learned in the previous hour; software is *licensed*. When you buy a program, you do not own the program; you only own the right to use it. You often cannot legally change it, sell it, or copy it (except for backup purposes). Some software does come with the license to revise the code but most software that you purchase off the shelf does not allow the modification of code.

There is a class of software and operating systems that not only allows modification of code, but encourages it. Open-source software makes the code available with the program so that improvements to the program can be made by the public in a collaborative manner. The Linux operating system is a famous example of open-source software.

Not only are there legalities involved, but also sometimes you cannot physically change the software. Programs come in two formats:

▶ Source code, such as the JavaScript program you created in the previous hour

▶ Compiled, executable code, such as apps you purchase for your phone or tablet

Once a program is written and compiled, programmers can no longer modify the program. Programs that are sold in stores do not usually include the source code. Therefore, companies cannot modify the programs they buy to make the program conform to their specific business. (Of course, programs that you write and compile, you can modify and re-compile because you will have access to your source code.)

So although it is expensive and time-consuming to write programs from scratch, many businesses prefer to do so, keeping large programming departments on hand to handle the programming load. A company might have several members of its data-processing staff spend a full year writing a program that is close, but not identical, to one that the company could buy. Companies also might utilize contract programmers for specific projects.

Despite the cost and effort involved, it is worth it to some companies not to have to conform to a program they buy from someone else. The program, once written, conforms to the company's way of doing business.

NOTE

Some companies have found that they can sell programs they develop to other firms doing similar business thereby recapturing some of their development costs. As you write programs for your company or for individuals, keep in mind the possible subsequent sale of your program to others.

Companies often measure the amount of time it takes to write programs in *people-years*. If it takes two people-years to write a single program, it is estimated that two people could write it in a single year, or one person would take two years. A 20-people-year project would take 20 people one year, or one person 20 years, or 10 people two years, and so forth. This measurement is only an estimate, but it gives management an idea of how it should allocate people and time for programming projects.

If you become a contract programmer, the people-year measurement is a great tool to use when pricing your service. You might give a customer an estimate of the price per people-year (or, for smaller projects, perhaps you would estimate the job in people-months or weeks). If you hire programmers to help you finish the program, you may finish early but you can still charge fairly for each person's labor due to the fact that you priced the programming job in people-years and not in calendar time.

CAUTION

Recently, a lot of attention has been given to the mythical people-years. Critics of this measurement state that computer firms do not generally estimate people-year measurements properly and that such a measurement is rarely meaningful. That may be, but just because people misuse the measurement does not make the measurement a bad way to gauge a project's completion when it is estimated correctly.

Programs, Programs, Everywhere

Why aren't all the programs ever needed already written? Search the Internet today and you'll see hundreds of programs for sale or free to download. There are programs for everything: word processing, accounting, drawing, playing games, editing and manipulating photos and videos, and so much more. It seems as if any program you need is within reach. Because computers have been around more than half a century, you would think that everybody would be about done with all the programming anyone would need for a long time.

To further complicate matters, Apple, Amazon, Android, and many other sites contain thousands of apps you can download and run on your tablet or mobile device. Some of these programs are free and some are for sale.

If all the programs needed were already written, you would not see the large listings of "Programmer Wanted" ads on job listing websites. The fact is that the world is changing every day, and businesses and people must change with it. Programs written five years ago are not up-to-date with today's practices. Also, they were written on computers much slower and more limited than today's machines. Finally, earlier programs were written just for personal computers, while companies must now interact with users that access resources via tablets and smartphones. As hardware advances are made, the software must advance with it.

There is a tremendous need for good programmers, today more than ever. As computers become easier to use, some people believe that programmers will become relics of the past. What they fail to realize is that it takes top-notch programmers to produce those easy-to-use programs. More importantly, it takes programmers to modify and improve upon the vast libraries of programs in use today. Even with economic slumps, the world is becoming more digitized daily and the demand for programmers will see an average increase as more people use computers more often.

Programs as Directions

If you have ever followed your GPS into unfamiliar territory, you know what it is like for your computer to follow a program's instructions. With only the instructions being called out, you can feel blind as you move from place to place, turning left and right, until you reach your destination or find that you made a wrong turn somewhere. Your computer, as the previous hour explained, is a blind and dumb machine waiting for you to give it directions. When you do, the computer acts out the instructions you give it without second-guessing your desires. If you tell your PC to do something incorrectly, it does its best to do so. Recall this definition of a program (from Hour 1, "Hands-On Programming"):

> *A program is a list of detailed instructions that the computer carries out.*

The term *detailed* in the previous definition is vital to making a machine follow your orders. Actually, the job of programming is not difficult; what is difficult is breaking the computer's job into simple and detailed steps that assume nothing.

Practice with Detailing Your Instructions

To get an idea of the thinking involved in programming, consider how you would describe starting a car to someone from the past. Suppose a cowboy named Heath, from the Old West, appears at your doorstep bewildered by the sights around him. After getting over the future shock, Heath wants to adapt to this new world. Before learning to drive your car, Heath must first learn to start it. When he is comfortable doing that, you will teach him to drive. Unlike a 16-year-old learning to drive, Heath has not grown up seeing adults starting cars so he really needs to master this process before going any further. Being the busy programmer you are, you leave him the following set of instructions taped to the car key:

1. Use this key.

2. Start the car.

How far would Heath get? Not very far. You gave correct instructions for starting a car but you assumed too much knowledge on his part. You must remember that he knows nothing about these contraptions called automobiles and he is relying on you to give him instructions that he can understand. Instead of assuming so much, these might be better instructions:

1. Attached is the key to the car. You need it to start the car.

2. With the key in hand, go to the car door that is closest to the front door of our home.

3. Under the door's black handle, you will see a round silver-dollar-sized metal place into which you can insert the key (with its rough edge pointing down).

4. After sticking the key into the hole as far as it will go, turn it to the right until you hear a click.

5. Turn the key back to the left until it faces the same way as it did when you inserted it, and remove the key.

6. Pull up on the black handle to open the door and get into the car. Be sure to sit in front of the round wheel (called a *steering wheel*) on the left-hand side of the front seat.

7. Close the door.

8. On the right side of the column holding the steering wheel, you will see a slot in which you can put the key.

Are you beginning to get the idea? This list of eight items is very detailed, and Heath hasn't even started the car yet. You still have to describe the gas pedal that he might have to press while he turns the key, in the correct direction of course. You also don't want to assume that Heath will turn *off* the car when he is done practicing, so you have to give him those directions as well. (Perhaps you should also warn your neighbors to stay off the streets for a while!)

If you are beginning to think this car-starting analogy is going a little too far, consider what you must do to tell a nonthinking piece of electronic equipment—a computer—to perform your company's payroll. A payroll program cannot consist of only the following steps:

1. Get the payroll data.

2. Calculate the payroll and taxes.

3. Print the checks.

To the computer, these instructions lack thousands of details that you might take for granted. It is the detailing of the program's instructions that provides for the tedium and occasional frustration of programming. Programming computers isn't difficult, but breaking down real-world problems into lots of detailed steps that a computer can understand is hard.

TIP

A typical payroll program might contain 20,000 or more lines of instructions. Don't let this deter you from learning to program, however. Large programming projects are written by teams of programmers; you will have plenty of help if you ever write such programs for a living. Also, new programming techniques and programming environments for today's computer languages make programming, even for the individual programmer working alone, much easier than ever before.

Closer to Home: A JavaScript Example

Consider the program output window shown in Figure 2.1. A JavaScript program produced this output.

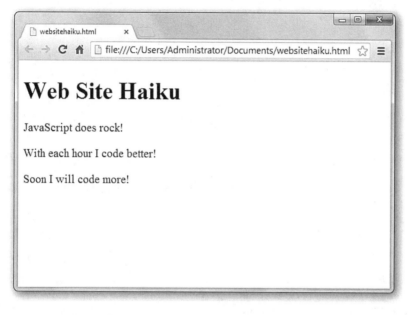

FIGURE 2.1
It takes detailed instructions to produce simple output.

What does it take to produce the three, simple lines of output? It takes detailed instructions in the JavaScript programming language. The computer cannot read your mind to know what you want. You must specifically tell JavaScript to print those three lines and even tell JavaScript that you want each line of the poem to start on a new line. Listing 2.1 shows the program that produced this output website.

LISTING 2.1   You must supply detailed instructions when you want the computer to do something.

```
<!DOCTYPE html>
<html>
<body>
```

```
▼ <h1>Web Site Haiku</h1>

<script>

// Three-line poem and the opening and closing
// <p> characters will make each line a
// separate one.

document.write("<p>JavaScript does rock!</p>");
document.write("<p>With each hour I code better!</p>");
document.write("<p>Soon I will code more!</p>");
</script>

</body>
</html>
```

Even though you don't yet know the JavaScript programming language, you've got to admit that the program in Listing 2.1 is rather simple to understand. Three `document.write` statements tell the computer to print three lines of output. All JavaScript program output from the write statement goes to the main website (the document).

TIP

Each JavaScript code snippet is placed in an .html file that has the opening and closing <html> and </html> tags, and then the <script> and </script> tags.

Sure, if you want to see the words in Figure 2.1, all you need to do is start WordPad or some other word processor and type the text into the document window. Nevertheless, a lot of programming work went into that word processor to allow you to put text in the document so easily. The idea in these early hours is to focus on creating programs that produce results.

Tools That Help

Many design tools exist to help you take large problems and break them down into detailed components that translate into programming elements. Hour 3, "Designing a Program," explains many of the methods that programmers use to get to a program's needed details. You'll find that programming is simple as long as you approach it systematically, as this text attempts to do. By combining theory with as much early, hands-on examples as possible, you'll understand what you're doing and learn how to program faster. If programming were truly difficult, there is no way so many computer advances could have been made over the last 60 years.

Programs Are Saved Instructions

The nice thing about programs you write is that you save them to disk after you write them. As with word-processed text, you store the programs you write in disk files as you did in the previous hour's lesson with the TYBeginProgram.html program. A program is to a computer as a recipe is to a cook. When a cook wants to make a certain dish, he or she finds the correct recipe and follows the instructions. When someone wants to execute a program, she or he instructs the computer to load the program from disk into memory and then run the program's instructions.

The computer's internal memory (*random access memory*, or *RAM*) is vital for holding program execution. Your computer's CPU cannot execute a program's instructions directly from the disk. Just as you cannot know what is in a book lying on a table until you read the book's contents into your memory (using your own CPU—your mind), your CPU cannot process a program's instructions until it loads the program from disk into main memory. Figure 2.2 shows the process of loading a program from the computer's disk (or disk-like storage such as a flash drive) into memory. As the figure shows, the CPU has direct access to memory but has no access to the disk drive. The disk is the long-term storage, and the memory is the short-term storage, where programs temporarily reside while the CPU executes them.

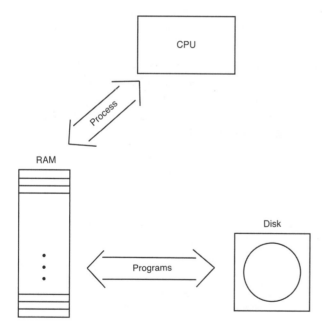

FIGURE 2.2
A program must be in memory before the CPU can execute the program's instructions.

As you already know, the program differs greatly from the output itself. The program is a set of instructions and the *output* is the result of those instructions. A recipe's output is the finished dish and the program's output is the printed output once the instructions are running.

Perhaps a specific example will further clarify what it means to a programmer for a user to use a program. If you use a word processor, then you probably follow steps similar to these:

1. You load the word-processing program from your hard drive into the computer's main memory. When you select the word-processing program's name from the menu or select its icon, you are instructing the computer to search the disk drive for the program and load it into main memory.

2. What you see onscreen is output from the program. You can produce more output by typing text on the screen. Everything that appears onscreen throughout the program's execution is program output.

3. After you type text, you may interact with other devices. You will probably issue a command to print the document (more than likely using the standard Windows File, Print menu option) to the printer and save the document in a data file on the disk.

4. When you exit the word processor, your operating system regains control. The word-processing program is no longer in memory, but it is still safely tucked away on disk.

As you can see, the results of a program's execution make up the output. The instructions themselves are what produce those results. Figure 2.3 gives an overview of the program-to-output process. Modern-day programs produce output in many different ways. Programs play music, talk to other computers over the phone lines, and control external devices. Output sent to the screen and printer still makes up the majority of today's program output.

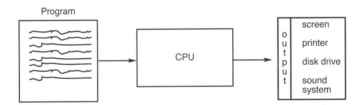

FIGURE 2.3
The program comes from disk, executes, and then sends its results to any of the many output devices, such as the disk, screen, or printer (or more than one of them from within the same program).

When a program is in memory, it is not there alone. Your operating system always resides in memory. If it did not, you could neither load a program from disk nor run it because the operating system itself is what actually loads programs to and from memory when you issue the correct command. Limited memory often poses a problem for larger programs. Recall that a program processes data, and the data and the program must be in memory before the program can easily process the data.

Figure 2.4 shows what a typical computer installation's memory looks like when a program is running. The operating system takes a big chunk, the program must be there too, and finally there must be room for data.

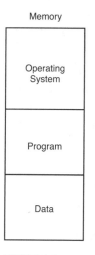

FIGURE 2.4
A typical memory layout shows that the operating system shares memory with executing programs.

The more memory your PC has, the faster your programs run. The extra memory means that the operating system will have to swap less to and from disk as the program operates. Some programs are even contained in memory in their entirety the whole time that the program runs. As a programmer, you should run with ample memory, as much as 256MB or 512MB, so that you can properly test your running programs while still keeping your programming environment loaded.

Art or Science?

A debate that you often see in computer literature is whether programming is an art or a science. Through the years, there have been advances made in programming that, if followed, improve a program's accuracy, readability, and *maintainability* (the process of changing the program later to perform a different or additional set of tasks). Most of these advances are nothing more than suggestions; that is, programmers don't have to use them to write programs that work.

Two of the most important advances in programming have been more philosophically based than engineered. They are *structured programming* and *object-oriented programming*. This book explores these two programming advances thoroughly in the hours that follow. They both offer ways that a programmer can write a program to make it better. Again, though, these are just suggested approaches to programming; programmers can (and many do) ignore them.

There are many ways to write even the smallest and simplest programs. Just as authors write differently and musicians play differently, programmers each have a unique style. Therefore, you would think that programming is more of an art than a science. On the continuum of science to art, you would be closer to being correct than those few who argue that programming is more of a science.

Nevertheless, as more advances are made in developing programming approaches, as has already been done with structured programming and object-oriented programming, you should see a shift in thinking. With the proliferation of computers in today's world, there is a massive educational effort in process to train tomorrow's programmers. Because programming is still a young industry, many advances are still left to be made.

Some of the biggest proponents of moving away from the artful approach to a more scientific approach, using structured and object-oriented programming, are the companies paying the programmers. Companies need to react quickly to changing business conditions, and they need programs written as quickly and as accurately as possible. As advances in computer programming are discovered, more companies are going to adopt policies that require their programmers to use more scientific and time-proven methods of writing better programs.

Speak the Language

The instructions you give in your programs must be in a language the computer understands, which, as you learned from Hour 1, is machine language. At its lowest level, a computer is nothing more than thousands of switches flipping on and off lightning fast. A switch can have only one of two states; it can be *on* or *off*. Because either of these two states of electricity can be controlled easily with switches, many thousands of them control what your computer does from one microsecond to another.

If it were up to your computer, you would have to give it instructions using switches that represent on and off states of electricity. Actually, that is exactly the way that programmers programmed the early computers. A panel of switches, such as the one shown in Figure 2.5, had to be used to enter all programs and data. The next time you find yourself cursing errors that appear in programs you write, think of what it would have been like programming 55 years ago.

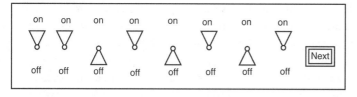

FIGURE 2.5
Programmers used a panel of switches to program early computers.

The on and off states of electricity are represented as 1s and 0s at the computer's lowest level. This representation has a name: *binary*. You can control what your computer does if you know the correct pattern of 1s and 0s required to give it commands. You can program a computer simply by issuing 1s and 0s if you have the correct system tools. Of course, programming in the binary digits of 1s and 0s is not much better than flipping up and down switches on the switch panel, so there has to be a better way.

CAUTION

Computers are not going to learn a human's spoken language any time soon, despite what you might see in science fiction movies. You have to learn a programming language if you want the computer to do what you want, and you must interpret or compile that language into machine language.

Computers Cannot Handle Ambiguity

Spoken languages are too ambiguous to computers. People's brains can decipher sentences intuitively, something a nonthinking machine cannot do. There are some inroads being made into *artificial intelligence*, which is the science of programming computers so that they can learn on their own. It also includes programming them to understand a spoken language such as English. Despite recent advancements, artificial intelligence is many years away (if it is even possible for computers to understand simple English commands).

Consider the following sentence:

> **Time flies like an arrow.**

Your mind has no trouble understanding the parts of this sentence. You know that it is an analogy, and the parts of speech make total sense to you. *Time* is a noun and the verb describes the action it performs: it *flies*, and it does so *like an arrow*. If you teach the computer to accept these descriptions of this sentence, it will work fine until it runs into something like this:

> **Fruit flies like an orange.**

Think about this for a moment. Again, you have no problem understanding this sentence, even though it is completely different from the other one. The computer taught to decipher the first sentence, however, is going to throw its cables up in frustration at the second sentence because none of the parts of the sentence are the same. The word *flies* is now a noun and not an action verb. The phrase *like an orange* is no longer a description of the action, but rather both the verb (*like*) and the object receiving the action (*an orange*). As you can see from these two sentences alone, understanding simple sentences that most people take for granted poses a tremendous problem for programmers trying to "teach" a computer to understand a language such as English.

Here's another example.

> **The pop can has a lid.**

Computers have extreme problems with statements such as this one because the sentence appears to have a subject-verb agreement problem. Does the sentence state that the can of pop has a lid or that the pop can have a lid? If it's the latter, then *has* should be *have*. The human mind can easily distinguish these problems and knows that the can of pop has a lid, but given today's technology, machines simply cannot easily do so.

Therefore, computers and people are at opposite ends of the spectrum. People want to speak their own language but computers want to stick to their language comprised of 1s and 0s. There has to be some kind of go-between. Programming languages were created to try to appease both the computer and the person programming the computer. You've seen from JavaScript that programming languages use words similar to those that people use, but programming languages have a highly specific syntax that allows little room for the ambiguity that is so prevalent in spoken languages. The computer can take a programming language and translate it to its machine language of 1s and 0s; the human programmer can learn, remember, and use the programming languages more effectively than 1s and 0s because programming languages appear similar to spoken languages, although more precise and simple.

Computers Speak Many Languages

You are going to learn a lot about several programming languages in this 24-hour course. You may have heard of some of the languages before. Over the years since the first computer language was invented, hundreds of programming languages have been written but there are only a handful that have prevailed to dominate the rest. Table 2.2 lists several programming languages that have gained more than obscure notoriety through the years.

TABLE 2.2   Many programming languages have appeared through the years.

Machine Language	Assembler
Algol	PL/I
PROLOG	LISP
COBOL	Forth

Machine Language	Assembler
RPG	RPG II
Pascal	Object Pascal
HTML	Ada
C	C++
C#	FORTRAN
SmallTalk	Eiffel
BASIC	Visual Basic
APL	Java
Python	PHP
JavaScript	Ruby

The computer is like a modern-day tower of Babel, indirectly responsible for more programming languages than were ever needed. Most people considered to be computer experts might only know a handful of programming languages—from three to five—and they probably know only one or two very well. Therefore, don't let the large number of languages deter you from wanting to learn to program.

There are lots of reasons why there are so many programming languages. Different people have different preferences, some languages are better than others depending on the tasks, and some people have access to only one or two of the languages. For example, HTML is a language that programmers use for developing websites. FORTRAN was used in the past for highly mathematical applications although other languages have supplanted FORTRAN in many programming departments. Java, JavaScript, and PHP, combined with HTML, are great languages for putting interaction on web pages. The emergence of agile development methodology has resulted in an increase in the use of Ruby programming.

Summary

There are several ways to obtain programs for computers, but to really make computers do what you want, you have to write the programs yourself. Most programs that you purchase are merely licenses to use but not customize the programs. Companies need programs that enable them to do business the way they prefer and do not force them to change their practices to conform to the programs.

Before you can program, you must learn a programming language. You may want to learn several languages, but your work and interest goals will determine which languages you learn.

Perhaps you want to specialize in Internet languages or perhaps you have a long-term Python contract. You'll find that the more languages you learn, the easier it will be for you to pick up additional languages.

The next hour describes some of the background needed for proper program design.

Q&A

Q. Why do programs have to be so detailed?

A. Programs are detailed because computers are machines. Machines do not have intelligence. A computer blindly follows your instructions, step by step. If you do not give detailed instructions, the computer can do nothing.

Workshop

The quiz questions are provided for your further understanding.

Quiz

1. What are the three ways to acquire a new program?

2. Why do businesses often write their own programs, despite the extra expense required?

3. Why must programmers know a programming language?

4. Why do computers not understand human language?

5. Which is more ambiguous, human language or computer language?

6. True or false: To be useful, a programmer should know at least five programming languages.

7. Why is RAM-based internal memory so important to a running program?

8. Which languages from Table 2.2 do you think are derived from the C programming language?

9. Why might a programmer specialize in only one programming language?

10. What is open-source software?

Answers

1. You can buy a program that's already written, buy a program with source code and modify the program, or write your own program from scratch.

2. Companies want their programs to conform to the way they do business.

3. Programmers must use programming languages to create programs.

4. Computers only understand a very low-level machine language and are not advanced enough to recognize higher languages.

5. Human language has more ambiguity than computer language.

6. False; a programmer might only know one or two languages and still be extremely useful and productive.

7. The more RAM your computer contains, the more of your program and data that can fit into memory at the same time and the faster your program executes.

8. C++ and C# are derived from the C language.

9. A programmer might specialize in only one programming language because the programmer's company may use only one language. Also, the more specialized the programmer is, the better the programmer will be in that skill. Nevertheless, most programmers are familiar with several languages and prosper more because of that knowledge.

10. Open-source programs are distributed with their source code along with the executable files. Users are encouraged to alter the code and improve the program, as long as they share their code changes with the community.

Designing a Program

Programmers learn to develop patience early in their programming careers. They learn that proper design is critical to a successful program. Perhaps you have heard the term *systems analysis and design*. This is the name given to the practice of analyzing a problem and then designing a program from that analysis. Complete books and college courses have been written about systems analysis and design. Of course, you want to get back to hands-on programming—and you'll be doing that very soon. However, to be productive at hands-on programming, you first need to understand the importance of design. This chapter attempts to cover program design highlights, letting you see what productive computer programmers go through before writing programs.

The highlights of this hour include

- ► Understanding the importance of program design
- ► Mastering the three steps required to write programs
- ► Using *output definition*
- ► Comparing top-down and bottom-up designs
- ► Seeing how flowcharts and pseudocode are making room for RAD
- ► Preparing for the final step in the programming process

The Need for Design

When a builder begins to build a house, the builder doesn't pick up a hammer and begin on the kitchen's frame. A designer must design the new house before anything can begin. As you will soon see, a program should also be designed before it is written.

A builder must first find out what the purchaser of the house wants. Nothing can be built unless the builder has an end result in mind. Therefore, the buyers of the house must meet with an architect. They tell the architect what they want the house to look like. The architect helps the buyers decide by telling them what is possible and what isn't. During this initial stage, the price is always a factor that requires both the designers and the purchasers to reach compromise agreements.

After the architect completes the plans for the house, the builder must plan the resources needed to build the house. Only after the design of the house is finished, the permits are filed, the money is in place, the materials are purchased, and the laborers are hired can any physical building begin. As a matter of fact, the more effort the builder puts into these preliminary requirements, the faster the house can actually be built.

The problem with building a house before it is properly designed is that the eventual owners may want changes made after it is too late to change them. It is very difficult to add a bathroom in the middle of two bedrooms *after* the house is completed. The goal is to get the owners to agree with the builder on the final house prior to construction. When the specifications are agreed on by all the parties involved, there is little room for disagreement later. The clearer the initial plans are, the fewer problems down the road because all parties agreed on the same house plans.

Sure, this is not a book on house construction, but you should always keep the similarities in mind when writing a program of any great length. You should not go to the keyboard and start typing instructions into the editor before designing the program any more than a builder should pick up a hammer before the house plans are finalized.

TIP

The more up-front design work that you do, the faster you will finish the final program.

Thanks to computer technology, a computer program is easier to modify than a house. If you leave out a routine that a user wanted, you can add it later more easily than a builder can add a room to a finished house. Nevertheless, adding something to a program is never as easy as designing the program correctly the first time.

User-Programmer Agreement

Suppose you accept a job as a programmer for a small business that wants to improve its website. (After you've gone through these 24 hours, you'll understand programming better and you'll even learn how to write web programs in Java.) The website changes that the owners want sound simple. They want you to write some interactive Java routines that enable their users to look at an online inventory and to print order lists that the users can bring into the store for purchases.

So, you listen to what they want, you agree to a price for your services, you get an advance payment, you gather the existing web page files, and you go to your home office for a few days. After some grueling days of work, you bring your masterpiece web pages back to show the owners.

"Looks good," they say. "But where is the credit card processing area? Where can the user go to order our products online? Why don't you show the products we've back-ordered and that are unavailable? Why haven't you computed sales tax anywhere?"

You've just learned a painful lesson about user-programmer agreements. The users did a lousy job at explaining what they wanted. In fairness to them, you didn't do a great job at pulling out of them what they needed. Both of you thought you knew what you were supposed to do, and neither knew in reality. You realize that the price you quoted them originally will pay for about 10% of the work this project requires.

Before you start a job and before you price a job, you must know what your users want. Learning this is part of the program design experience. You need to know every detail before you'll be able to price your service accurately and before you'll be able to make customers happy.

NOTE

Proper user-programmer agreement is vital for all areas of programming, not just for contract programmers. If you work for a corporation as a programmer, you also will need to have detailed specifications before you can begin your work. Other corporate users who will use the system must sign off on what they want so that everybody knows up front what is expected. If the user comes back to you later and asks why you didn't include a feature, you will be able to answer, "Because we never discussed that feature. You approved specifications that never mentioned that feature."

The program maintenance that takes place after the program is written, tested, and distributed is one of the most time-consuming aspects of the programming process. Programs are continually updated to reflect new user needs. Sometimes, if the program is not designed properly before it is written, the user will not want the program until it does exactly what the user wants it to do.

Computer consultants learn early to get the user's acceptance, and even the user's signature, on a program's design before the programming begins. If both the user and the programmers agree on what to do, there is little room for argument when the final program is presented. Company resources are limited; there is no time to add something later that should have been in the system all along.

Steps to Design

There are three fundamental steps you should perform when you have a program to write:

1. Define the output and data flows.

2. Develop the logic to get to that output.

3. Write the program.

Notice that writing the program is the *last* step in writing the program. This is not as silly as it sounds. Remember that physically building the house is the last stage of building the house; proper planning is critical before any actual building can start. You will find that actually writing and typing in the lines of the program is one of the easiest parts of the programming process. If your design is well thought out, the program practically writes itself; typing it in becomes almost an afterthought to the whole process.

Step 1: Define the Output and Data Flows

Before beginning a program, you must have a firm idea of what the program should produce and what data is needed to produce that output. Just as a builder must know what the house should look like before beginning to build it, a programmer must know what the output is going to be before writing the program. Anything that the program produces and the user sees is considered output that you must define. You must know what every screen in the program should look like and what will be on every page of every printed report.

Some programs are rather small, but without knowing where you're heading, you may take longer to finish the program than you would if you first determined the output in detail. Suppose you wanted to add a JavaScript-based program that allowed visitors to a website to enter contact information. To start, you should make a list of all fields that the program is to produce onscreen. Not only would you list each field, but you also would describe the fields. Table 3.1 details the fields on the program's window.

TABLE 3.1 Fields that your contact management program might display

Field	Type	Description
Contacts	Scrolling list	Displays the list of contacts
Name	Text field	Holds contact's name
Address	Text field	Holds contact's address
City	Text field	Holds contact's city
State	Text field	Holds contact's state
Zip	Text field	Holds contact's zip code
Home Phone #	Text field	Holds contact's phone number
Cell Phone #	Text field	Holds contact's mobile number
Email	Text field	Holds contract's email address
Stage	Fixed, scrolling list	Displays a list of possible stages this contact might reside in, such as being offered a special follow-up call or perhaps this is the initial contact

Field	Type	Description
Notes	Text field	Miscellaneous notes about the contact such as whether the contact has bought from the company before
Filter Contacts	Fixed, scrolling list	Enables the user to search for groups of contacts based on the stage the contacts are in, enabling the user to see a list of all contacts who have been sent a mailing
Edit	Command button	Enables the user to modify an existing contact
Add	Command button	Enables the user to add a new contact
OK	Command button	Enables the user to close the contact window

Many of the fields you list in an *output definition* may be obvious. The field called Name obviously will hold and display a contact's name. Being obvious is okay. Keep in mind that if you write programs for other people, as you often will do, you must get approval of your program's parameters. One of the best ways to begin is to make a list of all the intended program's fields and make sure that the user agrees that everything is there. Perhaps your client has specific interests, like wanting the Twitter handle of contacts as well. By communicating with your client, you will get a better idea of what you need to add to the program.

As you'll see in a section later this hour named "Rapid Application Development," you'll be able to use programs to put together a model of the actual output screen that your users can see. With the model and with your list of fields, you have double verification that the program contains exactly what the user wants.

Input windows such as the Contacts program data-entry screen are part of your output definition. This may seem contradictory, but input screens require that your program place fields on the screen, and you should plan where these input fields must go.

The output definition is more than a preliminary output design. It gives you insight into what data elements the program should track, compute, and produce. Defining the output also helps you gather all the input you need to produce the output.

CAUTION

Some programs produce a huge amount of output. Don't skip this first all-important step in the design process just because there is a lot of output. With more output, it becomes more important for you to define it. Defining the output is relatively easy—sometimes even downright boring and time-consuming. The time you need to define the output can take as long as typing in the program. You will lose that time and more, however, if you shrug off the output definition at the beginning.

The output definition consists of many pages of details. You must be able to specify all the details of a problem before you know what output you need. Even command buttons and scrolling list boxes are output because the program will display these items.

In Hour 1, "Hands-on Programming," you learned that data goes into a program and the program outputs meaningful information. You should inventory all the data that goes into the program. If you're adding JavaScript code to a website to make the site more interactive, you will need to know if the website owners want to collect data from the users. Define what each piece of data is. Perhaps the site allows the user to submit a name and email address for weekly sales mailings. Does the company want any additional data from the user such as physical address, age, and income?

Object-Oriented Design

Throughout this 24-hour tutorial, you will learn what *object-oriented programming (OOP)* is all about. Basically, OOP turns data values, such as names and prices, into objects that can take on a life of their own inside programs. Part III, "Object-Oriented Programming with Java" covers the basics of OOP.

A few years ago, some OOP experts developed a process for designing OOP programs called *object-oriented design (OOD)*. OOD made an advanced science out of specifying data to be gathered in a program and defining that data in a way that was appropriate for the special needs of OOP programmers. Grady Booch was one of the founders of OOD. It is his specifications almost two decades ago that continue to help OOP programmers collect data for the applications they are about to write and to turn that data into objects for programs.

In the next hour, Hour 4, "Getting Input and Displaying Output," you'll learn how to put these ideas into a program. You will learn how a program asks for data and produces information on the screen. This *I/O (input and output)* process is the most critical part of an application. You want to capture all data required and in an accurate way.

Something is still missing in all this design discussion. You understand the importance of gathering data. You understand the importance of knowing where you're headed by designing the output. But how do you go from data to output? That's the next step in the design process—you need to determine what processing will be required to produce the output from the input (data). You must be able to generate proper data flows and calculations so that your program manipulates that data and produces the correct output. The final sections of this hour will discuss ways to develop the centerpiece—the logic for your programs.

All output screens, printed reports, and data-entry screens must be defined in advance so you know exactly what is required of your programs. You must also decide what data to keep in files and the format of your data files. As you progress in your programming education, you will learn ways to lay out data files in formats they require.

When capturing data, you want to gather data from users in a way that is reasonable, requires little time, and has prompts that request the data in a friendly and unobtrusive manner. That's where prototyping (discussed next) and rapid application development can help.

Prototyping

In the days of expensive hardware and costly computer usage time, the process of system design was, in some ways, more critical than it is today. The more time you spent designing your code, the more smooth the costly hands-on programming became. This is far less true today because computers are inexpensive and you have much more freedom to change your mind and add program options than before. Yet the first part of this hour was spent in great detail explaining why up-front design is critical.

The primary problem many new programmers have today is they do absolutely no design work. That's why many problems take place, such as the one mentioned earlier this hour about the company that wanted far more in their website than the programmer ever dreamed of.

Although the actual design of output, data, and even the logic in the body of the program itself is much simpler to work with given today's computing tools and their low cost, you still must maintain an eagle eye toward developing an initial design with agreed-upon output from your users. You must also know all the data that your program is to collect before you begin your coding. If you don't, you will have a frustrating time as a contract programmer or as a corporate programmer because you'll constantly be playing catch-up with what the users actually want and failed to tell you about.

One of the benefits of the Windows operating system is its visual nature. Before Windows, programming tools were limited to text-based design and implementation. Designing a user's screen today means starting with a programming language such as Visual Basic, drawing the screen, and dragging objects to the screen that the user will interact with, such as an OK button. Therefore, you can quickly design *prototype screens* that you can send to the user. A prototype is a model, and a prototype screen models what the final program's screen will look like. After the user sees the screens that he or she will interact with, the user will have a much better feel for whether you understand the needs of the program.

JavaScript includes prototyping tools, much like Windows programming languages such as Visual C++ and Visual Basic do. For comparison, Figure 3.1 shows the Visual Basic development screen. The screen looks rather busy, but the important things to look for are the Toolbox and the output design window. To place controls such as command buttons and text boxes on the form that serves as the output window, the programmer only has to drag that control from the Toolbox window to the form. So to build a program's output, the programmer only has to drag as many controls as needed to the form and does not have to write a single line of code in the meantime.

Toolbox   Drag controls here   Already-placed controls

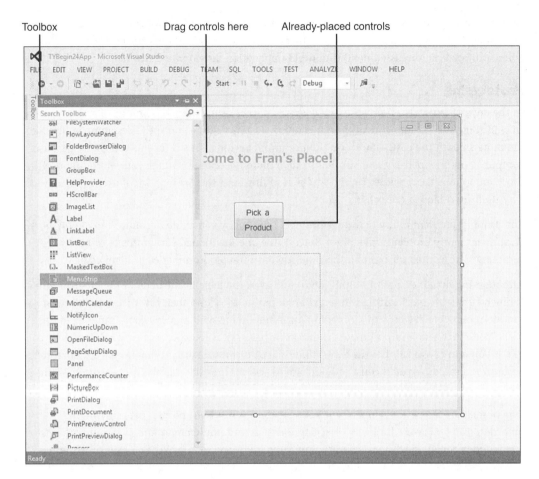

FIGURE 3.1
Program development systems such as Visual Basic provide tools that you can use to create output definitions visually.

Once you place controls on a Form window with a programming tool such as Visual Basic, you can do more than show the form to your users. You actually can compile the form just as you would a program and let your user interact with the controls. When the user is able to work with the controls, even though nothing happens as a result, the user is better able to tell if you understand the goals of the program. The user often notices if there is a missing piece of the program and can also offer suggestions to make the program flow more easily from a user's point of view.

CAUTION

The prototype is often only an empty shell that cannot do anything but simulate user interaction until you tie its pieces together with code. Your job as a programmer has only just begun once you get approval on the screens, but the screens are the first place to begin because you must know what your users want before you know how to proceed.

Rapid Application Development

A more advanced program design tool used for defining output, data flows, and logic itself is called *rapid application development*, or *RAD* for short. Although RAD tools are still in their infancy, you will find yourself using RAD over the span of your career, especially as RAD becomes more common and the tools become less expensive.

RAD is the process of quickly placing controls on a form—not unlike you just saw done with Visual Basic—connecting those controls to data, and accessing pieces of prewritten code to put together a fully functional application without writing a single line of code. In a way, programming systems such as Visual Basic are fulfilling many goals of RAD. When you place controls on a form, as you'll see done in far more detail in Hour 20, "Programming with Visual Basic 2012," the Visual Basic system handles all the programming needed for that control. You don't ever have to write anything to make a command button act like a command button should. Your only goal is to determine how many command buttons your program needs and where they are to go.

But these tools cannot read your mind. RAD tools do not know that, when the user clicks a certain button, a report is supposed to print. Programmers are still needed to connect all these things to each other and to data, and programmers are needed to write the detailed logic so that the program processes data correctly. Before these kinds of program development tools appeared, programmers had to write thousands of lines of code, often in the C programming language, just to produce a simple Windows program. At least now the controls and the interface are more rapidly developed. Someday, perhaps a RAD tool will be sophisticated enough to develop the logic also. But in the meantime, don't quit your day job if your day job is programming, because you're still in demand.

TIP

Teach your users how to prototype their own screens! Programming knowledge is not required to design the screens. Your users, therefore, will be able to show you exactly what they want. The prototyped screens are interactive as well. That is, your users will be able to click the buttons and enter values in the fields even though nothing happens as a result of that use. The idea is to let your users try the screens for a while to make sure they are comfortable with the placement and appearance of the controls.

Top-Down Program Design

For large projects, many programming staff members find that a top-down design helps them focus on what a program needs and helps them detail the logic required to produce the program's results. *Top-down design* is the process of breaking down the overall problem into more and more detail until you finalize all the details. With top-down design, you produce the details needed to accomplish a programming task.

The problem with top-down design is that programmers tend not to use it. They tend to design from the opposite direction (called *bottom-up design*). When you ignore top-down design, you impose a heavy burden on yourself to remember every detail that will be needed; with top-down design, the details fall out on their own. You don't have to worry about the petty details if you follow a strict top-down design because the process of top-down design takes care of producing the details.

TIP

One of the keys to top-down design is that it forces you to put off the details until later. Top-down design forces you to think in terms of the overall problem for as long as possible. Top-down design keeps you focused. If you use bottom-up design, it is too easy to lose sight of the forest for the trees. You get to the details too fast and lose sight of your program's primary objectives.

Here is the three-step process necessary for top-down design:

1. Determine the overall goal.

2. Break that goal into two, three, or more detailed parts; too many details cause you to leave out things.

3. Put off the details as long as possible, then keep repeating steps 1 and 2 until you cannot reasonably break down the problem any further.

You can learn about top-down design more easily by relating it to a common real-world problem before looking at a computer problem. Top-down design is not just for programming problems. Once you master top-down design, you can apply it to any part of your life that you must plan in detail. Perhaps the most detailed event that a person can plan is a wedding. Therefore, a wedding is the perfect place to see top-down design in action.

What is the first thing you must do to have a wedding? First, find a prospective spouse (you'll need a different book for help with that). When it comes time to plan the wedding, the top-down design is the best way to approach the event. The way *not* to plan a wedding is to worry about the details first, yet this is the way most people plan a wedding. They start thinking about the dresses, the organist, the flowers, and the cake to serve at the reception. The biggest problem with trying to cover all these details from the beginning is that you lose sight of so much; it is too easy to forget a detail until it's too late. The details of bottom-up design get in your way.

What is the overall goal of a wedding? Thinking in the most general terms possible, "Have a wedding" is about as general as it can get. If you were in charge of planning a wedding, the general goal of "Have a wedding" would put you right on target. Assume that "Have a wedding" is the highest-level goal.

NOTE

The overall goal keeps you focused. Despite its redundant nature, "Have a wedding" keeps out details such as planning the honeymoon. If you don't put a fence around the exact problem you are working on, you'll get mixed up with details and, more importantly, you'll forget some details. If you're planning both a wedding and a honeymoon, you should do two top-down designs, or include the honeymoon trip in the top-level general goal. This wedding plan includes the event of the wedding—the ceremony and reception—but doesn't include any honeymoon details. (Leave the honeymoon details to your spouse so you can be surprised. After all, you have enough to do with the wedding plans, right?)

Now that you know where you're heading, begin by breaking down the overall goal into two or three details. For instance, what about the colors of the wedding, what about the guest list, what about paying the minister...*oops,* too many details! The idea of top-down design is to put off the details for as long as possible. Don't get in any hurry. When you find yourself breaking the current problem into more than three or four parts, you are rushing the top-down design. Put off the details. Basically, you can break down "Have a wedding" into the following two major components: the ceremony and the reception.

The next step of top-down design is to take those new components and do the same for each of them. The ceremony is made up of the people and the location. The reception includes the food, the people, and the location. The ceremony's people include the guests, the wedding party, and the workers (minister, organist, and so on—but those details come a little later).

TIP

Don't worry about the time order of the details yet. The top-down design's goal is to produce every detail you need (eventually), not to put those details into any order. You must know where you are heading and exactly what is required before considering how those details relate to each other and which come first.

Eventually, you will have several pages of details that cannot be broken down any further. For instance, you'll probably end up with the details of the reception food, such as peanuts for snacking. (If you start out listing those details, however, you could forget many of them.)

Now move to a more computerized problem; assume you are assigned the task of writing a payroll program for a company. What would that payroll program require? You could begin by listing the payroll program's details, such as this:

▶ Print payroll checks.

▶ Calculate federal taxes.

▶ Calculate state taxes.

What is wrong with this approach? If you said that the details were coming too early, you are correct. The perfect place to start is at the top. The most general goal of a payroll program might be "Perform the payroll." This overall goal keeps other details out of this program (no general ledger processing will be included, unless part of the payroll system updates a general ledger file) and keeps you focused on the problem at hand.

Consider Figure 3.2. This might be the first page of the payroll's top-down design. Any payroll program has to include some mechanism for entering, deleting, and changing employee information such as address, city, state, zip code, number of exemptions, and so on. What other details about the employees do you need? At this point, don't ask. The design is not ready for all those details.

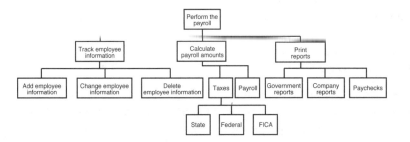

FIGURE 3.2
The first page of the payroll program's top-down design would include the highest level of details.

There is a long way to go before you finish with the payroll top-down design, but Figure 3.2 is the first step. You must keep breaking down each component until the details finally appear.

Only when you and the user gather all the necessary details through top-down design can you decide what is going to comprise those details.

Step 2: Develop the Logic

After you and the user agree to the goals and output of the program, the rest is up to you. Your job is to take that output definition and decide how to make a computer produce the output. You have taken the overall problem and broken it down into detailed instructions that the computer can carry out. This doesn't mean that you are ready to write the program—quite the contrary. You are now ready to develop the logic that produces that output.

The output definition goes a long way toward describing *what* the program is supposed to do. Now you must decide *how* to accomplish the job. You must order the details that you have so they operate in a time-ordered fashion. You must also decide which decisions your program must make and the actions produced by each of those decisions.

Throughout the rest of this 24-hour tutorial, you'll learn the final two steps of developing programs. You will gain insight into how programmers write and test a program after developing the output definition and getting the user's approval on the program's specifications.

CAUTION

Only after learning to program can you learn to develop the logic that goes into a program, yet you must develop some logic before writing programs to be able to move from the output and data definition stage to the program code. This "chicken before the egg" syndrome is common for newcomers to programming. When you begin to write your own programs, you'll have a much better understanding of logic development.

In the past, users would use tools such as *flowcharts* and *pseudocode* to develop program logic. A flowchart is shown in Figure 3.3. It is said that a picture is worth a thousand words, and the flowchart provides a pictorial representation of program logic. The flowchart doesn't include all the program details but represents the general logic flow of the program. If your flowchart is correctly drawn, writing the actual program becomes a matter of rote. After the final program is completed, the flowchart can act as documentation to the program itself.

Flowcharts are made up of industry-standard symbols. Plastic flowchart symbol outlines, called *flowchart templates*, are still available at office supply stores to help you draw better-looking flowcharts instead of relying on freehand drawing. There are also some programs that guide you through a flowchart's creation and print flowcharts on your printer.

Although some still use flowcharts today, RAD and other development tools have virtually eliminated flowcharts except for depicting isolated parts of a program's logic for documentation purposes. Even in its heyday of the 1960s and 1970s, flowcharting did not completely catch on. Some companies preferred another method for logic description called *pseudocode*, sometimes called *structured English*, which is a method of writing logic using sentences of text instead of the diagrams necessary for flowcharting.

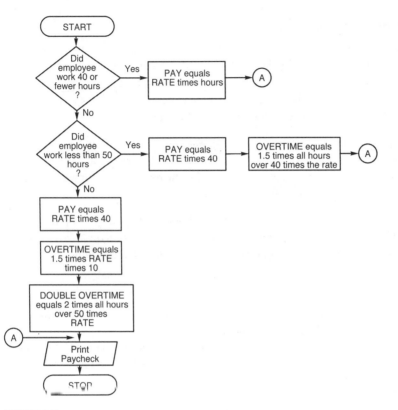

FIGURE 3.3
The flowchart depicts the payroll program's logic graphically.

Pseudocode doesn't have any programming language statements in it, but it also is not free-flowing English. It is a set of rigid English words that allow for the depiction of logic you see so often in flowcharts and programming languages. As with flowcharts, you can write pseudocode for anything, not just computer programs. A lot of instruction manuals use a form of pseudo-code to illustrate the steps needed to assemble parts. Pseudocode offers a rigid description of logic that tries to leave little room for ambiguity.

Here is the logic for the payroll problem in pseudocode form. Notice that you can read the text, yet it is not a programming language. The indention helps keep track of which sentences go together. The pseudocode is readable by anyone, even by people unfamiliar with flowcharting symbols:

```
For each employee:
   If the employee worked 0 to 40 hours then
     net pay equals hours worked times rate.
   Otherwise,
     if the employee worked between 40 and 50 hours then
```

```
      net pay equals 40 times the rate;
      add to that (hours worked -40) times the rate times 1.5.
   Otherwise,
      net pay equals 40 times the rate;
      add to that 10 times the rate times 1.5;
      add to that (hours worked -50) times twice the rate.
  Deduct taxes from the net pay.
Print the paycheck.
```

Step 3: Writing the Code

The program writing takes the longest to learn. After you learn to program, however, the actual programming process takes less time than the design if your design is accurate and complete. The nature of programming requires that you learn some new skills. The next few hourly lessons will teach you a lot about programming languages and will help train you to become a better coder so that your programs will not only achieve the goals they are supposed to achieve, but also will be simple to maintain.

Summary

A builder doesn't build a house before designing it, and a programmer should not write a program without designing it either. Too often, programmers rush to the keyboard without thinking through the logic. A badly designed program results in lots of bugs and maintenance. This hour described how to ensure that your program design matches the design that the user wants. After you complete the output definition, you can organize the program's logic using top-down design, flowcharts, and pseudocode.

The next hour focuses on training you in your first computer language, JavaScript.

Q&A

Q. At what point in the top-down design should I begin to add details?

A. Put off the details as long as possible. If you are designing a program to produce sales reports, you would not enter the printing of the final report total until you had completed all the other report design tasks. The details fall out on their own when you can no longer break a task into two or more other tasks.

Q. Once I break the top-down design into its lowest-level details, don't I also have the pseudocode details?

A. The top-down design is a tool for determining all the details your program will need. The top-down design doesn't, however, put those details into their logical execution order. The pseudocode dictates the executing logic of your program and determines when things happen, the order they happen in, and when they stop happening. The top-down design simply determines everything that might happen in the program. Instead of pseudocode, however, you should consider getting a RAD tool that will help you move faster from the design to the finished, working program. Today's RAD systems are still rather primitive, and you'll have to add much of the code yourself.

Workshop

The quiz questions are provided for your further understanding.

Quiz

1. Why does proper design often take longer than writing the actual program?

2. Where does a programmer first begin determining the user's requirements?

3. True or false: Proper top-down design forces you to put off details as long as possible.

4. How does top-down design differ from pseudocode?

5. What is the purpose of RAD?

6. True or false: You will not have to add code to any system that you design with RAD.

7. Which uses symbols, a flowchart or pseudocode?

8. True or false: You can flowchart both program logic as well as real world procedures.

9. True or false: Your user will help you create a program's output if you let the user work with an output prototype.

10. What is the final step of the programming process (before testing the final result)?

Answers

1. The more thorough the design, the more quickly the programming staff can write the program.

2. A programmer often begins defining the output of the proposed system.

3. True.

4. Top-down design enables a program designer to incrementally generate all aspects of a program's requirements. Pseudocode is a way to specify the logic of a program once the program's design has already been accomplished with tools such as top-down design.

5. RAD provides a way to rapidly develop systems and move quickly from the design stage to a finished product. RAD tools are not yet advanced enough to handle most programming tasks, although RAD can make designing systems more easy than designing without RAD tools.

6. False. RAD requires quite a bit of programming in many instances once its work is done.

7. A flowchart uses symbols.

8. True.

9. True.

10. The final step of programming is writing the actual code.

Getting Input and Displaying Output

Input and output are the cornerstones that enable programs to interact with the outside world. In the previous hour, you learned how important the output process is to programming because through output, your program displays information. A program must get some of its data and control from the user's input, so learning how to get the user's responses is critical as well.

The highlights of this hour include

- ▶ Displaying output in JavaScript

- ▶ Printing multiple occurrences per line

- ▶ Separating output values

- ▶ Using variables to hold information

- ▶ Getting data in JavaScript

- ▶ Prompting for data input

- ▶ Sending output to your printer

Printing to the Screen with JavaScript

JavaScript has a variety of methods to display output to a web page. Which you choose will depend on your goal. Almost every program you write will output some data to the screen. Your users must be able to see results and read messages from the programs that they run.

There are several ways to output to the screen. One of the easiest way to print words on the website is to enclose them in quotation marks after a `document.write` statement. The following four statements embedded in an HTML document print names on the screen:

```
<script>
document.write("Sally Brown<br>");
document.write("John Wilson");
</script>
```

These statements produce the following output:

```
Sally Brown
John Wilson
```

Remember that for any JavaScript statements, you need to bracket them with the <script> and
</script> tags. You may also be wondering about the <br> tag at the end of the Sally Brown
name. This signals to the browser to jump down to the next line, inserting a line break. Without
it, your output would look like this:

```
Sally BrownJohn Wilson
```

The quotation marks are not printed—they mark the string to be printed. You may be wondering, "What if I wanted to print quotation marks?" JavaScript has an easy solution. If you enclose
your string to be printed in single quote marks, you can then include the double quotation
marks as something to print. For example, if you added the line

```
document.write('"what if I wanted to print quotation marks?"');
```

The output would be

```
"what if I wanted to print quotation marks?"
```

Whether you use single or double quotation marks, understand that numbers and mathematical
expressions will print as is inside the string. JavaScript will not do any math within a string. If
you write

```
document.write("5 + 7");
```

JavaScript doesn't print 12 (the result of 5 + 7). Because quotation marks enclose the expression, the expression prints exactly as it appears inside the quotation marks. The document.
write statement produces this output:

```
5 + 7
```

If, however, you print an expression without the quotation marks, JavaScript prints the result of
the calculated expression.

```
document.write(5 + 7);
```

does print 12.

Consider the program in Listing 4.1. The program prints the radius of a circle, as well as the area of the entire circle and half of the circle.

LISTING 4.1   **Printing results of calculations**

```
<!DOCTYPE html>
<html>
<body>

<script>
// Filename: AreaHalf.html
// Program that calculates and prints the area
// of a circle and half circle
document.write("The area of a circle with a radius of 3 is ");
document.write(3.1416 * 3 * 3);
document.write("<br>The area of one-half that circle is ");
document.write((3.1416 * 3 * 3) / 2);
</script>

</body>
</html>
```

NOTE

Don't worry too much about understanding the calculations in this hour's programs. The next hour, Hour 5 "Data Processing with Numbers and Words," explains how to form calculations in JavaScript.

Here is the output you see if you run the program in Listing 4.1:

```
The area of a circle with a radius of 3 is 28.2744
The area of one-half that circle is 14.1372
```

Remember that each `document.write` statement will continue printing on the same line unless you add a `<br>` tag for a line break or a `<p>` tag for a new paragraph.

Storing Data

As its definition implies, *data processing* means that your programs process data. That data must somehow be stored in memory while your program processes it. In JavaScript programs, as in most programming languages, you must store data in *variables*. You can think of a variable as if it were a box inside your computer holding a data value. The value might be a number, character, or string of characters.

NOTE

Actually, data is stored inside memory locations. Variables keep you from having to remember which memory locations hold your data. Instead of remembering a specific storage location (called an *address*), you only have to remember the name of the variables you create. The variable is like a box that holds data and the variable name is a label for that box so you'll know what's inside.

Your programs can have as many variables as you need. Variables have names associated with them. You don't have to remember which internal memory location holds data; you can attach names to variables to make them easier to remember. For instance, `Sales` is much easier to remember than the 4,376th memory location.

You can use almost any name you want, provided that you follow these naming rules:

- ▶ Variable names must begin with an alphabetic character such as a letter.

- ▶ Variable names can be as long as you need them to be.

- ▶ Uppercase and lowercase variable names differ; the name `MyName` and `MYNAME` are two different variables.

- ▶ After the first alphabetic character, variable names can contain numbers and periods.

CAUTION

Avoid strange variable names. Try to name variables so that their names help describe the kind of data being stored. `Balance04` is a much better variable name for an accountant's 2004 balance value than `X1y96a`, although JavaScript doesn't care which one you use.

Here are some examples of valid and invalid variable names:

Valid	Invalid
Sales04	Sales-04
MyRate	My$Rate
ActsRecBal	5ActsRec
row	Prompt

CAUTION

Don't assign a variable the same name as a JavaScipt command or JavaScript will issue an invalid variable name error message.

Variables can hold numbers or *character strings*. A character string usually consists of one or more characters, such as a word, name, sentence, or address. JavaScript lets you hold numbers or strings in your variables.

Assigning Values

Many JavaScript program statements use variable names. Often, JavaScript programs often do little more than store values in variables, change variables, calculate with variables, and output variable values.

When you are ready to store a data value, you must name a variable to put it in. You must use an assignment statement to store values in your program variables. The assignment statement includes an equal sign (=) and an optional command `var`. Here are two sample assignment statements:

```
sales = 956.34

var rate = .28
```

TIP

The `var` keyword is optional and requires more typing if you use it. However, many other programming languages require that you use a keyword to first declare a variable, so it's good programming practice to use the optional `var` keyword.

Think of the equal sign in an assignment statement as a left-pointing arrow. Whatever is on the right side of the equal sign is sent to the left side to be stored in the variable there. Figure 4.1 shows how the assignment statement works.

Variable

FIGURE 4.1
The assignment statement stores values in variables.

If you want to store character string data in a variable, you must enclose the string inside quotation marks. Here is how you store the phrase "JavaScript programmer" in a variable named myJob:

```
myJob = "JavaScript programmer"   // Enclose strings in quotation marks
```

After you put values in variables, they stay there for the entire run of the program or until you put something else in them. A variable can hold only one value at a time. Therefore, the two statements

```
age = 67;
age = 27;
```

result in age holding 27, because that was the last value stored there. The variable age cannot hold both values.

You can also assign values of one variable to another and perform math on the numeric variables. Here is code that stores the result of a calculation in a variable and then uses that result in another calculation:

```
pi = 3.1416;
radius = 3;
area = pi * radius * radius;
halfArea = area / 2;
```

▼ TRY IT YOURSELF

You can use the *alert* method to print values stored in variables. Print the variable names without quotes around them. Listing 4.2 contains code similar to Listing 4.1, but instead of printing calculated results directly, the program first stores calculations in variables and prints the variables' values using the alert method, instead of `document.write`.

LISTING 4.2   `alert` **sends output of calculations and other data to the screen.**

```
<!DOCTYPE html>
<html>
<head>
        <title>Calculating the Area of a Circle</title>
</head>
<body>
        <script>

        // Filename areacircle2.html
        // program that calculates and prints the area
        // of a circle and half circle
```

```
        var pi = 3.14159; // mathematical value of PI
        var radius = 3; // radius of the circle

        // calculate the area of the whole circle
        var area = pi * radius * radius;

        alert("The area of a circle with a radius of 3 is "+ area);

        alert("The area of a half circle is " + area/2);

    </script>
</body>
</html>
```

Getting Keyboard Data with `Prompt`

So far, the programs you've created have used specific pieces of information and data coded right into your programs. Even variables have been defined with specific values, such as the radius of the circle in Listing 4.1. While this is interesting, it's ultimately limiting. To make programs more valuable, you need to get information from your user.

The *prompt* method is the opposite of alert. The prompt method receives values from the keyboard. You can then assign the values typed by the user to variables. In the previous section, you learned how to assign values to variables. You used the assignment statement because you knew the actual values. However, you often don't know all the data values when you write your program.

Think of a medical reception program that tracks patients as they enter the doctor's office. The programmer has no idea who will walk in next and so cannot assign patient names to variables. The patient names can be stored in variables only when the program is run.

When a program reaches a prompt call, it creates a dialog box that stays until the user types a value and presses the OK button. Here is a prompt:

```
prompt("What is your favorite color?");
```

When program execution reaches this statement, the computer displays a dialog box with the message you type in the quotation marks. The dialog box is a signal to the user that something is being asked and a response is desired. The more clear you make the statement you send to the prompt, the easier it will be for the user to enter the correct information.

▼ TRY IT YOURSELF

The program in Listing 4.3 is a third attempt at the area of a circle program, but this time the user gets to enter the radius of the circle. Now that the user can enter the radius of different-sized circles, this program has far more value.

NOTE

It might start to get a little dull to keep writing variations of the same program, but it's a great way to understand new commands and techniques by making just subtle changes to your code to achieve the same, or slightly different, results.

LISTING 4.3 Using `prompt` to get the value of a circle's radius

```
<! DOCTYPE html>
<html>
<head>
        <title>Calculating the Area of a Circle</title>
</head>
<body>
        <script>

        // Filename areacircle2.html
        // program that calculates and prints the area
        // of a circle and half circle

        var pi = 3.14159; // mathematical value of PI
        // Ask the user for the size of the circle
        var radius = prompt("What is the radius of the circle? ");

        // calculate the area of the whole circle
        var area = pi * radius * radius;

        // Making these parts of the message to user strings
        // both demonstrates strings and makes the alert fit
        // more cleanly on a single line.

        var message1 = "The area of a circle with a radius of ";
        var message2 = " is "
        alert(message1 + radius + message2 + area);

        alert("The area of a half circle is " + area/2);

        </script>
</body>
</html>
```

If the user runs this program, the prompt statement produces the dialog box featured in Figure 4.2.

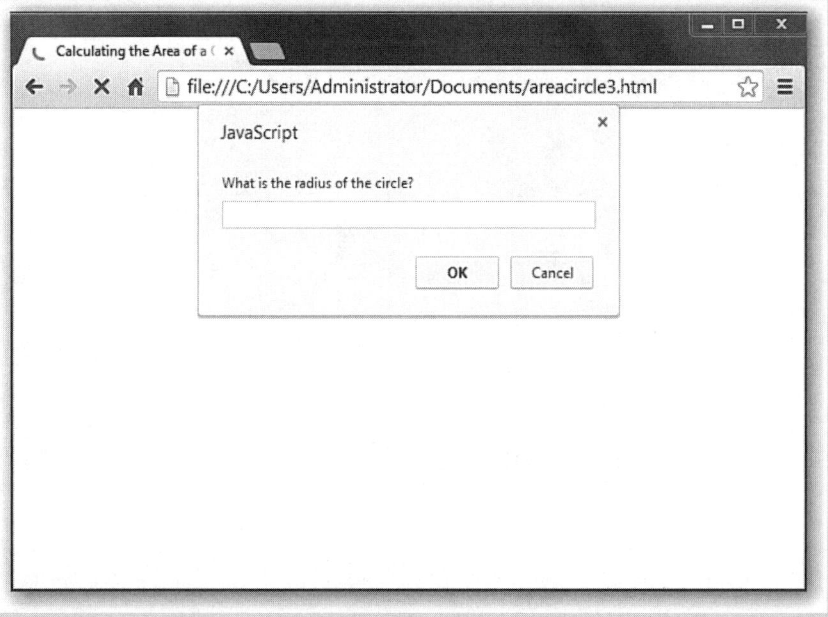

FIGURE 4.2
The program will not advance until the user enters a value and then hits Enter.

Once the user enters a value for the radius, the program proceeds as it did before, first showing the area of an entire circle and then the area of a half circle.

Inputting Strings

Unlike many programming languages, a variable in JavaScript can hold either a number or a string. Any type of variable, numeric or string, can be entered by the user through a prompt dialog box. For example, this line waits for the user to enter a string value:

```
var fname = prompt("What is your first name");
```

When the user types the name in response to the question, the name is put into the `fname` variable.

CAUTION
_____

If the user only presses OK, without entering a value in response to the prompt, JavaScript puts a value called *null* into the variable. A null value is a zero for numeric variables, or an empty string for string variables. An empty string—a string variable with nothing in it—is literally zero characters long.

▼ TRY IT YOURSELF

Listing 4.4 is a simple program that once again takes user input and again stores the information in variables. This time you are prompting the user for strings (and two of them).

LISTING 4.4   Using prompts to get a user's first and last names

```
<! DOCTYPE html>
<html>
<head>
     <title>Name entering program</title>
</head>
<body>
     <script>

     // Filename entername.html
     // program that asks the user's first and last
     // name and then displays it in a last, first format

     // Ask the user for their first name
     var fname = prompt("What is your first name? ");

     // Ask the user for their last name
     var lname = prompt("What is your last name? ");

     // Make a commaseparation variable for
     // last name, first name format

     var commasep = ", ";
     alert("First name first: " + fname + " " + lname);
     alert("Last name first: " + lname + commasep + fname);

     </script>
</body>
</html>
```

TIP

JavaScript's ability to combine the string asking the user to enter information and the prompt for the data itself is not a feature all programming languages share. When you use other languages (such as C), you may have to have a separate output statement telling the user what you need and an input statement to receive the information.

This program gets two strings from the user, a first name and a last name, and then combines them in two different formats in alert statements. There are other ways to combine strings, and they'll be covered in the next lesson. The other issue is that there is no checking to ensure your user entered the correct information. With strings, the program will accept numbers and treat them as strings. So if your user enters "Johnny" as their first name and "5" as their last name, JavaScript will set the full name as "Johnny 5."

While numbers can be treated as strings, the opposite is not true for strings being entered as numbers. In Listing 4.3, if the user enters a series of letters for the radius, the program will return NaN as the area of the circle. NaN stands for "Not a Number" and can be used to ensure the information is correct for the needed calculation. This is known as data validation, and will be covered in more detail in Hour 6, "Controlling Your Programs."

TRY IT YOURSELF ▼

Listing 4.5 shows a program that a small store might use to compute totals at the cash register. The prompt methods in this program are required; only at runtime will the customer purchase values be known. As you can see, getting input at runtime is vital for real-world data processing.

LISTING 4.5 You can use `prompt` to simulate a cash register program for a small store.

```
<! DOCTYPE html>
<html>
<head>
        <title>Fran's Place</title>
</head>
<body>
        <script>

        // Filename: Storereg.html
        // A more practical use of input and output
        // Asks users for specific info on sold items

        document.write("Welcome to Fran's Place!<br>");
        document.write("Let's proceed to checkout!<br><br>");
        candy = prompt("How many candy bars did they buy?");
        soda = prompt("How many cans of soda did they buy?");
        gas = prompt("How many gallons of gas did they buy?");

        // This section will take each value and
        // multiply it by the current cost per item
```

▼

```
candytotal = candy * 1.00;
sodatotal = soda * 1.50;
gastotal = gas * 3.879;

subtotal = candytotal + sodatotal + gastotal;

// Don't forget sales tax! 7.25% in this example
tax = subtotal * .0725;

receipt = "Item      Qnt    Total\n";
receipt += "-------------------------------\n";
receipt += "Candy     " + candy + "     $" + candytotal;
receipt += "\n";
receipt += "Soda      " + soda + "     $" + sodatotal;
receipt += "\n";
receipt += "Gas       " + gas + "     $" + gastotal;
receipt += "\n";
receipt += "-------------------------------\n";
receipt += "Subtotal    $" + subtotal;
receipt += "\nTax         $" + tax;
receipt += "\nTotal       $" + (subtotal+tax);
receipt += "\n\nHAVE A GREAT DAY!\n";

alert(receipt);
```

```
      </script>
  </body>
</html>
```

Figure 4.3 shows the output of this program. As you can see, the program could be helpful for a small store. However, the information could use some additional formatting and cleaning up, but once you learn some additional features of JavaScript (and HTML), you can quickly and easily build interactive programs and websites for almost any need you have personally or professionally.

You may be wondering about the 13 lines that build up the receipt variable before it is outputted to an alert box. This is a method to create a single, albeit long, string for one alert. For each item you are printing detail (candy, soda, gas), you are essentially building up the receipt with the exact same two lines of code, with the exception of the product quantity and variable totals. Later on, in Hour 6, you will learn some tricks to loop through identical or similar code lines with fewer total lines. This might not seem like a big deal when only dealing with three products, but what if you had 20 or more? Then you can really improve your coding efficiency by taking advantage of loops.

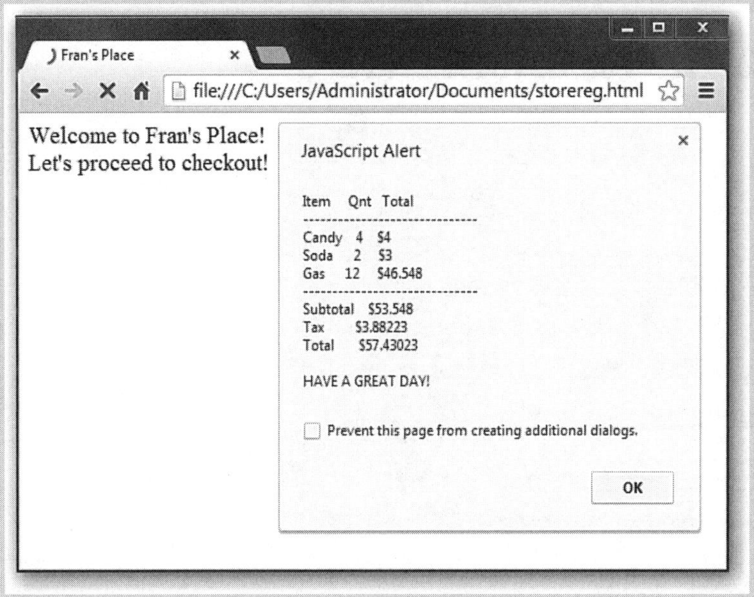

FIGURE 4.3
Running the cash register program produces this output.

Capturing Mouse Events

JavaScript does not just interact with the keyboard entries from users. In addition, there are methods of understanding when the user either clicks the mouse on a specific button or passes into a particular region. These types of actions are called *events*, and they will trigger and action if you have written code for something to happen when the events occur. For example, if the user clicks the mouse over a button on a web page form, the button's onClick event is triggered only if you have written code for it.

A rollover effect can apply to buttons or text on the Web page. If text contains a rollover, the text can change color or change in another way when the user points to the text. Often, such rollover effect is used for menu selection. Figure 4.4 shows a web page with JavaScript-enabled text before the user moves the mouse pointer over one of the text items. Figure 4.5 shows how the Author Links text changes when the user moves the mouse pointer over the text. This roll-over effect is possible only because the JavaScript that contains code to handle the rollover comes to the user's computer inside the HTML web page. The code must run on the user's computer to respond immediately to the mouse movement.

FIGURE 4.4
A web page with JavaScript looks like any other until the user activates a JavaScript scriptlet.

FIGURE 4.5
When the mouse pointer moves over text with a rollover effect, the JavaScript code changes the text's appearance.

Listing 4.6 contains the code that produces a command button's rollover effect. (You will not be able to reproduce this actual effect because you won't have graphics to use for the before and after rollover effects.) Not all the code will be clear even after you complete this hour; JavaScript can't be taught or learned in one short hour, but you're simply trying to grasp the fundamentals of how JavaScript activates such command buttons.

LISTING 4.6 **A JavaScript script that performs a button change when the user points to the button**

```
<! DOCTYPE html>
<html>
<head>
     <title>Image Test</title>
</head>
<body>
<img src="img1.gif" alt="img1"onmouseover="this.src='img2.gif';"
onmouseout="this.src= 'img1.gif';" />
</body>
</html>
```

This code probably looks a bit complicated, but when you type it in and load the page, it generates some cool results. However, make sure you have two image files, named img1.gif and img2.gif in the same directory as the code. It doesn't matter what they are, but similar sizes are best. The first, img1.gif, will be displayed when you load the web page. When you move your mouse cursor over the image, it will change to img2.gif, and when you move the mouse cursor off the image, it is back to your original image.

NOTE

Again, there is so much you can do with input and output in JavaScript, but we're just looking to cover programming basics. If you want to learn more, please pick up a tutorial devoted to the language—your websites will thank you if you do!

Summary

Proper input and output can mean the difference between a program that your users like to use and one they hate to use. If you properly label all input that you want so that you prompt your users through the input process, the user will have no questions about the proper format for your program. In addition to data entry, JavaScript provides methods that allow you to alter your website depending on the positioning of a visitor's cursor position, adding another level of interactivity to your programs.

The next hour describes in detail how to use JavaScript to program calculations using variables and the mathematical operators, as well as some handy string-manipulation tricks.

Q&A

Q. What is the difference between an alert dialog box and a prompt dialog box?

A. Alert shares information with the website visitor, while a prompt asks the user to enter specific information.

Q. Why don't I have to tell JavaScript what type of variable I want to use?

A. JavaScript is just that smart! Actually for most programming languages, you need to specify the type of variable, and if you try to put a different type of data in that variable, you can get an error or unpredictable results. JavaScript will change the variable type on the fly, so you can use the same variable as a string in the beginning of the program and then a number later. This is not the best idea, however. You should keep your variables focused on a specific type and a specific job.

Workshop

The quiz questions and exercises are provided for your further understanding.

Quiz

1. How do you print words in the output window?

2. How would you write an alert method that printed the sum of 10 and 20?

3. Declare a variable named movie and assign the last movie you saw in theaters to it.

4. True or false: You use the same code to jump down a line in both `document.write` and alert methods.

5. What is a variable?

6. How do you print the contents of variables?

7. What is a prompt?

8. Write a simple program that asks the user for their birthday in three separate prompts— one for month, one for date, and one for year, and then combine the three into a Month date, year format that you put up on the screen in an alert.

9. What do the onmouseover and onmouseout events do?

10. What does NaN stand for?

Answers

1. Use `document.write` to display words in an output window. If you want to create a dialog box with the displayed words, use the alert method.

2. `alert(10 + 20);`

3. (Obviously this should vary based on your most recent cinema-viewing experience.) For me:

   `var movie = "The Wolverine";`

4. False. For `document.write`, you use the `<br>` code, and this would not work in an alert (you would print `<br>` to the screen. If you want to jump down a line, use the escape character "`\n`" (don't feel bad if you got this wrong—we didn't cover it yet).

5. A variable is a named storage location.

6. You can use either `document.write` or `alert` or a number of other methods to print the contents of a variable.

7. A prompt describes the information that a user is to type.

8. Here is one possible solution:

```
<!DOCTYPE html>
<html>
<body>

<h1>Birthday Bash</h1>

<script>

bYear = prompt("What year were you born?");
bMonth = prompt("What month were you born?");
bDay = prompt("What day were you born?");

bMessage = "You were born on " + bMonth + " " + bDay
          + ", " + bYear + "!";
alert(bMessage);

</script>

</body>
</html>
```

9. The `onmouseover` event will trigger some code when the user's mouse pointer passes into a specific object (like an image, banner, or block of text). The `onmouseout` event will trigger some code when the user's mouse pointer leaves that object.

10. `NaN` stands for "Not a Number."

Data Processing with Numbers and Words

Without an in-depth knowledge of characters, strings, and numbers, you won't be able to understand any programming language. This doesn't mean that you must be a math whiz or an English major. You must, however, understand how languages such as JavaScript represent and work with such data.

In this hour, you will learn more about how JavaScript performs its mathematical calculations. In addition, you will learn how JavaScript represents and works with strings. Along the way, you will discover functions and powerful built-in routines that perform many of the programming chores for you.

The highlights of this hour include

- ▶ Merging strings together
- ▶ Understanding internal representation of strings
- ▶ Mastering the programming operators
- ▶ Digging into JavaScript's functions

Strings Revisited

Like most programming languages, JavaScript has excelled in their support of strings. Hardly any programming language before BASIC was created in the 1960s supported string data except in a rudimentary form. BASIC was created for beginners, but it offered advanced support for strings.

Even since the first BASIC language, programming languages have been slow to adopt string support beyond a rudimentary level. C++, one of the newer programming languages of the past 50 years and one of the most used, did not directly support strings. To work with strings in C++ (and its earlier rendition C), programmers had to do some fancy footwork to get around the fact that the fundamental string data type was not supported.

Merging Strings

You can merge or *concatenate* (programmers rarely use a simple word when a longer word will confuse more people) two strings together simply by placing a plus sign between them. Without going into too much detail, Listings 4.4 and 4.5 in Hour 4, "Getting Input and Displaying Output," used string concatenation before outputting the result to the screen.

▼ TRY IT YOURSELF

To see the concept in more detail, consider the short program in Listing 5.1. The program asks the user for the user's hometown and home state names, using two prompt methods, then prints the full location by concatenating them together with a comma and space between them to separate the names.

LISTING 5.1   Merging two strings together is simple.

```
<! DOCTYPE html>
<html>
<head>
        <title>Home town and state</title>
</head>
<body>
        <script>

        // Filename mergetown.html
        // program that asks the user's hometown and state
        // and then displays it in a town, state format

        // Ask the user for their hometown
        var town = prompt("What town are you from?");

        // Ask the user for their state
        var state = prompt("In what state were you born?");

        // Make a comma-separator variable for
        // last name, first name format

        var fullLocation = town + ", " + state;
        alert("So you are from " + fullLocation);

        </script>
</body>
</html>
```

Figure 5.1 shows the final output of the program after the user has entered a town and state.

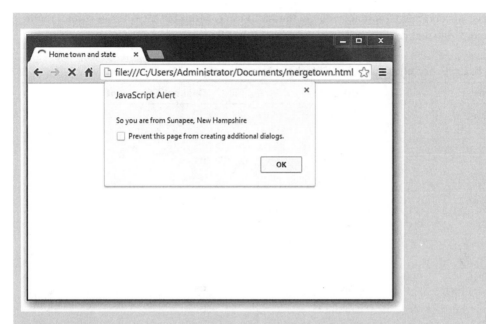

FIGURE 5.1
String concatenation lets you build one larger string by combining any number of smaller strings.

When using concatenation, you can either combine variables or string literals as demonstrated in Listing 5.1. Two variables are joined with a literal comma plus space in the middle. The specific example also demonstrates that users don't have to limit input in a prompt to a single word. After all, states, like New Hampshire in the example, and cities, if the user was born in Salt Lake City, can be made up of one or more words.

The ASCII Table

To fully understand strings, you must understand how your computer represents characters internally. A concept that will come into major play while you program in any language is the *ASCII table* (pronounced *ask-ee*). Although the reason for the ASCII table and how to take advantage of your knowledge of the ASCII table will increase as you hone your programming skills, you should take a few moments for an introduction to this important character-based table.

Years ago, somebody wrote all the various combinations of eight binary 1s and 0s, from 00000000 to 11111111, and assigned a unique character to each one. The table of characters was standardized and is known today as the ASCII table. Table 5.1 shows a partial listing of the ASCII table that contains 256 entries. ASCII stands for *American Standard Code for Information Interchange*. Some ASCII tables use only the last seven *bits* (called the *7-bit ASCII table*) and keep the far left-hand bit off. As you might surmise, a bit is a 1 or a 0. Eight bits form a *byte,* which is a character in computer terminology due to the ASCII table. Seven-bit ASCII tables cannot represent as many different characters as can today's 8-bit ASCII tables.

TABLE 5.1   Every character possible has its own unique ASCII value.

Character	ASCII Code	Decimal Equivalent
Space	00100000	32
0	00110000	48
1	00110001	49
2	00110010	50
3	00110011	51
9	00111001	57
?	00111111	63
A	01000001	65
B	01000010	66
C	01000011	67
a	01100001	97
b	01100010	98

Each ASCII value has a corresponding decimal number associated with it. These values are shown at the right of the eight-bit values in Table 5.1. Therefore, even though the computer represents the character "?" as 00111111 (two off switches with six on switches), you can refer, through programming, to that ASCII value as 63 and your computer will know you mean 00111111. One of the advantages of high-level programming languages is that they often let you use the easier (for people) decimal values and the programming language converts the value to the 8-bit binary value used inside the computer.

As you can tell from the ASCII values in Table 5.1, every character in the computer, both uppercase and lowercase letters, and even the space, has its own unique ASCII value. The unique ASCII code is the only way that the computer has to differentiate characters.

Every microcomputer uses the ASCII table. Large mainframe computers use a similar table called the *EBCDIC table* (pronounced *eb-se-dik*). EBCDIC stands for *Extended Binary Coded Decimal Interchange Code*. The ASCII table is the fundamental storage representation of all data and programs that your computer manages. A new coding scheme called *Unicode* is now beginning to see some use. Unicode spans far more than the 256 character limit of the ASCII or EBCIDIC tables to take into account languages such as the Japanese-based *kanji* and others that require numerous characters to represent. Unicode assigns hundreds of numbers to hundreds and even thousands of possible characters depending on the language being represented.

When you press the letter *A*, that *A* is not stored in your computer; rather, the ASCII value of the letter *A* is stored. As you can see from the ASCII values in the previous table, the letter *A* is represented as 01000001 (all eight switches except two are off in every byte of memory that holds a letter *A*).

TIP
_____
The ASCII table is not very different from another type of coded table you may have heard of. Morse code is a table of representations for letters of the alphabet. Instead of 1s and 0s, the code uses combinations of dashes and dots to represent characters.
_____

As Figure 5.2 shows, when you press the letter *A* on your keyboard, the *A* does not go into memory, but the ASCII value of 01000001 does. The computer keeps that pattern of on and off switches in that memory location as long as the *A* is to remain there. As far as you are concerned, the *A* is in memory as the letter *A*, but now you know exactly what happens.

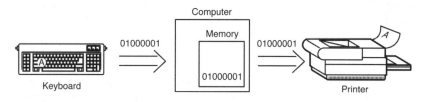

FIGURE 5.2
The letter *A* is not an *A* after it leaves the keyboard.

As Figure 5.2 illustrates, when you print a document from your word processor, the computer prints each "character" stored in that memory location; the computer's CPU sends the ASCII code for the letter *A* to the printer. Just before printing, the printer knows that it must make its output readable to people, so it looks up 01000001 in its own ASCII table and prints the *A* to paper. From the time the *A* left the keyboard until right before it printed, it was not an *A* at all, but just a combination of eight 1s and 0s that represents an *A*.

Performing Math with JavaScript

JavaScript performs mathematical calculations in the same way as most programming languages. Therefore, once you understand the way JavaScript calculates, you'll understand how virtually every other computer language calculates. Table 5.2 lists the JavaScript math operators with which you should familiarize yourself.

TABLE 5.2   JavaScript math operators are simple.

Operator	Description
()	Groups expressions together
*, /, %	Multiplication, division, and modulus
+, -	Addition and subtraction

The order of the operators in Table 5.2 is important. If more than one of these operators appears in an expression, JavaScript doesn't always calculate the values in a left-to-right order. In other words, the expression

```
v = 5 + 2 * 3
```

stores the value 11 in v, not 21 as you might first guess. JavaScript doesn't perform calculations in a left-to-right order, but rather in the order given in Table 5.2. Because multiplication appears before addition in the table, JavaScript computes the 2 * 3 first, resulting in 6; it then computes the answer to 5 + 6 to get the result of 11.

TIP

The order in which operators are evaluated is often called *operator precedence*. Just about every programming language computes expressions based on a precedence table. Different programming languages might use different operators from the ones shown in Table 5.2, although almost all of them use parentheses and the primary math operators (*, /, +, and -) in the same way as JavaScript does.

Parentheses have the highest operator precedence. Any expression enclosed in parentheses is calculated before any other part of the expression. The statement

```
v = (5 + 2) * 3
```

does assign the value of 21 to v because the parentheses force the addition of 5 and 2 before its sum of 7 is multiplied by 3.

Unlike some programming languages, JavaScript does not have an exponentiation operator to raise a number to a particular power. To do that, you would have to call Math.pow(a, b), with a being the number multiplied by itself b times. For example, if you wanted to know 4 x 4 x 4, sometimes written as 4^3, you would call Math.pow(4, 3), which would return the answer of 64.

You can also raise a number to a fractional power with the Math.pow method. For example, the statement

```
x = Math.pow(81, 0.5);
```

raises 81 to the one-half power, in effect taking the square root of 81. If this math is getting deep, have no fear; some people program in JavaScript for years and never need to raise a number to a fractional power. But if you need to, you can thank JavaScript for doing the heavy lifting for you.

The forward slash (/) divides one number into another. The statement

```
d = 3 / 2 ;
```

assigns 1.5 to d.

To sum up (pardon the pun) math operators, Listing 5.2 contains a program that prints the result of calculations that use many of the JavaScript operators described in this lesson. The output of the program is shown in Figure 5.3 after the program listing.

LISTING 5.2   **JavaScript calculations follow the order of operator precedence.**

```
<! DOCTYPE html>
<html>
<head>
        <title>Mathcheck</title>
</head>
<body>
        <script>

        // Filename mathcheck.html
        // program that asks for two numbers
        // and then performs various math operations on them

        // Ask the user for their hometown
        var a = prompt("Enter the first num?");

        // Ask the user for their state
        var b = prompt("Enter the second num?");

        c = parseFloat(a) + parseFloat(b);
        document.write(a+' + '+ b +' = '+ c +'<br>');
        c = a - b;
        document.write(a+' - '+ b +' = '+ c +'<br>');
        c = a * b;
        document.write(a+' X '+ b +' = '+ c +'<br>');
        c = a / b;
        document.write(a+' / '+ b +' = '+ c +'<br>');
        c = a % b;
```

```
            document.write(a+' % '+ b +' = '+ c +'<br>');
            c = Math.pow(a,b);
            document.write(a+'^'+ b +' = '+ c+'<br>');

        </script>
    </body>
</html>
```

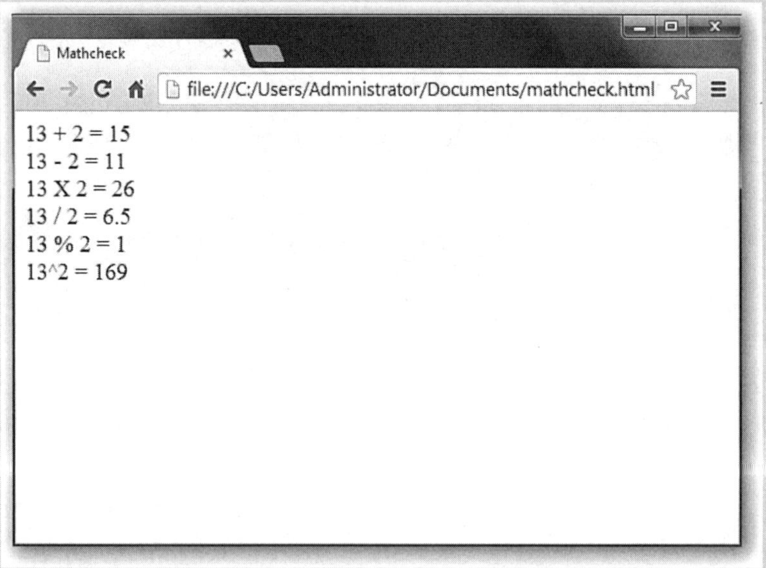

```
13 + 2 = 15
13 - 2 = 11
13 X 2 = 26
13 / 2 = 6.5
13 % 2 = 1
13^2 = 169
```

FIGURE 5.3
Viewing the output of the calculations.

There is probably one line of this listing that is confusing to you:

```
c = parseFloat(a) + parseFloat(b);
```

This line, designed to add a and b, is the most complicated math operation in the listing despite addition generally being the easiest type of math to understand. Why is that? Remember earlier when you learned that the plus sign can be used to combine two strings? If JavaScript thinks either of your numbers is a string, it will combine the two instead of adding them. To be safe, any time you get a number via user input from a prompt, you can convert the number using either `parseInt()` or `parseFloat()`. Those are complicated-sounding names, but all they do is take the variable or string literal given to them and make them either integers (`parseInt`) or floating-point numbers (`parseFloat`). Generally, `parseFloat` is the best choice, as it covers both integers and floating-point numbers equally well, where if you use `parseInt` and the number is a floating-point, JavaScript will cut off the decimal.

Here's a few examples of the two, using literals instead of variables:

```
x = parseInt(56); // x = 56
x = parseInt("4 guys pizza"); // x = 4
x = parseInt("12.8 or so"); // x = 12
y = parseFloat(56); // y = 56
y = parseFloat("4 guys pizza"); // y = 4
y = parseFloat("12.8 or so"); // y = 12.8
```

NOTE

These parse methods only work if a number starts the string. If the last example was "about 12.8," the function would return NaN, which stands for "Not a Number."

You don't have to be a math expert to use JavaScript; it does all the math for you. You only have to understand how JavaScript performs the math so that you can properly set up the equations you need to calculate.

How Computers Really Do Math

At their lowest level, computers cannot subtract, multiply, or divide. Neither can calculators. The world's largest and fastest supercomputers can only add—that's it. They perform the addition at the bit level. Binary arithmetic is the only means by which any electronic digital-computing machine can perform arithmetic.

The computer makes you think it can perform all sorts of fancy calculations because it is lightning fast. The computer can only add, but it can do so very quickly.

Suppose you want the computer to add seven 6s together. If you asked the computer (through programming) to perform the calculation

```
6 + 6 + 6 + 6 + 6 + 6 + 6
```

the computer would return the answer 42 immediately. The computer has no problem performing addition. The problems arise when you request that the computer perform another type of calculation, such as this one:

```
42 - 6 - 6 - 6 - 6 - 6 - 6 - 6
```

Because the computer can only add, it cannot do the subtraction. However (and this is where the catch comes in), the computer can *negate* numbers. That is, the computer can take the negative of a number. It can take the negative of 6 and represent (at the bit level) negative 6. After it has done that, it can *add* –6 to 42 and continue doing so seven times. In effect, the internal calculation becomes this:

```
42 + (-6) + (-6) + (-6) + (-6) + (-6) + (-6) + (-6)
```

Adding seven –6s produces the correct result of 0. In reality, the computer is not subtracting. At its bit level, the computer can convert a number to its negative through a process known as *2's complement*. The 2's complement of a number is the negative of the number's original value at the bit level. The computer has in its internal logic circuits the ability to rapidly convert a number to its 2's complement and then carry out the addition of negatives, thereby seemingly performing subtraction.

NOTE

Here's another kind of 2's complement: *That's a very fine two you have there.*

Because the computer can add and simulate subtraction (through successive adding of negatives), it can simulate multiplying and dividing. To multiply 6 times 7, the computer actually adds 6 together seven times and produces 42. Therefore,

```
6 * 7
```

becomes this:

```
6 + 6 + 6 + 6 + 6 + 6 + 6
```

To divide 42 by 7, the computer subtracts 7 from 42 (well, it adds the *negative* of 7 to 42) until it reaches 0 and counts the number of times (6) it took to reach 0, like this:

```
42 + (–7) + (–7) + (–7) + (–7) + (–7) + (–7)
```

The computer represents numbers in a manner similar to characters. As Table 5.3 shows, numbers are easy to represent at the binary level. After numbers reach a certain limit (256 to be exact), the computer will use more than one byte to represent the number, taking as many memory locations as it needs to represent the extent of the number. The computer, after it is taught to add, subtract, multiply, and divide, can then perform any math necessary as long as a program is supplied to direct it.

TABLE 5.3 The first 20 numbers can be represented in their binary equivalents.

Number	Binary Equivalent
0	00000000
1	00000001
2	00000010
3	00000011
4	00000100
5	00000101
6	00000110

Number	Binary Equivalent
7	00000111
8	00001000
9	00001001
10	00001010
11	00001011
12	00001100
13	00001101
14	00001110
15	00001111
16	00010000
17	00010001
18	00010010
19	00010011
20	00010100

NOTE

The first 255 binary numbers overlap the ASCII table values. That is, the binary representation for the letter *A* is 01000001, and the binary number for 65 is also 01000001. The computer knows by the context of how your programs use the memory location whether the value is the letter *A* or the number 65.

To see an example of what goes on at the bit level, follow this example to see what happens when you ask the computer to subtract 65 from 65. The result should be 0, and as you can see from the following steps, that is exactly what the result is at the binary level:

1. Suppose you want the computer to calculate the following:

   ```
    65
   -65
   ```

2. The binary representation for 65 is 01000001 and the 2's complement for 65 is 10111111 (which is –65 in *computerese*). Therefore, you are requesting that the computer perform this calculation:

   ```
    01000001
   +10111111
   ```

3. Because a binary number cannot have the digit 2 (there are only 0s and 1s in binary), the computer carries 1 any time a calculation results in a value of 2; 1 + 1 equals 10 in binary. Although this can be confusing, you can make an analogy with decimal arithmetic. People work in a base-10 numbering system. Binary is known as base-2. There is no single digit to represent 10; we have to reuse two digits already used to form 10, namely 1 and 0. In base 10, 9 + 1 is 10. Therefore, the result of 1 + 1 in binary is 10 or "0 and carry 1 to the next column."

```
 01000001
+10111111
100000000
```

4. Because the answer should fit within the same number of bits as the two original numbers (at least for this example—your computer may use more bits to represent numbers), the ninth bit is discarded, leaving the 0 result. This example shows that binary 65 plus binary negative 65 equals 0, as it should.

TIP

You can see a complete ASCII table at this web address: http://www.AsciiTable.com/

Using the ASCII Table

By understanding the ASCII table available, you can print any character by referring to its ASCII number. For instance, the capital letter *A* is number 65. The lowercase *a* is 97. Since you can type letters, numbers, and some special characters on your keyboard, the ASCII table is not needed much for these. However, you cannot use the keyboard to type the Spanish Ñ or the cent sign (¢), under normal circumstances. You print these with the `String.FromCharCode` method, which converts a number to its corresponding ASCII character. The format of `String.FromCharCode` is

```
String.FromCharCode(ASCII number)
```

The following `document.write` statement prints a capital N with a tilde over it, followed by a lowercase N, also with a tilde, and then the upside-down question mark that begins questions in Spanish. These characters would come in handy if you decide to translate your website to Spanish:

```
document.write(String.fromCharCode(209,241,191));
```

Here is the output:

Ññ¿

If you want to covert more than one character at a time, just separate the numbers with commas in the call to `String.fromCharCode()`.

The first 31 ASCII codes represent *nonprinting* characters. Nonprinting characters cause an action to be performed instead of producing characters.

Overview of Methods

Methods are built-in routines that manipulate numbers, strings, and output. You can accomplish some pretty cool goals with string functions, but before you do, you need to understand a bit about arrays, as they will help you better use strong methods.

Understanding Arrays

Just as words and sentences are a collection of single letters, strings are a collection of characters, including words, spaces, letters, and any other special characters you choose to type or add using the ASCII function discussed earlier in this lesson. When you assign a string to a variable, such as

```
var hometown = "Salt Lake City, Utah"
```

JavaScript considers that an array of characters and lets you access either the whole name, or individual elements of that name. If you call the alert method sending it hometown

```
alert(hometown);
```

as you can probably guess, your output will be a dialog box displaying

```
Salt Lake City, Utah
```

What is probably not obvious is what would happen if you called the alert method sending it hometown[3], such as

```
alert(hometown[3]);
```

If you did this, you would get a single letter in the dialog box

```
t
```

Now you may have figured out that the number in brackets would refer to a specific letter or character in the string. (Good job if you did!) But even then you might think, why not the letter l? After all, it is the third character in the name of the city. While that is true, JavaScript (and most programming languages) start their counting with 0 instead of 1. So the S is hometown[0], the a is hometown[1], and the t is hometown[3]. You may be wondering what character corresponds to hometown[4]. It is the space, with the L being hometown[5]. When figuring arrays,

JavaScript counts every character, including spaces. In this `hometown` variable, spaces are the 4, 9, and 15 spots in the array, and the comma is the 14.

This may seem confusing, but understanding arrays is important for almost every programming language. (Some more than others—C, for example, does not have a string data type, so to work with strings in C, you need to create an array of characters.) For now, just know that every single character in your strings corresponds to a specific number and that if you're counting them to figure it out, start with 0 and include all spaces, characters, letters, and numbers.

The next sections cover some of JavaScript's string and math methods.

String Methods

Once you've defined a string, you can then access some built-in JavaScript methods to alter your strings. This section will not cover all the string methods, just some of the more interesting ones. Feel free to explore online of a JavaScript tutorial to cover some of the others.

Making strings all capital or all lowercase letters

Two methods can be used to take a string and change the case of all the letters. Any non-letter characters are just ignored. The two methods, `toLowerCase()` and `toUpperCase()`, will create a new string, leaving the original string untouched. Taking the previous example, if the variable `hometown` is equal to "Salt Lake City, Utah", the following two calls

```
newtown1 = hometown.toLowerCase();
```

```
newtown2 = hometown.toUpperCase();
```

will result in `newtown1` holding the string "salt lake city, utah" and `newtown2` holding the string "SALT LAKE CITY, UTAH." The original string remains the same.

The string methods discussed in this section must always be called with a period (.) between the name of the string and the specific method. You've already been using this format, specifically with `document.write`, but instead of a general top-level object-like document, you are using the method of a specific object you created (in this case a string variable). You've also already seen this with the `Math.pow` method of generating exponential results.

Replacing part of a string

Another valuable string function is one that lets you replace part of a string. Say the good folks of Utah decide to be more health-conscious and rename their capital Blue Lake City. You can use the `replace()` method to create a new string that switches words in a string. You can either make a new string as demonstrated in the previous section, or overwrite your existing string. If `hometown` is still equal to "Salt Lake City, Utah", the code line

```
hometown = hometown.replace("Salt", "Blue");
```

would result in `hometown` now being equal to "Blue Lake City, Utah". You don't have to replace entire words, either.

```
hometown = hometown.replace("lt", "lty");
```

would result in `hometown` now being equal to "Salt Lake City, Utah. One additional note about `replace`. It only changes the first instance it finds of the substring you were trying to replace. So if your hometown was "New York, New York", calling

```
hometown = hometown.replace("New", "Old");
```

would result in `hometown` being equal to "Old York, New York". If you wanted to change the "New" in the state as well, you'd have to call `replace` a second time. These methods are powerful and useful, but you should experiment with them in order to ensure you get the intended results.

Other valuable string methods include `length`, which returns the number of characters in a string; `indexOf`, which finds where a specific value occurs in a string; `lastIndexOf`, which finds the last time a specific value occurs in a string; `split`, which breaks a string into several smaller strings (useful to take a sentence and break it by spaces, so you get each individual word); and `substr`, which will make a substring based on the numbers you provide (for example, if you provided "Salt Lake City, Utah," and 5, 11, the method would return "Lake Ci" as the substring). Some of these may seem to have little value, but as you develop scripts and programs, you'll find them more useful than you'd initially guess.

Numeric Functions

There are several functions supplied by JavaScript that perform math routines, and this section introduces you to some of those. Two, `parseInt()` and `parseFloat()`, were already covered and are a great way to ensure that numbers are not mistaken for strings. Lots of your own code is saved if you use these functions.

One common numeric function is the `Math.floor()` method. `Math.floor()` returns the integer whole value of the numbers you put in the parentheses. If you put a decimal number inside the parentheses, `Math.floor()` converts it to an integer. For example,

```
document.write(Math.floor(8.93));
```

puts an 8 (the method's return value) on the screen. `Math.floor()` returns a value that is equal to or less than the argument in the parentheses. It does not round numbers up. If you would like to round off to the nearest integer, use the `Math.round()` method. If you were to create the following statement

```
document.write(Math.round(8.93));
```

you would get 9 as an answer.

TIP
_____

With all math functions, you can use a variable or expression as the function argument.
_____

`Math.floor()` and `Math.round()` work for negative arguments as well. The following line of code

```
document.write(Math.floor(-7.6));
```

prints `-8`. This might surprise you until you learn the complete definition of `Math.floor()`. It returns the highest integer that is less than or equal to the argument in parentheses. The highest integer less than or equal to –7.6 is –8.

You don't have to be an expert in math to use many of the mathematical functions that come with JavaScript. Often, even in business applications, the following method comes in handy:

```
Math.abs(numeric value)
```

The `Math.abs()` method, called the *absolute value* method, can be used in many programs as well. `Math.abs()` returns the absolute value of its argument. The absolute value of a number is simply the positive representation of a positive or negative number. Whatever argument you pass to `Math.abs()`, its positive value is returned. For example, the line of code

```
document.write(Math.abs(-5) + " "+ Math.abs(-5.75)+" "+ Mat.bs(0)+" "+Math.
abs(5.7));
```

produces the following output:

```
5 5.75 0 5.7
```

The following advanced math methods are available if you need them:

```
Math.atn(numeric value);
Math.cos(numeric value);
Math.sin(numeric value);
Math.tan(numeric value);
Math.exp(numeric value);
Math.log(numeric value);
```

These are probably some of the least-used functions in JavaScript. This is not to belittle the work of scientific and mathematical programmers who need them; thank goodness JavaScript supplies these functions! Otherwise, programmers would have to write their own versions.

The `Math.atn()` function returns the arctangent of the argument in radians. The argument is assumed to be an expression representing an angle of a right triangle. If you're familiar with trigonometry (and who isn't, right?), you may know that the result of all arctangent calculations always falls between -π/2 and +π/2 and the `Math.arc()` function requires that its argument also fall within this range. `Math.cos()` always returns the cosine of the angle of the argument expressed in radians. `Math.sin()` returns the sine of the angle of the argument expressed in radians. `Math.tan()` returns the tangent of the angle of the argument expressed in radians.

TIP

If you need to pass an angle expressed in degrees to these functions, convert the angle to radians by multiplying it by $(\pi/180)$. (π is approximately 3.141592654.)

If you understand these trigonometric functions, you should have no trouble with the `Math.exp()` and `Math.log()`. You use them the same way. If you do not understand these mathematical functions, that's OK. Some people program in JavaScript for years and never need them.

`Math.exp()` returns the base of natural logarithm (*e*) raised to a specified power. The argument to `Math.exp()` can be any constant, variable, or expression less than or equal to 88.02969. *e* is the mathematical expression for the value 2.718282. The following program shows some `Math.exp()` statements:

```
document.write(Math.exp(1));
document.write(Math.exp(2));
document.write(Math.exp(3));
document.write(Math.exp(4));
document.write(Math.exp(5));
```

Here is the output produced by these five `document.write` statements:

```
2.71828183
7.3890561
20.0855369
54.59815
148.413159
```

Notice the first number; *e* raised to the first power does indeed equal itself.

`Math.log()` returns the natural logarithm of the argument. The argument to `Math.log()` can be any positive constant, variable, or expression. The following program line demonstrates the `Math.log()` function in use:

```
document.write(Math.log(3));
```

Here is the output:

```
1.098612
```

Summary

You now understand how JavaScript calculations work. By utilizing the math operators and by understanding the math hierarchy, you will know how to compose your own calculations.

By understanding the ASCII table, you not only better understand how computers represent characters internally, but you also understand how to access those ASCII values by using the `String.fromCharCode()` method. Many of JavaScript's methods are universal—similar functions exist in many languages that you'll learn throughout your programming career.

Q&A

Q. In JavaScript, do I have to know all the values that I will assign to variables when I write the program?

A. Data comes from all sources. You will know some of the values that you can assign when you write your programs, but much of your program data will come from the user or from data files.

Q. What kinds of data can variables hold?

A. Variables can hold many kinds of data, such as numbers, characters, and character strings. As you learn more about programming, you will see that numeric data comes in all formats and, to master a programming language well, you must also master the kinds of numeric data that are available. Some programming languages, such as Visual Basic and C, support variables that hold time and date values as well.

Workshop

The quiz questions and exercises are provided for your further understanding.

Quiz

1. What is the result of the following expression?

   ```
   (1 + 2) * 4 / 2
   ```

2. What is the result of the following expression?

   ```
   (1 + (10 - (2 + 2)))
   ```

3. What is a method?

4. What is the output from the following `document.write` statement?

   ```
   document.write(Math.floor(-5.6));
   ```

5. What is the output from the following `document.write` statement?

```
document.write(Math.pow(3,4));
```

6. Write a `document.write` method call that replaces the "Liberty Basic" in "Teach Yourself Liberty Basic" to "JavaScript".

7. Name the three trigonometric functions mentioned in this hour.

8. What is the difference between `Math.round()` and `Math.floor()`?

9. What does the following statement print?

```
document.write(String.fromCharCode(65,67,69));
```

Answers

1. 6

2. 7

3. A method is a section of code designed to perform a specific task.

4. -6

5. 81

6. CompLang = "Teach Yourself Liberty Basic";

```
document.write(CompLang.replace("Liberty Basic","JavaScript"));
```

7. The three trigonometric functions are `sin()`, `cos()`, and `tan()`.

8. `Math.floor()` will return the integer value of a number passed to it. `Math.round()` will return the integer value of the number if the decimal portion is less than .5 or the next highest integer if the decimal portion is .5 or higher.

9. ACE

Controlling Your Programs

This hour's lesson extends your knowledge of JavaScript by showing you how to compare values and repeat sections of JavaScript programs. A user's responses or calculated data can control the flow of your program. This lesson teaches you how to write programs that make decisions. The code sometimes needs to repeat sections in order to complete the processing of several data values. You'll learn how to create a loop to do just that.

With the concepts that you learn in this lesson, you can write powerful programs to do what you need done. You will find yourself thinking of new ideas and new ways to use your computer.

The highlights of this hour include the following:

- ▶ Making decisions with JavaScript
- ▶ Using the `if` statement
- ▶ Changing decisions with the `else` statement
- ▶ Repeating sections of code
- ▶ Using the `for` loop
- ▶ Using `while` and `do...while` loops

Comparing Data with `if`

JavaScript provides the ability for your program to make a choice and to perform one or another action depending on a condition. A JavaScript decision statement has two possibilities. To decide which path to take in a JavaScript program, you must use the `if` statement. Most programming languages have an `if` statement that works exactly like JavaScript's. Therefore, once you learn how JavaScript supports the `if` statement, you will be able to apply the same principles for most other computer languages as well.

Listing 6.1 shows you an example of a program that contains an `if` statement. Even though you have never seen a JavaScript `if` statement before, you will probably have little trouble figuring out what this program does.

LISTING 6.1 Use an `if` statement when you want your program to make a decision.

```
<! DOCTYPE html>
<html>
<head>
      <title>Ifbranch</title>
</head>
<body>
      <script>

      // Filename ifbranch.html
      // program that decides how much of a bonus
      // to pay a salesperson

      // Get the name and sales of the salesperson
      var salesname = prompt("What is the name?");
      var salestot = prompt("What were his or her sales?");

      if (salestot < 5000)
      {
            bonus = 0;
            daysOff = 0;
      }
      else
      {
            bonus = 100;
            daysOff = 2;
      }
      document.write(salesname+" earned a bonus of $");
      document.write(bonus+" as well as "+daysOff);
      document.write(" Days Off<p>");
      </script>
</body>
</html>
```

Look at the following two sample runs of the program. Pay attention to the fact that the program calculates a different bonus based on the salesperson's total sales. The first sample run follows:

```
What is the salesperson's name? Jim
What were the total sales made last month? 3234.43
Jim earned a bonus of $0 as well as 0 days off.
```

The salesperson did not get a bonus because the sales were not high enough. Consider the difference in the following:

```
What is the salesperson's name? Jane
What were the total sales made last month? 5642.34
Jane earned a bonus $25 as well as 2 days off.
```

The program offers complete control over one of two options via the if statement. Figure 6.1 shows you the flowchart of this program. As Hour 3, "Designing a Program," explained, programmers rarely use flowcharts to design programs anymore, but flowcharts are helpful in teaching how statements logically work. The diamond in the flowchart represents a *decision symbol* and shows the operation of JavaScript's if statement.

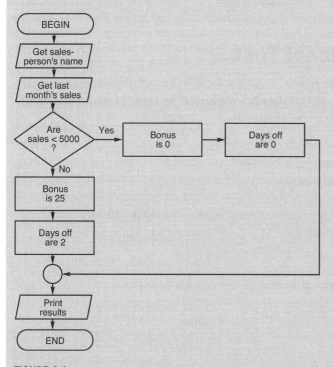

FIGURE 6.1
The flowchart's decision symbol illustrates the nature of the salesperson program's if statement.

The `if` statement works just like it reads. If the statement to the right of the `if` is true, the block of statements following `if` executes. If the statement to the right of `if` is not true, the block of statements following the `if` is ignored. If an `else` statement block follows the `if` and the statement to the right is not true, the `else` block executes instead. The `else` is optional; without it, you are testing to see whether you will execute a single block of statements. For example, the following is an `if` statement that prints a message only if the statement to the right of `if` is true. If it is not, and there is no `else`, the program continues on. Although you need to put a semicolon (;) at the end of most JavaScript statements, do not place one at the end of the `if` statement. That will prevent your program from running the way you want.

```
if (age < 18)
    document.write("You are not old enough");
```

NOTE

The parentheses around the statement to the right of the `if` are not required, but they clarify what exactly is being tested. This statement to the right of `if`, typically enclosed within parentheses, is called a *relational test*.

Writing the Relational Test

The `if` statement reads just as it does in plain English: *If something is true, do one thing; otherwise do something else.* You do not always add an *else* after a spoken *if*, and you do not have to have one in JavaScript either. Consider the following statements:

> *If I make enough money, I'll retire early.*
>
> *If you're out late, call me, else you'll get in trouble.*
>
> *If you're in town, we'll eat dinner together.*

As a programming language, JavaScript is fairly strict about how you make the `if` test. The relational test, the statement to the right of the `if`, usually includes one of the symbols from Table 6.1.

TABLE 6.1   `if` statement relational operators determine how the `if` behaves.

Operator	Description	Example
<	Less than	if (sales < maxSales)
>	Greater than	if (amount > 100.00)
==	Equal to	if (age == 21)

Operator	Description	Example
>=	Greater than or equal to	if (grade >= 90)
<=	Less than or equal to	if (price <= 1.00)
!=	Not equal to	if (year != 2004)

You learned about math operators in Hour 5, "Data Processing with Numbers and Words." JavaScript supplies these relational operators so you can test certain conditions with `if` statements. There are always two possibilities with the relational operators. Something is either less than something else, or it is not. Something is either greater than something else, or it is not. Something is either equal to something else, or it is not.

TIP

The two possibilities that the relational operators enable provide the means for duplicating the two-legged decision symbol in a flowchart. A decision symbol has two possible outcomes, and so does the `if`. `if` is either true or false.

TRY IT YOURSELF ▼

The statements following `else` can be any JavaScript statement or multiple statements. Your programs can even contain one more `if` statements within `else` clauses in its block. Listing 6.2 contains a set of `if` statements that print different messages depending on when in the month the user was born depending on the day the user enters.

LISTING 6.2 You can nest several `if` statements to check a series of conditions.

```
<! DOCTYPE html>
<html>
<head>
     <title>Ifbranch</title>
</head>
<body>
     <script>

     // Filename ifbranch2.html
     // program that demonstrates multiple
     // if and else statements

     // Get the name and sales of the salesperson
     var bdate = prompt("What day were you born?");
```

```
        if (bdate <= 7)
        {
                document.write("The first week of the month");
        }
        else if (bdate <= 18)
        {
                document.write("The middle of the month");
        }
        else if (bdate <= 31)
        {
                document.write("The end of the month");
        }
        else
        {
                document.write("I don't think that's right");
        }
        </script>
</body>
</html>
```

As this snippet demonstrates, you can validate some input values to make sure the user entered what you expected. If the user enters a day of the month higher than 31, the last `else` executes and tells the user they probably entered invalid data.

NOTE

JavaScript allows for multiple `if...else if...else if` layers, but there is another way to handle several possible conditions or values to a single variable, the `switch` statement.

Looping Statements

Looping statements are another important feature of any programming language. JavaScript supplies three statements that control loops. Your computer will never get bored. It will loop over and over, quickly repeating statements as long as you need it to.

Loops have many uses. You might need a loop to ask the user for several people's data, to calculate a combined total, or to print several lines of data. JavaScript's three primary looping statements are

▶ `for` loops

▶ `while` loops

▶ `do...while` loops

The following sections describe these looping statements.

Using the `for` Loop

The for loop is actually a block of statements enclosed between braces following the initial for statement. Before you look at a for loop, an analogy to things in everyday life might be helpful. As with the if, a for loop is a natural way of expressing an idea. Consider the following description:

```
For each of today's invoices:
        check the accuracy of the invoice,
        add the total amount to the daily sales total.
```

You can sense from this description of invoice totaling that a repetitive process happens. If there are five invoices, the process repeats for each invoice.

The computer's for loop works just like the for-each concept in the invoice description (that's why it's called for). To ease you into the method of for loops, Listing 6.3 shows a simple loop that explains the for statement.

LISTING 6.3 Use `for` to control a counting loop.

```
<! DOCTYPE html>
<html>
<head>
        <title>forloop</title>
</head>
<body>
        <script>

        // Filename forloop.html
        // program that prints 10 numbers using
        // a for loop

        for (i = 1; i <= 10; i++)
        {
                document.write(i+"<br>");
        }
        </script>
</body>
</html>
```

Here is the output from Listing 6.3's program:

1
2
3

```
4
5
6
7
8
9
10
```

The `for` statement can save a programmer time and effort by repeating a line or block of code. The `for` statement is broken into three parts enclosed in parentheses to the right of the `for`. Generally, the first part sets up a counter variable, and the second tests the counter variable using a relational operator like the ones in Table 6.1. In Listing 6.3, the variable i is set to 1, and 1 is clearly less than 10. Because the statement is true, the block of code inside the braces prints below the for statement. In this case, there's only a single line of code in the block, but it prints the current value of i, 1.

Once the block finishes executing, the third part of the `for` statement executes. In this case, a math operator new to you, the increment operator, runs. The increment operator (++) adds one to the variable, increasing i from 1 to 2. Now the `for` statement returns to the second part of the parenthetical section, and again tests the relational statement there. 2 is still less than 10, so once again the block of code executes, printing the current value of i, 2. Once the block is completed, the third portion of the `for` loop kicks in again, incrementing i by 1 to 3, and testing and looping continue until i is not less than or equal to 10, at which point the loop would terminate and the program would proceed to the next section of code.

NOTE

You don't have to increase your test variable by 1. You can use a different operator (+=) to increase the value by any number. The statement i += 2 increases the counter by two and if you changed i++ to i += 2 in Listing 6.3, you would only print the odd numbers.

Listing 6.4 shows a program that does exactly the same thing as Listing 6.3, but without using a for loop. You can see that the for loop makes repetitive statements much easier to code. (Consider how much easier it would be to use a for statement to print the numbers from 1 to 200, instead of writing 200 lines of code to print those numbers if you used the method in Listing 6.4.)

LISTING 6.4   **Printing without a `for` loop gets tedious.**

```
<! DOCTYPE html>
<html>
<head>
      <title>noforloop</title>
</head>
```

```
<body>
        <script>

        // Filename noforloop.html
        // program that prints 10 numbers without
        // the benefit of a for loop

                i = 1;
                document.write(i+"<br>");
                i = 2;
                document.write(i+"<br>");
                i = 3;
                document.write(i+"<br>");
                i = 4;
                document.write(i+"<br>");
                i = 5;
                document.write(i+"<br>");
                i = 6;
                document.write(i+"<br>");
                i = 7;
                document.write(i+"<br>");
                i = 8;
                document.write(i+"<br>");
                i = 9;
                document.write(i+"<br>");
                i = 10;
                document.write(i+"<br>");

        </script>
</body>
</html>
```

You do not have to print the value of the loop variable as done in Listing 6.4. Often, a for loop controls a set of statements, determining the number of times those statements repeat, without using the control variable for anything else. Listing 6.5, controlled by a for loop, prints a message 15 times.

LISTING 6.5 Printing a message several times in a loop is efficient.

```
<! DOCTYPE html>
<html>
<head>
        <title>formessage</title>
</head>
<body>
        <script>
```

```
// Filename formessage.html
// program that prints a message
// 15 times

for (i = 1; i <= 15; i++)
{
        document.write("HAPPY BIRTHDAY!<br>");
}
</script>
</body>
</html>
```

Another example will make this clearer. Look at the program in Listing 6.6. A teacher might use it to print a grade sheet. The program asks the teacher how many test scores are to be entered. It uses that answer to loop through a series of statements asking for the next child's name and grade. As the teacher enters the data, the values are printed to the printer. At the end of the program, there is a complete listing of names and grades. (In Hour 9, "Programming Algorithms," you will learn how to program an accumulator to add all the grades together and to print a class average.)

LISTING 6.6 A teacher's grade-printing program is easy to follow when you use a loop.

```
<! DOCTYPE html>
<html>
<head>
        <title>Grading Papers</title>
</head>
<body>
        <script>

        // Filename gradingpapers.html
        // program asks how many students are in a class
        // and then gets their names and grades

        var names = new Array();
        var grades = new Array();
        var students = prompt("How many kids in the class?");

        for (i = 0; i <students; i++)
        {
                names[i] = prompt("Enter student name:");
                grades[i] = prompt("What was their test grade?");
        }
        for (i = 0; i < students; i++)
```

```
        {
              document.write(names[i]+" got a "+grades[i]+"!<br>");
        }
        </script>
</body>
</html>
```

Now after running the program, the user gets a prompt box asking for a number of students in the class (for the example, 5 was entered). The program loops through a series of additional prompts asking for names and grades of each student. After the data entry is complete, the following information appears on the web page (yours will match the data you enter):

```
Katie got a 94!
Maddie got a 93!
Chris got a 87!
Andrew got a 78!
Ben got a 81!
```

A quick note about one extra method used in this program. Just as you learned in the last chapter that a word is an array of characters, you can also create and use arrays of names or numbers. These come in handy when you need a collection of similar numbers, like grades in this program, or monthly expense totals. You could obviously create separate variables for each item, but one variable name with multiple numbered versions is so much easier to handle, particularly if you get larger number needs. What if you had 5,000 customers, and needed to keep a balance for each? Would you prefer to create 1 name with 5,000 copies or 5,000 different variables? The latter, right? And in JavaScript if you want to create an array of any type of data, you just need to call the `new Array()` method.

This program calls it twice, once for an array of student names and once for an array of grades. The program then runs through two `for` loops, with the first to get the input and the second to print out the data. If the teacher has 5 students, the `for` loops will loop 5 times. If the teacher inputs that there are 10 students, the program loops 10 times. With just 12 lines of JavaScript, you've managed to create a pretty powerful piece of code.

Controlling the `for` Loop

There are additional ways you can control a `for` loop. You can make the control variable increment by a value other than 1 each time through the loop. You can also make the count variable count down instead of up.

Listing 6.7 shows you a program that counts down from 10 to 1 and then prints "Blast Off!" at the end of the loop. To carry out the countdown, a negative value had to be used in the third part of the `for` statement (just as the ++ operator increases a variable by 1, the -- operator, also known as the decrement operator, decreases a variable by 1). Each time through the loop, −1 is added to i, which causes the descending count.

LISTING 6.7 Counting down from 10 to 1 is simple with a `for` loop.

```
<! DOCTYPE html>
<html>
<head>
        <title>Countdown!</title>
</head>
<body>
        <script>

        // Filename countdown.html
        // program uses a for loop to
        // countdown instead of up


        for (i = 10; i > 0; i--)
        {
                document.write(i+"...<br>");
        }
        document.write("BLAST OFF!");
        </script>
</body>
</html>
```

Here is the output from the program:

```
10...
9...
8...
7...
6...
5...
4...
3...
2...
1...
Blast Off!
```

The `for` loop offers much loop control, but it is designed to count through the control loop's value. You don't have to increase or decrease your counter variable by 1 in the third part of your `for` loop. You can increase it by 2 (`i += 2`), 5 (`i += 5`), decrease by 2 (`i -= 2`), 0.5 (`i -= .5`), or any amount.

You can nest one loop inside another. Such nested constructs can seem rather advanced to beginning programmers, but the nested loops are simple to understand if you consider what happens when you need to perform a loop more than once. You *could* write the loop twice, back to back, or you could enclose the loop inside another loop that executes its body twice. Hour 9 explains nested loops in more detail.

Not all your loops can be determined by a counting variable. Sometimes you need loops that loop while a certain condition is true or until a certain condition is met. The loops described in the next section often prove more effective when that is your programming goal.

Using the `while` Loop and `do...while` Loops

The `while` loop supplies a way to control loops through a relational test. The loop's relational test uses the same relational operators used with `if` statements (refer back to Table 6.1 for a complete listing of relational operators).

Suppose the teacher with the grade-printing program doesn't know exactly how many students took the test, and doesn't want to take the time to count them. Because the total number of tests must be specified to control the `for` loop properly, another method is required. Listing 6.8 shows you the same program, but controlled by a `while` loop. Notice that the `while` continues looping while a certain condition is true. The condition is the teacher's answer in response to having more tests to enter.

LISTING 6.8   You can control the grade program with a `while` loop.

```
<! DOCTYPE html>
<html>
<head>
       <title>Grading Papers</title>
</head>
<body>
       <script>

       // Filename gradingpapers.html
       // program loops until the teacher does
       // not have any additional students

       var names = new Array();
       var grades = new Array();
       var ans = 'Y';
       i = 0;
       total = 0;
       while (ans == 'Y')
```

```
        {
                names[i] = prompt("Enter student name:");
                grades[i] = prompt("What was their test grade?");
                total += parseFloat(grades[i]);
                ans = prompt("Do you have another grade? (Y/N)");
                i++;
        }
        for (j = 0; j < i; j++)
        {
                document.write(names[j]+" got a "+grades[j]+"!<br>");
        }
        average = total / j;
        document.write("<p>The class average was "+average);
        </script>
</body>
</html>
```

This program keeps looping until the teacher indicates that there are no more grades to enter. Notice that the `while` is followed by a relational test, the result of which (true or false) determines whether the loop repeats again or quits. So if the conditional statement is false the first time, the block of code will not run at all. In this program, we've guaranteed the code will run one time by setting the `ans` variable to 'Y' to trigger the first pass through the loop. This is where a `do...while` loop can be more efficient. The only difference between a `while` loop and a `do...while` loop is the placement of the test expression. In the code you just saw, the condition is tested and then the code runs. A `do...while` loop will run at least once before the condition is tested. The following snippet is the `while` from the previous program rewritten as a `do...while` loop:

```
do
{
        names[i] = prompt("Enter student name:");
        grades[i] = prompt("What was their test grade?");
        total += parseFloat(grades[i]);
        ans = prompt("Do you have another grade? (Y/N)");
        i++;
} while (ans == 'Y');
```

This would make more sense for your grading program—you would not have to set `ans` equal to 'Y' before the loop, and you'd run the code at least one time, which should almost always happen (unless every single student was sick on a particular day. Senior skip day, anyone?).

One added bonus to this program was the addition of a `total` variable, which got the value of all grades and then was divided by the number of students that took the test in order to get an average grade—an extra piece of information your program calculates for the teacher to add some additional programming value.

TIP

When using a `while` or `do...while` loop, make sure that somewhere in the block of code you are altering the variable you are testing in the relational statement. Otherwise, you may get yourself caught in an infinite loop and your program will not end.

Summary

Congratulations! You can now enter data into a JavaScript program and format the resulting output. You have also mastered the true power of any programming language—looping. The programs you saw in this lesson are getting to be powerful, yet you have seen that programming is easy. You have learned how the relational operators are used with the `if` statement so that a JavaScript program can make decisions based on the data. In addition, the looping constructs enable sections of your program to repeat as long as necessary.

The next hour shows you how to analyze your programs to locate errors that might appear in them. You'll learn bug-catching secrets so that you can write more accurate programs more quickly.

Q&A

Q. Does it matter whether I select `while`, `do...while`, or `for` statements when I'm writing loops?

A. Generally, `for` loops are useful when you must count values or iterate the loop's body for a specified number of times. The `while` loop is useful for iterating until or while a certain condition is met, and a `do...while` loop is best when you know a block of code needs to run at least once. If you are counting up or down, a `for` loop is easier to write and is slightly more efficient than an equivalent `while` loop. Ultimately though, you can use whatever style of loop you prefer.

Q. How does `if` compare to `for`?

A. Both the `if` statements and the `for` statements, as well as the `while` and `do...while` statements, rely on conditional values to determine their job. Nevertheless, an `if` statement is never considered to be a loop. Always keep in mind that an `if` statement executes its body of code at most one time, and possibly never if the `if` is false to begin with. Even if the `if` condition is true, the `if` statement never executes its body more than one time, unlike the looping statements that can repeat their code bodies many times.

Workshop

The quiz questions and exercises are provided for your further understanding.

Quiz

1. How does a conditional operator differ from a mathematical operator?

2. What is a loop?

3. True or false: Code inside an `if` statement might never execute.

4. True or false: Code inside `for` loops always executes at least once.

5. How can you make a `for` loop count down?

6. How many times does the following `for` loop print?

```
for (i = 2; i <= 19; i += 3)
   {
      document.write(i);
   }
```

7. Which loop, `while` or `for`, is best to use when you want to execute the loop a fixed number of times?

8. Where does the conditional appear in the `while` loop?

9. What is the difference between a `while` and `do...while` loop?

10. What method do you need to call in order to declare an array?

Answers

1. A conditional operator tests how two values compare, whereas a mathematical operator calculates an answer based on the values.

2. A loop is a set of instructions that repeat.

3. True. If the conditional tested by the `if` statement is false, the code inside the `if` statement will be skipped.

4. False. If the `for` loop's counter variable is already past the limit before the loop begins, the `for` loop will not execute and control passes to the statement that follows the loop's next statement.

5. Use a negative increment to make a `for` loop count down.

6. The loop executes six times.

7. Use the `for` loop when you want to execute a loop a fixed number of times.

8. The conditional appears after the `while` command.

9. Set the conditional to `true` before entering the loop.

10. The `new Array()` method.

HOUR 7
Debugging Tools

Programs are easy to write. *Correct* programs are a different story. Locating program bugs can be difficult. When you are working with tools that compile or interpret your programs, debugging tools will be built in to the compilation or interpretation process, making your life much easier. Although the compiler or interpreter locates syntax errors for you, logic errors often take extra time to locate, and you must be the one to locate such problems before your users locate the problems. For example, when a payroll amount comes out incorrectly due to a bug, you will need to locate the problem as soon as possible.

Although your debugging skills will improve as your programming skills improve, you can help reduce bugs that appear and make debugging simpler by learning to write programs in a way that will make them easier to maintain and update. When you write clear and concise code, you'll debug your programs faster. Many sophisticated debugging tools exist in today's programming languages. This hour shows you how to access debugging tools available to JavaScript developers so that you can try them yourself. Although in comparison to some of the more comprehensive development suites JavaScript debugging is rather limited, you do get good exposure to the capabilities of debuggers by working through the process. The highlights of this hour include

- ▶ Looking in the past to the first computer bug

- ▶ Learning the difference between logic and syntax errors

- ▶ Seeing the importance of writing clear and concise code

- ▶ Using the JavaScript console to help locate errors

- ▶ Stepping through a program one line at a time

The First Bug

The term *bug* has an interesting origin. The late U.S. Navy Admiral Grace Hopper was one of the early pioneers of computer hardware and software. She helped to design and write the first COBOL compiler for the military. *COBOL* (Common Business-Oriented Language) was a language later used by most business programmers of the 1960s and 1970s. Admiral Hopper was working on a military computer system in the early 1950s and, while printing a report, the printer stopped working. Admiral Hopper and her coworkers set out to find the problem.

After spending a lot of time without finding any problems in the program or in the data, Admiral Hopper looked inside the printer and noticed that a moth had lodged itself in a printer's relay switch, keeping the printer from operating properly. As soon as the *bug* (get it?) was removed, the printer worked perfectly. The moth did not fare as well, but it did go down in computer history as the first computer bug.

NOTE

Michael Crichton may have used Admiral Hopper's true story as the basis for his nail-biting suspense novel ***Andromeda Strain***, a story that had a small printer problem that almost caused disaster.

Accuracy Is Everything

You are now well aware that the computer is a machine that cannot deal well with ambiguity. A programmer's plague is the collection of errors that show up in code. Perhaps as you've entered JavaScript programs in the earlier hours, you've run across problems that occurred as you mistyped a character or two. Bugs can creep into code. Programmers must ensure that they do not write programs that contain errors, although this is not always as easy as it might seem.

When breaking the programming problem into detailed instructions, programmers often leave things out or code the wrong thing. When the program runs, errors appear because the programmer didn't plan for a particular event, used an incorrect calculation, or typed a line of code incorrectly.

TIP

Some of the most common bugs you will encounter, and often the most difficult to spot, involve mistyping or omitting punctuation marks, including forgetting that second quotation mark, brace, or parenthesis, or not ending a JavaScript statement with a semicolon. If your program doesn't run the way you intended (or run at all), double-checking all your special characters like these is often a good place to start.

The debugging process is what a programmer goes through to exterminate the bugs from a program. As a programmer writes a program, he or she often runs the program in its unfinished state (as much as it can be run) to catch as many bugs as possible during the program's development. Incrementally running the program as more and more of the code is completed helps eliminate bugs from the finished program. Still, the majority of the bugs can be found only after the program is completely written.

Beginning programmers often fail to realize how easy it is for bugs to creep into code. Expect them and you will not be surprised. Many early programming students have taken a program into the instructor saying, "The computer doesn't work right," when in reality, the program has a bug or two. When you begin to write programs, expect to have problems you will have to correct. Nobody writes a perfect program every time.

Depending on the length of a program, the time it takes the programmer (or programmers) to correct problems is often almost as long as the time taken to write the program originally. Some errors are very difficult to find.

There are two categories of computer bugs: syntax errors and logic errors. To learn the difference, take a few moments to find the two errors in the following statement:

> **There are two errrors in this sentence.**

TIP
_____

Found only one problem? Need a clue? Not yet; look again for two mistakes before going further.
_____

The first error is obvious. The word *errrors* is misspelled; it should be spelled *errors*. The second problem is much more difficult to find. The second problem with the statement is that the entire premise of the statement is incorrect. There is only *one* error in the statement and that error is the misspelled word *errrors*. Therefore, the logic of the statement itself is in error.

This problem demonstrates the difference between a *syntax error* and a *logic error*. The syntax error is much easier to find. As you learned in Hour 1, "Hands-On Programming," syntax errors often appear as misspelled programming language commands and grammatical problems with the way you use the programming language. Logic errors occur when your program is syntactically correct, but you told it to do something that is not what should really be done.

Compilers and interpreters locate your program's syntax errors when you try to compile your program. This is another reason syntax errors are easier to spot: Your computer tells you where they are. When a computer runs into a syntax error, it halts and refuses to analyze the program further until you correct the syntax error. Listing 7.1 shows a JavaScript program that does not work because of a syntax error. It's one of the first programs you wrote, one to compute the area of a circle. However, a character has been removed from the original code to create the error. Figure 7.1 shows the blank page of code because of the error. At the bottom of the screen, the JavaScript console has been opened in Google's Chrome web browser (use the menu and navigate to Tools -> JavaScript Console, or type Control-Shift-J.) The console will be covered in more detail later in the lesson, but you can see it has identified a syntax error in the code and gives you the line number (13) of the listing where the problem exists. It doesn't clearly tell you the problem, but it's a start.

LISTING 7.1   Even a simple program can have an error in it.

```
<!DOCTYPE html>
<html>
<head>
      <title>Calculating the Area of a Circle</title>
</head>
<body>
  <script type="text/javascript">

  // Filename: AreaCircle1.html Program that calculates and
  // prints the area of a circle and half circle
  document.write("The area of a circle with a radius of 3 is ");
  document.write(3.1416 * 3 * 3);
  document.write("<br>The area of one-half that circle is );
  document.write((3.1416 * 3 * 3) / 2);

  </script>
</body>
</html>
```

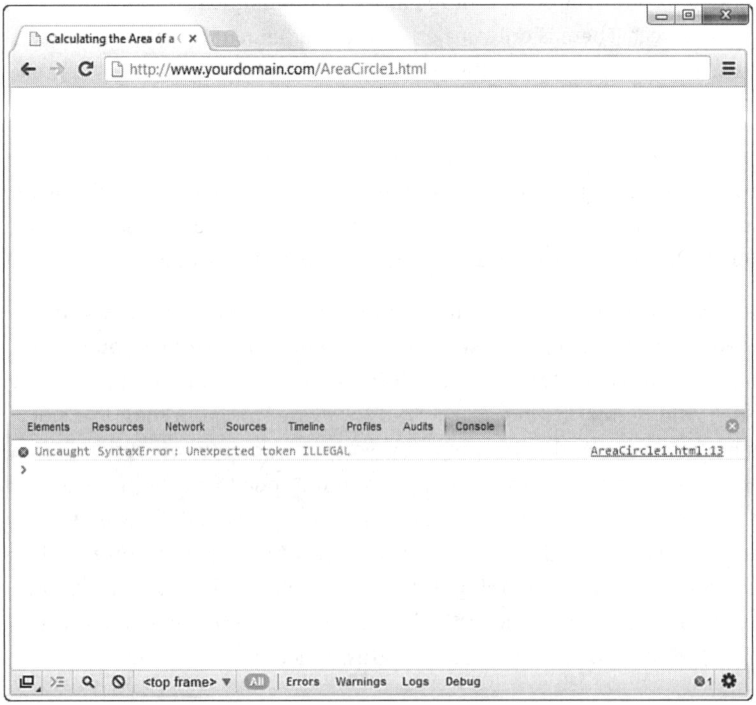

FIGURE 7.1
The JavaScript console can be helpful in identifying errors in your code. The console in Chrome is shown here.

Other browsers contain different views of the JavaScript console, as seen in Figure 7.2, which is the console in Firefox.

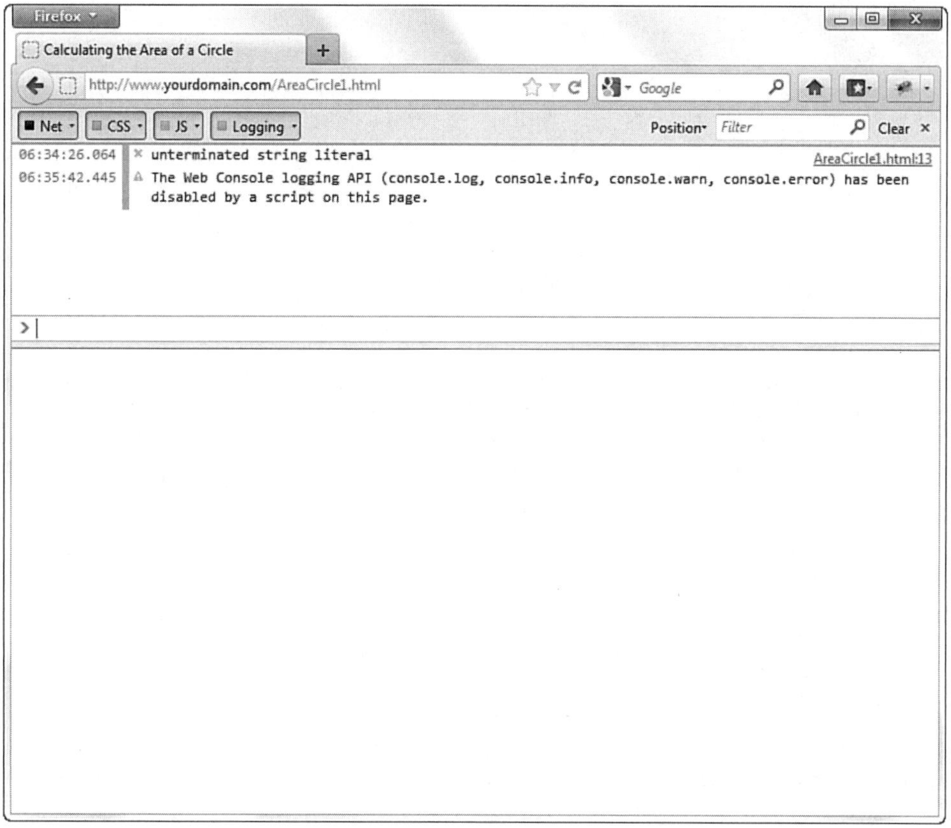

FIGURE 7.2
The JavaScript console can be helpful in identifying errors in your code. The console in Firefox is shown here.

Additionally, browsers such as Chrome and Firefox allow you to install add-on programs, including additional feature-rich debuggers such as Firebug, shown in Figure 7.3. You can learn more about Firebug at http://getfirebug.com/.

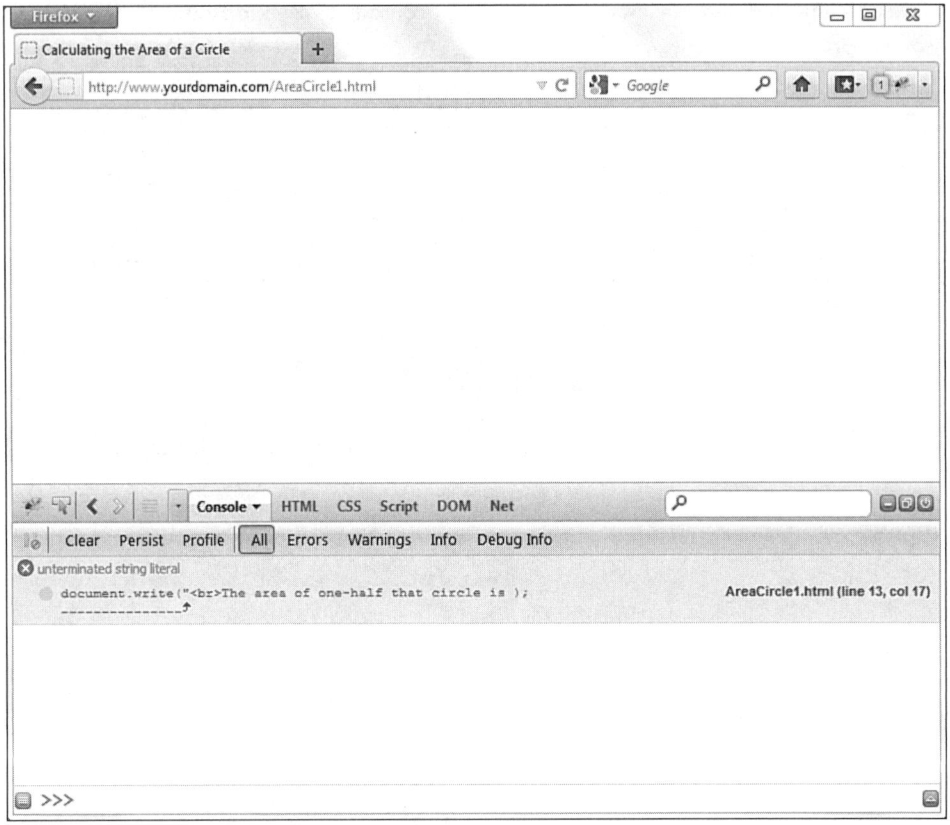

FIGURE 7.3
The JavaScript console can be helpful in identifying errors in your code. The Firefox add-on called Firebug is shown here.

Suppose you're writing a program to print invoices for your company's accounts receivable department. Because of an error, the computer prints all the invoices with a balance due of –$1,000. In other words, according to the invoice, every customer has a $1,000 credit. Your computer did its job, acting out your program's instructions. The program obviously contained no syntax errors because it ran without stopping. The logic errors, however, kept it from working properly.

Extensive testing is critical. The programmer wants to get all the errors out so the program will work correctly when the user finally uses it. The larger the program, the more difficult this is. Exterminating program bugs is just part of the daily job programmers tackle.

NOTE

There is a third kind of error called a ***runtime error***. Runtime errors are actually almost always caused by logic mistakes because the programmer failed to predict and therefore handle a potential problem. Runtime errors can occur if a program attempts to write to a disk without first checking to ensure that the disk is mounted. A runtime error can occur, for instance, if the program divides by zero (division by zero is undefined mathematically). The more you program, the more you will learn to head off potential runtime errors that can occur.

Write Clear Programs

As you write programs, keep in mind the future maintenance that will be required. Sometimes, a program might be in use for a long time before a bug appears because a certain combination of factors occurred. Perhaps an unexpected data value appears, such as a negative value in an age field that should never be negative. Perhaps an operating system update causes a program to stop working.

Not only might bugs appear down the road, but programs often also need to be modified as the needs of the program change. When you write your programs, write clear and concise code. Every time you write a new line of code, consider whether a comment is needed to explain that line or to introduce a new section. Add extra whitespace characters to your program.

Consider the C program shown in Listing 7.2. The program is a valid, legal, C program that works on many C compilers that you might use. Yet, the program is horribly written. The program works and contains no syntax or logic errors, but the program is virtually impossible to maintain easily. The program is rather short but even advanced C programmers will have to hesitate to decipher the code if they are to make changes to it.

LISTING 7.2 **This C program contains no errors but is extremely difficult to maintain.**

```
/* Filename: CFIRST.C Initial C program that
demonstrates the C comments and shows a few variables
 and their declarations */
#include <stdio.h>
main() {int i,j;/* These 3 lines declare 4 variables */
char c;float x;i=4;/* i and j are assigned integer values */
j=i+7;c='A';/* All character constants are enclosed in
single quotes */x=9.087;/* x requires a floating-point
value since it was declared as a floating-point variable */x=
x*4.5;/*Change what was in x with a formula */
/* Sends the values of the variables to the screen */printf("%d %d %c %f",i,
j,c,x);return 0;/* End programs and functions this way*/}
```

Whether you know C or not, you must admit that Listing 7.2 is bunched together and difficult to read. By adding whitespace and extra lines, the program automatically becomes easier to understand even for non–C programmers as Listing 7.3 demonstrates.

TIP

You'll find that much of C programming is clear to you thanks to your JavaScript experiences. If you want to learn C, you will still have to learn about some of the way C works, including some of the lines in Listings 7.2 and 7.3, but you'll certainly have a head start.

LISTING 7.3   This C program with better spacing is far clearer to understand.

```
/* Filename: CFIRST.C
   Initial C program that demonstrates the C comments
   and shows a few variables and their declarations */
#include <stdio.h>

main()
{
    int i, j;    /* These 3 lines declare 4 variables */
    char c;
    float x;

    i = 4;       /* i and j are assigned integer values */
    j = 1 + '/;
    c = 'A';     /* All character constants are
                    enclosed in single quotes */
    x = 9.087;   /* x requires a floating-point value since it
                    was declared as a floating-point variable */
    x = x * 4.5; /* Change what was in x with a formula */

 /* Sends the values of the variables to the screen */
    printf("%d %d %c %f", i, j, c, x);

    return 0;    /* End programs and functions with return */
}
```

Practice Debugging with JavaScript

Popular web browsers such as Chrome and Firefox contain debugging tools that can help you locate and correct problems in your JavaScript. As you saw earlier in the lesson, you can invoke the JavaScript console in your web browser while any page has been loaded. The console will inform you of syntax errors the moment you run a program that contains at least one syntax error. To see this in action, follow these steps:

1. Open your text editor.

2. Type the following code exactly as written here:

```
<!DOCTYPE html>
<html>
<head>
      <title>Bug Hunt!</title>
</head>
<body>
  <script type="text/javascript">

      document.write("This program contains some buggs.");
      Document.write("This line may have a problem.");

  </script>
</body>
</html>
```

3. Save the file as bughunt.html and then open it in your browser. You will see only the first line of code, as shown in Figure 7.4.

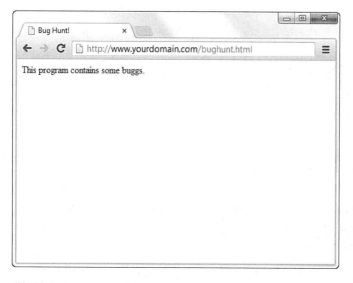

FIGURE 7.4
Only one line of code prints, when you expected two. It's a bug!

4. Now, invoke the JavaScript console by going to the menu and selecting Tools -> JavaScript Console or by typing Control+Shift+J. You should see the console with an error displayed, as shown in Figure 7.5.

FIGURE 7.5
The console shows where the bug is, and what it is.

5. The console shows the error is:

```
Uncaught TypeError: Object function Document() { [native code] } has
no method 'write'.
```

This line of code may be hard to understand, but even if you find it confusing, it can cause you to reexamine the line where things have gone wrong, and perhaps get you to realize the incorrect capitalization of Document.

Note that JavaScript has no problem with the first line, even though the line has a misspelling (the word *buggs* contains an extra letter *g*) because the problem is not part of an instruction to JavaScript. The problem is an error of misspelling and appears inside the quoted string. JavaScript prints exactly what is in the string because the string is a properly-formed string, just misspelled.

If you fix your error and reload the page, you will see the bug has been cleared and nothing new appears in the console log, as in Figure 7.6.

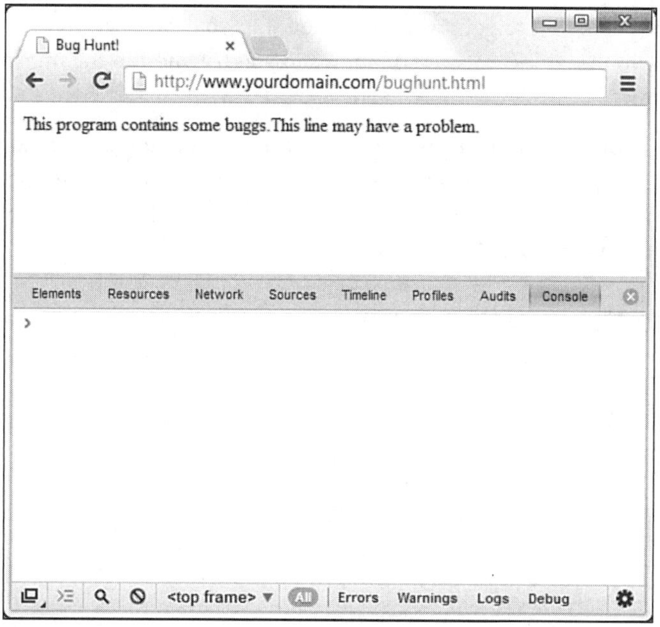

FIGURE 7.6
Your JavaScript bug has been fixed, but your spelling error has not.

Let's go through a runtime error. Create a new text file and type the following code exactly as written here:

```
<!DOCTYPE html>
<html>
<head>
        <title>Bug Hunt 2!</title>
</head>
<body>
  <script type="text/javascript">

        var i = 0;
        var j = 9;

        document.write("i divided by j is "+i/j);
        document.write("<br>j divided by i is "+j/i);
```

```
    </script>
  </body>
</html>
```

Save the code as bughunt2.html and upload it to your website or load it in your browser. In the the first line, dividing 0 by 9 gives you the correct answer, 0. But when you try and flip the numbers and divide 9 by 0, you get Infinity.

As you can see in Figure 7.7, nothing appears in the console because this type of bug (a runtime error) doesn't stop the execution of the program. Instead, it just provides you with an unexpected result. In cases like this, the console can't help you—you have to use your eyes and your brain to realize that isn't the result you expected or want.

FIGURE 7.7
This runtime error does not produce an entry in the console.

JavaScript's Console Log

As you've seen, every time a JavaScript error occurs, it is printed in the console. For as long as you have that console open, you can see a running log of the errors; if you reload the page with the same error, it will print the error again. However, you can also specifically print your own error messages to the console log.

Using the Console API (application programming interface), you can insert your own logging statements so as to help you better understand the errors that are occurring. In Listing 7.5, you can see some of these API methods in use, displayed in Figure 7.8.

LISTING 7.5 Logging into the Console in JavaScript

```
<!DOCTYPE html>
<html>
<head>
      <title>Console Logging</title>
</head>
<body>
  <script type="text/javascript">

  console.log("Hello World!");
  console.error("Server is  not responding",500);
  console.warn("Danger, Will Robinson!");
  document.write("Look down there in the console. Nothing to see here.");

  </script>
</body>
</html>
```

The general console.log() statement places the text you type within the parentheses directly into the log. Using console.error() allows you to specify the string and server error type to display; this appears with an additional warning icon in the console log itself. Finally, in this example, you see the use of console.warn() to display text with a yellow warning icon (as opposed to the red icon, or no icon at all).

FIGURE 7.8
Showing examples of custom logging.

Although this example is simple—it's not even logging within the context of a real program, after all—you can begin to see the usefulness of being able to set specific logging statements to display at different points in your program.

Additional Debugging Techniques

As mentioned earlier in this lesson, when you use programming environments more power-ful than the JavaScript console, such as sophisticated development suites or even just inte-grated development environments (you'll learn more about these in Hour 24, "The Future of Programming"), most of the debugging aids are similar to those that you now know. These addi-tional tools allow you to change source code during debugging to see how your changes immedi-ately affect the output. Also, you can change variables as the program runs.

The following list is a partial sample of some of the features you'll find in most of today's debug-ging systems:

▶ Analyzing variables at runtime and viewing those variables in a window separate from the output.

▶ Changing contents of variables during the execution of the program so that the rest of the program acts as though the code had assigned those values.

▶ You can set *breakpoints* throughout the program so that the program runs at normal speed until your preset breakpoint is reached. At that time, you can single-step through the rest of the code.

▶ You can set *watch variables* that halt the program's execution when the watch variables receive a specific value or range of values.

▶ You can skip statements that you don't want to execute during debugging.

In addition to the usual fare of debugging features, many tools allow you to retrace your steps through a program. When you need to see exactly which parts of a program have executed up to a breakpoint, you can look at the *call stack*. The call stack appears in a dialog box and shows all procedures that have executed in the program to that point. If you double-click a procedure name, the code window opens to that procedure, and all variable values are still intact so that you can see what values have been computed.

Be sure to explore the development tools available to you for your programming language and development environment of choice—they are numerous!

Summary

This hour showed how you can use debugging tools to locate problems in your programs. You used the JavaScript console to learn the skills related to debugging, but those same skills will transfer rapidly to other languages and tools. Learning how to debug pays dividends when you need to track bugs. Although the debugging tools cannot locate specific logic bugs on their own, they make locating logic bugs easier for you to do.

Q&A

Q. How can single-stepping help me debug a program when it takes so long to step through a large application?

A. By executing a program one line at a time, you can analyze variable and control values at your pace. Remember that you don't have to single-step through every statement, but only the statements that you want to analyze. After you view values, you then can run the rest of the program or set a breakpoint later in the code and run the program at normal speed to that set breakpoint. Single-stepping not only helps you ensure that data values are correct, but you can also monitor the execution of a program to make sure that the program's statements execute in the order that you intended.

Q. Can I debug a compiled program?

A. Unfortunately, the debugging tools only work with source code. The source code is needed to display variable names and locate program statements. As a good programmer, you will keep a copy of all source code you compile into user's programs so you can locate and fix bugs that you or the user find later.

Workshop

The quiz questions are provided for your further understanding.

Quiz

1. True or false: The first bug in a computer program was literally a bug.

2. What is one of the most common causes of a bug?

3. What are the two main categories of bugs?

4. What are the differences between the two?

5. How do you open the JavaScript console in Chrome?

6. Name three methods that allow you to write to the console.

7. What does single-stepping mean?

8. What are watch variables?

9. If your program compiles without errors and executes without stopping at a runtime error, are you assured that the program is bug-free?

10. Do all web browsers have a JavaScript console?

Answers

1. True (a moth, to be precise).

2. Mistyping a bit of punctuation in your code, such as a semicolon.

3. The two types are syntax errors and logic errors.

4. A logic error is a mistake in program logic, whereas a syntax error is a mistake in program grammar or spelling.

5. Menu -> Tools -> JavaScript Console, or type Control+Shift+J

6. `console.log()`, `console.error()`, `console.warn()`

7. To single-step means to walk through the program's execution one statement at a time, analyzing the results of each statement.

8. Watch variables are variables you set up to monitor during a program's debugging session.

9. Just because a program compiles and runs does not mean that you have fully debugged the program. Sometimes, an error appears long after the program is in use due to a special set of data values that are entered.

10. Yes, but it may differ in appearance from browser to browser.

Structured Techniques

Now you are familiar with the steps to take before programming. You also know how to do some programming, having a little JavaScript in your programming bag of tricks. In this hour's lesson, you begin honing your programming skills. From Hour 3, "Designing a Program," you now know that two steps must always precede writing the program—defining the output and data as well as developing the logic. After you develop the logic, you can write the program, using one of the many available programming languages.

This hour guides you into being a more structured programmer, writing clearer code, and writing code that is maintainable. Your future as a programmer depends on your being able to write code that others can change and manage.

The highlights of this hour include the following:

► Understanding the importance of structured programming

► Analyzing the three structured-programming constructs

► Testing a program

► Checking a program in stages

► Using parallel testing to eliminate downtime

Structured Programming

Structured programming is a philosophy stating that programs should be written in an orderly fashion without a lot of jumping to and fro. If a program is easy to read, the program is easier to change. People have known for many years that clear writing style is important, but it became obvious to computer people only after nearly 20 years of using nonstructured techniques.

In the late 1960s, programming departments began to wallow in programming backlogs that grew at tremendous rates. More people were writing more programs than ever, but many programmers had to be hired to maintain the previously written programs.

TIP

You cannot hear the importance of writing readable and maintainable programs too often. By using a conscientious approach (instead of the old "throw a program together" approach that some program-mers use), you help ensure your future as a programmer. Companies save money when a program-mer writes code that is easily maintained.

When you finish a program, you are finished only for the time being. That program's assump-tions about the job that it performs will change over time. Businesses never remain constant in this global economy. Data processing managers began to recognize that the programming maintenance backlog was beginning to take its toll on development. Programmers were pulled away from new projects in order to update older projects. The maintenance was taking too long.

By the way, the programming backlog of the 1960s has never really gotten better. Companies all around the world keep contract programmers and programming staff on hand to develop the new systems that they need. A backlog of computer projects seems to be the norm in the com-puter world. Constant change in the world means that an organization's data processing has to change as well.

Roots of Structured Programming

During the maintenance crisis of the 1960s, data processing people began looking for new ways to program. They weren't necessarily interested in new languages but in new ways to write pro-grams that would make them work better and faster and, most important, make them readable so that others could maintain the programs without too much trouble. Structured-programming techniques were developed during this time.

There is some debate as to exactly when beginning programmers should be introduced to struc-tured programming. Some people feel that programmers should be trained in structured pro-gramming from the beginning. Others feel beginners should learn to program any way that gets the job done, and then they should adapt to structured programming.

You've seen what flowcharts are, and the rest of this hour will use those tools to show you what structured programming is all about. As mentioned in Hour 3, flowcharts are not used so much anymore to design complete programs but are used for showing small logic flows. It is a good idea to incorporate structured-programming techniques into your code-writing process. Many of today's languages naturally lend themselves to structured-programming techniques because their commands and structure mirror the structured-programming rules you'll learn in the next sections.

Looking at Structure

Just because a program is well written and easily read doesn't necessarily mean it's struc-tured. Structured programming is a specific approach to programming that generally produces well-written and easily read programs. Nothing can make up for a programmer rushing to finish a program by proceeding in what he thinks is the fastest way. You often hear, "Later, I'll make it structured, but for now, I'll leave it as it is." *Later* never comes. People use the program until one day, when changes have to be made, the changes turn out to take as long as or longer than it would take to scrap the entire program and rewrite it from scratch.

Structured programming includes the following three constructs:

▶ Sequence

▶ Decision (also called *selection*)

▶ Looping (also called *repetition* or *iteration*)

A *construct* (from the word *construction*) is a building block of a language and one of a language's fundamental operations. As long as a programming language supports these three constructs (most modern languages do), you can write structured programs. The opposite of a structured program is known as *spaghetti code*. Like spaghetti that flows and swirls all over the plate, an unstructured program—one full of spaghetti code—flows all over the place with little or no structure. An unstructured program contains lots of *branching*. A branch occurs when a program goes this way and that with no particular order.

Jumping Around

Most programming languages enable you to branch with a `goto` statement. The `goto` works just as it sounds: it tells the computer to go to another place in the program and continue execution there. While JavaScript reserved the keyword goto (meaning you cannot use it as a variable or function name), It does not have a `goto` statement, so you don't have to worry about learning what it does and then not using it. However, if you work with other languages you will see this technique used, but it should be avoided whenever possible.

The three structured-programming constructs aren't just for programs. You will find that you can use them for flowcharts, pseudocode, and any other set of instructions you write for others, whether those instructions are computer-related or not. The three structured-programming constructs ensure that a program doesn't branch all over the place and that any execution is controlled and easily followed.

The following three sections explain each of the three structured-programming constructs. Read them carefully and you'll see that the concept of a structured program is easy to understand. Learning about structure before learning a language should help you think of structure as you develop your programming skills.

Sequence

Sequence is nothing more than two or more instructions, one after the other. The first few programs you wrote in JavaScript use sequence. The sequential instructions are the easiest of the three structured-programming constructs because you can follow the program from the first statement to the last within the sequence. Figure 8.1 shows a flowchart that illustrates sequence.

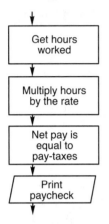

FIGURE 8.1
The sequence structured-programming construct executes the program in order.

To show that you can represent any kind of logic using pseudocode as well as a flowchart, here is pseudocode that matches the sequence of the flowchart:

```
Get the hours worked.
Multiply the hours by the rate.
Subtract taxes to compute net pay.
Print paycheck.
```

NOTE

Some programmers prefer to see pseudocode when looking at logic instead of flowcharts because of pseudocode's compact nature and its closeness to actual computer code.

Because computers must have the capability of making decisions and performing repetitive tasks, not all your programs can consist of straight sequential logic. When sequence is available, however, it makes for straightforward program logic.

Decision (Selection)

You have seen the *decision* construct before. In JavaScript, when you wrote an if statement, you were using the structured-programming decision construct. At the point of such a decision, the program must take off in one of two directions. Obviously, a decision is a break from the sequential program flow, but it's a controlled break.

By its nature, a branch must be performed based on the result of a decision (in effect, the code must skip the code that is not to execute). Based on new data, the program might repeat a decision and take a different route the second time, but again, you can always assume that the decision code not being executed at the time is meaningless to the current loop.

Figure 8.2 shows a flowchart that contains part of a teacher's grading program logic. The flowchart illustrates the use of the decision construct.

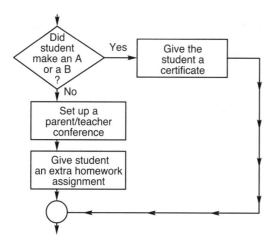

FIGURE 8.2
The decision structured-programming construct offers one of two choices.

Here is the pseudocode for the decision shown in the flowchart:

```
If the student makes an A or B,
   give the student an achievement certificate.
Otherwise:
   set up a parent-teacher conference;
give the student extra homework.
```

Looping (Repetition and Iteration)

Perhaps the most important task of computers is *looping* (the term for repeating or iterating through lines of program code as you did in Hour 6, "Controlling Your Programs"). Computers repeat sections of a program millions of times and never become bored. Computers are perfect companions for workers who have lots of data to process, because the computer can process the data, repeating the common calculations needed throughout all the data, and the person can analyze the results.

Looping is prevalent in almost every program written. Rarely do you write a program that is a straight sequence of instructions. The time it takes to design and write a program isn't always worth the effort when a straight series of tasks is involved. Programs are most powerful when they can repeat a series of sequential statements or decisions.

Figure 8.3 shows a flowchart that repeats a section in a loop. Loops only temporarily break the rule that says flowcharts should flow down and to the right. Loops within a flowchart are fine because eventually the logic will stop looping.

CAUTION

Be aware of the dreaded infinite loop. An *infinite loop* is a never-ending loop. If your computer goes into an infinite loop, it continues looping, never finishing, and sometimes it's difficult to regain control of the program without rebooting the computer. Loops should always be prefaced with a decision statement so that eventually the decision triggers the end of the loop and the rest of the program can finish.

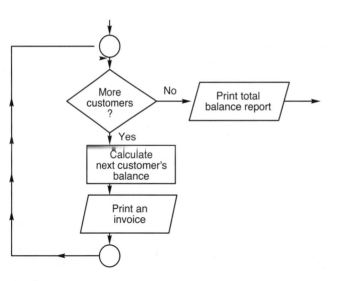

FIGURE 8.3
The looping structured-programming construct repeats parts of the program.

Here is the pseudocode for the flowchart:

```
If there are more customers,
   do the following:
     calculate the next customer's balance;
     print an invoice.
Otherwise,
   print the total balance report.
```

As you can see, eventually there won't be any customers, and the loop (beginning with do) will stop looping so that the rest of the logic can take over.

None of these structured-programming constructs should be new to you because you worked with them in the JavaScript programs. As long as you keep these three constructs in mind while you develop your program's logic, and as long as you resist the temptation to start branching all over the program, you will write well-structured, easy-to-maintain programs and secure your position as a programmer for many years to come.

Packaging Your JavaScript Code into Functions

When writing your programs, you often find that you have to perform specific jobs repeatedly. To save time, you can create a function and then re-use it in any JavaScript program you write. These resusable bits of code are similar to the methods you have seen to date, like the math and string methods. Writing functions is not limited to JavaScript either; it is a fundamental practice of structured programs in most other languages as well.

Creating Functions

Suppose you noticed you always needed to cut your variable values in thirds (perhaps you have three kids and need to divide everything equally among them). Rather than constantly write the code needed to divide your variables in three, you decide to create a function to do it for you. The following code would do it for you:

```
function cutthird (x) {
        var y = x / 3;
        return y;
}
```

The x in the parentheses can be any value. You can replace it with an actual number (6) or a variable. The function will take that number, divide it by 3, and then return the new value. The keyword return is probably new to you. If your function is going to perform some operation on a variable, you need to get the new value back to your original code. The return keyword tells your program to send some value back to the calling function. Now to use the function in your code, you could call it in the following manner:

```
candy = prompt("How many pieces of candy in the bag?");
var candyperkid = cutthird(candy);
document.write("Each kid gets " + candyperkid + " pieces");
```

So in this case you've created a new variable, candyperkid, and set it to the value that your function calculates. You can then call the function as often as you want, just as you can call any string or math method as often as you want.

▼ TRY IT YOURSELF

Let's say you are building a website for your own small business. You would like each page you create to have your company's name, mailing address, phone number, and email at the top. Seems like a great place to add a function! So let's return to Fran's Place, the small store used in Hour 4, "Getting Input and Displaying Output" (see Listing 8.1).

LISTING 8.1 Building a simple informational function

```
<! DOCTYPE html>
<html>
<head>
    <title>Fran's Place</title>
</head>
<body>
    <script>

    // Filename: Storeinfo.html
    // A function that lists the info
    // for Fran's Place in a typical function

    function storeInfo() {
    document.write("Welcome to Fran's Place!<br>");
    document.write("103 Main Street<br>");
    document.write("Wabash, IN 48673<br>");
    document.write("Open daily 7AM-10PM<br>")
    document.write("Call us at 260-555-1244<br>");
    document.write("Visit our website www.fransplace.com<br>");
    }

    // Call the function to test it

    storeInfo();

    // Now you can put whatever store info you want
    document.write("<p><p>Apples on Sale!<br>");
    document.write("3 lbs. for $2.00!<br>");


    </script>
</body>
</html>
```

Now, this shows a different function, one that neither receives any arguments (like `candy` in the previous example), nor returns a value. It just prints information to the web page and then moves on.

Typing your functions in the same file that uses them doesn't really save you any time. However, you can create files that collect your functions in organized groups that make sense. In the next example, you're going to create two files. The first, storefunction.js (see Listing 8.2), will be used to keep your functions related to a common purpose (keeping store data) and the second (see Listing 8.3) will be an HTML file similar to what you've been creating so far.

LISTING 8.2   Collecting your functions into a .js file

```
// Filename: storefunctions.js
// A file that collects the functions
// for Fran's Place in a single file

function storeInfo() {
 document.write("Welcome to Fran's Place!<br>");
 document.write("103 Main Street<br>");
 document.write("Wabash, IN 48673<br>");
 document.write("Open daily 7AM-10PM<br>")
 document.write("Call us at 260-555-1244<br>");
 document.write("Visit our website www.fransplace.com<br>");
}
```

LISTING 8.3   storeinfo2.html. Similar function as Listing 8.1, but adding a separate file with the function

```
<! DOCTYPE html>
<html>
<head>
      <title>Fran's Place</title>
      <script src='storefunctions.js'></script>
</head>
<body>

      <script>

      // Filename: Storeinfo2.html
      // A function that lists the info
      // for Fran's Place in a typical function


      // Call the function to test it
```

```
        storeInfo();
        document.write("<p><p>Apples on Sale!<br>");
        document.write("3 lbs. for $2.00!<br>");



    </script>
</body>
</html>
```

Once you create a .js file with your saved code, to include it you just need to use the script src line, `<script src='storefunctions.js'></script>`. This assumes that the .js file is in the same folder as your HTML file. If it isn't, you can add the file path to your file name such as

`<script src='c:/My Documents/code/store/storefunctions.js'></script>`

You can place this command in the head of your HTML file, or you can place it in the body of the HTML file.

Now it may not seem like you're saving much time if you compare the work you would put into Listing 8.1 versus Listings 8.2 and 8.3. But this is the simplest example and only has one func-tion. Perhaps you'll decide to add another function, such as turning the cash register prompts from Hour 4 into a function. That could be added to your storefunction.js file.

Another value of collecting a function into a single file is if you need to alter your information for your store. Perhaps you decide to stay open to 11 every night instead of 10. If you've created 20 web pages for your store and each individual page has that information, you need to change all 20. If the 20 pages all use the function file, changing it there will cause all the web pages to be updated.

Testing the Program

When you finish writing the actual program code with your structured format and your func-tions, you aren't completely done with the program. You must turn to the task of debugging the program using the methods described in Hour 7, "Debugging Tools." You know that you need to eliminate as many bugs from the program as possible. For obvious reasons, you don't want the user to do this. You don't want the user of your program finding all kinds of mistakes that you made. Therefore, you must thoroughly test the program.

Knowing how to debug is only the first step in writing trouble-free programs. You already know what to do if bugs appear, but before you release a program for use, you need to ensure that you have put that program through thorough testing so that few, if any, bugs ever appear.

Here are the typical testing steps that programmers should follow before distributing a final version of a program to users:

1. Perform desk checking.

2. Perform a beta test.

3. Compare the results of the beta test against the old system's parallel test results.

Desk Checking

Most programmers go through a series of desk checks on their programs. *Desk checking* is the process of sitting in front of a computer and checking the program by using as many different scenarios of data as possible to find weak spots and errors in the code. During desk checking, programmers should try extreme values, type bad input, and generally try their best to make the program fail. Programmers should also try every option available in the program, using different combinations to see what happens in all situations.

Beta Testing

When desk checking is completed and programmers are as confident as they can be about the program's correctness, programmers should set up a group of users to try the program. This is known in the industry as the *beta testing* stage. The more beta testers (test users of the program) you find to test the program, the better the chance that errors will be found. Users often try things the programmer never thought of while writing the program.

Beta Testing Now Exists on a Grand Scale

More and more companies are openly inviting the public to help beta-test products. Microsoft, for example, is extremely open about distributing beta-test copies of its applications and operating systems long before the final release is available for sale. Most of these beta versions are available for download over the Internet. These beta-test products give reviewers and testers an early peek at the software, which also helps Microsoft because these testers can inform Microsoft of bugs they find.

As the beta audience grows, so does the time a company takes for the test. The problem is that today's software is highly complex, requiring as many as a few hundred programmers to produce a product, such as a new version of Windows. A large-scale beta test is about the only way that these companies can discover some of the bugs that must be fixed before the product is released.

Parallel Testing

The user should never abandon an old system and switch to the new program right away. *Parallel testing* should be performed. For instance, if you write a payroll program to replace the manual payroll system for a dry cleaner, the dry cleaner shouldn't receive a copy of your program and use only that. Instead, the dry cleaner should continue its manual payroll system and use your program at the same time. Although this means that the payroll function takes a little longer each pay period, you can compare the results of the program with those of the manual system to see whether they match.

Only after several pay periods of well-matched parallel testing should the user feel confident enough to use the program without the manual backup.

During this testing period, programmers might have to make several changes to the program. Expect that changes will be necessary, and you won't feel disappointed or lose your programming confidence. Programmers rarely write a program correctly the first time. It usually takes many attempts to make programs correct. The thorough testing described in this section doesn't ensure a perfect program. Some errors might appear only after the program has been used for a while. The more testing you do, the less likely it is that errors will creep up later.

Profiling Code

A *profiler* is a program that monitors the execution of your program, looking for sluggish code that might be optimized for speed or size. Many of today's compilers are optimizing compilers that try to take your code and turn it into the fastest possible machine code, but there is always room for improvement. On average, 5% of a program takes 95% of the program's execution time. The profiler can help you improve the speed and efficiency of your program

Advanced programming systems such as Visual C++ come with profiling tools that help you locate sluggish areas of your program. You cannot always speed up a program, but if parts of a program are slowing down the overall operation, you might be able to optimize the code to keep the program flowing smoothly. A profiler can also help you pinpoint when files get so large that faster disk drives and more memory might be beneficial to the operation of a program.

Getting Back to Programming

You're probably ready to get back into the foray of programming. That's good, because it's time to do just that. You now have some groundwork that many newcomers to programming never get. You know the importance of writing clear and concise code. You also know the importance of testing the program before you put the program into production, and you know how to debug any problems that you might find.

The rest of this part of the book focuses on improving your programming skills by teaching you some fundamental programming topics such as data searching, graphics, and programming for the Windows environment.

Summary

The programming process requires more than sitting at the keyboard. Proper design is important, as are structured-programming techniques and proper testing. You and others can easily maintain a well-written program. Because of the changing world and the high maintenance requirements of programs, you should attempt to learn structured-programming techniques that help clarify programs. The three structured-programming constructs that you are now familiar with are sequence, decision, and looping. You also can save time and avoid repetition of code by creating functions.

The next hour explains some advanced programming concepts that you can apply to search for data. You'll be back in front of the keyboard for a few more hours with JavaScript to get you ready for the next step, which begins the third part of this book: object-oriented programming.

Q&A

Q. How much testing is enough?

A. You can never test too much, but resources and the user's request for the program certainly bear on the decision to stop testing. If you know bugs exist in the program, you must remove them, so testing will help ensure that you've fixed all that you can fix.

Q. What tools are available to help me test my program?

A. Most of today's integrated debuggers are highly efficient at helping you spot and remove errors in your programs. You saw some of these in the previous hour when you used JavaScript's debugger to locate problems, examine values, and test programs.

Workshop

The quiz questions are provided for your further understanding.

Quiz

1. Why is the programming backlog still around?

2. Why do some programmers prefer to use and view pseudocode for logic design instead of flowcharts?

3. What is the opposite of spaghetti code?

4. What are the three structured-programming constructs?

5. Although not in JavaScript, what statement do other programming languages use for branching?

6. Why can excessive branching be bad?

7. Write a function that takes an amount and calculates 6 percent sales tax on the amount and returns that value.

8. Which comes first, desk checking or beta testing?

9. What is the difference between parallel testing and beta testing?

10. What is a profiler?

Answers

1. Computers are used more and more, and new programs need to be written while older programs need to be updated.

2. Flowcharts can consume far too much space on paper for large systems and are cumbersome to draw.

3. Clean, easily maintainable, well-structured code is the opposite of spaghetti code.

4. The three structured programming constructs are sequence, decision, and looping.

5. The `goto` statement branches to another part of the program.

6. Too much branching makes a program difficult to follow and maintain.

7. Yours might look slightly different, but as long as you get to the right answer, style is personal:

```
function calculateTax(product)
{
    var taxrate = .06;
    tax = product * taxrate;
    return (tax);
}
```

8. Desk checking must precede beta testing.

9. When one parallel tests, the old system is used in conjunction with the new system and the results are compared.

10. A profiler analyzes a program for inefficient code.

HOUR 9
Programming Algorithms

In this hour, you will learn about programming algorithms that are common across all programming languages. An *algorithm* is a common procedure or methodology for performing a certain task. In mathematics, algorithms provide step-by-step methods for solving a problem in a finite number of steps that can require some repetition. To keep things simple, you'll see the algorithms in JavaScript, but the concepts you learn here are important no matter which programming language you use.

You will learn how to use your programs to count data values and accumulate totals. This is a technique that's been touched upon in earlier lessons, but this hour will formalize your understanding of the topic. The computer is a perfect tool for counting values such as the number of customers in a day, month, or year or the number of inventory items in a department's warehouse. Your computer also is capable of lightning-fast accumulations of totals. You can determine the total amount of a weekly payroll or the total amount of your tax liability this year.

Computers are masterful at sorting and searching for data. When you sort data, you put it in alphabetical or numerical order. There are different methods for doing this, and this hour presents the most common one. There are also many ways to search a list of data for a specific value. You might give the computer a customer number, have it search a customer list, and then have it return the full name and account balance for that customer. Although computers are fast, it takes time to sift through thousands of data items, especially when searching through disk files (your disk is much slower than memory). Therefore, it behooves you to gain some insight into some efficient means of performing a search.

After you master the sorting and searching techniques, this hour finishes by taking a topic you were introduced to in the last lesson and going a bit further with it—functions.

The highlights of this hour include:

- ▶ Counting with counter variables
- ▶ Storing data in array variables
- ▶ Totaling with accumulator variables
- ▶ Swapping the values of two variables

- ▶ Understanding ascending and descending sorts
- ▶ Using the bubble sort
- ▶ Searching for values in unsorted lists
- ▶ Searching by the binary search
- ▶ Using functions to divide the jobs in your program
- ▶ Nesting loops to improve a program's effectiveness

Counters and Accumulators

When you see a statement such as the following, what do you think?

```
number = number + 1
```

Your first impression might be that the statement isn't possible. After all, nothing can be equal to itself plus one. Take a second glance, however, and you will see that in a programming language such as JavaScript, the equal sign acts like a left-pointing arrow. The assignment statement, in effect, says "Take whatever is on the right side of the equal sign, evaluate it, and put it in the variable to the left of the equal sign." Most of the other programming languages also use assignment statements that work like the JavaScript assignment.

When JavaScript reaches the statement just shown, it adds 1 to the contents in the variable named number. If number is equal to 7 to begin with, it is now equal to 8. After it adds the 1 and gets 8, it then stores 8 in number, replacing the 7 that was originally there. The final result is one more than the initial value.

When you see a variable on both sides of an equal sign, and you are adding 1 to the variable, you are *incrementing* that variable's value. You might remember from earlier listings that adding 1 to a variable is useful. Many programmers put such an assignment statement inside a loop to count items. The variable used is called a *counter*. Every time the loop repeats, 1 is added to the counter variable, incrementing it. When the loop finishes, the counter variable has the total of the loop.

JavaScript (and other programming languages like C) have several ways to add 1 to a variable, and you've seen most of them already. Each of the following three statements add 1 to the variable count:

```
count = count + 1;
count += 1;
count++;
```

When adding 1, the third is the most efficient, but it can only be used to add 1. The first two choices can add any number to your variable—you just need to change the 1 to the number you'd like to add. That includes integers or floating point numbers. You can also add a variable in that spot as well, as the following line of code would add newAmount to count:

```
count += newAmount;
```

Subtracting 1 is just as easy. Again the following three statements all subtract 1 from the variable count, and again you can use the first two to subtract any number by replacing the 1 with that number:

```
count = count - 1;
count -= 1;
count--;
```

TRY IT YOURSELF ▼

The program in Listing 9.1 uses a counter. The program lets the user keep guessing at a number until it is guessed correctly. This program gives the user a hint as to whether the guess was too low or too high. The program counts the number of guesses. The tries variable holds the count.

LISTING 9.1 A number-guessing game can use a counter variable.

```
<! DOCTYPE html>
<html>
<head>
      <title>Guessing Game</title>
</head>
<body>
      <script>

      // Filename guessinggame.html
      // Generates a random number between 1 and 100
      // keeps getting guesses until the user is
      // correct.

      var compNum = Math.floor(Math.random()*100)+1;
      var tries = 0;
      alert("IT'S THE GUESSING GAME!");
      alert("I am thinking of a number from 1 to 100");
      do {
            guess = prompt("What do you think the number is?");
            if (guess < compNum) {
                  document.write(guess+" is too low! Try again");
```

```
                       document.write("<br>");
              }
         else if (guess > compNum) {
                       document.write(guess+" is too high! Try again");
                       document.write("<br>");
         }
              tries++;
         } while (guess != compNum);
         alert("You guessed the number in "+tries+" guesses!");
         </script>
</body>
</html>
```

Figure 9.1 shows a sample run of this program. Without the counter, the program would be unable to tell the user how many guesses were tried.

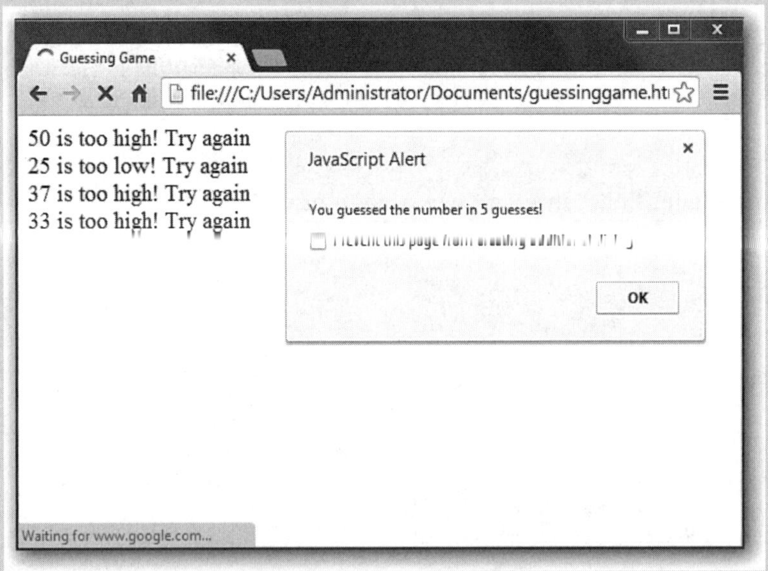

FIGURE 9.1
The number-guessing game's counter keeps track of the number of tries.

Array Variables

Anytime you find yourself writing two or more sets of statements and the only differences are the variable names, you are probably not taking advantage of a better programming style. The program to check grades that you wrote in Hour 6, "Controlling Your Programs," was far more effective because you used arrays for both the names of the students and their test scores.

TIP

Another advantage to using an array for a set of similar variables is that you can take advantage of the powerful loop statements you learned in Hour 6. The goal of programming is to make your life simpler, not harder. Whenever you can put repetitive code into a loop, you save wear and tear on your fingers.

Reserving Array Space

In many programming languages, you declare arrays the same way you declare other variables—you just need to add brackets to the name with the size of the array (how many elements) between the brackets. This is not the case with JavaScript. As you may remember from Hour 6, you declare an array in JavaScript by calling the new Array() method. The following line of code declares an array named customers:

```
var customer = new Array();
```

If you know the size of the array you need, you can put that number inside the parentheses:

```
var MonthlySales = new Array(12);
```

You can also initialize the array's elements by including them in the array call:

```
var Months = new Array("January", "February", "March");
```

Although this example would create a three-element where Months[0] is equal to "January", Months[1] is equal to "February", and Months[2] is equal to "March". If you wanted an array with all the months specified, you'd have to list them, or you could create a 12-element array and then fill the names in later.

▼ TRY IT YOURSELF

Listing 9.2 shows a complete program for storing monthly sales totals. It creates the array, asks for all the sales, and prints all the values. Without arrays, there isn't an easy way to duplicate this program, short of having 12 differently named sales variables and inputting them with 12 different statements.

LISTING 9.2   This sales program stores data in arrays for each month.

```
<! DOCTYPE html>
<html>
<head>
      <title>Sales Report</title>
</head>
<body>
      <script>

      // Filename monthlysales.html
      // program gets sales for each month
      // and then prints out the monthly totals
      var months = new Array(12);
      var monthSales = new Array(12);
      months[0] = "January";
      months[1] = "February";
      months[2] = "March";
      months[3] = "April";
      months[4] = "May";
      months[5] = "June";
      months[6] = "July";
      months[7] = "August";
      months[8] = "September";
      months[9] = "October";
      months[10] = "November";
      months[11] = "December";

      for (i = 0; i < 12; i++)
      {
            checker = "What were sales for the month of ";
            checker += months[i];
            monthSales[i] = prompt(checker);
      }
      for (i = 0; i < 12; i++)
      {
            document.write(months[i]+"'s sales were $");
            document.write(monthSales[i]+"<br>");
```

```
      }
   </script>
</body>
</html>
```

Figure 9.2 shows the results of running Listing 9.2.

FIGURE 9.2
Looping through the two arrays prints the months and the sales totals.

Parallel Arrays

The months and sales totals demonstrate a popular use of arrays. The months[] and monthSales[] arrays are known as *parallel arrays*. That is, the arrays each have the same number of elements, and each element in one corresponds to an element in the other.

With parallel arrays, you can store arrays with any type of data. Although a single array can hold only one type of data, you can have several parallel arrays that correspond to each other on a one-to-one basis. Using parallel arrays, you can keep track of an entire set of names, addresses, phone numbers, and salaries in a payroll program.

Accumulators for Total

An *accumulator* is similar to a counter in that the same variable name appears on both sides of the equal sign. Unlike counter variables, accumulators usually add something other than 1 to the variable. Use accumulators for totaling dollar amounts, sales figures, and so forth. You can use a total to expand on the monthly sales program and produce total yearly sales and average monthly sales for the bottom of the report.

To compute an average, you must accumulate the monthly sales, adding one at a time to an accumulator (the totaling variable). Because an average is based on the total number entered, you must also count the number of sales entered. After all the sales are entered, the program must divide the total amount of the sales by the total number of months. This produces an average. The program in Listing 9.3 shows you how to do this. The counting and accumulating processes shown in this program are used frequently in data processing, regardless of the programming language you use.

LISTING 9.3 A sales-reporting and averaging program can use an accumulator for sales totals.

```
<! DOCTYPE html>
<html>
<head>
      <title>Sales Report</title>
</head>
<body>
      <script>

      // Filename salesreport.html
      // program gets monthly sales totals and then
      // calculates total sales and average per month
      var months = new Array(12);
      var monthSales = new Array(12);
      months[0] = "January";
      months[1] = "February";
      months[2] = "March";
      months[3] = "April";
      months[4] = "May";
      months[5] = "June";
      months[6] = "July";
      months[7] = "August";
      months[8] = "September";
      months[9] = "October";
      months[10] = "November";
      months[11] = "December";
      var totalSales = 0;
      for (i = 0; i < 12; i++)
      {
```

```
            checker = "What were sales for the month of ";
            checker += months[i];
            monthSales[i] = prompt(checker);
            // Add the monthly sales to the totalSales
            // Use parseFloat to ensure it's treated
            // like a number
            totalSales += parseFloat(monthSales[i]);
        }
        for (i = 0; i < 12; i++)
        {
            document.write(months[i]+"'s sales were $");
            document.write(monthSales[i]+"<br>");
        }
        document.write("<p>Total sales for the year are $");
        document.write(totalSales+"<br>");
        var avgSales = totalSales/12;
        document.write("Average monthly sales are $");
        document.write(avgSales+"<br>");
        </script>
    </body>
</html>
```

Figure 9.3 shows the results of running Listing 9.3.

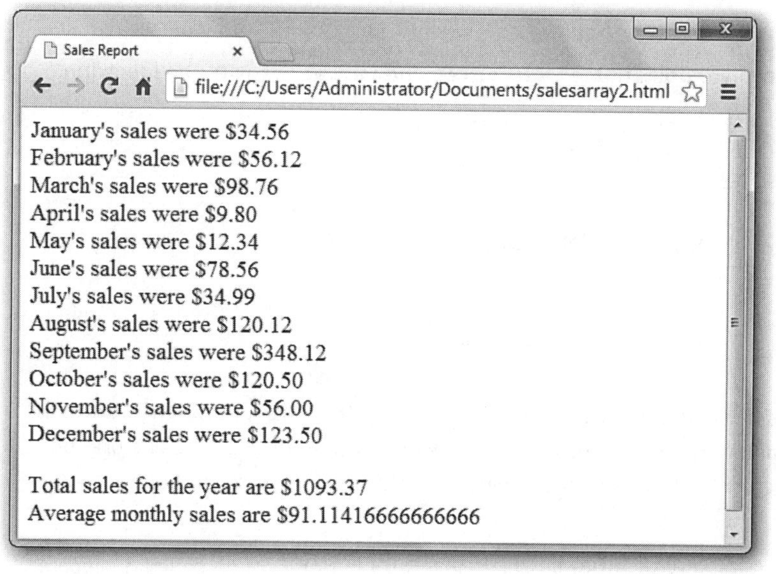

FIGURE 9.3
You can use accumulator variables to calculate totals and averages.

Swapping Values

The cornerstone of any sorting algorithm is data swapping. As you sort data, you have to rearrange it, swapping higher values for lower values. As Figure 9.4 shows, swapping values simply means replacing one variable's contents with another's and vice versa.

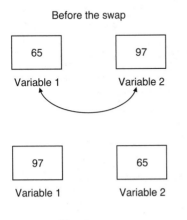

Before the swap

Variable 1   Variable 2

Variable 1   Variable 2

After the swap

FIGURE 9.4
Swapping the values of two variables.

Suppose you assigned two variables named `variable1` and `variable2` with the following statements:

```
variable1 = 65;
variable2 = 97;
```

The concept of swapping them is simple. How would you do it? If you said the following, you would not quite be correct:

```
variable1 = variable2;
variable2 = variable1;
```

Can you see why these two assignment statements don't swap the values in the two variables? The first statement assigns `variable2` to `variable1`, which wipes out `variable1`'s original value. The second statement is then redundant because both variables already hold the same value after the first statement.

An accurate approach to swapping variables is to use a third variable, often called a *temporary variable* because you don't use its value once you swap the original variables. Here is the code to perform the swapping accurately:

```
temp = variable1;
variable1 = variable2;
variable2 = temp;
```

Sorting

The following list of numbers isn't sorted:

    10
    54
    34
    21
    23

Here is the list sorted in *ascending order* (from lowest to highest):

    10
    21
    23
    34
    54

Here is the list sorted in *descending order* (from highest to lowest):

    54
    34
    23
    21
    10

You can also sort character string data, such as a list of names. Here is a list of five sorted names (unless otherwise specified, an ascending sort is always used):

    Adams, Jim
    Fowler, Lisa
    Kingston, William
    Stephenson, Mike
    Williams, Pete

Using the Bubble Sort

There are several ways to sort lists of data. The most popular one for beginning programmers is called the *bubble sort*. The bubble sort isn't the most efficient sorting algorithm. As a matter of fact, it is one of the slowest. However, the bubble sort, unlike other sorting algorithms (such as the heap sort and the quick sort) is easy to understand and to program.

The data that you want to sort is typically stored in an array. Using the array subscripts, you can rearrange the array elements, swapping values until the array is sorted in the order you want.

In the bubble sort, the elements of an array are compared and swapped two at a time. Your program must perform several passes through the array before the list is sorted. During each pass through the array, the bubble sort places the lowest value in the first element of the array. In effect, the smaller values "bubble" their way up the list, hence, the name bubble sort.

After the first pass of the bubble sort (controlled by an outer loop in a nested `for` loop, as you will see in the following program), the lowest value of 10 is still at the top of the array (it happened to be there already). In the second pass, the 21 is placed right after the 10 and so on until no more swaps take place.

▼ TRY IT YOURSELF

The program in Listing 9.4 shows the bubble sort used on the five values shown earlier.

LISTING 9.4   You can sort a list of values with the bubble sort.

```
<! DOCTYPE html>
<html>
<head>
        <title>Bubble Sort</title>
</head>
<body>
        <script>

        // Filename bubblesort.html
        // uses the bubble sort algorithm to sort a
        // set of values

        var values = new Array(10, 54, 34, 21, 23);
        var temp;

        // Outer loop
        for (pass = 0; pass < 5; pass++)
        {
```

```
                // Inner loop for comparisons
                for (ctr = 0; ctr < 5; ctr++)
                {
                        if (values[ctr] > values [ctr+1])
                        {
                                temp = values[ctr];
                                values[ctr] = values[ctr+1];
                                values[ctr+1] = temp;
                        }
                }
        }
        // After both loops, now print the sorted loop

        document.write("Here is the loop after sorting...<br>");
        for (i = 0; i < 5; i++)
        {
                document.write(values[i]+"<br>");
        }
        </script>
</body>
</html>
```

Here is the output from the program in Listing 9.4:

```
Here is the array after being sorted...
10
21
23
34
54
```

Analyzing the Bubble Sort

To give you a better understanding of the bubble sort routine used in this program, Figure 9.5 shows you a flowchart of the bubble sort process. By using the flowchart and by following the program, you should be able to trace through the bubble sort and better understand how it works. At the heart of any sorting algorithm is a swapping routine, and you can see one in the body of the bubble sort's for loops.

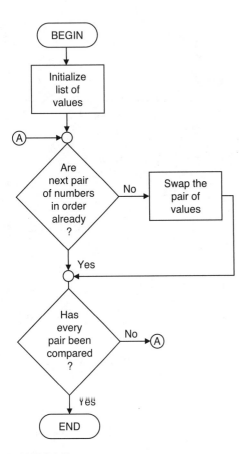

FIGURE 9.5
The flowchart of the bubble sort routine shows the swapping of values.

TIP

If you want a descending sort, you only have to change one statement in Listing 9.4's program—the first statement inside the `for` loops. Instead of swapping the values if the second item of the pair is lower, swap them if the second item of the pair is higher. The new line looks like this:

```
if (values(ctr) < values(ctr + 1))
```

Searching Arrays

There are many methods for searching arrays for a specific value. Suppose you have several parallel arrays with inventory data. The first array, `partNo[]`, holds all your inventory item part numbers. The second array, `desc[]`, holds the description of each of those parts. The third array, `price[]`, contains the price of each corresponding part. You might keep all the inventory data on the disk and then read that data into the parallel arrays when it is time to work with the data.

One use for an inventory program that uses parallel arrays is a look-up routine. A user could type a part number, and the computer program would search the `partNo[]` array for a match. When it finds one (for example, at element subscript number 246), you could then print the 246th element in the `desc[]` and `price[]` arrays, which shows the user the description and price of the part number just entered.

There are several ways to search an array for values. The various searching methods each have their own advantages. One of the easiest to program and understand, the *sequential search*, is also one of the least efficient. The search method you decide on depends on how much data you expect to search through and how skilled you are at understanding and writing advanced searching programs. The next few sections walk you through some introductory searching algorithms that you might use someday in the programs you write.

Performing the Sequential Search

The sequential search technique is easy but inefficient. With it, you start at the beginning of the array and look at each value, in sequence, until you find a value in the array that matches the value for which you are searching. (You then can use the subscript of the matching element to look in corresponding parallel arrays for related data.)

TIP

The array being searched doesn't have to be sorted for the sequential search to work. The fact that sequential searches work on unsorted arrays makes them more useful than if they required sorted arrays because you don't have to take the processing time (or programming time) to sort the array before each search.

Figure 9.6 shows a flowchart of the sequential search routine (as with most flowcharts in this hour, only the sequential search routine is described, not the now-trivial task of filling the array with data through disk input/output [I/O] or user input). Study the flowchart and see if you can think of ways to improve the searching technique being used.

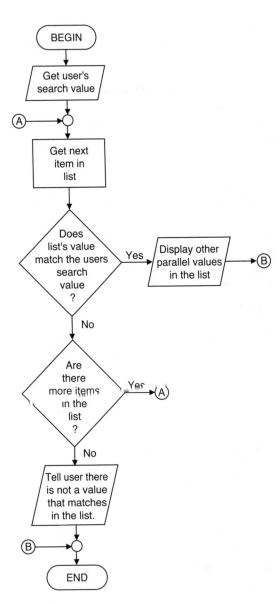

FIGURE 9.6
Flowcharting the sequential search technique.

The program in Listing 9.5 shows you the sequential search algorithm coded in JavaScript. The inventory arrays described earlier are used in the program. The listing shows only a partial program because the arrays are assumed to have the data already in them. The program asks the user for the part number, and then the sequential search routine finds the matching description and price in the other two arrays. After you study the program, you should find that the sequential search is very easy to understand.

LISTING 9.5   A sequential search can help an inventory application.

```
// Filename: searchseq.html
// Sequential search for an item's description and price.
// (This assumes the arrays have been filled elsewhere.)


// This code would be part of a larger inventory program.


// This program assumes that the variable named TotalNumber
//    contains the total number of items in the inventory,
//    and therefore, in the arrays as well.
// First, get the part number the user wants to look up
  searchPt = prompt("What is the number of the part you want to see?");
  foundPart = 0; // a flag to know if the part is found
  for (i = 0; i < TotalNumber; i++)      // Look through all inventory items
  {
    if (partNo[i] = searchPt)
      {
        document.write("Part Number "+searchPt+"'s description is");
        document.write(desc[i]);
        document.write("With a price of "+price[i]);
        foundPart = 1; //Turn on the flag
        break;    // Quits the for loop once the part # is found
      }
  }
// Now check the found part flag to see whether we found the part
  if (foundPart == 0)
  {
    document.write("** Sorry, but that part number is not in the inventory.");
  }
```

Performing the Binary Search

If your array is already sorted, there is another technique that offers tremendous searching speed advantages over either of the sequential searches shown in the previous sections. This technique is known as the *binary search*. The binary search is more complex to understand and program than the sequential search, but, as with most things in the programming world, it is worth the effort in many cases.

The binary search technique uses a divide-and-conquer approach to searching. One of the primary advantages of the binary search is that with every comparison you make, you can rule out one-half of the remaining array if a match isn't found. In other words, if you are searching for a value in a 100-element array, and the first comparison you make fails to match, you only have at most 50 elements left to search (with the sequential search, you would still have a possible 99 elements left to search). On the second search, assuming there is no match, you rule out one-half of the remaining list, meaning that there are only 25 more items to search through.

The multiplicative advantages of a binary search will surprise you. If you have a friend write down a number from 1 to 1,000 and then use the binary search technique to make your guesses (your friend will only have to tell you if you are "too low" or "too high" with each guess), you can often zero in on the number in 5 to 15 tries. This is an amazing feat when there is a pool of 1,000 numbers to choose from!

The binary search technique is simple. Your first guess (or the computer's first try at matching a search value to one in the list) should be exactly in the middle of the sorted list. If you guess incorrectly, you only need to know if you were too high or low. If you were too high, your next guess should split the lower half of the list. If you were too low, you should split the higher half of the list. Your new list (one-half the size of the original one) is now the list you split in the middle. Repeat the process until you guess the value.

Suppose your friend thinks of the number 390. Your first guess would be 500 (half of 1,000). When your friend says "too high," you would immediately know that your next guess should be between 1 and 499. Splitting that range takes you to your second guess of 250. "Too low," replies your friend, so you know the number is between 251 and 499. Splitting that gives you 375. "Too low" means the number is between 376 and 499. Your next guess might be 430, then 400, then 390 and you've guessed it. One out of 1,000 numbers, and it only took six guesses.

Listing 9.6 uses the binary search technique to find the correct inventory value. As you can see from the code, a binary search technique doesn't require a very long program. However, when you first learn the binary search, it takes some getting used to. Therefore, the flowchart in Figure 9.7 will help you understand the binary search technique a little better.

LISTING 9.6   A binary search can speed searching tremendously.

```
// Filename: searchbin.html
// Binary search for an item's description and price.
// (This assumes the arrays have been filled
//   and SORTED in PartNum order elsewhere.)

// This code would be part of a larger inventory program.
// ** This program assumes that the variable named TotalNumber
//     contains the total number of items in the inventory,
//     and therefore, in the arrays as well.

// First, get the part number the user wants to look up
  searchPt = prompt("What is the number of the part you want to see?");
  first = 0;  // Set the lower bound of your search
  last = TotalNumber - 1;   // The upperbound of the search
  found = 0; // The flag that the part was found

  while (first <= last)
  {
    mid = Math.floor((first + last) / 2)   // Set the middle and make it an int
    if (searchPt == PartNo[mid])
    {
      document.write("Part number "+searchPt+"'s description is ");
      document.write(Desc[mid]+"<br>");
      document.write("With a price of $"+price[mid]);
      found = 1; // Turn the flag on
      break; // Exit the while loop
    }
    else if (searchPt < PartNo[mid])  // Check the lower half of the array
      last = mid - 1;
    else
      first = mid + 1 // Check the upper half of the array
  }

  if (found == 0) // The part was not in the array
  {
    document.write("<p>");
    document.write("** Sorry, but that part number is not in the inventory.");
  }
```

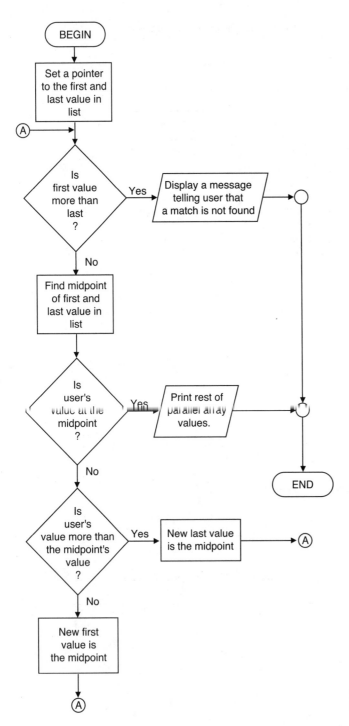

FIGURE 9.7
Flowcharting the binary search.

Taking Functions Further

Introduced in Hour 6, user-created functions deserve a bit more discussion. A function is like a detour; it is a side trip your program makes for a few statements, often accomplishing a specific task, and then the program gets back on the path it was executing and continues from there.

The function is a set of code that works as a unit, as a method works. Functions (also called subroutines in some programming languages) are available for all languages, and aren't difficult to understand. The algorithms presented in this hour make perfect candidates for functions. A function turns your program into a collection of modules that you can integrate. Instead of one long program, your program becomes lots of little sets (functions) of code.

Understanding the Need for Subroutines

Suppose you're writing a program that prints your name and address several times. Without using a function, you would write code similar to the snippet shown in Listing 9.7. The program repeats the same printing code over and over.

LISTING 9.7 A program outline that doesn't use functions can be hard to maintain.

```
// Long program that prints name and address throughout
// (The rest of the code is not shown.)

//  Program statements go here

document.write("Mark Cunningham<br>");
document.write("1244 West Oak<br>");
document.write("Canton, NH  63443<br>");

//  More program statements go here

document.write("Mark Cunningham<br>");
document.write("1244 West Oak<br>");
document.write("Canton, NH  63443<br>");

//  More program statements go here

document.write("Mark Cunningham<br>");
document.write("1244 West Oak<br>");
document.write("Canton, NH  63443<br>");

//  More program statements go here

document.write("Mark Cunningham<br>");
document.write("1244 West Oak<br>");
```

```
document.write("Canton, NH   63443<br>");

//  Rest of program finishes up here
```

CAUTION

Not only is repeating the same code tedious, but by requiring more typing, it lends itself to errors. If you only have to type in the code once, but can still execute that code repeatedly whenever you want (as in a function), your chances of typing errors decrease. Also, if your address ever changes, you only have to change it in one place (inside the subroutine), not everywhere it appears in the program.

If you put the `document.write` statements in a function, you would save yourself some typing. It would also be easier to transfer the code to another program. All you have to do is write the function and then call it as often as you'd like.

Listing 9.8 is an improved version of the previous program outline. Notice that a statement begins the subroutine's name and address printing code. This is a label that you make up that names the subroutine's location.

LISTING 9.8 **A program outline that uses functions is simple.**

```
<! DOCTYPE html>
<html>
<head>
        <title>Function Example</title>
        <script>
        function printAddress() {
            document.write("Mark Cunningham<br>");
            document.write("1244 West Oak<br>");
            document.write("Canton, NH   63443<br>");
          }
      </script>
</head>
<body>
        <script>
    // Long program that prints name and address throughout
    // (The rest of the code is not shown.)

    //  Program statements go here

    printAddress();  // Runs the function

    //  More program statements go here
```

```
printAddress();   // Runs the function

//  More program statements go here


printAddress();   // Runs the function

//  More program statements go here
```

TIP

As mentioned is Hour 6, you can put your commonly used functions in a separate .js file that you can then add to any .html file that needs to use that function.

TRY IT YOURSELF ▼

The purpose of the function is to execute the same block of code more than once. Grouping a routine into a function makes a lot of sense; it helps organize your program. Listing 9.9 shows a complete program with three functions. The subroutines perform the following tasks:

1. Ask the user for a list of numbers.

2. Sort the numbers.

3. Print the numbers.

As you can see, the first part of the program is nothing more than a calling procedure that controls the execution of the functions. By breaking your program into functions such as this program does, you can help zero in on code later if you want to change something. If you want to change to a different sorting method, you can quickly find the sorting routine without having to trace through a bunch of unrelated code.

LISTING 9.9 A program that uses functions for everything is easier to maintain and understand.

```
<! DOCTYPE html>
<html>
<head>
      <title>Function Program</title>

      <script>

      // Get the values to sort
      function askForData(values, size) {
            for (i = 0; i < size; i++) {
            values[i] = parseFloat(prompt("Enter a number:"));
            }
      }
```

```
        // You should recognize the sorting double for loop
        function sortData(values,size) {
                for (pass = 0; pass < size; pass++) {
                        for (ctr = 0; ctr < size; ctr++) {
                                if (values[ctr] > values[ctr+1])
                                {
                                        temp = values[ctr];
                                        values[ctr] = values[ctr+1];
                                        values[ctr+1] = temp;
                                }
                        }
                }
        }

        function printData(values, size) {
                for (i = 0; i< size; i++) {
                        document.write(values[i]+"<br>");
                }
        }
        </script>
</head>
<body>
        <script>

        // Filename functionprogram.html
        // uses the program functions to
        // get a set of values and then sort them

        var size = prompt("How many numbers do you want to use?");
        Values  = new Array(size);

        // Get the data
        askForData(Values, size);

        document.write("Before sorting<br>");
        printData(Values, size);

        // Now sort the numbers
        sortData(Values, size);

        // Print the data again, to show the sort results
        document.write("After sorting<br>");
        printData(Values, size);

        </script>
</body>
</html>
```

TIP

By asking users how many numbers they want to enter, the program has far more value than a program that can only sort a set number of values. Printing the numbers before and after the sort shows the value of functions, as you've called the function twice in the program, but only had to write the code once.

Nested Loops

As with almost all statements, you can nest two or more loops inside one another. Several listings in this hour have done just that, including Listing 9.9. As a programmer, you must make sure you understand the concept of nested loops. Anytime your program needs to repeat a loop more than once, use a *nested loop*. Think of the inside loop as looping "faster" than the outside loop. The inside loop iterates faster because the counter variable of the inside loop goes through all its iterations before the outside loop's first iteration has completed. Because the outside loop doesn't repeat until its block of code is complete. When the outside loop finally does iterate a second time, the inside loop starts all over again.

So if you have an outer loop that is set to run 5 times, and an inner loop that is set to run 10 times, the inner loop executes a total of 50 times. The outside loop iterates five times, and the inside loop executes 10 times for each of the outer loop's iterations.

Summary

The techniques you learned in this hour will be useful throughout your entire programming career. Sorting, searching, and functions are needed for useful data processing. The computer, thanks to your programs, can do these mundane tasks while you concentrate on more important things.

The next hour gives you a break from algorithms and shows you how to write some programs that use graphics. Programming can be fun and graphics are quite possibly the most fun part of programming.

Q&A

Q. How do functions improve a program's accuracy?

A. A program is easier to write and maintain when you group routine code together in functions. The functions help you focus on specific parts of the program that you need to change or fix if bugs exist in the code. When your whole program is comprised of small routines, in functions, you make your code more modular and you help ensure that code in one part of the program doesn't affect code in another part of the program.

Workshop

The quiz questions are provided for your further understanding.

Quiz

1. What is an accumulator?

2. True or false: The following statement is an accumulator statement:

   ```
   num = num - 1
   ```

3. What is the difference between the terms *ascending sort* and *descending sort*?

4. Why is a third variable needed when you want to swap the values of two variables?

5. Which sort is the easiest to write and understand?

6. True or false: A counter statement is a special kind of accumulator statement?

7. What is the simplest kind of search technique?

8. Which is more efficient: the binary search or the sequential search?

9. Write a function that takes a number, doubles it, adds 2, and returns the new value.

10. True or false: Using functions saves typing the same code over and over throughout a program.

Answers

1. An accumulator is a variable whose value is updated.

2. False. Although the statement might actually be using an accumulator variable, the statement happens to be decreasing the value stored there, whereas accumulators are usually added to.

3. An ascending sort puts lists in order from low to high and a descending sort puts lists in order from high to low.

4. The third variable is needed to hold one of the values temporarily.

5. The bubble sort is one of the simplest sorts to write and understand.

6. True.

7. A sequential search is the simplest search technique.

8. The binary search is far more efficient than the sequential search.

9. Again, your execution may be slightly different:

```
function changenumber(x)
{
        var y = x * 2;
        z = y + 2;
        return (z);
}
```

10. True.

Having Fun with Programming

Now is the time to sit back and have some fun with JavaScript. Sure, programming is fun in itself, and you already know how easy and enjoyable writing programs with JavaScript can be. Nevertheless, there is more you can do with JavaScript than writing data-processing programs for business and engineering. You can also use JavaScript to jazz up your websites.

The material you master in this hour gives you the framework for adding pizzazz to your programs. You will get an idea of how game programmers do their jobs. You will learn some fundamental concepts that you need in order to write programs that capture a user's attention.

The highlights of this hour include:

▶ Rotating images on a page

▶ Adding interactivity to your web photos

▶ Using the onmouseover Event

▶ Adding a ticker to your website

Rotating Images on a Page

Static pages can be boring pages. If you are a business trying to attract customers or someone showing off your favorite photos of your children, your garden, or your dog, a single photo is nice, but a series of photos can be even better. You can use your knowledge of arrays and other programming constructs to create a photo rotation for a page.

▼ TRY IT YOURSELF

For this project, you need a series of photos that you want to display. While not necessary, putting them all in the same folder as your code will make part of the listing easier. This sample program (shown in Listing 10.1) will use six photos, named alice.jpg, john.jpg, maggie.jpg, nieces.jpg, family1.jpg, and familyhike.jpg. You would change those names in the code to the names of the photos you want to use.

LISTING 10.1   Adding a photo rotator to your web page is easy with JavaScript.

```
<!DOCTYPE html>
<html>
<head>
        <title>Family Photos!</title>
        <script>

        // First, create an array of images to rotate
        var famPhotos = new Array();
        famPhotos[0] = new Image();
        famPhotos[0].src = "alice.jpg";
        famPhotos[1] = new Image();
        famPhotos[1].src = "john.jpg";
        famPhotos[2] = new Image();
        famPhotos[2].src = "maggie.jpg";
        famPhotos[3] = new Image();
        famPhotos[3].src = "nieces.jpg";
        famPhotos[4] = new Image();
        famPhotos[4].src = "familyhike.jpg";
        famPhotos[5] = new Image();
        famPhotos[5].src = "family1.jpg";

        var i=0;
        function rotator() {
                document.getElementById("image1").src = famPhotos[i].src;
                i++;
                if (i==famPhotos.length) {
                        i = 0;
                }
                setTimeout(function() { rotator(); }, 2000);
        }

        </script>
</head>
<body onload = "rotator('image1', famPhotos);" >
<h1>FAMILY PHOTO TIME</h1>
Our family had a great summer! Here's some photos of what we did...
```

```
<div id="img"> <img id="image1" height="600px" width="400px"
    border="5" style="border-color:white;" /></div>
</body>
</html>
```

Figure 10.1 shows the resulting page when you run this program (obviously you will not get the same photo, unless your wife and children are dead ringers for mine!).

FIGURE 10.1
With JavaScript, you can enhance the graphical elements of your website.

By setting up an array of images in the header, you can easily go back and add more or delete some pictures as needed. When you declare your array, you first let JavaScript know an element is an image with the new `image()` function and then you can set the `.src` for each element in the array to a .jpg image. Again, if your .jpg photos are in the same directory as the .html file, you don't need to type in the entire file directory path. You can also use a web address there for your file names. Adding additional photos is as simple as adding two additional lines, a subsequent new `image()` call, and then a file location setting.

When your array is set, it's time to create a function to rotate the images in your array. Despite being less than 10 lines of code, the rotator function probably looks a bit intimidating. It shouldn't. The method `document.getElementbyId` is used to set `image1` to the first element in your array of photos, `famPhotos[0]`. It gets this one because before you defined the function, you set `i` to 0. However, once it sets `image1` to `famPhotos[0]`, it now increments the variable `i` by 1. This means the next time the function is called, it will set `image1` to the second element in your array of photos, `famPhotos[1]`. This will keep setting the image to a new element in your array of photos until it reaches the last element. That's when the handy `if` statement jumps in. If `i` is incremented to one past the last element of the array, the `if` statement will automatically reset `i` to 0 and we can loop through the images in the photo array again from the beginning.

The last line of code, `setTimeout`, is just a handy JavaScript function that will keep calling your rotator function (and therefore place a new photo on the page), but will wait a set amount of time. The last number, currently set to 2,000, is the delay and is equal to milliseconds. So 2,000 is a 2-second delay. Feel free to experiment with this number to create different transition delays. Be careful to not use too small of a number—I got a bit of a headache watching my photos rotate every 200 milliseconds.

That's it for the function. All that's left is to call the function in the body of the HTML document. The function is called within the body definition by way of the onload event. This ensures the code function runs as soon as everything is loaded on the page. Within the body, we use a little HTML (which will be covered in greater detail in Hour 16, "HTML5 and CSS3") to set a heading for the page and a little text before `image1` is placed. The information that follows `image1` on that line sets the width and height of the image as well as the size and color of the image's border. You can also experiment with these numbers (and colors) to get different effects.

NOTE
_____

All images will have the same aspect ratio, so if you mix portrait and landscape pictures, some photos will be stretched to fit the box. So your photos will look best if you choose a set of photos that are either all portrait or all landscape.

_____

Adding Interactivity to Your Web Photos

Another way to add value to your web page is to make your graphics and photos interactive. The best web pages are not static, but give the user a chance to interact. Thinking back to our small store example from earlier hours—it would be nice to create a page with photos of products in inventory. Obviously, you could also put the product information, such as description and price next to or under the photos, but you could make a cleaner page if the page only had photos and the information would come up if the user clicked on the photo. Again, JavaScript can make it possible thanks to the onclick() method. Within each photo placement line, you can add the onclick() method that runs some chunk of JavaScript code when the user clicks a specific photo.

TRY IT YOURSELF ▼

Listing 10.2 is a simple example that demonstrates how to use the onclick() method with different photos. Three functions are defined in the header section for the three photos that will be placed in the HTML section of the code. Again for you to run this code, you need to place photos in the same folder as your code. The ones in this example are named product1.jpg, product2.jpg, and product3.jpg. If you want to use differently named photos, just change the names in the listing to match your choices.

LISTING 10.2 **Adding interactivity to your web photos**

```
<!DOCTYPE html>
<html>
<head>
        <title>Product Information</title>
        <script>
        function Product1Info() {
        alert("Summer product! On sale until Labor Day for $9.99.");
        }
        function Product2Info() {
        alert("One of our bestsellers! A bargain at $19.50.");
        }
        function Product3Info() {
        alert("Everyone could use one of these at $1.99!");
        }

        </script>
</head>
<body>
<h1>Fran's Place<br>Shop our inventory!</h1>
We've got everything you need!<br>
<img src ="product1.jpg" height="300px" width="200px"
border="5" style="border-color:blue;" onclick="Product1Info()" /></div>
<img src ="product2.jpg" height="300px" width="200px"
border="5" style="border-color:red;" onclick="Product2Info()" /></div>
<img src ="product3.jpg" height="300px" width="200px"
border="5" style="border-color:black;" onclick="Product3Info()" /></div>

</body>
</html>
```

Figure 10.2 shows the results of running the code in Listing 10.2.

FIGURE 10.2
You can run code that presents as much information as you want when the web user clicks an image.

Like the last example, this program mixes HTML and JavaScript. If you want to add real power and pizzazz to your web pages, you need to become familiar with each, particularly the exciting combination of HTML 5 and CSS 3, the topics of Hour 16. The `onclick()` method used in this example is useful with any object, not just images as demonstrated here. You can also build a function of JavaScript code to run if users click buttons, banners, or blocks of text.

TIP

The three photos placed on the page each used a different-color border (red, blue, and black). Normally, consistently colored borders would make for a more elegant web design, but this was done to show you the variety of color you can add to your page.

The code presented here is also as simple as can be—a single line of information presented to the screen in an `alert()` method. That's not to denigrate a simple line of information—sometimes, that's all that you need. However, if you want to present more information, or build a more complex function that executes upon clicking, you can do that as well.

Capturing the Position of the Mouse

Giving your website visitors additional information when they click a photo or some other object on your page is a nice way to add complexity to your website. However, you can give additional data without even requiring a click from the user. As covered back in Hour 3, "Designing a Program," JavaScript has a built-in method that captures the position of the mouse and can trigger some code if the user moves the mouse pointer over a specific photo or other object.

TRY IT YOURSELF ▼

Let's go back to the example in the last section, but instead of giving the user additional information about a product if they click one of our product images, the name and price appear in an alert box on the page if they pass their pointer onto a product photo. Listing 10.3 will be simple to follow after what you just did in Listing 10.2.

LISTING 10.3   **Adding a different interactivity to your web photos with the** `onmouseover` **event.**

```
<!DOCTYPE html>
<html>
<head>
        <title>Product Information</title>
        <script>
        function Product1Info() {
        alert("Summer product! On sale until Labor Day for $9.99.");
        }
        function Product2Info() {
        alert("One of our bestsellers! A bargain at $19.50.");
        }
        function Product3Info() {
        alert("Everyone could use one of these at $1.99!");
        }

        </script>
</head>
<body>
<h1>Fran's Place<br>Shop our inventory!</h1>
We've got everything you need!<br>
```

```
<img src ="product1.jpg" height="300px" width="200px"
border="5" style="border-color:blue;" onmouseover="Product1Info()" /></div>
<img src ="product2.jpg" height="300px" width="200px"
border="5" style="border-color:red;" onmouseover="Product2Info()" /></div>
<img src ="product3.jpg" height="300px" width="200px"
border="5" style="border-color:black;" onmouseover="Product3Info()" /></div>

</body>
</html>
```

The code is virtually identical to the last example. The only difference is that the `onclick` methods in each of the three photo placements have been replaced with `onmouseover` methods instead. Now users don't need to click in order to get the information—they just need to pass their pointers over the page. Now the alert box can be a little clunky because visitors cannot do more on the page until the box is dismissed. As an additional project, it is worth trying to alter the code in the functions to place text on the page instead of in an alert box.

TIP

If you want the text to disappear when the mouse pointer leaves the image or object, there is a second method, `onmouseout`, that you can use to trigger different code when the mouse is no longer in the specific area. Often the two methods are used in concert to achieve a specific "on and off" effect.

Adding a Repeating News Ticker to Your Website

Another cool feature you could add to your website is one of those news-style tickers that repeats information over and over. If you're a small business, perhaps you could put your shop's hours or address and phone numbers. If you are building a family website, you can add a reminder to your children to do their chores and homework, hoping that repetition will eventually sink in (take it from me, it won't).

▼ TRY IT YOURSELF

Let's return to Fran's Place, our little store from previous hours and the last two examples. But instead of building a clean example like we've done in previous cases, let's add the ticker code to the last example. After all, when you start to build your programs and websites, it's unlikely that they'll do just one job—they will accomplish multiple goals and purposes. So this example (see Listing 10.4) will still have the three product photos that generate alert boxes when users pass their pointer into the photo's area, but the page will also have a box below the photos in which a few messages rotate through.

LISTING 10.4   Our website for our small store is starting to get a bit robust.   ▼

```
<html>
<head>
<title>Welcome to Fran's Place</title>

<script>

// Set the scrolling message, and you can add as many pieces
// as you want
var scrollMsg = "We are open Daily from 9AM to 10PM...";
scrollMsg += "We've got the largest variety of products";
scrollMsg += " in the tri-state area...";
scrollMsg += "Our prices will not be beat!...";

//Our three product information functions
function Product1Info() {
      alert("Summer product! On sale until Labor Day for $9.99.");
      }
      function Product2Info() {
      alert("One of our bestsellers! A bargain at $19.50.");
      }
      function Product3Info() {
      alert("Everyone could use one of these at $1.99!");
      }

//The scrolling function
var beginPos = 0;
function scrollingMsg() {
document.msgForm.scrollingMsgBox.value =
scrollMsg.substring(beginPos,scrollMsg.length)+scrollMsg.substring(0,beginPos);
beginPos = beginPos + 1;
if (beginPos > scrollMsg.length) {
beginPos = 0
}
window.setTimeout("scrollingMsg()",90)
}

</script>

</head>
<body BGCOLOR="WHITE" onload="scrollingMsg()">
<h1>Fran's Place<br>Shop our inventory!</h1>
We've got everything you need!<br>

<img src ="product1.jpg" height="300px" width="200px"
border="5" style="border-color:blue;" onmouseover="Product1Info()" /></div>
```

```
<img src ="product2.jpg" height="300px" width="200px"
border="5" style="border-color:red;" onmouseover="Product2Info()" /></div>
<img src ="product3.jpg" height="300px" width="200px"
border="5" style="border-color:black;" onmouseover="Product3Info()" /></div>
<form name="msgForm">
<input type="text" name="scrollingMsgBox" size="88">
</form>

<p> </p>
<p><b>Thanks for Shopping at Fran's Place</b>.</p>
</body>
</html>
```

Figure 10.3 shows the results of running the code in Listing 10.4.

FIGURE 10.3
By adding several different interactive features, you can create a website that people will want to visit repeatedly.

So much of this code has now been present for the past three examples, but there is some new code to discuss. Within the header, a string variable named scrollMsg is created and any and all information you want to appear on your ticker is added to the string using the string concatenation operation (+=). Remember that using this operator will add the string listed on the right side of the operator to the end of the string indicated on left side of the operator. So you can use the concatenation operator to build a string of significant size. A larger scroll of information will keep visitors interested longer. The value to putting the string up in the header is that you can easily find it to change the information as needed, such as a new special of the week or extended hours around the holidays.

The function scrollMsg follows and takes the completed scrollMsg string and prints it to the created text box starting with the first character in the string thanks to the beginPos counter being set to 0 before the function is called. When the string is printed, the beginPos counter is incremented by 1 and then after a short delay, the function is called again. This time the string is printed in the text box starting from the second character in the string, and the counter is incremented again. By continually printing the string advanced by a single character, a scrolling, animated effect occurs. The function would only print the message once except for the if statement that follows the incrementing of the beginPos counter. Each time the function runs, this if statement checks whether the counter is higher than the length of the string. If it is, there's no more string to print. So the counter is set back to 0, and the rotation can begin again, giving the illusion of a neverending repeating ticker.

The setTimeout method you used in the photo rotator is used here to scroll the message. Again, the number at the end of the setTimeout call sets the delay between the function calls, therefore setting the speed of the scroll. Again, feel free to experiment with this number to set a pace you feel is right.

Summary

After the first nine hours covered learning basic programming syntax and methodology using JavaScript code as examples, this hour returned to JavaScript's roots. People most often use JavaScript to add some fun interactivity to their website. While many people use existing web-creation tools to add the bells, whistles, and widgets to their sites, there is something extremely satisfying about creating the effects yourself.

The examples presented in this lesson are just scratching the surface. You can also use JavaScript to add animation, sound, video, and so much more. This book cannot cover it all—there's additional programming techniques and other languages still to be covered in this book, but there are numerous other options out there, including the previously mentioned *Sams Teach Yourself JavaScript in 24 Hours.*

That's not to say you are done with JavaScript—the next hour covers a few more advanced topics as a sendoff on the language before the book turns its attention to Java, OOP, and other topics.

Q&A

Q. If one or two of these interactive techniques are good, more would be better, right?

A. Be careful not to overdo interactivity and pizzazz on your website. Too much of it can be distracting and detract from the look and feel of a professional site. If your site has multiple pages, consider using one or two effects per page and spread them out that way. Another idea would be to change the interactivity on your page monthly so that it constantly feels fresh and updated. Old content, even if it is interactive, is an easy way to alienate your visitors. If you don't seem to care enough about your site to update it, why should they care enough to visit it?

Q. Will these types of effects work if my website visitors come via a mobile device, like a phone or tablet?

A. Mobile devices have led to an additional level of complexity in web development (and more work for web developers!). For now, continue to develop web pages the way you are, but as you get more proficient, you should start to consider developing mobile sites as well. When you do, go simple. Some of the best effects on full-page websites do not look good on smaller screens, if they work at all.

Workshop

The quiz questions are provided for your further understanding.

Quiz

1. What is the advantage of putting image files in the same folder as your JavaScript code?

2. Where do you place a function in the HTML body code if you want it to run as soon as the page loads?

3. What is the name of the method you can use to repeatedly call a function after a preset delay?

4. What measure of time is used for the delay in the method from question 3?

5. True or false: You can only set images up to be interactively clickable.

6. What method would be used to trigger code if a pointer leaves a specific object?

7. True or false: You cannot select the color of the banner around an image.

8. True or false: There is a limit of 10 images you can rotate through on a website.

  9. What is the difference between `onclick` and `onmouseover`?

10. How do you add a string to the end of another string?

Answers

  1. You don't have to type the entire file path to your image files if they are in the same file as your program file.

  2. Within the `<body>` declaration, you can add a function with the `onload` method and it will run as soon as the page loads.

  3. The `setTimeout()` method.

  4. Milliseconds.

  5. False. You can also set images to be interactive upon the mouse pointer going into the image.

  6. `onmouseout`.

  7. False. You can change the color of the border set around images.

  8. False. There is no limit to the number of images you can rotate through on a website.

  9. The `onmouseover` will trigger code when the mouse pointer passes into a specific object. You must click the object in order to trigger the code if you use the `onmouseclick` image.

10. You use the string concatenation method (`+=`). For example, if you have the string `name = "Bobby"`, and you want to add the last name "Smith" to the string name. You would write:

```
name += " Smith"
```

Notice the addition of the space at the beginning of the "Smith" string. If you didn't add that, `name` would then equal "BobbySmith".

HOUR 11
Advanced Programming

For just about the first half of this book, you've learned the methodology and mindset of effective programmers. While all the examples and discussion have covered JavaScript code, most of these concepts are fairly universal. Even better, the syntax of loops and conditional expressions that you learned are directly applicable to other languages like C, C++, and Java. If you want to move to Visual Basic, you just need to tweak your syntax a bit, but by learning the concepts, you're already most of the way there.

The last hour was not general programming, but more specific to what JavaScript can do to improve your website. This hour will cover more of the same, specifically adding improving the user's experience with cookies. After this hour, you will jump into object-oriented programming (OOP), as covered in Java.

The highlights of this hour include:

▶ Defining cookies

▶ Writing cookies

▶ Reading cookies

▶ Deleting cookies

JavaScript's Programming Weakness

When you program, an important skill to master is file management. All the great data-manipulation code in the world has little value if you are not saving the information to a file for later use. Programs that read data are limited if the data is hard-wired into the code or must be entered by the user. The real power of data-management programs often come from when they can read data from a disk file, make changes, and then write the altered or new information to a disk file. For this reason, most programming languages come with a robust set of file-management functions and methods.

This is not the case with JavaScript. There are severe limitations to the language's ability to create files on the computer's disk system. If you think about the general purpose of JavaScript, this limitation makes sense. If you are browsing the web, you don't want to give any site you visit the ability to start placing files on your hard drive. In the best-case scenario, your hard drive would start to fill with junk you probably don't want. In the worst-case scenario, unscrupulous and malicious hackers could wreak havoc on your machine. So some security is in order, otherwise people would probably turn off JavaScript in their browsers.

There is an exception to this rule. If you have websites you visit regularly, you often want them to remember vital information, including shopping history, preference, and in many cases usernames and passwords if you visit sites that restrict access to registered users. JavaScript can accommodate these needs thanks to cookies.

Snacking on Cookies

Not only are cookies delicious, they make your web-browsing life so much easier. When you patronize a site regularly, you don't want to waste your time re-entering your key information. If you buy products on a site, it's great to have your mailing address saved. Or if you looked at 10 products and put them in a shopping cart to consider purchasing later, most of the time you'd like those items to remain in your cart until you decide to either purchase them or manually remove them from your cart, even if you come back to the site weeks later.

NOTE
_____

Cookies are a sweet name, but I always thought these files should have been called breadcrumbs, as they can lead the user back to their original state, like Hansel and Gretel tried to do with breadcrumbs in the original fairytale.
_____

It you'd like to see how many cookies you have, they are generally located in your Temporary Internet Files. You will probably be a bit surprised with just how many are there. I don't like messing with files in that folder, so I made a copy of one and pasted it into my documents folder. Opening it with my text editor, here's what the file looks like:

```
B
8q7et818ihvh5&b=3&s=d6
yahoo.com/
2147484672
2019565568
30429292
1498382404
30282220
*
```

Fairly unreadable to you and me, right? The only thing that's clear from this jumbled collection of letters and digits is the website that placed this cookie on my hard drive, yahoo.com. But yahoo can take this cookie the next time I visit it, parse the information contained within it, and know certain information about my most recent visit. This knowledge will make for a smoother return trip for me, and you should want that for your web visitors as well.

So if you've created a commerce site, you need to add the capabilities for cookies into your web pages in order to maximize the value and interest in your site. Cookies are small files that your JavaScript program can leave on a user's computer, containing information that your web page can read and use the next time the user visits.

NOTE

As you may know, users have the ability to turn cookies off in their browsers—so you cannot assume cookies will be there.

In addition to not saving cookies in the first place, sometimes users delete cookie files when cleaning up their computers. So if you plan on integrating cookies into your website, you will have to write code that can work either with or without cookies—sounds like a job for our favorite conditional statement, `if`!

Accessing Cookies via `document.cookie`

If you are looking to create cookies, you need to work with the cookie property of the document object. Cookies are limited stings of data. A cookie consists of a name and its set value:

```
username=Rebecca
```

Cookies can store multiple pieces of information, allowing you to keep additional data. For example, you can store the last time the user visited your site, or if you had three stores, you can remember which store location is the closest to your visitor. Then when they return to your site, you can use this data to make their web experience more personalized. Think of it as similar to patronizing a restaurant repeatedly and the feeling you get when they greet you by name and know your favorite dish.

Cookies do have some limitations. Spaces are not allowed in them and many of the punctuation characters, including parentheses, exclamation points, the number sign, and the dollar sign, are not allowed. Before you think no characters other than digits and letters are allowed, it's not that simple (is it ever?)—you can use the at symbol (@) as well as +, -, and /, as well as a few others. Don't worry about memorizing which symbols can and cannot be used in a cookie; JavaScript has built-in methods that replace the not-allowed characters with their hexadecimal equivalent as well as a second method that will convert a cookie with hexadecimal characters back to their original values. For example, if you ask a user for their first name, and they enter "Mary Lou", setting the string through the escape method will turn the string into "`Mary%20Lou`". The % symbol is a clue that the next two digits represent a converted character—in this case,

20 is a space. You may be able to guess from this that the percent symbol (%) is also a not-allowed character in cookies, and % is changed to %25.

TIP

You may be saying, "Whoa! What the heck is hexadecimal?" It is a number system that has the digits 0–9 plus A through F. So while 1–9 are the same as our base-10 number system, the number after 9 isn't 10, it's A (or 0A as you will often see it). 11, 12, 13, 14, 15, 16, 17 is 0B, 0C, 0D, 0E, 0F, 10, 11 in hexadecimal. If this explanation isn't helping, don't fret. You ultimately don't have to worry about getting hexadecimals right—your computer takes care of it for you.

Just as `escape(string)` will turn a specific string into an acceptable format to be stored in a cookie, `unescape(string)` will take a converted string and turn it back to normal. This will become more clear when you see the code example later in this hour.

The Parts of a Cookie

While the lesson mentioned that a cookie consisted of a name and a value, there is more to cookies. Table 11.1 lists the different parts of a cookie, as well as their corresponding value.

TABLE 11.1 The properties of a cookie

Property	Description
cookieName	The name of the cookie, from `name=value`
cookieValue	The value of the cookie name, from `name=value`
domain	An optional attribute that tells the browser the cookie's website. The default is the site setting the cookie.
path	Specifies the directory in which the cookie is available. This attribute is also optional, and its default is the entire domain.
expires	Specifies the date on which the cookie will be deleted. Also optional, but with no date, the cookie will only be active while the current browser is open. The date must be set in Universal Coordinated Time (UTC), which is the same as Greenwich Mean Time (GMT).
Secure	While rarely used, this attribute, if set, will only retrieve a cookie with a secure server.

Writing Cookies

To write a cookie, you just need to set a string with the data above to the `document.cookie`. The following small function is a simple chunk of code that asks for a name and then saves it as a cookie:

```
function writeCookie()
{
        var custName = prompt("What is your name?");
        //Now make sure all characters in the name are cookie legal!
        cookieName = escape(custName);
        //Will now set a cookie with a cookieName of name
        // and a cookieValue of the cookieName string post escape method
        document.cookie = "name=" + cookieName;
        alert("We've created the cookie name="+cookieName);
}
```

If you put that function in the header of an HTML file and then call it from the body of your HTML file, you will be prompted to enter a name. If you enter a standard first name, you'll see that name. So I'm going to enter my stage name, D!J Skribble23(), a combination of letters, numbers, and a few odd punctuation marks. JavaScript will tell me it is setting the cookie name=D%21J%20Skribble23%28%29.

However, this cookie will expire as soon as the browser closes. That's not a valuable cookie. Let's say you want to keep the cookie for about three months after it's created. To do that, you need to add the following code lines to your function above (after the alert line, but before the closing brace):

```
        var expDate = new Date();
        expDate.setTime(expDate.getTime() + (90*24*3600*1000));
        var expireDate = expDate.toUTCString();
        document.cookie += "; expires="+expireDate;
```

Hopefully these lines aren't too confusing. The first line creates a variable named expDate and populates it with today's date using the new Date() method, which automatically sets your variable to the current day and time. However, we don't want that to be the expiration date—we want the cookie to not expire until 90 days in the future. So we will use the setTime method to set a new time on our expDate variable by using the getTime method to get the current time and then add enough to move the time 90 days in the future. That's what that string of numbers does. It takes the number of days (90) times the number of hours in a day (24) times the number of seconds in an hour (3,600) times the number of milliseconds in a second (1,000). Thankfully, JavaScript will do all that multiplying for you. Now expDate has the time 90 days in the future, but as mentioned in Table 11.1, the time must be in UTC format. Luckily, JavaScript has a method that will do that conversion for you, toUTCString. Now you can use the concatenation operator (+=) to add an "expires=" and your expiration date to your cookie, which has a name and an expiration date.

Great, so we can easily set a cookie name with little work. But how valuable is that if we cannot read the cookie's value and do something with it. The next section discusses how to read cookies.

Reading Cookies

To read a cookie, you have to write code that can make sense of the string in the `document.` `cookie` attribute. If it's just a simple "name=value" single-cookie string, that would be straightforward. However, things like that are rarely straightforward, and you need to be prepared to deal with more complicated data (or no data at all, if your web visitor has deleted cookies or not allowed cookies to be saved in the first place). Luckily, if the data is complicated thanks to the presence of additional attributes like the ones listed in Table 11.1, JavaScript has a number of string methods that make your data-reading life easier.

How will you know if you have multiple attributes in your cookie string? Each is separated with the semicolon. JavaScript has a method that splits a larger string into an array of smaller strings, using a character you specify. For example, say you have the following cookie string:

```
cookieString="name=Sandy;domain=www.jamemc.com;path=/documents";
```

If you use the split method and assign it to an array as follows:

```
var cookieArray = cookieString.split(";");
```

you would create a 3-item array with the following elements:

```
cookieArray[0] = "name=Sandy";
cookieArray[1] = "domain=www.jamemc.com";
cookieArray[2] = "path=/documents";
```

You are now in a position to look for a specific `name=value` pair within your array of cookie values. You just need to loop though the elements of the array and check whether the beginning of a specific element matches the name you are looking for. The following `readCookie` function will loop through the exploded out array created from `document.cookie` and check whether the `name=` exists within the code

```
function readCookie()
{

        // Get all the cookies pairs in an array
        var cookarray  = document.cookie.split(';');

        // Now set up the element we want to find
        cooksearch = "name=";
        //Loop through the array elements
        for(var i=0; i<cookarray.length; i++) {
                var startcook = cookarray[i];
                if (startcook.indexOf(cooksearch) == 0) {
                        var aa = cooksearch.length;
                        var bb = startcook.length;
                        Cname = unescape(startcook.substring(aa, bb));
```

```
                alert("Found cookie! " + Cname );
            }
        }

}
```

NOTE

Testing this type of code can be difficult on a local machine, as many browers will not allow local files to fully load for security reasons. Loading the sample program onto a web server is the most effective method for testing.

This code will loop through each of the pieces of your `document.cookie` and search for a substring that matches the one you are looking to find. Using a `for` loop that goes from 0 to the number of elements in the array, each element is checked whether they're a match. If there is, a new variable, `Cname`, is set to the string (after you've run the `unescape()` method on the substring to ensure there weren't any character conversions when the cookie was initially saved). This code then generates an alert box to tell the user the name was found, but that's a poor use of the information. It would be far better to return `Cname` to the point in the code.

Deleting Set Cookies

If you'd like to delete a cookie in JavaScript, all you need to do is set the expire to a time in the past. That will trigger the browser to delete the cookie as it has expired.

For example, to change the date to 90 days before, you can use the same code as last time, but subtract our mathematical formula instead of adding it:

```
function deleteCookie() {
    var expDate = new Date();
    expDate.setTime(expDate.getTime() - (90*24*3600*1000));
    var expireDate = expDate.toUTCString();
    cookieString += "; expires="+expireDate;
}
```

TRY IT YOURSELF ▼

Let's put this all together in an example that takes a user's name and saves it in a cookie. The code will check to see whether the cookie already exists, and if it does, it will parse out the name and use it in a "welcome back" greeting. Rather than just do that, the cookie functions are integrated into the Fran's Place website from the previous hour, so now this page has a scrolling text box, interactive photos, and cookies:

```
<!DOCTYPE html>
<html>
<head>
<script>
// Set the scrolling message, and you can add as many pieces
// as you want
var scrollMsg = "We are open Daily from 9AM to 10PM...";
scrollMsg += "We've got the largest variety of products";
scrollMsg += " in the tri-state area...";
scrollMsg += "Our prices will not be beat!...";

//Our three product information functions
function Product1Info() {
        alert("Summer product! On sale until Labor Day for $9.99.");
        }
        function Product2Info() {
        alert("One of our bestsellers! A bargain at $19.50.");
        }
        function Product3Info() {
        alert("Everyone could use one of these at $1.99!");
        }

//The scrolling function
var beginPos = 0;
function scrollingMsg() {
document.msgForm.scrollingMsgBox.value =
scrollMsg.substring(beginPos,scrollMsg.length)+scrollMsg.substring(0,beginPos);
beginPos = beginPos + 1;
if (beginPos > scrollMsg.length) {
beginPos = 0
}
window.setTimeout("scrollingMsg()",100)
}

function readCookie(c_name)
{
        var c_value = document.cookie;
        var c_start = c_value.indexOf(" " + c_name + "=");
        if (c_start == -1)
          {
               c_start = c_value.indexOf(c_name + "=");
          }
        if (c_start == -1)
          {
               c_value = null;
          }
        else
          {
               c_start = c_value.indexOf("=", c_start) + 1;
```

```
                var c_end = c_value.indexOf(";", c_start);
                if (c_end == -1)
                  {
                        c_end = c_value.length;
                  }
                c_value = unescape(c_value.substring(c_start,c_end));
          }
        return c_value;
}

function writeCookie(c_name,value,exdays)
{
        var exdate=new Date();
        exdate.setDate(exdate.getDate() + exdays);
        var c_value=escape(value) + ((exdays==null) ? "" : "; expires="+exdate.
        ➥toUTCString());
        document.cookie=c_name + "=" + c_value;
}

function checkCookie()
{
        var username=readCookie("username");
        if (username!=null && username!="")
        {
                alert("Welcome again " + username);
        }
        else
        {
                username=prompt("Please enter your username:","");
                if (username!=null && username!="")
                  {
                        writeCookie("username",username,365);
                  }
          }
}
function loadfunctions()
{
        scrollingMsg();
        checkCookie();
}
</script>
</head>
<body BGCOLOR="WHITE" onload="loadfunctions()">

<h1>Fran's Place<br>Shop our inventory!</h1>
We've got everything you need!<br>

<img src ="product1.jpg" height="300px" width="200px"
border="5" style="border-color:blue;" onmouseover="Product1Info()" /></div>
```

```
<img src ="product2.jpg" height="300px" width="200px"
border="5" style="border-color:red;" onmouseover="Product2Info()" /></div>
<img src ="product3.jpg" height="300px" width="200px"
border="5" style="border-color:black;" onmouseover="Product3Info()" /></div>
<form name="msgForm">
<input type="text" name="scrollingMsgBox" size="88">
</form>

<p> </p>
<p><b>Thanks for Shopping at Fran's Place</b>.</p>
</body>
</html>
```

The first time a user visits the site, they see the dialog box in Figure 11.1.

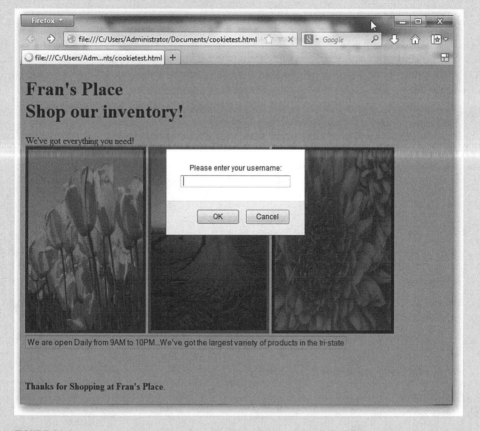

FIGURE 11.1
Cookies can become part of any of your websites.

However, with subsequent visits, they are greeted with a personalized dialog-box greeting instead of the prompt as seen in Figure 11.2.

FIGURE 11.2
Who doesn't like being remembered?

NOTE

The screen in Figure 11.2 looks a bit different than the one in Figure 11.1 because I checked the code with two different browsers, Chrome (Figure 11.1) and Internet Explorer (Figure 11.2). It works under both, but it is nice to double-check and see the subtle display differences that occur depending on what browser a visitor uses to come to your site.

One additional code note here. Again this program uses the `onload()` function during the body declaration. However, I wanted to load two distinct methods—both the scrolling message box method `scrollingMsg()` and the new method to check for a cookie `checkCookie()`. So I created a new holding method `loadfunctions()`, which is called when the page loads and it in turn, calls my two methods. You can put several functions in such a holding function, but don't overdo it as it can slow the loading time of your page.

Summary

In this hour, you learned how to personalize the web-browsing experience of your visitors using cookies. While you do occasionally hear some people complain about cookies, they are a common part of the web-browsing experience and almost every page you surf will place cookies on your device. With the ever-increasing speed of processors and size of storage, the amount of lag created by these extra files is imperceptible.

As mentioned at the beginning of the hour, this is almost your last foray into JavaScript. You will now jump to a section on OOP using Java before then surveying some additional programming languages and Internet-development tools—if you are missing JavaScript by then, you will be reunited for one last lesson. You can also go in other directions with JavaScript by picking up a tutorial like *Sams Teach Yourself JavaScript in 24 Hours,* which will teach you how to use JavaScript libraries, as well as how to add animation and multimedia files to your web pages using JavaScript.

Q&A

Q. Should I worry about the security of cookies?

A. The fears about the security of cookies are largely overblown. Cookies will share aspects of your browsing history with web developers, but they will not share secure information like passwords and account numbers.

Q. How many cookies can I create on my website?

A. While you can create multiple cookies on a website, there is a limit of 20 cookies and 4 kilobytes of cookie data. For most small websites, this is more than enough cookies and storage space. If you find a need to go over the former, you can use some clever methods to store multiple pieces of information in a single cookie, but that is a bit beyond the scope of this book. The information, if you need it, is easy to find in other JavaScript tutorials, and involves combining information into a single cookie and then breaking it back up when you read the cookie.

Workshop

The quiz questions are provided for your further understanding.

Quiz

1. What is the value of cookies to web pages?

2. True or false: The following line of code would set a cookie for a visitor's name:

   ```
   cookie.document(visitorname==bob);
   ```

3. What punctuation character separates different cookies and cookie attributes?

4. What attributes must be in all cookies?

5. If you use the `expires` attribute, what format must the date be in?

6. How do you delete a cookie?

7. Why do you need to use the `escape()` and `unescape()` methods when reading and writing cookies?

8. True or false: All cookies must have the `secure` attribute set.

Answers

1. Cookies allow a website to remember specific data so the visitor doesn't need to re-enter the information.

2. False. The cookie property belongs to the document type, not the other way around. Second, you need to use the assignment operator (=) instead of the equality operator (==). The correct format is

   ```
   document.cookie = "name=bob;";
   ```

3. You use the semicolon (;) to separate different cookies or cookie properties.

4. The `cookieName` and `cookieValue` attributes must be in all cookies.

5. For all cookies, the expiration date must be set in Universal Coordinated Time (UTC).

6. Set the expiration date for the cookie to a time that has already passed.

7. Certain characters are not allowed in a cookie, so the `escape()` method converts those characters to hexadecimal format. When reading a cookie, the `unescape` method will turn those hexadecimal-formatted characters back to their original format.

8. False. The `secure` attribute is optional.

Programming with Java

The Java language is a shapeshifter that has been used for three dramatically different purposes in its nearly 20-year history.

First, it was a simple language perfectly suited to run on embedded devices like appliances and as small programs embedded on web pages.

Next, it grew into a sophisticated general-purpose language that ran on web servers, powering websites, relational databases, and other Internet servers behind the scenes.

Finally, it has become a mobile language for creating apps, small programs that run on phones and tablets using the Android operating system. There are a staggering number of devices in the world running Java programs—more than three billion—and many of them are the phones we carry with us all day long.

For this introductory hour, it will be most instructive to go back to Java's roots and see how it got started as a killer way to add some interactivity to the web.

The world of web pages gained an unexpected boost in capabilities when the Java language was introduced in 1995. Originally designed to be used for such devices as digital TV set-top boxes, Java became the first widely available language used to make web pages dynamic with animation, games, and other constantly updated content. Java almost single-handedly rescued static web pages and turned the web into an interactive medium where users could interact with changing web pages.

Though today there are many other ways to make the web more interactive, including Macromedia Flash and HTML5, Java still can be used to create web pages that run like stand-alone computer programs. Despite its capabilities, Java is simple to learn. The inventors of Java used C and C++ as their model language. Java is no longer a small language, but it is an extremely robust one for creating programs that work without modification on many different kinds of computers, phones, tablets, and other devices.

The highlights of this hour include

- ▶ Seeing what Java is all about
- ▶ Running Java programs that travel with web pages

▶ Understanding the need for small Java programs

▶ Comparing Java to other languages

▶ Compiling Java programs

▶ Extending the built-in Java classes for your Java programs

Introducing Java

Colorful web browsers brought the Internet to the world by taking it out of the exclusive hands of scientific, military, and educational researchers. The new web browsers made the Internet accessible to everybody with simple navigational tools and an appealing graphical nature. Soon, millions of users all over the world were jumping from one website to another in a global medium of text, images, and hyperlinks.

Browsers filled the job requirements better than anyone could have imagined but grew stale due to the static nature of web pages. Despite the colorful and cross-linked pages that browsers made available to the world, the pages did not have enough action in them to keep users occupied. Browser technology was too static to make websites truly come alive.

NOTE

Think about this: As PCs became faster, became more graphical, and began supporting multimedia, viewing only pictures and text, which was at first unique online, became dull quickly. Users needed more interaction to keep their attention when online.

Users wanted more from the Internet than just a distributed set of interconnected graphical screens. Despite the web's hypertext nature, those hypertext links simply take you from one page to another without doing any work for you except eliminating the need to type long web page addresses. Users want real computing power coming at them from the websites they visit. For example, instead of reading cooking recipe, you might want to see the food being cooked by an expert or take an introductory, graphical tutorial on the steps required to make that food.

Java, developed by Sun Microsystems in the mid-1990s and managed today by Oracle by virtue of its acquisition of Sun in 2010, changed the way that websites operate. Java is a programming language with language features similar to C++. Fortunately, Java also contains many language features that are similar to JavaScript, such as the `for` loop, the `if` statement, and the `while` loop.

Java's Overnight Success

Upon its launch in 1995, Java was designed to be a better C++ than C++. Both C++ and Java are efficient programming languages that you can use to write almost any computer application. Java's initial emphasis, though, was online Internet programming. Java was a small and efficient language with safeguards in place to add security to online programs that C++ simply couldn't handle.

Today, Java works in many environments; some programmers develop large, complex applications in Java, and those applications have nothing to do with the Internet. Because Java was a lot like the C++ language already in use, this helped to ensure a rapid acceptance and usage within the programming world.

Instead of using web browsers to view data, with Java capabilities, browsers now can seamlessly download programs written in Java and execute those programs on the end user's computer as opposed to the remote server serving up the web page. When you view a Java-enabled web page, you see not only the usual graphical page, but you also are able to interact with Java programs that run on your own computer, brought to your computer via the web's connection.

You can write four kinds of Java programs:

▶ *Java applets* are small programs that travel with web page code and execute on the web user's computer.

▶ *Java applications* are complete standalone programs that don't require a web browser to execute.

▶ *Java servlets* are programs that run on a web server and are delivered to users as web pages.

▶ *Java apps* are small programs that run on smartphones and other mobile devices that have the Android operating system.

The first Java programs appeared as Java applets. The original goal of Java was to place executable code on web pages so that users could interact with websites in more compelling and attention-getting ways. As Java became more popular, programmers began using Java to write standalone programs that executed without the need for web browsers. For example, if you want to write a rental property management application that runs independently of an Internet connection, you could select Java as the programming language you use to develop the application.

Figure 12.1 shows a web page in which someone has embedded a Java applet. When the user surfs to the web page, the web page appears and a moment or two later the spaceship starts descending toward the surface of the moon. Web page authors create web pages using a formatting language called *HTML* (HyperText Markup Language). The applet rides from the server to the user's computer via the web page's HTML code. The applet actually executes on the user's computer and not on the serving computer. By executing on the user's machine, as opposed to the server's machine, the user can interact with the Java applet and the applet can respond to the user in real time.

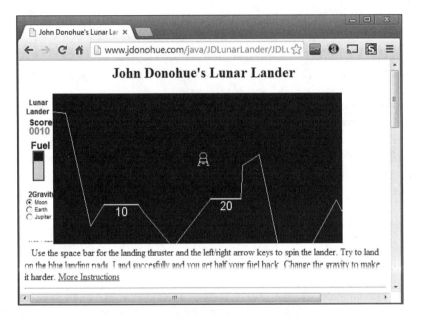

FIGURE 12.1
It's the Java applet that gives the spaceship the fuel needed to move.

NOTE

This applet by John Donohue recreates the early videogame Lunar Lander, released by Atari in 1979. Gamers today might find it hard to believe, but back then this was the state of the art in arcade games. We'd pump coin after coin into this game trying to fight gravity's cruel arithmetic and land safely by mastering four movements: tilt left, tilt right, flatten out, and fire the thrusters.

A program that used to require a giant arcade console now can be implemented as a Java applet.

To play the game, visit www.jdonohue.com/java.

Java Provides Executable Content

When working with Java, you'll often hear and read about *executable content*. Executable content is what Java is really all about. A web page contains executable content via web commands in the form of a Java applet. Any web page's content is executable on the target user's computer. Figure 12.2 shows an overview of a web document with two embedded Java applets. The language behind web pages is called *HTML* and you'll learn more about HTML in Hour 16, "HTML5 and CSS3."

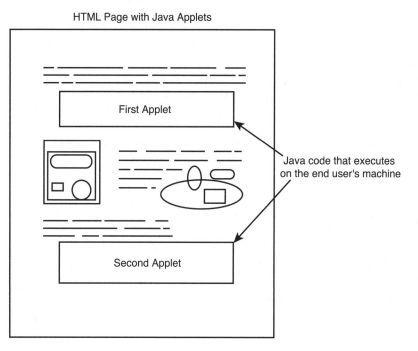

HTML Page with Java Applets

First Applet

Java code that executes
on the end user's machine

Second Applet

FIGURE 12.2
HTML serves up Java's executable content.

When the user enters the URL that displays the page shown in Figure 12.2 (or when the user clicks hypertext links to navigate to the page), the user's web-browsing software loads the HTML code, formats the page's text according to the HTML commands, displays any graphics images that appear on the page, and loads the executable content (as applets). The executable content executes either immediately or upon a predetermined event, such as a mouse click on the web page.

The best method of running Java applets is not always obvious to the user. When an applet is providing animation, the look of that animation is smooth because the animation program runs on the user's computer. Because of the applet, the speed of the animation is not dependent on the download time or on Internet traffic.

Before Java-enabled web pages, the user did have some interaction with the remote site. However, that interaction was severely limited. Web page animation was controlled by the user's animation software. If a computer system had no software that could display animation, that feature of the web page was lost for that system's user. If the user was to interact with the remote site in a question–answer session, such as order-taking, the user would often have to fill in the form completely before error-checking could be done to any of the user's responses. The user would have to trigger any and all interactions with the remote site; the response would then be limited to the remote site's speed and the current traffic flow on the Internet.

NOTE

The first way that web pages took user input was through simple forms that were transmitted using the *CGI* (*Common Gateway Interface*). When you go to a website's Contact Us page and you use the form to provide your name, email address, and a comment then click a Send button to submit it, there's a program collecting and transmitting that information with the CGI.

These programs are not usually Java applets. But some of them might be servlets, the programs mentioned earlier that are run by web servers.

Seamless Execution

Surely you have traveled to a website, downloaded software, and then logged off to execute that software. Java applets do this without requiring that you ever leave your browser. When you travel to a remote site, the Java applet runs without you doing anything at all. In addition, the software applet automatically downloads itself to your PC, runs when you trigger its execution, and then goes away when you leave the website without taking up permanent disk space. Think of the possibilities for software developers; users can test-drive your software without running an installation program and without needing to remove the software when the demonstration concludes.

Multi-Platform Executable Content

Now that you've seen how Java-enabled websites appear to the user, think about the requirements of such executable content. When you write a Java-based web page, you want the code to work on the user's computer no matter what kind of computer the user operates.

Whereas most language compilers, such as Visual C++, turn programs into machine-dependent executable programs, Java development tools don't go quite that far. All Java compilers translate your Java code into a special machine-independent module. The Java compiler first compiles the code into an in-between stage called *bytecode*. Your Java-enabled web-browsing software then translates this compiled bytecode into instructions that your computer executes.

No computer can directly read bytecode, but each computer's Java-enabled browser can. In other words, given a Java applet's bytecode, a PC can run the applet using a web browser, and an Android tablet can run that very same bytecode by using its own Java-enabled browser. All modern browsers can run Java applets with an enhancement offered by Oracle called the Java Plug-in, including Google Chrome, Microsoft Internet Explorer, Mozilla Firefox, and Apple Safari. The Java Plug-in is a computer-within-a-computer called the Java Virtual Machine (JVM) that interprets the machine-dependent bytecode and then translates that bytecode into machine-specific instructions a particular computer can understand (see Figure 12.3).

Running Java on the Virtual Machine

Figure 12.3 shows the Java compilation/translation scenario. You'll use the Java language to produce bytecode for a *virtual machine*, not a specific machine, because the bytecode is machine independent. The JVM is not a particular kind of computer but is an imaginary computer. Each computer must have a virtual machine interpreter to run Java code. The interpreter translates the compiled bytecode into specific instructions for that computer. Therefore, the Java compiler doesn't have to compile for any one computer, just bytecode for the virtual machine. The byte-code is sent to the web page that is to contain the applet, and when the user requests that web page, the user's web browser reads the bytecode and automatically interprets the bytecode into code readable by the user's computer. The user is unaware that all this took place; the web page is displayed and the executing applet is seen along with the rest of the web page's content.

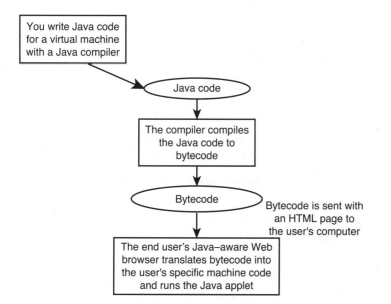

FIGURE 12.3
Your Java session produces compiled bytecode that a computer's JVM translates to run the program.

The web browser automatically runs the Java applet. Some applets run automatically, and some run in response to a user event such as a mouse click. It's important that you realize that the user doesn't necessarily know or care that a small program is running. To the user, the Java-based web page simply does more than one without Java. The page usually responds much more quickly, as fast as the user's computer can translate the Java bytecode into executable content. All traces of the program then go away when the applet ends, or when the user leaves the web page.

All Java programs are compiled into bytecode and run by a JVM on a user's computer. If you design a program with Java that must be downloaded and installed by a user, it requires a virtual machine on that computer. Oracle has a website where people can see if they have one installed. Visit www.java.com in a web browser and look for a "Do I Have Java?" link.

Java Usage Summary

As a newcomer to Java technology, you might appreciate a summary of the process one goes through when viewing a Java-enabled web page with a Java-aware web browser. Here are the steps that occur:

1. In a web browser, you enter a Java-enabled website's URL.

2. The serving computer sends the web page, in HTML format, to your web browser.

3. The HTML-based document's commands inform your web browser of the web page's Java-based executable content.

4. Your web browser downloads graphics images from the server if any graphics appear on the web page.

5. Depending on how the Java applet is to be triggered (either automatically or by a user's event), the server also will send the bytecode to your computer when the time is right.

6. Your browser's Java Plug-in interprets the bytecode and executes the Java-executable content.

7. When you leave the web page, the executable content goes away. (Some web browsers will keep the Java code in memory for a while in case you return to the page.)

Because the previous steps were based on the user's perspective, this is also a good time to explain what you, the Java programmer, will go through to create web pages with Java applets. Here are the general steps you'll follow:

1. Start your Java programming environment.

2. Write the Java applet.

3. Create the HTML web page that will contain the Java applet. Use appropriate HTML commands to indicate the applet and its parameters.

4. Compile the Java applet. Your Java development environment may offer a way to place the applet in its appropriate location for the HTML web page that will contain the applet.

5. If the compiler finds errors, fix them and recompile the file.

6. Test and debug the applet.

7. Store the applet and HTML on your web server, where they await a user's request.

You'll Start with Standalone Java

Although up to this point you've learned about Java applets rather than for standalone applications, you won't be learning Java from the applet perspective just yet. You'll find that it's easier to learn Java by mastering the standalone Java language first and then moving to applets, which you'll do in Hour 15, "Applets and Web Pages." While learning the Java language, the web page information would simply sidetrack you from mastering the language commands.

The Java language wasn't originally intended to be a competitor to C++ and the other languages people use to write non-web, standalone applications, but Java has surpassed its authors' hopes and dreams and become a major competitor in the programming language field.

Developers quickly learned that Java is a great language in its own right. Standalone Java applications run from a program window and not from a web browser as Java applets do. A Java application looks and acts just like any application written in any traditional programming language.

When Is Java Not Java?

Although JavaScript and Java have similar names and a few commands and operators overlap, JavaScript is little like Java. Even though both work inside the HTML of web pages, add interactivity to web pages, and share some language elements, JavaScript is deployed differently than Java and generally serves different purposes.

JavaScript began as a small language with which you can cause buttons and other web page elements to move and change as the mouse is clicked and keys are pressed. JavaScript also enables you to create menus and other web page interactive features. It later was put to use creating Asynchronous JavaScript and XML (AJAX) applications that function like static web pages but pull data dynamically in response to user input. But you cannot write JavaScript applications that stand by themselves outside of the web pages encompassing them. Java is a more powerful, complex language that can be used on full-blown standalone applications or applets.

Java's Interface

Java's interface elements—items such as check boxes and command buttons—can take on different appearances to match different computer platforms or can look the same on all of them. This is called the program's look and feel. Programs can look the same on Macs as they do on Windows computers. When other languages are used (such as C++), interface elements typically take on the parent computer's operating system style. If you really want your Java programs to achieve the specific look of a particular operating system, such as a Microsoft Windows 8 operating system, you can designate a look and feel for your program that takes on the operating system's style.

Over time, Java has become even more portable across different kinds of hardware. With each major release (eight so far), the Java language grows, adding a richer set of supporting libraries so you code less and get more done faster. Using these libraries, programmers can more easily maintain Java software because less coding means less work when a change must be made to a program. Java includes support a fantastic library called Swing that lets you place windows, dialog boxes, and other graphical user interface elements in a program without much effort. Of course, you could ignore Swing and do it all the hard way and not get any sleep. But by taking advantage of Swing, you'll put interactive code together faster.

Just look at some of the standard features found in Java that aren't available in some languages:

▶ **Drag and drop**—Enables users to move items from one screen location or program to another by dragging those items with the mouse.

▶ **Sound**—Adds sound effects to spice up your programs.

▶ **Network support**—Allows access to other computers on a user's network after getting proper security clearance from the user.

▶ **Collections**—Stores data in advanced data structure repositories such as linked lists.

▶ **2D and 3D graphics**—Dazzles the audience with eye-catching creations.

▶ **Database API**—An *API* is an acronym for *Application Programming Interface* (programmers never use easy words when hard ones sound smarter) and Java supports Java Database Connectivity (JDBC), a heavy-duty database API that enables your code to access, report, and retrieve from a data source such as a company database.

▶ **Timers**—Enables you to drop time-keeping routines into your programs that produce timed input responses, clocks, calendars, and other time-related operations.

Security Issues

Security should always be your concern when writing programs run over the Internet. In practice, Java-enabled applets can be prone to security problems if the proper precautions aren't in place. After all, when you visit a Java-enabled web page, you aren't always sure if an applet is running or what exactly an applet is trying to do to your computer's disk or memory.

Fortunately, Java was designed to be a network-based programming language. Therefore, security is inherent in the language, both for the developer and for the Internet user. What follows are some of the default security-related protections built into the Java language:

▶ A Java applet is not allowed to venture into the user's memory areas where it doesn't belong.

▶ A Java applet cannot create, read, rename, copy, or write files on the user's file system.

▶ A Java applet cannot connect to additional machines on the user's network.

▶ A Java applet cannot call system routines on the user's system.

CAUTION

You can locally load and run a Java applet from your own browser by loading an applet from your own disk drive or network. In the case of a locally loaded applet, the applet generally has permission to read and write to the local file system. In addition, some applet viewers do let the user specify a list of files that a web applet can access.

As you can see, Java developers do understand the need for security, and the most obvious security footholds are barred from an applet's access. As more people write Java applets, additional security concerns are sure to enter into the picture.

Java changes as technology and computers change. Modern Java compilers support all the modern security methods such as *digital signatures* (signing documents online), *public* and *private keys* (encryption of data to hide it from others), and *site certificates* whereby your web browser checks to ensure the software is valid and certified to be safe.

Give Java a Spin

Now that you know more about Java, you can take a look at a Java-enabled web page. Use a browser to locate this website: www.javaonthebrain.com/java/cars.

When you go to this website, if your browser has the Java Plug-in, you quickly see the splash screen of a puzzle game developed by Karl Hörnell called Autocrazy. Figure 12.4 shows the web page and the puzzle game being played.

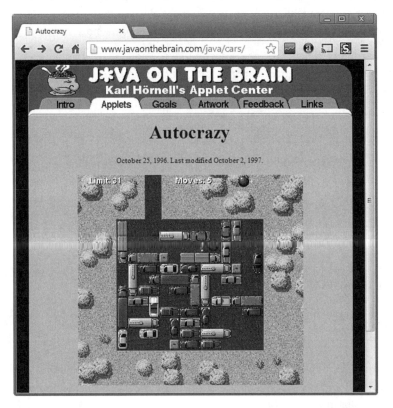

FIGURE 12.4
Java applets can enliven a web page.

The game loads automatically, displaying a splash page animation of cars moving around an insanely crowded and disorganized parking lot. Click the Play button to see the cars arranged in a puzzle where a user controls the movement of each vehicle. Click a car to move it in forward (the front half) or reverse (the back), if such movement is possible.

The goal is to clear a path for the white convertible with brown seats to leave the lot in as few moves as possible.

Java is the once and future king of fun little games like this one. In the '90s, thousands of games were created as Java applets and presented on web pages like this one. As other game development alternatives such as Flash arose, Java faded as a game programmer's favorite.

But then Android phones came along, and now millions of Java games are running on those phones and other mobile devices as apps. Every game you play on an Android device was written with Java.

Java Language Specifics

Java is not a difficult language to learn, though becoming proficient requires time to learn how to exploit the huge amount of Java code offered by Oracle and other providers that have been made available so you don't have to reinvent the wheel on your own program. Java includes several prebuilt procedures that are often used to perform standard operations such as I/O, connecting to web servers, and accessing databases. Java is an *OOP (object-oriented programming)* language and is similar to C++ in many ways. Both languages have common keywords, comments, and built-in functions. Java's OOP nature means that you can extend language objects that others write to complete applications faster.

TIP
___
Given Java's C++ roots, once you learn Java, you will already know a lot about C++. However, Java's developers did try to make Java better than C++. For example, Java, unlike C++ (or C) but similar to JavaScript, supports the string data type. Java also leaves out some features of C++ that are difficult to learn and error prone to use, such as pointers.
___

Java Example

Listing 12.1 shows a very simple Java program so that you can familiarize yourself with the format of the language. This particular program bears little resemblance to JavaScript programs, but you'll soon see that your knowledge of that language will speed your mastery of Java.

LISTING 12.1 Your first Java program may look cryptic.

```
// A simple Java applet

import java.applet.*;      // required support files
import java.awt.*;

// Main class
public class Simple extends Applet {
```

```
public void init() {
    resize(320, 240);    // applet's window size
}

public void paint(Graphics g) {
    // change subsequent text color to red
    g.setColor(Color.red);
    // write a simple message in the window
    g.drawString("Free the bound periodicals!", 75, 100);
}
}
```

When embedded inside a web page as you'll learn how to do in Hour 15, Listing 12.1 is simple and displays the message "Free the bound periodicals!" in red on the screen's browser, 75 pixels from the right edge and 100 pixels from the top of the screen. The screen in this case would be whichever Java-enabled web browser is used to view the page with the HTML code that contains this applet.

Before going into the specifics of Listing 12.1, take a moment to consider these points:

▶ Comments, the explanatory remarks for programmers, begin with two forward slashes—//.

▶ All Java programs are case-sensitive. Therefore, if you initially name a variable intSum, don't refer to that variable later as INTSUM because Java will not recognize that both are the same.

▶ Java is a free-form language. You can indent and include lots of whitespace to make your programs easier to read and maintain (or exclude it, if you like making things harder for yourself later).

▶ A semicolon generally follows each complete executable line. No semicolons follow comments or braces, however. Also, a class or procedure's definition line (the first line in a class or procedure) doesn't end with a semicolon because these statements define classes and procedures but don't execute or produce output.

▶ A pair of braces encloses a group of lines that Java treats as a single block of code. Generally, a block can appear anywhere that a single statement can appear. The braces also designate start and stop points for procedures.

These Java-coding principles apply to small as well as large standalone Java programs.

Analyzing the Code

Some of the details of Listing 12.1 should be easy to understand. In the listing, comments help divide the sections of the applet from one another as well as document some lines in the code.

The `import` commands in Listing 12.1 appear in almost every Java program that you'll write. The `import` command is somewhat analogous to the C and C++ `#include` preprocessor directive, but `import` is a Java command and not a language directive. Another difference is that `import` does not import code, despite its name. Instead, it makes it easier to refer to existing classes from special class packages provided by your Java compiler. Remember that in OOP, a class defines an object. A *package* is a collection of classes that are logically grouped together. For example, graphics routines often appear in a package. You can refer to the graphics objects from the class as long as you import that package.

The `import` command follows these two formats:

```
import specificPackage.specificClass;

import specificPackage.*;
```

When you know the name of a class that you want to use, you can specify that name inside the `import` command. The `specificPackage` is the name of the class package from which you want to import the class named `specificClass`. For example, if you want to import a class package file named `nu.xom.Builder`, you'd do this:

```
import nu.xom.Builder;
```

The second format of `import` uses the `*` wildcard character to specify that you want to import *all* classes from a class package. Listing 12.1 uses this `import` format for its imported classes. The `java.applet` class package is a necessary class for you to use when the applet is to be embedded in a web page. Therefore, you'll always import `java.applet` and all its classes at the top of every applet that you write. The `java.awt` class package contains many graphics routines that enable you to send output to a web page's applet window. Instead of printing text onscreen, your applet must *draw the text* pixel by pixel. Listing 12.1 contains a `drawString()` function that is a class procedure defined in the `java.awt` class package.

If you don't use `import`, you must refer to classes by their full names all the time, which consists of the package and class name.

The following line from Listing 12.1 defines a class named `Simple`:

```
public class Simple extends Applet {
```

The opening brace in this `public` statement begins the body of the applet's `Simple` class and the class doesn't terminate until the closing brace. A statement such as this `public` statement must appear in your applet because your applet is actually an entirely new class, from the predefined Applet class, that you are extending. In this example, the applet is taking the generic class called Applet (defined in the java.applet class package) and extending the class by naming the copy Simple; the code in the body of Simple is the added functionality for this newly extended class. Without the added code, Simple would be no different from the built-in Applet class and the applet would appear in the web page but could do nothing. The new code is what makes the applet perform.

The next few lines in Listing 12.1 define a new method called init(). (*Methods* act much like functions except that you apply the methods to objects such as the screen window object.) In reality, the listing is redefining a method that already exists. When the subclassed Applet became Simple, a method named init() came with the Applet class but it does nothing except prepare the applet to run. init() is a method that's applied to the Simple class. Every Java applet programmer *must* redefine init() and almost every applet includes the resize() function in the body of init() as done here:

```
public void init() {
    resize(320, 240);    // applet's window size
}
```

The resize() method simply informs your class of your applet's window size in the target web page. You also can insert any other code inside init() that you want executed after the initial loading of the applet. resize() requires two arguments: an *x* and a *y* coordinate. Enter the coordinates in pixels. In Listing 12.1, the resize() function is defining the Java applet's window size (the window will appear inside the web page on the user's machine) as 320 pixels wide by 240 pixels high.

The paint() method should appear in every applet that you create and paint() should follow init(). Your applet executes paint() every time your applet window needs redrawing. If the user hides the applet's window with another window and then unhides it later, the hidden portion must reappear and it is paint() that determines what happens every time the window is redrawn. As long as you've supplied a paint() method—and you must for anything to be displayed—you can be assured that your applet window will reappear properly with the text, colors, and whatever else that paint() puts on the window.

In Listing 12.1, the paint() method looks like this:

```
public void paint(Graphics g) {
    // change subsequent text color to red
    g.setColor(Color.red);
    // write a simple message in the window
    g.drawString("Free the bound periodicals!", 75, 100);
}
```

Unlike `init()`, `paint()` requires an argument inside its parentheses. The argument is a value that the `paint()` method operates on. Although `Graphics g` is a strange argument, the argument represents your web page's graphical applet window. Whatever `paint()` does to the value named g happens to your applet's window.

The `setColor()` method, therefore, sets the color for all text that will subsequently appear on the output window, g, until another `setColor()` appears. Although the window's background remains gray (you can change the background color if you want), text that appears will be red. After the applet sets the text color to red, four red words appear in the applet's window due to this line:

```
g.drawString("Free the bound periodicals!", 75, 100);
```

`drawString()` is a commonly used Java method that sends text strings to the applet's window. `drawString()` respects the color set by `setColor()` so the text, "Free the bound periodicals!" will appear in red. Notice the g before the method name. You could, if you opened several different windows with an applet, send text to different windows by prefacing `drawString()` with each window's designated context name, such as g used here. The two arguments that end the `drawString()` method indicate how wide and high, in pixels, the text is to appear.

You now know all there is to know about Listing 12.1's applet. If you're still somewhat confused, don't panic because the next few hours cover the language in more detail. Java statements can be tricky due to the object and class situations brought on by OOP.

Get Ready to Begin

The best way to get into Java programming quickly is to install an integrated development environment (IDE) that has been designed for Java programmers. There are several excellent IDEs for Java, some that can be downloaded over the Internet at no cost and others that are commercial products.

One of the best is NetBeans, a free IDE offered by Oracle that began many years ago under the name Forte for Java. NetBeans is available from the website www.netbeans.org.

If you've not yet installed NetBeans for Java, see Appendix B, "Using the NetBeans Integrated Development Environment" (available for download after registering this book at informit.com/register), and follow the installation instructions. You will then be ready to write your first Java program in the next hour.

Summary

The goal of this hour was to introduce you to the Java language with a primer on applets, the simplest type of Java programs. Java adds a jolt to web pages by sending these small interactive programs along with web pages. Part of this introduction was a language overview. Unlike more traditional programming languages such as C++, a Java program is sometimes part of something else, most notably a web page. The program travels with the web page to a user's machine and executes using the user's own computing power.

You may not understand much of the Java language yet, but you can understand a simple Java program better now that you've finished this lesson. An applet is actually a subclass, an inherited version of a predefined class, that comes with the Java compiler. You add functionality to the Java `Applet` class to make the program your own.

Q&A

Q. Do I embed my Java program code directly inside the HTML code on my web page?

A. No. HTML is only for formatting a web page's appearance and for placing the applet in the correct location, but your compiled applet, in bytecode, travels along with a web page to the destination computer. HTML always appears and downloads in source code format, whereas a Java program always downloads in bytecode format. Therefore, the two files must travel separately to the user's computer.

Q. Can a user stop my Java program from executing?

A. Certain web-based security features can keep Java applets that arrive with a web page from executing on the user's machine. Although the Java language includes built-in security controls to keep Java authors from invading a user's machine from the Internet, the user can still keep the applet from executing by setting certain browser options.

Workshop

The quiz questions are provided for your further understanding.

Quiz

1. True or false: The faster the user's computer is, the faster the Java applet that appears with the web page runs.

2. True or false: The faster the user's computer is, the faster the Java applet downloads on the user's machine.

3. What is the language behind web page formatting called?

4. What is bytecode?

5. Why is the concept of a Java Virtual Machine (JVM) important?

6. How does the Java language provide security support for the end user who views Java-enabled web pages?

7. What is the purpose of the `import` command?

8. How do you send text to the screen in a Java applet?

9. Why is the `paint()` method important?

10. What specifies a Java comment in Java programs?

Answers

1. True.

2. False. The bandwidth and size of the Java applet determines how fast the Java applet loads.

3. HTML is the language that formats web pages.

4. Bytecode is the language into which Java compiles Java code.

5. By emulating a virtual machine, any computer in the world can run any compiled Java program.

6. Java handles security in many ways. For example, Java must receive proper security clearance from the user before accessing a network, cannot access memory space that it has no right to, cannot create, read, rename, copy, or write files on the end user's computer, and Java applets cannot call internal system routines on the end user's system.

7. The `import` command brings object libraries into the Java program.

8. The `drawString()` function writes characters to the screen.

9. The `paint()` method determines what happens when a window is redrawn.

10. Java comments begin with `//` or are enclosed inside a `/*` and `*/` pair.

HOUR 13
Java's Details

In this hour, you will gain a deeper understanding of the Java programming language. Java has its roots in C and C++. Once you become familiar with Java, you will then be familiar with much of C and C++. Java has become the most widely used programming language in the world, overtaking C++.

Java is actually simpler to learn than C++ because many of the skills of Java programming come from knowing which internal prebuilt Java procedures to run. As you saw in the previous hour's overview, when you want to print a message in color, you don't have to do much more than find the name of the prebuilt procedure that first sets the color, find the name of the procedure that prints in an output window, and then use those procedures in your program.

The highlights of this hour include

- ▶ Seeing how Java treats literals
- ▶ Declaring variables
- ▶ Understanding operators
- ▶ Controlling programs with `if` statements
- ▶ Validating user input
- ▶ Looping with the `for` and `while` statements

Defining Java Data

JavaScript supports numeric and string data types. Most languages, including Java, break data down further into several different types. Data can be either *literals*, constant values that do not change such as your first name or date of birth, and *variables*, which, as you know already from JavaScript, are named storage locations for data that can change.

Java Literals

A literal is just a number, character, or string of characters. Several kinds of Java literals exist. Java supports *integer* (whole numbers without decimal places) and *floating-point* (numbers with decimal place) literals. Here are some valid integer literals:

```
23    -53819    0
```

Here are sample floating-point literals:

```
90544.5432211    -.0000324    -2.354    67.1
```

Integer literals can use the _ underscore character to make them more readable:

```
7_500_000    8_650_300_000
```

The _ just makes the value easier for humans to understand. You can see at a glance that the first number is 7.5 million without needing to count the zeroes. The Java compiler ignores the underscores.

Java also supports two *Boolean* literals. These Boolean literals are `true` and `false`. You'll use Boolean literals to test or set Boolean values to `true` or `false` to determine if certain events are to occur.

A character literal is a single character. You must enclose character literals inside single quotation marks. The following are character literals:

```
'J'    '@'    '4'    'p'
```

A character literal doesn't have to be alphabetic. You cannot compute with a number inside a character literal. Therefore, '4' is a character literal but 4 is an integer literal. If you need to represent several characters as a single literal, use a string literal as described at the end of this section. Programmers work with literals all the time, such as when printing a corporation's name on a report.

Java supports special character literals called *escape sequences*. Due to the nature of some character literals, you cannot always represent a character inside single quotation marks. For example, a tab character can appear on a screen to move the cursor forward a few characters to the next tab stop. But to store a tab character in a variable, you cannot assign the tab key directly to a variable—you must use an escape sequence to represent the tab character. These escape characters do consume more than one position inside the single quotes, such as '\n', but they only take one character's storage location as do all character literals. Table 13.1 lists some Java escape sequences.

TABLE 13.1 Java's escape sequence characters represent nontypable characters.

Escape Sequence	Represents
`'\f'`	Form feed
`'\n'`	Newline (linefeed followed by a carriage return)
`'\t'`	Tab (horizontal)
`'\007'`	Ring the PC's speaker
`'\''`	Single quotation mark
`'\"'`	Quotation mark

NOTE

Remember that Java came from C and C++. C and C++ support the same data types as Java (except for strings) as well as the same escape sequences. As you learn more about Java's operators and control statements throughout the rest of this hour, virtually all you learn is applicable in C and C++ as well.

You can use an escape character to move the cursor down a line with the newline escape sequence, or you could use one to place a single quotation mark on a window. You could not represent a single quote by placing it inside two single quotes like this: `' ' '`.

Specify string literals by enclosing them in quotation marks. All the following items are string literals:

```
"This is a string."      "12345"      ""      "q"
```

TIP

You can place an escape sequence character inside a string. Therefore, the following string literal contains starting and ending quotation marks due to two escape sequences that represent the quote marks: `"\"Java\""`.

Java Variables

As in JavaScript, you're in charge of naming Java variables. You must inform Java that you need to use a variable by declaring that variable before you use it. When you declare a variable, you tell Java the name and data type of that variable. Java then reserves storage for that variable throughout the variable's lifetime. A variable's life may be for the entire program (as is the case with *global* variables) or may exist only for a few lines of code (as is the case with *local* variables), depending on how and where you declare the variable. Once you declare a variable, Java protects that variable's data type; that is, you cannot store a string in an integer variable.

Integer Variables

Table 13.2 lists the four kinds of integer variables Java supports. The integer variable you use depends on what you're going to store in that variable. For example, if you're going to store a child's age in a variable, you could do so in a `byte` variable. If you are going to store intergalactic distances, you need to use a `long` integer.

TABLE 13.2 Java variable sizes determine which integer variable you use.

Data Type	Storage Needed	Data Range
byte	1 byte	-127 to 128
short	2 bytes	-32,767 to 32,768
int	4 bytes	-2,147,483,647 to 2,147,483,648
long	8 bytes	-9.2233 times 10 to the 18th power to 9.2233 times 10 to the 18th power

A byte of memory represents a single character of storage. Therefore, you can store approximately 16 million characters, or byte integers, in 16 million bytes of free memory.

Generally, you'll find variable declarations near the beginning of Java programs and procedures. To declare a variable, use Table 13.2's first column to tell Java the kind of variable you require. The following statement declares an integer variable named numKeys:

```
int numKeys;   // defines a 4-byte integer variable
```

Remember to follow your variable declarations, as with all Java statements, with semicolons. The following statements define four variables, one for each type of Java integer:

```
byte a;
short b;
int c;
long d;
```

You can define several variables of the same data type on one line like this:

```
int x, y, z;   // defines 3 integer variables
```

CAUTION

Java declares variables but does not initialize variables for you. Therefore, don't assume zero or blanks are in numeric and string variables. Be sure to initialize each variable with a value before you use that variable inside a calculation.

Use the assignment operator, =, to assign values to your variables. You can assign a variable an initial value at the same time you define a variable. The following statements declare four variables and initialize three of them:

```
byte f = 32;
int c, d = 7639;    // defines but does not initialize c
long highCount = 0;
```

Floating-Point Variables

Table 13.3 lists the two kinds of floating-point variables that Java supports. You'll use the larger floating-point variable to represent extremely large or small values with a high degree of accuracy. Generally, only scientific and mathematically related programs need the `double` data type. For most floating-point calculations, `float` works just fine.

TABLE 13.3   **Java supports two floating-point variable data types.**

Data Type	Storage Needed	Decimal Accuracy
float	4 bytes	6 decimal places
double	8 bytes	14 decimal places

The following statements declare and initialize floating-point variables that can hold decimal numbers:

```
float w = -234.4332F;
float x = 76545.39F;
double y = -0.29384848458, z = 9283.11223344;
```

The first two values are followed by an uppercase F, which indicates that they are `float` values instead of `double`. Java's default for decimal numbers is `double`.

Boolean Variables

Use the `boolean` keyword to declare Boolean variables. A Boolean variable can hold only `true` or `false`. The following statements declare and initialize three Boolean variables:

```
boolean hasPrinted = false;
boolean gotAnswer = false, keyPressed = true;
```

These conditional values specify whether or not an event took place.

Character Variables

Declare character variables with the `char` keyword as the following statements do:

```
char firstInitial;
char lastInitial = 'Z';
```

You may assign any of the character literals you learned about earlier this hour, including escape sequences, to character variables. The following statements store the letter A in a variable and a tab character in another variable:

```
c1 = 'A';
tabChar = '\t';
```

String Variables

Java does not actually support string variables, and neither do C or C++, but Java includes a built-in class that defines string data as variables so you can declare string variables just as you can the other data types. Use the `String` keyword (notice the uppercase S; most programmers use an initial uppercase letter for names of classes) to declare string variables. You cannot directly change a string variable once you declare and initialize the variable but you can use built-in functions to change string variables.

The following statements declare three strings:

```
String s;                        // no initialization
String langName = "Java";        // an initialized string
String warning = "Don't press Enter yet!"; // initialized
```

Arrays

Java supports arrays, which are lists of zero or more variables of the same data type, as you learned in Hour 5, "Programming Algorithms." All array subscripts begin at 0, so a 10-element array named ara utilizes these array elements: ara[0] through ara[9]. Of course, you don't have to name arrays ara; you can assign any name you wish to an array.

To define an array, use the `new` command. The following statements define three arrays:

```
int countList[] = new int[100];    // declare an array of 100 elements
double temps[] = new double[30];   // declare 30 double elements
char initials[] = new char[1000]; // declare 1,000 characters
```

Although their declarations require more typing than non-array variables, once you've declared arrays, you can use the array elements just as you use other variables. For example, the following statements work with individual array elements:

```
countList[0] = 10;
countList[50] = 394;
temps[2] = 34334.9298;
initials[1] = 'a';
initials[2] = initials[1];
```

Operators

Java supports several mathematical and conditional operators. You don't have to be a math expert to understand them but Java's operators are somewhat more involved than JavaScript's due to Java's heavier reliance on operators (the same holds for C and C++).

The Primary Math Operators

Table 13.4 contains Java's primary math operators.

TABLE 13.4   Java supports fundamental math operators.

Operator	Name	Sample
+	Addition	`4 + count`
-	Subtraction	`gross - net`
*	Multiplication	`pay * taxRate`
/	Division	`bonus / factor`
%	Modulus	`bonus % factor`

You can use parentheses to group calculations together. Java normally computes division and multiplication in a formula before addition and subtraction, but the following makes sure the addition is computed first so an average can result:

```
average = (sales1 + sales2 + sales3 + sales4) / 4;
```

The modulus operator returns the remainder when you divide one integer into another. The assignment operator evaluates from right to left so you can combine multiple assignments as in this statement:

```
a = b = c = d = e = 0;   // Stores 0 in all five variables
```

Increment and Decrement Operators

As you learned in Hour 9, your programs will often keep track of running totals or count down or up to a value such as a total score. To add one or subtract one from a variable, you can use Java's increment (++) and decrement (--) operators as follows:

```
runningTotal++;  // adds 1 to variable
countdown--;     // subtracts 1 from variable
```

You may place increment and decrement operators inside expressions such as this:

```
answer = aVar++ * 4;
```

You can place increment and decrement operators on either side of a variable. If you place them on the left, *prefix* notation occurs and Java computes the increment or decrement before other operators. If you place them on the right, *postfix* notation occurs and Java computes the increment and decrement after other operators.

Assuming x contains 5 before the next statement, answer receives the value of 12:

```
answer = ++x * 2;   // evaluate prefix first
```

The next statement performs a different calculation, however, due to the postfix notation. Java does not update x until after x is evaluated in the rest of the expression:

```
answer = x++ * 2;   // evaluate postfix last
```

In this expression, answer will contain 10 because the multiplication occurs before x increments. As with the prefix version, x always ends up with 6 before the statement completes. The choice of prefix or postfix depends on how you formulate the expression. If, for example, you used the same variable more than once on the right side of the equal sign, you should use postfix notation if you increment the variable so the expression is accurate. In other words, the following assignment statement uses postfix increment because age is incremented after it's used for the assignment:

```
ageFactor = age++ * .45 + age;   // uses postfix
```

This statement uses the value of age twice in the calculation and then, after assigning the answer to ageFactor, increments the value in age. If prefix had been used, age would first be incremented before being used in the expression.

Arithmetic Assignments

Often, you will update, or change, the value of a variable based on that variable's existing value. For example, suppose you are keeping track of a 10-question polling result. Every time the user answers a polling questionnaire, you'll add 10 to a running total. Any time you want to modify the value of a variable, while using that variable's current value in the expression, put the variable on both sides of the assignment operator. The following statement adds 10 to the variable named totalAnswers:

```
totalAnswers = totalAnswers + 10;   // adds 10
```

You can divide a variable by two, as done with aVar here:

```
aVar = aVar / 2.0;
```

This updating of variables occurs so frequently that the Java language borrowed common C and C++ operators called *arithmetic assignment* operators. Table 13.5 explains these.

TABLE 13.5   Java's arithmetic operators shortcut the updating of variables.

Operator	Sample	Description
+=	n += 2	Adds to a variable
-=	netPay -= 10.0	Subtracts from a variable
*=	pay *= .7	Multiplies a variable's contents
/=	bonus /= scale	Divides a variable's contents
%=	num %= 1	Computes the remainder based on a variable's current contents

Given Table 13.5's operator listing, the following statements use the arithmetic assignments to produce the same results described before the table:

```
totalAnswers += 10;    // same as totalAnswers = totalAnswers + 10;
aVar /= 2.0;           // same as aVar = aVar / 2.0;
```

Comparison Operators

Table 13.6 describes Java's conditional operators. These operators do not perform mathematical operations but return a Boolean `true` or `false` result that indicates how one data value relates to another. You should have little trouble understanding these operators, as they are similar to JavaScript's comparison operators.

TABLE 13.6   Java's comparison operators compare how data values relate to one another.

Operator	Sample	Description
==	sales == max	Tests for equality
!=	profit != goal	Tests for inequality
<	n < m	Tests for less than
>	amt > 0	Tests for greater than
<=	top <= bottom	Tests for less than or equal to
>=	age >= 21	Tests for greater than or equal to

CAUTION

Don't confuse the equality operator, ==, with the assignment, =. Java, C, and C++ use = for assignment and == to test for equality.

The Conditional Operator

The *conditional operator* is the only Java operator that requires three values. The conditional operator actually combines *if-then-else* logic into a simple, clear operation. The conditional operator returns one of two values depending on the result of a comparison operator.

Here is the general format of the conditional operator:

```
(comparison) ? true result : false result;
```

Often, you'll assign a conditional to a variable as in the following statement:

```
minVal = (a < b) ? a: b;   // stores the lesser of a or b
```

If the comparison of (a < b) results in true, a is assigned to minVal. Otherwise, if (a < b) is false, the conditional assigns b to minVal. Although you'll learn about Java's if statement later this hour, Java's if statement is close enough to JavaScript's if statement that you can understand much of it now. As a comparison, and to help strengthen your understanding of the conditional operator, here is the identical logic using if-else statements:

```
if (a < b)
    minVal = a;
else
    minVal = b;
```

Use a conditional when you must make a fairly simple calculation based on the result of a comparison, such as (a < b) here. In most instances, a multi-statement if-else is easier to maintain than a conditional statement that tries to do too much.

Programming Control

Now that you know how to define Java data and work with its operators, you need to know how to manipulate that data through program control. Java programmers group statements together in *blocks* of code. A block of code is one or more statements enclosed within a pair of braces such as this:

```
{
    count++;
    System.out.println("The count is now higher");
}
```

Blocks can contain other blocks so you can *nest* one block inside another. The indention of the block's body helps to show where blocks begin and end in long programs.

Learn the Format

As you learn programming languages, you'll see how statements are formatted or put together. A general notation is often used to show you how to code a programming language statement.

Italicized words are placeholders that you fill in with your own values. The non-italicized words, such as `if`, are required. If any part of the format appears inside square brackets, with the exception of array brackets, that part of the statement is optional.

The following format shows that `if` is required but the `else` portion is optional. You fill in the italicized placeholder code with other programming statements:

```
if (condition) {
    block of one or more Java statements;
} else {
    block of one or more Java statements;
}
```

The `if` and `if-else` Statements

Here is the general format of the `if` statement:

```
if (condition) {
    block of one or more Java statements;
}
```

CAUTION

Never put a semicolon at the end of the condition's parenthesis! Semicolons go only at the end of the executable statements. The condition does not terminate the `if` statement but only introduces the `if`. If you placed a semicolon after the condition, then a *null statement* would execute, meaning nothing would happen no matter how the condition tested and the block would always execute.

Consider the following `if` statement:

```
if (age >= 21) {
    g.drawString("You have authorization for the payment", 25, 50);
    makePmt(pmt);
}
// rest of program goes here
```

The two statements in the body of the `if` execute only if `age` contains a value of 21 or more. If `age` is less than 21, the block of code does *not* execute. Whether or not the block executes does not keep the subsequent statements in the program from continuing.

A common use of `if` is *input verification*. When you ask the user for a value, you should check the value to make sure the user entered a reasonable answer. For example, the following code asks the user for his or her age. If the user enters zero or a negative value, the program's `if` statement displays an error message and prompts the user again:

```
getAge(age);  // calls a procedure to get the user's age
if (age <= 0) {
    // the following lines output to the user's screen
    System.out.println("You entered a bad age value.");
    System.out.println("Try again please.");
    getAge(age);
}
// code goes here to process the age
```

The `if-else` adds an `else` block to the `if` statement. Here is the format of the `if-else` statement:

```
if (condition) {
  block of one or more Java statements;
} else {
  block of one or more Java statements;
}
```

If the condition evaluates to true, the first block of Java statements executes. If, however, the condition evaluates to false, the second block of Java statements executes.

The section of Java code in Listing 13.1 computes a payroll amount based on the following general rules:

▶ If the employee works 40 or fewer hours, the employee gets paid an hourly rate times the number of hours worked.

▶ If the employee works from 40 to 50 hours, the employee gets paid one-and-one-half times the hourly pay for all hours over 40.

▶ If the employee works more than 50 hours, the employee gets paid twice the hourly rate for those hours over 50.

LISTING 13.1   Using `if-else` to compute an employee's overtime

```
// assume all variables are declared and initialized
// to 0 in earlier code

// check for double-time first
if (hours > 50) {
    doubleTime = 2.0 * payRate * (hours - 50);
    // 1.5 pay for middle 10 hours
    halftime = 1.5 * payRate * 10.0;
} else {
    // no double because no hours over 50
```

```
        doubleTime = 0.0;
}

// check for time-and-a-half
if ((hours > 40) && (hours <= 50)) {
    halftime = 1.5 * payRate * (hours - 40);
}

// compute regular pay for everybody
if (hours <= 40) {
     regPay = hours * payRate;
} else {
   regPay = 40 * payRate;
}

// add the parts to get total gross pay
totalPay = regPay + halftime + doubleTime;
```

NOTE

You'll notice a new operator in Listing 13.1, the *and* operator, `&&`. `&&` combines two conditions. Both conditions must be true for the entire `if` to be true. Therefore, `if ((hours > 40) && (hours <= 50))` means the hours must be over 40 and less than or equal to 50 for the `if` to be true.

The `while` Loop

Java supports several kinds of loops. The `while` loop continues as long as a condition is true. Here is the format of the `while` loop:

```
while (condition) {
    block of one or more Java statements;
}
```

While the *condition* remains true, the block repeats, but as soon as the *condition* becomes false, the loop body stops executing. It's incumbent upon you to modify the *condition* inside the loop's body or the loop will never stop.

In some cases, the body of the `while` loop will never execute. If the *condition* is false upon entering the loop, Java skips the loop's body and continues with the rest of the program. Earlier, you saw how an `if` statement can inform a user if the user enters invalid data. With looping, you can take the user's input validation a step further: You can keep asking the user for an answer until the user enters a value that falls within your program's expected range.

The following code uses a `while` loop to keep asking the user for an age value until the user enters a value greater than zero:

```
getAge(age);  // calls a procedure to get the user's age
while (age <= 0) {
    // user didn't enter proper age
    System.out.println("\nYou entered a bad age value.");
    System.out.println("Try again please.");
    getAge(age);
}
System.out.println("\nThank you");
// when execution gets here, age contains a positive value
```

Here is an example of the output:

```
How old are you? -16
<beep>

You entered a bad age value.
Try again please.
How old are you? 0
<beep>

You entered a bad age value.
Try again please.
How old are you? 22

Thank you
```

The `for` Loop

The simplest `for` loop in Java works very much like JavaScript. Here is the general format of the `for` loop:

```
for (startExpression; testExpression; countExpression) {
    block of one or more Java statements;
}
```

Java evaluates the `startExpression` before the loop begins. Typically, the `startExpression` is an assignment statement (such as `ctr = 1;`), but the `startExpression` can be any legal expression you specify. Java evaluates the `startExpression` only once, at the top of the loop, just before the loop begins.

CAUTION

Although semicolons appear twice in the `for`'s parenthetical control statement, you should never put a semicolon after the `for`'s closing parenthesis or the `for` loop will never repeat its body of code.

The `for` statement tests its condition at the top of the loop. Here's the way the test works:

- If the *testExpression* is true when the loop begins, the body of the loop executes.

- If the *testExpression* is false when the loop begins, the body of the loop never executes.

A count is one of the quickest ways to see how the `for` loop operates. Consider the following `for` loop:

```
for (int ctr = 1; ctr <= 13; ctr++) {
    System.out.print(ctr);
    System.out.print(" ");

}
```

When the code runs, here is what the user sees:

```
1 2 3 4 5 6 7 8 9 10 11 12 13
```

You don't have to increment the *countExpression*. You can increment or decrement the variable by any value each time the loop executes. The following code prints all even numbers below 20:

```
System.out.println("Even numbers below 20:");
for (int num = 2; num <= 20; num+= 2) {  // adds 2 each loop iteration
    System.out.println(num);
}
```

From Details to High-Level

Throughout this hour, you've been studying the details of the Java language. If you've made it through without too many scars, you will be surprised at how much you also know of C and C++ when you look at a program written in one of those two languages.

Two areas of Java programming that this hour did not concentrate on are

- Input and output (I/O)

- Object-oriented programming (OOP) concepts

It was important to focus on the language specifics in this hour. Now that you have done that, you are ready to tackle the other side of Java. Fortunately, I/O is rather simple in Java because the built-in library routines that come with Java enable you to get the user's input and display output relatively easily. As you learn about Java I/O in the next hour, you'll also learn about how Java supports OOP.

Summary

The goal of this hour was to teach you about Java operators and the language's fundamental commands. You now understand how to control Java programs and how to form mathematical expressions in Java. You saw how knowledge of JavaScript helped you master Java more quickly due to the similarities between the programming languages.

When you finish the next hour, you will put everything together and begin using NetBeans to enter and test the programs you write.

Q&A

Q. Why should I use escape characters?

A. Escape characters were more important before windows-type environments due to the row and column textual nature of older computer screens, but you'll still use escape characters in modern-day Java (and C and C++) programs to represent characters that you cannot type directly from your keyboard, such as a carriage return character.

Q. Which should I use, the conditional operator or the `if` statement?

A. Although you saw both the conditional operator and an equivalent `if` statement for comparison in this hour, the two are for different purposes. The `if` statement can be much more complex than the conditional statement because you can use the `else` and blocks to execute many statements depending on the complexity of the problem you're coding. Use the conditional for short, one-statement conditional bodies that produce results that you'll assign to other variables. Most of the time, a multiline `if-else` statement is easier to maintain than a complex conditional statement.

Workshop

The quiz questions are provided for your further understanding.

Quiz

1. True or false: You can change a Java literal just as you can change the value of a variable.

2. How would you store a quotation mark in a character variable named `aQuote`?

3. How many integer data types does Java support?

4. What is the lowest subscript in a Java array?

5. How many different values can a Boolean variable hold?

6. Describe what the modulus operator does.

7. Rewrite the following code in Java using only one variable and one operator:

   ```
   sum = sum * 18;
   ```

8. What is in the value of `y` when the following code completes?

   ```
   int x, y;
   x = 4;
   y = ++x + 3 * 2;
   ```

9. What is wrong with the following `for` loop?

   ```
   for (int num = 1; num > 20; num++); {
       System.out.println("Hello!");
   }
   ```

10. True or false: You must increment the `for` loop's variable by one each time through the loop.

Answers

1. False. You cannot change a literal.

2. Store the escape character for the quotation mark.

3. Java supports four integer data types: `byte`, `short`, `int`, and `long`.

4. The first subscript in a Java array is `0`.

5. A Boolean variable can hold one of two possible values.

6. The modulus operator returns the integer remainder of a division between two integers.

7. `sum*=18;`

8. `11`

9. The semicolon at the end of the `for` statement causes the loop to execute without ever doing anything but looping. Once the loop finishes, the `System.out.println()` executes one time.

10. False. You can increment, decrement, or change the loop variable by whatever value you want.

HOUR 14
Java Has Class

In this hour, you will learn all about Java classes after performing some hands-on programming with the NetBeans integrated development environment (IDE). This, perhaps, is one of the heaviest hours in this 24-hour tutorial due to the nature of object-oriented programming (OOP).

Most Java programming revolves around an object's class data and methods. Java contains all kinds of rules and conventions for specifying class data and methods. In this hour, you'll learn how methods perform their work and you'll see how to set up data that responds to those methods.

The highlights of this hour include

- ▶ Working inside the NetBeans IDE
- ▶ Displaying Java output in windows
- ▶ Using classes to define objects
- ▶ Understanding how methods behave
- ▶ Passing and returning arguments
- ▶ Overloading methods to ease programming duties

Using NetBeans to Run a Java Program

You probably don't want to wait any longer to begin coding in Java. You've now got enough of the language's background to begin with some hands-on work.

Listing 14.1 contains a Java source program that asks for two numbers and displays the sum of them. Considering that a pocket calculator could do this in four button presses, the Java source code might seem rather long for such a simple calculation. Some overhead is required for Java applications, and the OOP mechanisms, such as private data members, add some code, as you'll see throughout the last half of this hour (hence, the apparent wordiness of the code). Fortunately, the wordiness does not increase in direct proportion to an application's requirements.

This program is a standalone application and is not a Java applet that appears inside a web page. Java applets use the same Java language as standalone Java applications but require some extra code to make the applet work inside a web page, as you'll learn about in the next hour, Hour 15, "Applets and Web Pages."

LISTING 14.1 This simple Java program adds two numbers together.

```
public class Calculator {

    /**
     * @param args the command line arguments
     */
    public static void main (String args[]) {
        int intSum;              // holds the sum

        // compute sum
        intSum = 14 + 35;

        // show user the sum
        System.out.println("The total is " +  intSum);

        System.exit(0);          // stops the execution
    }
}
```

To create Listing 14.1's program, just follow these steps:

1. Start NetBeans. A startup dialog appears for a few moments and the IDE opens with a Start Page displayed in the main editing window, as shown in Figure 14.1. Java programs you create with NetBeans belong to projects, so you must create one. Click the New Project button shown in Figure 14.1.

2. In the New Project dialog, select Java in the Categories pane and Java Application in the Projects pane; then Click Next.

3. In the Project Name field, enter FirstProject (or anything else you like). Deselect the Create Main Class box and make a note of the value in the Project Location text field. This is the place on your disk where NetBeans saves all the Java programs you put in this project.

4. Click Finish. NetBeans creates the project and adds it to the Projects pane, which is on the left-hand side right below the New Project button.

5. With a project open, you're ready to begin creating a Java program. Click New File, a button adjacent to New Project. The New File dialog opens.

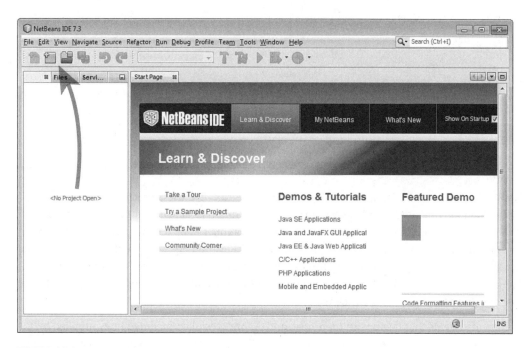

FIGURE 14.1
Creating a new project in NetBeans.

6. Choose `Java` from the Categories pane and `Java Main Class` from File Types; then click Next. You are telling NetBeans that you want to create a standalone Java application. All Java programs use `main` as the starting point of the program's execution. `main` is the name of a method, or routine, and some small Java programs contain only a `main` method. NetBeans will actually build part of the `main` procedure for you so that you don't have to type the entire program in Listing 14.1.

7. In the Class Name field, enter `Calculator`. This will be the name of the program.

8. Click Finish. NetBeans builds the outline of your program shown in Listing 14.2.

LISTING 14.2   NetBeans builds an outline of your code so you have less to type.

```
/*
 * To change this template, choose Tools | Templates
 * and open the template in the editor.
 */

/**
 *
 * @author Greg Perry
```

```
 */
public class Calculator {

    /**
     * @param args the command line arguments
     */
    public static void main(String[] args) {
        // TODO code application logic here
    }

}
```

NetBeans adds several comments and uses the same syntax as C uses, which is still supported by the Java language. All text between an opening /* and a closing */ pair of characters, even if the words span multiple lines, is considered by the compiler to be a comment. NetBeans adds several comments to your code that begin with asterisks just to help separate the comments from actual executable program code. You can also use the newer-style comments that begin with //. The advantage of the old style is that each comment line doesn't have to begin with //, only the first one, in multiple lines of comments.

Commented items that begin with an ampersand, @, are special commented lines supplied by NetBeans that you should replace with something other than the default values, such as putting your name after the text @author. Of course, because they're inside comments, you can put anything you want there. But as Hour 3, "Designing a Program," explained, maintenance is vital when working in a group of programmers, and each programmer should put his or her name in the source code along with a version number of the code to show what was worked on. For now, you can remove these comment lines preceded by the ampersand by selecting and deleting them as you would do in a word processor.

The class name chosen for a Java program determines its filename. So because this class is called Calculator, the filename is Calculator.java. All Java source code ends in the .java filename extension.

Within the file, NetBeans creates a method, the regular main method.

The main method has the words public static void before the name to define how this method is to be viewed. These keywords basically tell the compiler that main is a public method that can be seen from the rest of the files in the project, if the project has additional files and the main method returns no values.

Values, called *arguments*, are placed inside main's parentheses in order to be passed to main from other places. When your programs have multiple methods, each one can transfer values back and forth through this argument list. main's argument list is there in case you want to send values from the operating system to the program when the program first starts. In most cases you won't do this, but a string array exists in the main method just in case.

Java created this program shell for you so that your only job is to fill in the source code with the rest of Listing 14.1's code, compile the program, and see the results. To finish the program, follow these steps:

1. Delete the comment `// TODO code application logic here` and at that same spot, type `main`'s body of code as shown in Listing 14.3.

LISTING 14.3   Type this to complete the `main` procedure that NetBeans began for you.

```
public static void main(String args[]) {
    int intSum;             // holds the sum

    // compute sum
    intSum = 14 + 35;

    // show user the sum
    System.out.println("The total is " +  intSum);

    System.exit(0);         // stops the execution
}
```

2. Your program should now look like the one in Listing 14.4. Although you may have changed, added, or deleted some comments, your non-comment code should exactly match that of the listing.

LISTING 14.4   The completed version of the `Calculator` program

```
/**
 *
 * @author Greg Perry
 */
public class Calculator {

    /**
     * @param args the command line arguments
     */
    public static void main(String args[]) {
        int intSum;             // holds the sum

        // compute sum
        intSum = 14 + 35;

        // show user the sum
        System.out.println("The total is " +  intSum);

        System.exit(0);         // stops the execution
    }
}
```

3. You can now run the program. NetBeans compiles the program automatically if there are no errors. To run it, hit Shift-F6 or choose the menu command Run, Run File. If you don't see the Output window, click the Output tab at the bottom of the editing window where you entered the program's source code. The output window shows the following program result:

```
The total is 49
```

Going GUI

You've successfully run your first Java program, but the output is text-based and does not take advantage of a graphical environment very well. Listing 14.5 contains the same program as the previous one except for two added lines that take advantage of Swing. Swing is a Java library that enables you to add message boxes, get input from input boxes, and add windowlike features to your program, among many other capabilities.

Create a new Java program following the same steps undertaken with `Calculator`, except to make `SwingCalculator` the Class Name when you're asked for it in the New File dialog.

LISTING 14.5 **Move away from the text mode into windowed features.**

```java
import javax.swing.*;

/**
 *
 * @author Greg Perry
 */
public class SwingCalculator {

    /**
     * @param args the command line arguments
     */
    public static void main(String[] args) {
        int intSum;              // holds the sum

        // compute sum
        intSum = 14 + 35;

        // show user the sum
        JOptionPane.showMessageDialog(null, "The total is " +  intSum);

        System.exit(0);          // stops the execution

    }
}
```

When you execute your program, the message box shown in Figure 14.2 appears. That's better and more modern than outputting straight text, isn't it? Click the message box's button to close the message box window when you're done.

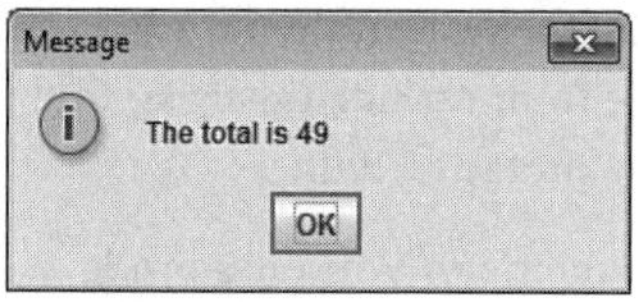

FIGURE 14.2
Swing powers a Java program's graphical user interface (GUI).

The Java libraries, such as Swing, are full of objects you can bring into your own code and use. Part of the fun of getting to know Java is figuring out what all the language can do for you through the use of these object-oriented library routines. Need to add a command button or other feature to your program? Look for an object library that supplies that feature and just plug the object into your program! That's one of the beauties of Java and OOP.

NOTE

The Swing object library can be used by this program because of the `import` command that imports, or brings into your program, all the windowlike objects from the library named `javax.swing`. One of the many features of this library is the `JOptionPane` program that enables you to send output to a windowed message box instead of as text in a window as you did in the previous section using `System.out.println`. `System` is actually an object, your computer, and `out` is a subobject, or a *derived* object, that represents a text window.

Java and OOP

Java is an *OOP* (*object-oriented programming*) language, and just about everything you do works with an object of some kind. An object is a place where more than one variable resides with methods that do things to (and with) those variables. Objects give their variables special treatment such as protecting the variables' details from the rest of the code, but still, an object is a place where two or more variables often appear together in a group.

Consider this object declaration:

```
public class Employee {
    protected String firstName[15] = new String;
    protected String lastName[15] = new String;
    protected float salary;
    protected int age;
    // rest of object's declaration follows
}
```

Although several variables are declared here, two as arrays, they are collected together into the class called `Employee`. Just as the integer data type is not a variable but defines data, neither is `Employee` a variable; it is a class that declares what subsequent variables will look like. The class simply defines the format of an object that you generate from that class just as the integer data type defines the format of a variable that you generate from the integer data type. The `protected` keyword tells Java that those members are not accessible from outside the class; that is, only code that you subsequently place inside the class can use the protected data.

Figure 14.3 shows how the `Employee` object's data values appear in memory. Variables inside objects are called *members* but they're really just variables. After the variable members are defined in the object, the rest of the declaration often contains procedures called *methods*, which are routines that act upon the object's data.

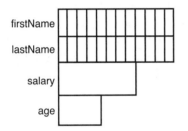

FIGURE 14.3
Objects can contain lots of variables and their data types don't have to match.

Overview of Classes

All Java programs are actually objects themselves. The entire Java program you write is an object. There exists a special top-level object called `java.lang.Object`. Your program is a derivation from that object. When you *derive* one object from another, or inherit an object from another, the derived object takes on all the properties of its parent object, the higher-level object.

Here is the line that derived from this special Java application object in this hour's earlier programs:

```
public class Calculator extends java.lang.Object {
```

In other words, you created a Java application, an object, from the `java.lang.Object` object. More specifically, you created a new class by inheriting from the `java.lang.Object` class. You extended a new object from an existing one that represented a generic Java application.

Why Inherit?

You inherit to eliminate redundant coding. When you inherit from a class, your derived class (sometimes called the subclass) inherits all methods and data values from the parent class.

Therefore, with the simple `extends` keyword, your new class that you inherit from a parent class gains all the parent's power, behaviors, and data.

When you define methods and data members in the inherited class, that class becomes stronger than its parent class because the inherited class now has extended abilities.

An object is more than a variable. An object is an active variable that, with its data and methods, not only has characteristics from the data values but also can perform operations on that data with its member code. As you pursue your programming career and learn more about objects, you will learn how languages such as Java specifically activate objects so that you can use those objects in other programs you write. You can reuse objects in a second program that you previously wrote simply by copying the object's class definition to your new program.

Unlike the built-in data types, such as `int`, if you perform a math operation on one of your objects, you'll have to teach Java how to do the math by writing a method that performs the work. Once you supply the code, however, calculating with the objects is basically as easy to do as calculating with the built-in types.

Listing 14.6 demonstrates a class with data values (often called *data members* or just *members*) and methods (procedures inside the class).

LISTING 14.6   A class can have both data members and procedure methods.

```
// The Box Class

class Box {      // a new class, so there is no
      // extension or inheritance from another class
    float area;      // a class data member
    int colorCode;  // a class data member

    void calcArea(float width, float length) {
        // computes a value from data passed to the object
        area = width * length;
    }

    void setColor(int colorValue) {
        // sets a color for the object
        colorCode = colorValue;
    }
}
```

`Box` is a class with four members: two of `Box`'s members are data members (`area` and `colorCode`) and two are methods (`calcArea()` and `setColor()`). `Box` is not an object, just a definition of the object (the class). You can, however, instantiate objects from the `Box` class, meaning you can define object variables.

NOTE

Box is not a fully working, complete class. You would need to add additional members to effectively define a full class with ample data and methods.

Java does not normally know what a Box is. Only after you declare the Box class, as in Listing 14.6, can you then define (instantiate) an object like this:

```
Box hatHolder;   // create variable for a new object
```

The new variable named hatHolder is an object variable. Can you see that, loosely speaking, an object is a lot like a variable? You first have to tell Java about the object's type by defining the object's class, and you then have to define one or more objects just as you can define one or more variables. Unlike a variable, however, the hatHolder objects contain more than a single data type; hatHolder is a combination int and float value along with two methods that manipulate those data values.

If you want to execute one of the object's methods, you only need to use the dot operator. Suppose you wanted to calculate the area of the hatHolder object. The following statement executes hatHolder's calcArea() method:

```
hatHolder.calcArea(4.3, 10.244);   // executes the calcArea method
```

In the previous hour, you learned how to use the new keyword to declare an array. new also defines objects. Here is how you would instantiate a Box object using new:

```
Box hatHolder = new Box();   // instantiates a new Box object
```

Always use the parentheses when you use new with object instantiation. You can instantiate two Box objects as follows:

```
Box slot1 = new Box();
Box slot2 = new Box();
```

You now can calculate the area for the second Box object:

```
slot2.calcArea(1.0, 5.0);   // sets the second object's area
```

You can specify the color for the first box as follows:

```
slot1.setColor(4);   // sets the first object's color
```

Do You Understand OOP?

The nature of objects and OOP sneaks up on you. Relax if you don't feel as though you're mastering objects as quickly as you learned the non-OOP Java language, such as for loops. This is your first book of programming! Complete books much thicker than this are devoted to the explanation of OOP concepts.

OOP requires a special kind of thinking that does not always come quickly. Throughout this hour, you'll familiarize yourself with OOP. When you're ready to return to OOP with Java or another OOP-based language such as C++, this introduction will pay dividends.

Methods Do the Work in Classes

Although you've seen methods in action, and although you know a little about what methods are all about, this section explains methods in a little more detail and fills in a few more pieces of the method puzzle.

A Method's Execution

Methods perform work. Methods operate on class data by using the controlling statements you learned about in the previous hour and also by utilizing variables to hold data. A method's argument list inside the method's parentheses may contain values or the list may be empty. If arguments exist, the code that calls the method must initialize those values and send the expected arguments and types.

TIP

Think of an argument as a variable that's passed from one statement to a method. Arguments act like variables.

Figure 14.4 shows how the code in one method calls another method and sends that called method two arguments. Java sends a copy of the argument but does not really send the argument variables themselves. Therefore, if the called method changes an argument in any way, the change is not noticed when the calling code regains control.

NOTE

Java is known as a *call-by-value* language because a called method can never change the calling method's argument data. The called method can use and modify the arguments within the called method's statements, but when control returns to the calling code, the variables sent as arguments to the methods are unmodified in the calling method.

Figure 14.4's receiving method takes two values, computes with them, prints their newly computed values, and then returns control to the calling class.

Here is the output from Figure 14.4's code:

```
In method...
a=456.000
b=4608.294930876

In calling class...
a=10.0
b=20.0
```

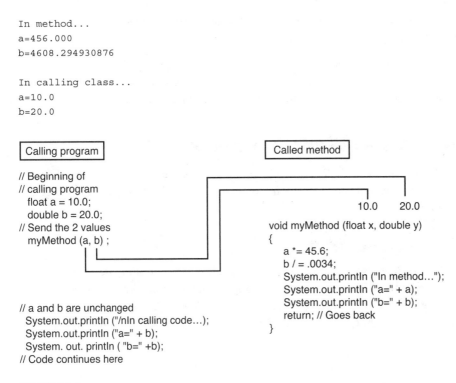

Calling program

```
// Beginning of
// calling program
   float a = 10.0;
   double b = 20.0;
// Send the 2 values
   myMethod (a, b) ;
```

Called method

```
                              10.0    20.0
void myMethod (float x, double y)
{
   a *= 45.6;
   b / = .0034;
   System.out.println ("In method...");
   System.out.println ("a=" + a);
   System.out.println ("b=" + b);
   return; // Goes back
}
```

```
// a and b are unchanged
   System.out.println ("/nIn calling code...);
   System.out.println ("a=" + b);
   System. out. println ( "b=" +b);
// Code continues here
```

FIGURE 14.4
The calling code sends two expected arguments to the called code

As you can see, the called method receives two values and changes those values but the changes last only inside the method. The calling class code's variables are not, and cannot be, changed by the method.

The method arguments in Figure 14.4 are named x and y even though the calling program names those variables a and b. The received names might or might not match those in the calling code because only values are passed and not variables. The biggest concern you must have when passing data to methods is to get the number of arguments and data types correct. The method is expecting a float followed by a double, as you can see from this method's declaration line:

```
void myMethod(float x, double y)
```

The calling code must provide two variables that match this pattern. The first definition line of a called method must always declare the arguments and their data types.

The passing of data between code and methods is not strictly one-way. A method can return a value to the calling code. Although you can send zero, one, or multiple arguments to a method, a method can only return one value. Figure 14.5 illustrates the return nature of methods.

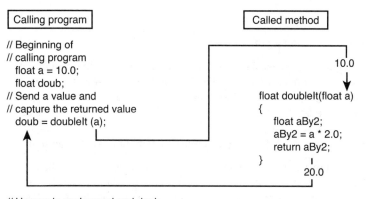

FIGURE 14.5
A called method can return only a single value.

Here is the output from Figure 14.5's program:

```
In calling class...
a=10.0
b=20.0
```

The doubleIt() method is a two-way method in that the calling code passes an argument and the method also returns a value back to the calling code. The called method does not change any value and returns the doubled value back to the calling code. The calling code captures the return value in the variable named doub.

If a method requires no arguments, leave the argument list empty.

Summary

You now have the basics of OOP. You should have a better idea what classes, methods, and data are all about. The new operator creates the class objects that your program can use. The object is much more than just a variable that holds data; objects contain methods so objects are more active than variables.

The next hour takes a quick tour of Java-based web applets. You'll see exactly how to embed a Java program inside a web page and how to set up the program to run when the user loads the page inside a web browser.

Q&A

Q. NetBeans has many options. How can I learn more about it?

A. NetBeans certainly is a comprehensive package with which you can develop many different kinds of Java programs. The online help system is complete and Oracle's web site at www. netbeans.org contains information about the IDE and all aspects of the Java language from the programmer's as well as the user's perspective.

Q. If I wanted to pass arguments to `main()` from my operating system, how would I do that?

A. Suppose you wrote a Java program that calculated the sales commission for any salesperson in your company. You could pass the salesperson's employee number to `main()` and the program would then calculate the appropriate commission after looking up that salesperson's sales data in the company files. Several ways exist to pass such an employee number. One way on Windows would be to place the program in your Start menu, right-click on the compiled program's filename, select Properties, and type the number to the right of the filename. All arguments passed to the program appear to the right of the filename when you execute the file in such a way.

Of course, changing the program's properties is certainly a tedious way to execute the program for all salespeople for whom you want to calculate commission. These command-line arguments actually were more important in the pre-Windows DOS operating system where typing filenames to execute programs was more common. In such an application today, you would make your program more usable if you forgo the command-line arguments in favor of prompting the user for the salesperson's employee number inside the program once the program starts.

Workshop

The quiz questions are provided for your further understanding.

Quiz

1. What alternative to the Java comment `//` can you use for commenting code?

2. What are arguments?

3. Where does the argument list reside in the `main()` procedure?

4. What does Swing add to Java programs?

5. What command brings Java object libraries into Java programs?

6. How does a class differ from an object?

7. True or false: All Java programs derive from a single Java object named `java.lang.Object`.

8. What takes place when you instantiate an object?

9. What happens when you extend an object from another?

10. True or false: If an argument list requires no arguments, you should keep the argument list empty.

Answers

1. You can enclose comments in /* and */.

2. Arguments are values passed between a calling procedure and a called procedure.

3. The `main()` argument list is there so that users can pass arguments from the operating system environment to the program.

4. Swing adds windowed controls to a program.

5. The `import` command brings Java object libraries into programs.

6. A class defines the way objects will look and behave.

7. True.

8. The program builds an object based on the class definition.

9. The extended object inherits the data and methods from the parent object.

10. False. Keep the argument list empty if the argument list requires no arguments. (You'll learn that you do place `void` inside empty argument lists in C and C++.)

HOUR 15
Applets and Web Pages

In this hour, you will learn how to embed Java applets inside web pages. As explained in Hour 12, "Programming with Java,", Java applets are small programs that travel with web page code and execute on the user's computer. Generally, you'll want to keep your applets small because they load with the user's web page. Unlike standalone Java applications, which can be much larger, the more efficient your applets are, the faster they load with a web page and the more likely your users are to be happy with the load time.

As you'll see, the Java language does not change whether you're programming an applet or any other kind of program. The way you set up a Java applet is different from the way you set up a standalone application but once you've set up the applet's outline, the code that does the work is straight Java.

The highlights of this hour include

- ▶ Using an appletviewer and web page for applets
- ▶ Generating the Java outline, or skeleton, for an applet
- ▶ Generating a Java applet skeleton that utilizes Swing
- ▶ Using HTML code to carry your applet to your users

About Writing Java Applets

When you write a Java program that you want transmitted over the Internet, remember that the program embeds itself in the web page. The language behind all web pages is HTML and you'll learn all about HTML—if you're not already familiar with it—in Hour 16, "HTML5 and CSS3." If you're not yet familiar with HTML, you don't need to understand much HTML to make Java applets work. This hour explains only the HTML commands needed to embed a Java applet because the focus for this section is primarily Java.

Although the Java language does not differ when you write Java applets versus other Java programs, you will need to set up your program differently when it is an applet.

Many Java developers use the *appletviewer* tool to test the applets they run. Instead of compiling the Java applet and transporting the applet to a web browser to test the applet, appletviewer enables the Java programmer to test applets without using a browser. Fortunately, you don't even need to use appletviewer to test the Java applets that you write because NetBeans enables you to test both applets and standalone Java programs from within the development system.

Creating a Java Applet

One of the best ways to learn how to create, test, and run Java applets is to create one yourself and go through the process of testing and running the applet. This hour spends some time walking you through the creation of a Java applet as well as testing the applet and viewing the applet inside a web browser.

The Java Applet Skeleton

Many Java applets follow the same pattern to set up the initial procedure and to work within a web page. If you want to create a Swing-enabled applet to take advantage of windows and dialog boxes, you will use the applet outline shown in Listing 15.1. Be warned, however, that programming with Swing requires that you learn some extra non-Java fundamentals. Swing makes it easier for you to place graphical user interface (GUI) controls on your applet but you must learn how Swing generates those controls. You can glean some information about Swing from NetBeans' online help.

If you use the NetBeans New File command to create a Swing-based Java applet, it creates this applet skeleton for you. The name of the applet, NewJApplet.java, will change if you have NetBeans create several applets over time because NetBeans will not overwrite existing files. A second Java applet's file and class name will be NewJApplet1.java, the next would be NewJApplet2.java, and so on.

LISTING 15.1   **A Swing-based Java applet uses this program outline.**

```
import javax.swing.JApplet;

/**
 *
 * @author Greg Perry
 */
public class NewJApplet extends JApplet {

    /**
     * Initialization method that will be called after the applet is loaded into
     * the browser.
     */
    public void init() {
```

```
        // TODO start asynchronous download of heavy resources
    }
    // TODO overwrite start(), stop() and destroy() methods
}
```

Listing 15.1 simply creates a Java applet using the Swing library so that subsequent statements that you add to the code will be able to access the Swing library. You may see other comments that NetBeans adds to the code if you generate this yourself; some comments have been removed from Listing 15.1 so you can focus on what's important for this section of the hour. To create this applet's outline:

1. With the project you began last hour open (named `FirstProject` or something of your own choosing), click the New File button or choose the menu command File, New File. The New File dialog opens.

2. Choose Java in the Categories pane and JApplet in the File Types pane, then click Next.

3. If you don't like the Class name provided by default, change it.

4. Click Finish. The Swing applet is created with the outline open for editing in the source code editor.

Inheriting from the class `javax.swing.JApplet` brings the Swing object libraries into your program. Loading these Swing classes causes your applet to load a little slower than it otherwise would and consumes more web page downloading bandwidth. Of course, the user interface elements such as message boxes that you gain with the Swing classes often outweigh the slight extra load times needed for Swing applets.

Finishing an Applet

As you gain familiarity with Java, you'll soon learn which object library or libraries you need to employ. For example, to use graphics in your Java applet, you'll need the `java.awt` package that includes the `Graphics` library you need for drawing text onto a window. Use the following command to import these libraries:

```
import java.awt.*;  // import the graphics library
```

NOTE

Importing a graphics library doesn't necessarily mean that you are writing a graphical applet. Many routines in the `java.awt.Graphics` library use graphics to produce non-graphical output, such as text. Placing text in a window, for example, is easily achieved when you use the `drawString()` method found in `java.awt.Graphics`.

The init() method is a method you'll want to put into your applets. When you inherit from the JApplet class, you inherit all methods from that class including one called the init() method; but the init() method that you inherit does nothing. You must redefine the method for your specific applet. Therefore, when you write an applet by extending the JApplet class, you will have to supply an init() method of your own.

TIP

resize() is always the first method executed in your applet. Put all initialization code inside init().

Almost every init() that you write will call the resize() method, just as the skeleton did and just as the complete applet in Listing 15.2 does. Notice the name, JANoSwng.java, indicating that the code contains no Swing routines. The resize() method simply informs your class of your applet's window size in the target web page. You also can insert other code inside init() that you want executed right after the initial loading of your applet. resize() requires two arguments: the first determines the width, in pixels, of your applet's window, and the second determines the height of your applet's window (see Figure 15.1).

LISTING 15.2   Completing the text-based Java applet

```
/*
 * JANoSwng java
 */
import java.applet.*;  // used for all applets
import java.awt.*;     // used to draw text onto window

public class JANoSwng extends Applet {
    /* creates a new applet */
    public void init() {
        resize(320, 240);  // applet's window size
    }

    public void paint(Graphics g) {
        // change subsequent text color to red
        g.setColor(Color.red);
        // write a simple message in the window
        g.drawString("Potrzebie!", 75, 100);
    }
}
```

Your Web Page

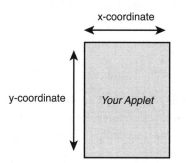

x-coordinate

y-coordinate

Your Applet

FIGURE 15.1
`resize()` determines the size of your applet's window.

Whenever your applet includes a method that also appears in the class method from which you extended your applet, as does `init()` in this case, your extended applet's method will always override the original class method. You can be assured that your `init()` will execute in place of the original `Applet` class's `init()`.

The `paint()` method also should appear in applets you create, at least those that do not use the Swing class, and `paint()` should follow `init()`. Your applet executes `paint()` every time your applet window needs redrawing. In a graphical environment, parts of your screen have to be redrawn quite often. For example, you might hide a window and, when you unhide the window, the hidden portion must reappear. Perhaps your user minimizes the web page down to a taskbar icon and then maximizes the window or resizes the window. As long as you've supplied a `paint()` method—and you must—you can be assured that your applet window will reappear properly with the text, colors, and whatever else appears there.

Look more closely at Listing 15.2's `paint()` lines:

```
public void paint(Graphics g) {
    // change subsequent text color to red
    g.setColor(Color.red);
    // write a simple message in the window
    g.drawString("Potzrebie!", 75, 100);
}
```

Unlike `init()`, `paint()` requires an argument inside its parentheses. The argument is a value that the `paint()` method operates on. Although `Graphics g` is a strange argument, the parameter represents your applet's web page graphical window. The `Graphics g` designation is a Java standard designation for your applet's window.

Whatever paint() does to the value named g happens to your applet's window. The g is known as a graphics *device context*. A graphical application does not actually write to your screen; instead, it writes to windows. The Graphics g argument tells your applet where to write, namely, the window inside the applet's enclosing web page.

The next line ought to make sense to you:

```
g.setColor(Color.red);
```

Remember that the g represents your web page applet's window. If you discern that this statement sets your applet window to red, you are almost correct. Actually, the statement sets all subsequent colors to red. Executing multiple setcolor() methods between each line of output, you are able to send different colors to the same window.

When you see a period following an object (the object, g, represents your applet's window), the value to the right of the period always will be a method or a value. You know that setColor() is a method because of the parentheses that follow its name. The setColor() method is an internal Graphics class method that sets all subsequent output to a specific color. The color must appear inside the parentheses. The color inside the parentheses is the setColor() argument.

Windows is capable of displaying several million colors. As with the *Windows Application Programming Interface* (*Windows API*), a set of routines that C++ programmers use when writing Windows programs, there are several ways to represent all the shades of colors that can appear on your screen. You can specify some standard colors easily. If you don't get too picky on just that right shade of yellow you've always loved on your sun porch, you can specify one of the colors from Table 15.1 for the argument inside setColor(). Notice that you must precede the color name with the Color object. The Color object is a symbolic object, defined inside the java.awt class package, which represents colors. You can specify a named value by following the Color and separating period with one of the named color values in Table 15.1.

TABLE 15.1 Use these color values to put colored text on the screen.

black	blue	cyan
darkGray	gray	green
lightGray	magenta	orange
pink	red	white
yellow		

As you can see, the syntax is a little tricky but `setColor()` is not necessarily hard to understand. For example, you could later print some green text on your applet's window by placing the following statement before you print the text:

```
g.setColor(Color.green);
```

After printing green text, you then could call `setColor()` once more to set the color back to red like this:

```
g.setColor(Color.red);
```

Referring back to Listing 15.2, once the applet sets the color red, the applet sends two words to the applet window with the following line:

```
g.drawString("Potrzebie!", 75, 100);
```

The `drawString()` method is commonly used to send strings to the applet's window. Because `drawString()` respects the color set by `setColor()`, the text, `"Potrzebie!"`, will appear in red. Notice the g before the method name. The g happens to be the name of this window, passed to the `paint()` routine like this:

```
public void paint(Graphics g)
```

The g refers to the graphics context which is the applet's window. Any name could be used. You could use any variable in place of g and then preface the methods inside `paint()` with that variable name.

The second and third parameters of `drawString()` represent the starting x, y coordinates where you want the text to appear. In other words, `init()` creates an applet window that runs 320 pixels across by 240 pixels down. Then `drawString()` starts drawing its text, "Potrzebie!", exactly 75 pixels down and 100 pixels across the applet window.

OOP-Based Coding

This applet's `setColor()` method demonstrates part of the object-based nature of OOP code. For example, in non-OOP languages, the procedures are more important than the data. In OOP languages, the data, or more accurately, the objects, have the primary focus. When you want to set the applet window's printing color, what is the object—the color, the `setColor()` method, or your applet's window? The applet's window is the object. The window is the target of the color-setting procedure.

The very first item in this applet's `setColor()` line is g, which represents your applet's graphical drawing window as described earlier in this section. Everything else on the line does something to that object. The object g, referring to your applet window, gets its color chosen with the setColor() method. Inside setColor(), another less-obvious object appears named Color. In other words, you want to set a particular color object to a particular color. The phrase Color.red does just that, it sets the object in question, Color, to red. That object, the red color, is then passed through the setColor() method to the graphic applet window named g.

Applets, unlike other types of Java programs, are not intended to be run directly. A web page must be created, the applet is placed on that page, and the page is loaded in a web browser.

For testing purposes, you can run an applet in NetBeans directly. With JANoSwng.java open in the source code editor, choose the menu command Run, Run File or hit Shift-F6. The applet is run by the appletviewer tool, which should look like Figure 15.2.

FIGURE 15.2
Your applet running in appletviewer.

The only thing that appletviewer displays is the applet window, which for this applet displays the text "Potrzebie!"

Placing the Applet Inside the Web Page

Remember that the primary purpose of an applet is to appear on an Internet user's computer when that user loads the web page that contains the applet. Listing 15.3 contains a sample HTML file that forms the skeleton of many HTML files that embed Java applets.

LISTING 15.3   An HTML file that carries a Java applet

```
<HTML>
  <HEAD>
    <TITLE>First Java Applet</TITLE>
  </HEAD>
```

```
<BODY BGCOLOR="#CCCCCC">
  <H1>First Java Applet</H1>
  <APPLET
    CODE = JANoSwng.class
    WIDTH=320
    HEIGHT=240 >
  </APPLET>
</BODY>
</HTML>
```

Don't get too caught up with the HTML at this time because in Hour 16, you'll learn what all the HTML code means. For now, just know that the `<APPLET>` command (called a *tag* in HTML terminology) tells the web page the name of the compiled Java class that is to be embedded and the width and height of the applet's window, which, not coincidentally, is the same width and height values that the applet's init() method prepares for.

NOTE

HTML also supports the `<OBJECT>` and `<EMBED>` tags to place Java applets on web pages, but the Java Plug-in recommends that the `<APPLET>` tag be used because it is the simplest to use.

The `<HTML>` and `</HTML>` tags always mark the beginning and end of an HTML file. The `<HEAD>` and `</HEAD>` tags mark the beginning and end of the web page's primary header, which usually contains a title and other information about that page. You can see that this header has a title, delimited with `<TITLE>` and `</TITLE>`, that simply contains the name of the Java applet. The `<BODY>` and `</BODY>` tags delimit the body of the web page and generally comprise the largest portion of the web page, including the page document's contents.

The `<BODY>` tag contains an attribute that's given a value like this: BGCOLOR="#CCCCCC". The BGCOLOR attribute sets the background color of a page, using the value "CC" for red, green, and blue. This makes the page gray, so that it does not blend in with the white applet window.

The `<H1>` and `</H1>` tags enclose a headline on the page at the largest size. (There also are `<H2>` through `<H6>` tags.)

Obviously, the lines that follow the `<H1>` tag specify the applet information. They are the following:

```
<APPLET
  CODE = JANoSwng.class
  WIDTH=320
  HEIGHT=240 >
</APPLET>
```

The `<APPLET>` tag requires extra settings that many of the other tag commands do not require. These settings are called *attributes*. The `<APPLET>` tag indicates that the web page is to load an applet at that particular page location; thus, the tag must contain the applet information, such as the applet name. The web page must have this correct information so that the page can properly locate the applet and display the applet in an appropriate window. The <APPLET> tag can span several lines for readability, as done here.

The CODE attribute names the class of the applet that is to execute. For now, remember that a class is generally the same as an applet program because most applets contain a single class and the class contains all the functioning applet code. Therefore, the class will generally be your Java filename (with the java extension).

The WIDTH and HEIGHT attributes always are required for all applets that you embed in a web page. The web browser must be told the size of your applet's window (the applet will appear on the page in a window). Finally, the </APPLET> ending tag indicates that the applet parameter information is complete.

CAUTION

The applet must reside in the same folder as the HTML file unless you preface the name with its location, as the following CODE attribute does: CODE="http://www.example.com/JavaApps/ JANoSwng.class"

To create an HTML file, you need a text editor. The text editor enables you to create a text file, similar to the way that a word processor enables you to create a document. The file should have the .html filename extension.

NetBeans can be used to create and edit HTML files. Click the New File button, choose the category Other and file type HTML Page, and click Next. Give the file a name (but leave off the .html extension—NetBeans will provide it automatically) and click Finish. The new HTML file opens for editing.

Viewing the Applet Inside the Web Page

Once you've compiled the Java applet, you may have to copy the compiled applet, called JANoSwng.class, to the same folder in which you've created your HTML source code. You now have, in the same folder, the HTML source code (you never compile HTML source code) and the compiled Java class file. Follow these steps to see your applet run in your web browser:

1. In your file system, go to the folder that contains the web page and JANoSwng.class.

2. Open the web page (such as by right-clicking it and using the Open With command to pick a browser).

3. Your applet should appear in its own window, such as the one in Figure 15.3.

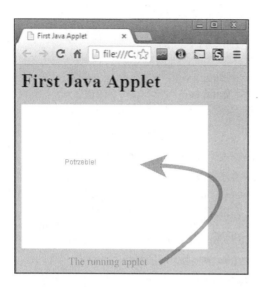

FIGURE 15.3
Your applet appears inside the browser window.

Summary

This hour provided a quick overview of how to work with Java applets. You understand how standalone Java applications work and you know how embedded Java applets work. You may not yet be a Java expert but you do know your way around the language and you are on your way to understanding object libraries.

You now have an idea of how applet authors create their applets and place those applets inside web pages using HTML code tags. The applets should be much smaller than regular, standalone Java applications because the Java applet must download to the user's computer with the web page and download times can be slow.

The next hour moves on to different programming languages and HTML5 and CSS3, the latest and greatest standards for creating web pages. Visual Basic, which you'll learn about in Hour 20, "Programming with Visual Basic 2012," is not a true object-oriented language as Java is, but you will see how parts of Visual Basic work with objects such as command buttons that you drag with your mouse onto the Windows screen.

Q&A

Q. **How much of an HTML expert must I be to use Java applets effectively?**

A. In some companies, people other than Java programmers write HTML code, so you don't have to know much HTML at all. Nevertheless, as you'll see in Hour 16, HTML is an extremely simple language, far simpler, actually, than JavaScript. So, many Java programmers learn HTML.

Q. **What's the best way to learn which Java library classes are available for me to use?**

A. One concern of all Java newcomers is knowing which class packages are available and learning how to use them. The chicken-before-the-egg paradox appears here because if you were first given a list of every class method name, how would you know when to use the methods and how would you know what each one did? Even with descriptions, you would experience information overload because many hundreds of methods exist and some are dual-purpose and overlap others in functionality.

Now that you know the language basics, such as data types, applet insertion, and control statements, much of learning more about Java requires analyzing other Java applications to see what object libraries programmers use most and to learn what those libraries do.

Workshop

The quiz questions are provided for your further understanding.

Quiz

1. Why do you want to keep your Java applets small?

2. What is the purpose of the appletviewer?

3. What features can the Swing library add to a Java applet?

4. What drawback, albeit a small one, does the Swing library sometimes give Java applets?

5. What does the `resize()` method do?

6. What does the `init()` method do?

7. What filename extension does a Java source applet use?

8. What filename extension does a compiled Java applet use?

9. What HTML command embeds a Java applet into the surrounding web page?

10. What do the HTML `WIDTH` and `HEIGHT` commands specify?

Answers

1. Keep Java applets small so they load quickly.

2. The appletviewer enables you to test Java applets without using a web browser.

3. The Swing library enables you to add command buttons, list boxes, text boxes, and other Windows controls to your Java applets and programs.

4. The Swing library can add overhead and size to an applet.

5. `resize()` determines the applet's window size.

6. `init()` is always the first procedure that an applet executes.

7. Java applet source code uses the .java extension.

8. Compiled Java applets use the .class extension.

9. The `<OBJECT>` tag (or the `<APPLET>` tag) embeds Java applets in web pages.

10. The two commands specify the width and height of the applet's window and often match the applet's `resize()` arguments.

HTML5 and CSS3

Hypertext Markup Language (HTML) is the code behind web pages. Using HTML, you place text, graphics, JavaScript, Java and other active content, and hyperlinks throughout web pages to give those pages the look you desire. You've been using some HTML to this point, as it serves as a wrapper around the JavaScript code you've been writing to learn basic programming. You needed some rudimentary HTML code to make the JavaScript run.

Unlike traditional programming languages (but like the JavaScript you've studied so far), HTML is interpreted as your web page loads. Your web page, formatted with HTML code, goes across the Internet to any user who requests it. That user's browser then interprets your HTML elements to format the page properly.

This hour introduces you to the world of HTML coding. You will learn how HTML formats text, graphics, and other web page elements. HTML is a fairly simple language because, instead of issuing commands to process data as you do with procedural languages such as C++, most HTML includes simple formatting instructions to adjust the appearance of the web page.

The highlights of this hour include

- ▶ Understanding how HTML formats web pages
- ▶ Recognizing HTML tags
- ▶ Working with HTML text
- ▶ Placing graphics on a web page
- ▶ Introducing CSS
- ▶ Generating web page hyperlinks

HTML Programming

A web page might contain text, graphics, icons and text containing links (also known as *hyperlinks* or *hot spots*), Java applets, JavaScript code, and multimedia content. One of the goals of web page designers is to make web pages appear uniform no matter what kind of computer the user uses (or, more accurately, which *platform* the user uses, which might be a PC, a tablet, or a phone, with one of a number of operating systems). Although the same web page still looks different on different computers and different browser versions, a steady progression is being made to a truly universal browser standard that will show all web pages uniformly (see the sidebar entitled, "W3C Attempts to Standardize HTML.") The *HTML* is a machine-independent language that web developers use to design web pages. A page's HTML listing is actually a set of text elements that, when viewed with a web browser, produces a web page that conforms to the look the author intended.

TIP

No matter what programming language you decide to master next, whether it is advanced Java, C++, or another, you should learn the fundamentals of HTML. HTML and JavaScript in concert can be used to accomplish some fairly impressive tasks. The Internet plays a huge role in computers today, and you'll almost certainly be connecting your programming efforts to the web eventually in some way. HTML is the primary web page language. All the other web page languages use HTML in some way. Fortunately, HTML is primarily a formatting and hyperlinking language that is rather simple to master, especially now that you understand the way JavaScript works.

Not only can simple HTML markup produce visually appealing web pages, many times beginners don't use HTML to produce a web page today; instead they rely on website-creation tools that allow them to choose basic templates and then make simple changes to the look and feel. These sites then translate the page you laid out into HTML elements. Microsoft Word and other word processors can often save documents (with formatted text as well as embedded tables, graphics, and multimedia) as HTML pages that Word translates to HTML code.

TIP

Using website-creation tools and Word can generate code for you, but you'll never learn without doing, and frankly the code that is automatically generated is often sloppy and poorly executed. You are far better off in the long run learning to write your own HTML from scratch.

W3C Attempts to Standardize HTML

The *World Wide Web Consortium*, known as *W3C*, is a standards committee supported and staffed by the computer industry. The goal of W3C is to define standards for HTML and HTML-based languages and web browsers.

Although web browsers and HTML language systems don't have to follow the W3C's suggestions for HTML coding, those that do will help to ensure that their website will have more of a chance of being seen properly in all web browsers. The committee makes many coding suggestions, and also defines new HTML elements that browser makers can adopt to make HTML coding easier and to make web pages richer with content. The most recent update is HTML5.

You can visit their website at www.w3.org and learn more about the consortium.

Following an HTML Example

Figure 16.1 shows a web page. The page looks rather simple and is free of clutter.

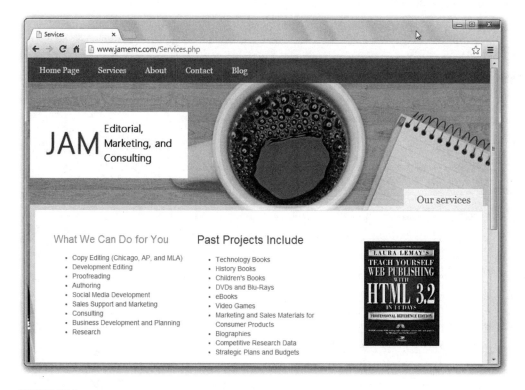

FIGURE 16.1
A web page created with HTML code.

Figure 16.2 contains some of the HTML markup that produced Figure 16.1's web page.

Take a moment to compare Figure 16.2's HTML markup to Figure 16.1's web page. The full HTML code required to display Figure 16.1 is even longer than what you see in Figure 16.2. The HTML code that you do see is rather advanced so the excerpt of this HTML listing looks a little forbidding. Nevertheless, as you keep comparing the HTML code to the web page, you'll begin to see some ways that the HTML language formatted and placed text on parts of the web page.

Be warned that Figure 16.2 contains virtually no whitespace and alignment that would make the page easier to maintain. Often, web pages generated with website creation programs are rather compact, as opposed to web pages that an HTML programmer designs from scratch. Before this hour is over, you will see simpler HTML code written by a programmer that demonstrates more readability. You'll inevitably find both kinds of HTML-based pages because many of the web pages you use today are generated by web page design programs instead of coded by hand in HTML. Actually, many web page programmers use a web page designing program to produce the initial HTML code, and then they modify the generated HTML code, often cleaning up the code's spacing to make the code more maintainable.

```
89    <li><font color="#857f7a">Copy Editing (Chicago, AP, and MLA)</font></li>
90    <li><font color="#857f7a">Development Editing</font></li>
91    <li><font color="#857f7a">Proofreading</font></li>
92    <li><font color="#857f7a">Authoring</font></li>
93    <li><font color="#857f7a">Social Media Development</font></li>
94    <li><font color="#857f7a">Sales Support and Marketing</font></li>
95    <li><font color="#857f7a">Consulting</font></li>
96    <li><font color="#857f7a">Business Development and Planning</font></li>
97    <li><font color="#857f7a">Research</font></li>
98  </ul></div></div><div style="display:block; float: left; overflow: hidden; width:33%;">
    <div class="ColumnMarginBox ColumnInner"><div style="display:block;overflow:hidden;" ><font
    style="font-size: 24px;" color="#005fbf"><span style="line-height: 1.3571428571428572;">Past
    Projects Include</span></font><br />
99    (ul)
100        <li><font color="#857f7a"><span style="line-height: 18px;">Technology Books</span></font>
    </li>
101        <li><font color="#857f7a"><span style="line-height: 18px;">History Books</span></font>
    </li>
102        <li><font color="#857f7a"><span style="line-height: 18px;">Children's Books</span></font>
    </li>
103        <li><font color="#857f7a"><span style="line-height: 18px;">DVDs and Blu-Rays</span></font>
    </li>
104        <li><font color="#857f7a"><span style="line-height: 18px;">eBooks</span></font></li>
105        <li><font color="#857f7a"><span style="line-height: 18px;">Video Games</span></font></li>
106        <li><font color="#857f7a"><span style="line-height: 18px;">Marketing and Sales Materials
    for Consumer Products</span></font></li>
107        <li><font color="#857f7a"><span style="line-height: 18px;">Biographies</span></font></li>
108        <li><font color="#857f7a"><span style="line-height: 18px;">Competitive Research
    Data</span></font></li>
109        <li><font color="#857f7a"><span style="line-height: 18px;">Strategic Plans and
    Budgets</span></font></li>
```

FIGURE 16.2
Part of the HTML markup that produced the web page.

You will notice that the HTML code snippet from the website used in Figure 16.1 uses lowercase for the tags (the HTML elements between angled brackets, < and >) and attributes (the words that specify how some of the tags look and behave, such as color). At one time, the W3C recommended all uppercase in tags and attributes. Most web pages use lowercase, or a mixture of both lowercase and uppercase HTML tags and attributes. Although the browser ignores case and doesn't care which you use, for all new web development, it's now strongly recommended to take the all-lowercase approach.

Displaying a Web Page

When you navigate to view a web page, the remote server sends to your browser only the HTML text, and the browser responds to the markup by formatting text appropriately and placing links and graphics images where the HTML code dictates they should appear. Your browser first receives the full HTML page and then receives whatever graphics images and multimedia content are needed to complete the page.

Browsers provide a Stop button that you can click, or you can press Esc, to keep from receiving graphics and multimedia images for those times when you don't want to wait on them but want to read the text that has already been sent to your browser. In place of the images and multimedia content, most browsers display an icon in place of the image showing where the image would appear if you had let the image load to your computer.

Command Tags

The terms within angled brackets, (< and >) are called *tag references* (or *tag commands*). Tag commands are central to the HTML program. Many commands contain a beginning and ending tag (a forward slash, /, always precedes an ending tag). A nonbracketed text item is a *literal* (a value that does not change), such as a title that is to appear on the web page. The tags primarily determine the placement of figures, the content of text, and links to other websites. For example, as you saw in many of your JavaScript programs, `<title>` marks the beginning of a title and `</title>` marks the end. In versions prior to HTML5, the presentation of content was also accomplished with HTML tags, however many of those tags have been *deprecated* (no longer supported in code compliant with HTML5), and those functions have been moved to cascading style sheets (CSS), which are touched upon later in the hour.

Many of the tags in Figure 16.2 are formatting tag codes that specify font style and size instructions for the web browser.

Tags don't contain formatted text; they offer formatting instructions that your web browser is to follow. Therefore, when your web browser sees the `<center>` tag, your web browser knows to center the text that runs up to the subsequent `</center>` ending tag as the following HTML code would do:

```
<center>Fran's Place</center>
```

The HTML code completely determines how text appears. Therefore, except for keeping your HTML code readable, no advantage exists for adding spacing. HTML ignores extra spaces that come before your web page's text. The following code produces the same, centered title that the previous code did even though the text itself has some extra spaces at the beginning:

```
<center>
    Fran's Place
</center>
```

You can document HTML code with the following comment tag:

```
<!-- This is an HTML comment -->
```

Everything between `<!--` and `-->` is treated as an HTML comment, even if the comment spans multiple lines. Like you have seen in other sections of this book, comments are for the benefit of the people reading the code and are ignored when the HTML is interpreted by the browser—the information between those character sets do not display on the page.

A Simpler Example

Many websites are a good deal simpler than the one previously shown. Don't get bogged down in advanced HTML commands when you first begin studying HTML because even simple HTML commands can produce quite attractive and complete web pages. For example, consider how simple Listing 16.1's HTML code appears. You should have little trouble following the HTML commands even if HTML is new to you. If you do find yourself unsure, don't worry. This is actually a code listing from later in the hour, and its particulars will be covered in more detail.

LISTING 16.1   Simple HTML commands can produce attractive web pages.

```
<!DOCTYPE html>
<html>
  <head>
    <title>Using styles</title>
<style>
  body
  {
     background-color:pink;
  }
  h1
  {
     color:orange;
     text-align:center;
  }
  img.imgBlue { border: 12px solid; color: blue; padding:5px;}
  p.ex1 {color:red; font-family:Georgia; font-size:20px;}
  p.ex2 {color:blue;font-family:Courier; font-size: 24px;}
  p.ex3 {color:green;font-size:8px;}
</style>
```

```
  </head>
  <body>
<h1>Let's try CSS with our HTML</h1>
<p class="ex1">Text using the ex1 attributes.</p>
<p class="ex2">Text using the ex2 attributes<br>
This is a second line still using ex2 as it isn't turned off yet.</p>
<p class="ex3">Hard to read, but this is the third style, ex3.</p>
<img src="img1.gif" class=imgBlue>
  </body>
</html>
```

This example code combines HTML and CSS and will be analyzed and run later in the hour. However, with your JavaScript experience, nothing about this quick example should seem too intimidating.

TIP

The next time that you are using your web browser, locate the menu option that lets you view the HTML source code. If you use Internet Explorer, the source display command is View, Source, and if you use Google Chrome, just right click your mouse on the page and select View Page Source from the menu.

Transferring a packet of HTML code, such as that in Listing 16.1, is much less time-consuming than transferring a graphics image of the web page. Your web browser reads the HTML commands and then formats the text or graphics images according to their instructions.

As stated earlier, several powerful web-design tools and sites exist to create web pages using modern graphical cut-and-paste methods; but you also can create a fancy web page simply by using a text editor and knowing the HTML language. Often, programmers use graphical tools to lay out the overall web page and then use a text editor to hone the HTML source code to finalize the page.

A Quick HTML Primer

All web pages require a fundamental set of HTML codes. Listing 16.2 shows the minimal HTML code needed to display a web page.

LISTING 16.2   The general format for all HTML web pages

```
<!DOCTYPE html>
<html>
  <!-- This is a comment -->
  <head>
    <title>The window's title bar text goes here</title>
```

```
  </head>
  <body>
    <!-- The bulk of the web page text, graphics, and HTML
       code goes here -->
  </body>
</html>
```

All listings start with the `<!DOCTYPE html>` tag (which you probably remember from your numerous JavaScript programs). This tag serves as a declaration to tell your browser what version of HTML is being used to author the web page. The angled bracket commands are the HTML command tags that format the page's data and instruct the browser on how to display the page. Many HTML tags appear in pairs, such as `<body>` and `</body>`. The closing tag, indicated with a slash (/), tells the browser where the tag command ends. However, some tags are singular—you do not need a closing tag.

Notice that the first tag in all web pages should be `<html>`, indicating the beginning of the HTML code. The end tag is `</html>`, indicating that the web page is through.

The heading section, enclosed with `<head>` and `</head>`, contains title bar information using the `<title>` and `</title>` tags and other preliminary web page data such as *metatags*, advanced HTML code that programmers can place inside web pages to get noticed by search engines. If you remember, you often defined JavaScript functions in the heading section of your HTML pages. If you don't use JavaScript, the title bar is the only text that appears in the heading section.

The body section, enclosed with `<body>` and `</body>`, includes the bulk of the web page content. The user is most interested in the data between these two tags.

HTML Text Formatting

To make text appear on the browser's screen, simply type the text inside the HTML code. Your web page body could include lines of text like this:

```
<body>
This text will appear
on whatever web browser screen
opens this HTML code.
</body>
```

Web browsers do not automatically format text. These three lines of text all appear on one line inside the browser, like this:

```
This text will appear on whatever web browser screen opens this HTML code.
```

As covered in the beginning of the book, if you want to add line breaks, you must include the `<br/>` tag (no ending `<br>` tag is needed). `<br/>` tells the web browser to break the line at that point and move to the next line. The following `<body>` section displays three lines of text:

```
<body>
This text will appear<br/>
on whatever Web browser screen<br/>
opens this HTML code.
</body>
```

Again, the text breaks onto three lines only because of the `<br>` tags and not because the lines happen to end there.

You can add italics, boldfacing, and underlining to your text. The following HTML code contains such formatting:

```
This line contains <u>two underlined</u> words.
This line contains <i>two italicized</i> words.
This line contains <b>two boldfaced</b> words.
```

CAUTION

Generally, web page designers refrain from using underlining on web pages because most hyperlinks appear as underlined text. Therefore, if you include underlined text that does not serve as a link to another web page, users may waste time trying to click on those underlined words to see what happens.

TRY IT YOURSELF ▼

The `<h>` tag controls the size of headlines that you use as titles on your page. You can use `<h1>` (the most important) through `<h6>` (the least important) to display headlines. Figure 16.3 shows the web page created by the HTML code in Listing 16.3.

LISTING 16.3   Examples of the `<h>` tag show how to change headline text size.

```
<!DOCTYPE html>
<html>
  <head>
    <title>Headline sizes</title>
  </head>
  <body>
    <!-- An automatic line break
        occurs after each headline -->
    <h1>Number 1 headline </h1>
    <h2>Number 2 headline </h2>
```

```
        <h3>Number 3 headline </h3>
        <h4>Number 4 headline </h4>
        <h5>Number 5 headline </h5>
        <h6>Number 6 headline </h6>
    </body>
</html>
```

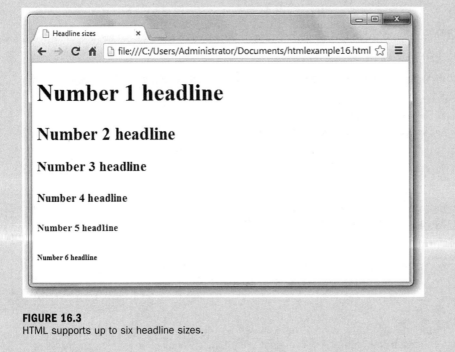

FIGURE 16.3
HTML supports up to six headline sizes.

Using CSS to Control How Your Text Looks

Versions of HTML before 5 used to use a `<font>` tag as an additional method to control the size of your text. HTML5 has eliminated this and you now need to use CSS to accomplish the same goal. CSS3 is the latest version of CSS, and these sheets can be used to control the appearance of your text on HTML web pages. This information can be included directly on your HTML page, or you can create a separate file with the information. Like you did with your JavaScript user-created functions, this is an excellent method to then re-use your favorite type styles, in terms of color, font size, font type, and more. The use of CSS3 with HTML5 enables web developers to use HTML to focus on the content of the document versus the presentation of that content, which can now be better controlled across a variety of formats with CSS.

There is so much to CSS in terms of what you can do with your web page. This lesson can only touch on some very basic points, as the goal of the book is to get you back into programming, but you should know of the presence and goals of CSS3, particularly with the release of HTML, which has deprecated (phased out) some of the previous font, table, color, and size tags and attributes of previous versions with the goal that these functions will be better executed with CSS. Obviously, the browser support of those tags from previous versions cannot simply end—there's literally millions of web pages out there written in earlier versions of HTML and they still need to be viewable. But you should design web pages with an eye to the future and not the past, so if you'd like to learn more about HTML5 and CSS3, please pick up *Sams Teach Yourself HTML and CSS in 24 Hours, 9th Edition.*

TRY IT YOURSELF ▼

While you will eventually want to consider creating your own files with your style information, the following example shown in Listing 16.4 puts the style information directly into your HTML document. The information should be placed in the header section of the file and needs to be surrounded by the `<style>` and `</style>` tags.

LISTING 16.4 **Examples of setting your own styles using CSS to control font color, size, and typeface**

```
<!DOCTYPE html>
<html>
 <head>
  <title>Using styles</title>
<style>
  body
  {
    background-color:pink;
  }
  h1
  {
      color:orange;
      text-align:center;
  }
  p.ex1 {color:red; font-family:Georgia; font-size:20px;}
    p.ex2 {color:blue;font-family:Courier; font-size: 24px;}
    p.ex3 {color:green;font-size:8px;}
</style>
 </head>
 <body>
 <h1>Let's try CSS with our HTML</h1>

 <p class="ex1">Text using the ex1 attributes.</p>
```

```
<p class="ex2">Text using the ex2 attributes<br>

This is a second line still using ex2 as it isn't turned off yet.</p>

<p class="ex3">Hard to read, but this is the third style, ex3.</p>
</body>
</html>
```

Now, there's no way the image you see in Figure 16.4 would be considered good design by anyone (honestly, be thankful the printed book is black-and-white). However, it's an excellent example of the way you can alter the attributes of headings, paragraphs, and the web page's background. In fact, as the example demonstrates, you can come up with multiple styles and designs for paragraphs. You just need to set a specific name for the class of paragraph and then call it within the body of your HTML text. The best way to figure out what styles work for you is to experiment. Once you find the combinations that work for you, you can create a file with that information as a .css file that you can then call in any HTML file you wish to use your new style combinations.

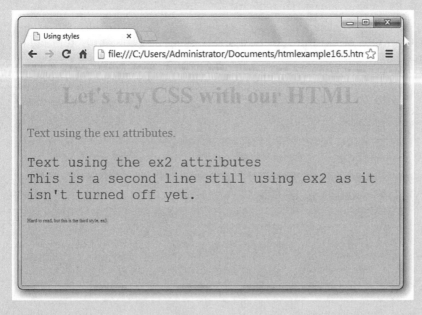

FIGURE 16.4
You have the ability to change a number of text attributes. Text size grows as you increase the font size.

NOTE

While you can specify colors in CSS using their names as shown in this simple example, you have far more flexibility when you use RGB notation. This involves passing three integers between 0 and 255, for example `rgb(255,0,255)`. The first value is red, the second green, and the third blue. Black would be achieved by setting all to 0 and white results from setting all to 255. In between, these three values can result in more than 16 million color combinations, far more than just using color names.

Including Graphics in Your Website with HTML

The `<img>` tag places images on your web pages when you use the `arc=` attribute with the tag. After you designate an image's location and filename, the image appears. Graphics are simple to display and the `<img>` tag is all you'll need for many of your web page graphics.

Here is a simple web page command that displays an image on the screen:

```
<img src="images/myphoto.jpg">
```

The image appears wherever this `<img/>` tag appears inside the HTML code. It's up to you to ensure that the image is formatted in a type of file that browsers can display. The common image formats are GIF, JPEG, and PNG, and most graphics programs produce images in these three formats.

Older versions of HTML allowed you to place a border around a graphic, in effect adding a framed image to your web page. However, HTML5 has phased out the `<border>` attribute, but CSS3 can help you out again. For example, adding the following line to the style section of the head:

```
img.imgBlue { border: 12px solid; color: blue; padding:5px;}
```

will put a solid blue border around the image if you add the class info to your image placement like this.

```
<img src="img1.gif" class=imgBlue>
```

Again, experimentation is the best way to learn about what is possible with CSS, but if you plan to make compelling sites, CSS can be just as powerful a tool for you as the programs you can write with JavaScript.

Using Hyperlinks

An *anchor* tag, indicated by `<a>` and `</a>`, creates a hyperlink to another page location. The browser that displays your web page creates an underlined link at the point of your HTML's `<a>` tag.

The following lines send the user to the Pearson Education website when the user clicks the hyperlink:

```
<a href="http://www.pearsoned.com">
Click for great learning
</a>
```

Everything between the `<a>` tag and the closing `</a>` tag comprises the anchor, and the `href` attribute forces the hyperlink. The four words, `Click for great learning`, will be underlined on the screen, and the user can click anywhere in that text to access the corresponding website.

You can even specify graphics and multiline text as hyperlinks. When the user clicks the hyperlink, the browser accesses the linked web page. The user can click the browser's Back button to access the current page.

The HTML statement that follows shows you how to use an image as a hyperlink. Remember that everything you place between the initial `<a href>` tag and attribute, along with the `</a>` ending tag is a hyperlink, whether you place graphics, text, or both there.

```
<a href="http://www.jamemc.com">
  <img src="images/Flag.gif">
</a>
```

When the web page appears that includes this statement, the user's mouse pointer will change to a hand when the user points to the image on the screen that is named `Flag.gif`. If the user then clicks the image, the browser opens the page located at www.jamemc.com.

Summary

By now, you have a preliminary understanding of how to use HTML and CSS to code and format web pages. Once you understand the general nature of HTML code, creating and formatting web pages becomes a simple matter. When you are ready to add tables, frames, and other advanced elements to your page, you'll need to master more advanced command tags, but you should have little trouble doing so as long as you build gradually on the knowledge you have already acquired. Using only the tags discussed in this hour, you can create nice-looking, although simple, web pages that contain text, graphics, and links to other sites.

Q&A

Q. Why do some HTML tags require both opening and ending tags while others do not use ending tags?

A. A command tag requires a beginning and ending tag when you are about to format a specific element on the web page. For example, when italicizing text, you must begin the italics with the `<i>` tag and the italicized text follows. Without the ending tag, `</i>`, all text on the rest of the web page would be italicized. Command tags such as line breaks, `<br/>`, do not format specific text or graphics and can stand alone because they cause a single action, a line break.

Q. Do I need web page designer software to practice learning HTML and CSS?

A. Just like you did with JavaScript, start Notepad and enter your HTML and CSS commands. Save your text with any of the following filename extensions: .htm, .html, .HTM, or .HTML, the case doesn't matter. If you don't specify the extension, Notepad will save your file as a text file with the .TXT extension. Web pages should always use one of the extensions just listed. You then can start your web browser, such as Google Chrome or Internet Explorer, and select File, Open and locate the file you just created. When you click OK, your HTML-based web page will appear. If you did not code something properly, you will not get an error, but the page will not look right.

Workshop

The quiz questions are provided for your further understanding.

Quiz

1. Why is a working knowledge of HTML so important for all programmers today?
2. For what does CSS stand?
3. What is a command tag?
4. How do you code an HTML comment?
5. What do the `<title>` and `</title>` command tags control?
6. How do you increase the size of headline text?
7. How do you increase the size of regular web page text?
8. Why would you specify alternate text for web page graphics?
9. True or false: You can turn both graphics and text into hyperlinks on a web page.
10. Why is it generally a bad practice to underline text on a web page?

Answers

1. HTML is used by Java programmers, as well as programmers of other languages, and the web is integrated into many programming environments today.
2. CSS stands for cascading style sheets.
3. A command tag is an HTML command.
4. An HTML command begins with `<!--` and ends with `-->`.

5. These tags define the title that appears inside the web page window's title bar.

6. Use the `<hn>` tag to increase headline text, replacing n with a number between 1 and 6. The `<h1>` tag is for the largest head, and each number makes a smaller sized head.

7. Use CSS to define the type, size, and weight of your text font.

8. So the alternative text appears if the user has turned off the web browser or if a visually impaired user is using a voice-enabled web browser.

9. True.

10. Unless the underlined text is a link to another element, underlines imply that a link exists where there is none.

HOUR 17
JavaScript and AJAX

As you've seen with the JavaScript examples so far in this book, JavaScript is a client-side programming language that allows you to display and interact with information in your web browser. AJAX, on the other hand, is a set of technologies (one of which is JavaScript) that allows you to move beyond the client-side boundaries of a web browser and work with files on a web server or with responses from server-side programs.

This hour introduces you to the basics of working with AJAX, including

- How AJAX enables JavaScript to communicate with server-side programs and files
- Using the XMLHttpRequest object's properties and methods
- Creating your own AJAX library
- Using AJAX to read data from an XML file
- Using AJAX to communicate with a server-side program

Introducing AJAX

Traditionally, one of the major limitations of JavaScript was that it couldn't communicate with a web server because it is a client-side technology—it stays within the browser. For example, you could create a game in JavaScript, but keeping a list of high scores stored on a server would require submitting a page to a server-side form, which JavaScript could not do (because, as you've learned, it wasn't meant to do that).

Speaking purely about user interactions, one of the limitations of web pages in general used to be that getting data from the user to the server, or from the server to the user, generally required a new page to be loaded and displayed. But in 2013, you likely run across websites every day that enable you to interact with content without loading a new page every time you click or submit a button.

AJAX (Asynchronous JavaScript and XML) is the answer to both these problems. AJAX refers to JavaScript's capability to use a built-in object, XMLHttpRequest, to communicate with a web server without submitting a form or loading a page. This object is supported by Internet Explorer, Firefox, Chrome, and all other modern browsers.

Although the term *AJAX* was coined in 2005, `XMLHttpRequest` has been supported by browsers for years—it was developed by Microsoft and first appeared in Internet Explorer 5. Nonetheless, it has only recently become a popular way of developing applications because browsers that support it have become more common. Another name for this technique is *remote scripting*.

NOTE

The term *AJAX* first appeared in an online article by Jesse James Garrett of Adaptive Path on February 18, 2005. It still appears here: www.adaptivepath.com/ideas/ajax-new-approach-web-applications.

The JavaScript Client (Front End)

JavaScript traditionally only has one way of communicating with a server—submitting a form. Remote scripting allows for much more versatile communication with the server. The *A* in AJAX stands for *asynchronous*, which means that the browser (and the user) aren't left hanging while waiting for the server to respond. Here's how a typical AJAX request works:

1. The script creates an `XMLHttpRequest` object and sends it to the web server. The script can continue after sending the request.

2. The server responds by sending the contents of a file or the output of a server-side program.

3. When the response arrives from the server, a JavaScript function is triggered to act on the data.

4. Because the goal is a more responsive user interface, the script usually displays the data from the server using the DOM (Document Object Model), eliminating the need for a page refresh.

In practice, this happens quickly, but even with a slow server, it can still work. Also, because the requests are asynchronous, more than one can be in progress at a time.

The Server-Side Script (Back End)

The part of an application that resides on the web server is commonly referred to as the *back end*. The simplest back end is a static file on the server, such as an XML or text file that holds data—JavaScript can request the file with `XMLHttpRequest`, and then read and act on its contents. More commonly, the back end is a server-side program running in a language such as PHP, Perl, or Ruby, and these server-side programs output results in XML or JSON (JavaScript Object Notation) format.

JavaScript can send data to a server-side program using GET or POST methods, the same two ways an HTML form works. In a GET request, the data is encoded in the URL that loads the program. In a POST request, it is sent separately and can contain more data.

XML

The *X* in AJAX stands for *XML* (Extensible Markup Language), the universal markup language upon which the latest versions of HTML are built. A server-side file or program can send data in XML format, and JavaScript can act on the data using its methods for working with XML.

Keep in mind that XML is just one way to send data, and not always the easiest. The server could just as easily send plain text, which the script could display, or HTML, which the script could insert into the page using the innerHTML property. Some programmers have even used server-side scripts to return data in JavaScript format, which can be easily executed using the eval function.

NOTE

JSON takes the idea of encoding data in JavaScript and formalizes it, and is a very popular method for transferring data. See www.json.org/ for details and code examples in many languages.

Popular Examples of AJAX

Although typical HTML and JavaScript is used to build web pages and sites, AJAX techniques often result in *web applications*—web-based services that perform work for the user. Here are a few well-known examples of AJAX:

▶ Google's Gmail mail client (http://mail.google.com/) uses AJAX to make a fast-responding email application. You can delete messages and perform other tasks without waiting for a new page to load.

▶ Amazon.com uses AJAX for some functions. For example, if you click on one of the Yes/No voting buttons for a product comment, it sends your vote to the server and a message appears next to the button thanking you, all without loading a page.

▶ Facebook (www.facebook.com), or any site allowing you to "like" something on Facebook, is probably the most prevalent use of AJAX in our daily lives. Every single time you click to "like" something, either on Facebook or elsewhere, you are using AJAX to communicate that click to a server-side script somewhere, which then seamlessly updates the "like" count, without reloading the page.

These are just a few examples. Subtle bits of remote scripting appear all over the web, and you might not even notice them—you'll just be annoyed a little bit less often at waiting for a page to load.

AJAX Frameworks and Libraries

Because remote scripting can be complicated, especially considering the browser differences you'll learn about briefly in this hour, several frameworks and libraries have been developed to simplify web application programming that leverages AJAX. Here are a few popular and feature-rich frameworks and libraries:

▶ **jQuery** (http://jquery.com/) is the most popular JavaScript library in use today with over 90% market share, and serves as the foundation for many of the AJAX functions and applications you encounter on a daily basis. The core library and the user interface extensions library allow you to rapidly build and deploy rich user interfaces or add a variety of attractive effects to existing components.

▶ **Prototype** (www.prototypejs.com/) is another JavaScript library that simplifies tasks such as working with DOM objects, dealing with data in forms, and remote scripting (AJAX). Prototype is also built into the Ruby on Rails framework for the server-side language Ruby, and the Script.aculo.us library plugs in to Prototype for rapid development of visual effects and user interface elements.

▶ **Backbone.js** (http://backbonejs.org) and **Ember.js** (http://emberjs.com) are both lightweight but powerful frameworks for rapid development of AJAX-based web applications, and are especially popular for the creation of single-page web applications.

Limitations of AJAX

Remote scripting is powerful, but there are some things it can't do, and some things to watch out for. Here are some of the limitations and potential problems of AJAX:

▶ The script and the XML data or server-side program it requests data from must be on the same domain, or steps must be taken to allow and secure cross-domain communication.

▶ Some older browsers and some less common browsers (such as some mobile browsers) don't support XMLHttpRequest, so you can't count on its availability for all users. While this is changing, it must still be accounted for.

▶ Requiring AJAX might compromise the accessibility of a site for disabled users.

▶ Users may still be accustomed to seeing a new page load each time they change something, so there might be a learning curve for them to understand an AJAX application. This too, is changing, through heavy personal use of social media sites which are themselves heavy users of AJAX.

As with other advanced uses of JavaScript, the best approach is to be unobtrusive—make sure there's still a way to use the site without AJAX support if possible, and use feature sensing to prevent errors on browsers that don't support it.

Using `XMLHttpRequest`

You will now look at how to use `XMLHttpRequest` to communicate with a server. This might seem a bit complex, but the process is the same for any request. Later, you will create a reusable code library to simplify this process.

Creating a Request

The first step is to create an `XMLHttpRequest` object. To do this, you use the `new` keyword, as with other JavaScript objects. The following statement creates a request object in some browsers:

```
ajaxreq = new XMLHttpRequest();
```

The previous example works with Firefox, Chrome, Internet Explorer 7 and 8, and other modern browsers, but not with Internet Explorer 5 or 6. It is up to you whether you want to support these browsers or not because their percentages of use are very low. However, some institutions might be stuck with a lot of IE6 browsers installed at workstations, so your mileage may vary.

NOTE
_____

From this point forward, the sample code will only support IE7 and beyond (modern browsers), but if you want to support these old browsers, you have to use ActiveX syntax:

```
ajaxreq = new ActiveXObject("Microsoft.XMLHTTP");
```
_____

The library section later this hour demonstrates how to use the correct method depending on the browser in use. In either case, the variable you use (`ajaxreq` in the example) stores the `XMLHttpRequest` object. You'll use the methods of this object to open and send a request, as explained in the following sections.

Opening a URL

The `open()` method of the `XMLHttpRequest` object specifies the filename as well as the method in which data will be sent to the server: `GET` or `POST`. These are the same methods supported by web forms:

```
ajaxreq.open("GET","filename");
```

For the GET method, the data you send is included in the URL. For example, this command opens (runs) a script file on the web server called search.php and sends the value "John" for the query parameter:

```
ajaxreq.open("GET","search.php?query=John");
```

Sending the Request

You use the send() method of the XMLHttpRequest object to send the request to the server. If you are using the POST method, the data to send is the argument for send(). For a GET request, you can use the null value instead:

```
ajaxreq.send(null);
```

Awaiting a Response

After the request is sent, your script will continue without waiting for a result. Because the result could come at any time, you can detect it with an event handler. The XMLHttpRequest object has an onreadystatechange event handler for this purpose. You can create a function to deal with the response and set it as the handler for this event:

```
ajaxreq.onreadystatechange = MyFunc;
```

The request object has a property, readyState, that indicates its status, and this event is triggered whenever the readyState property changes. The values of readyState range from 0 for a new request to 4 for a complete request, so your event-handling function usually needs to watch for a value of 4.

Although the request is complete, it might not have been successful. The status property is set to 200 if the request succeeded or an error code if it failed. The statusText property stores a text explanation of the error or "OK" for success.

CAUTION
_____

When using event handlers, be sure to specify the function name without parentheses. With parentheses, you're referring to the *result* of the function; without them, you're referring to the function itself.
_____

Interpreting the Response Data

When the readyState property reaches 4 and the request is complete, the data returned from the server is available to your script in two properties: responseText is the response in raw text form, and responseXML is the response as an XML object. If the data was not in XML format, only the text property will be available.

JavaScript's DOM methods are meant to work on XML, so you can use them with the `responseXML` property. For example, you can use the `getElementsByTagName()` method to extract data from XML.

Creating a Simple AJAX Library

You should be aware by now that AJAX requests can be a bit complex. To make things easier, you can create an AJAX library, or a JavaScript file that provides functions that handle making a request and receiving the result, which you can reuse any time you need AJAX functions.

Listing 17.1 shows the complete AJAX library, including the special case for very old browsers.

LISTING 17.1 The AJAX library

```
// global variables to keep track of the request
// and the function to call when done
var ajaxreq=false, ajaxCallback;

// ajaxRequest: Sets up a request
function ajaxRequest(filename) {
   try {
    // Firefox / IE7 / Others
    ajaxreq= new XMLHttpRequest();
   } catch (error) {
    try {
      // IE 5 / IE 6
      ajaxreq = new ActiveXObject("Microsoft.XMLHTTP");
    } catch (error) {
      return false;
    }
   }
   ajaxreq.open("GET", filename);
   ajaxreq.onreadystatechange = ajaxResponse;
   ajaxreq.send(null);
}

// ajaxResponse: Waits for response and calls a function
function ajaxResponse() {
   if (ajaxreq.readyState !=4) return;
   if (ajaxreq.status==200) {
      // if the request succeeded...
      if (ajaxCallback) ajaxCallback();
   } else alert("Request failed: " + ajaxreq.statusText);
   return true;
}
```

To use this library, follow these steps:

1. Save the library file as `ajax.js` in the same folder as your HTML documents and scripts.

2. Include the script in your document with a `<script src>` tag. It should be included before any other scripts that use its features.

3. In your script, create a function to be called when the request is complete, and set the `ajaxCallback` variable to the function.

4. Call the `ajaxRequest()` function. Its parameter is the filename of the server-side program or file. (This library supports GET requests only, so you don't need to specify the method.)

5. Your function specified in `ajaxCallback` will be called when the request completes successfully, and the global variable `ajaxreq` will store the data in its `responseXML` and `responseText` properties.

The next two sections explain a bit more about the library's core functions.

The `ajaxRequest` Function

The `ajaxRequest` function handles all the steps necessary to create and send an `XMLHttpRequest`. First, it creates the `XMLHttpRequest` object. As noted before, this requires a different command for older browsers, and will cause an error if the wrong one executes, so try and `catch` are used to create the request. First the standard method is used, and if it causes an error, the ActiveX method is tried. If that also causes an error, the `ajaxreq` variable is set to `false` to indicate that AJAX is unsupported.

The `ajaxResponse` Function

The `ajaxResponse` function is used as the `onreadystatechange` event handler. This function first checks the `readyState` property for a value of 4. If it has a different value, the function returns without doing anything.

Next, it checks the `status` property for a value of 200, which indicates the request was successful. If so, it runs the function stored in the `ajaxCallback` variable. If not, it displays the error message in an alert box.

Creating an AJAX Quiz Using the Library

Now that you have a reusable AJAX library, you can use it to create JavaScript applications that take advantage of remote scripting. This first example displays quiz questions on a page and prompts you for the answers.

Rather than including the questions in the script, this example reads the quiz questions and answers from an XML file on the server as a demonstration of AJAX.

CAUTION

This example requires the use of a web server. It will not work on a local machine due to browsers' security restrictions on remote scripting.

The HTML File

The HTML for this example is straightforward. It defines a simple form with an Answer field and a Submit button, along with some hooks for the script. The HTML for this example is shown in Listing 17.2.

LISTING 17.2   The HTML file for the quiz example

```
<!DOCTYPE html>
<html lang="en">
  <head>
   <title>Ajax Quiz Test</title>
   <script type="text/javascript" src="ajax.js"></script>
  </head>
  <body>
    <h1>Ajax Quiz Example</h1>
    <form method="post" action="">
    <p><input type="button" value="Start the Quiz" id="startq" /></p>
    <p><strong>Question:</strong></p>
    <span id="question">[Press Button to Start Quiz]</span></p>
    <p><strong>Answer:</strong></p>
    <input type="text" name="answer" id="answer" /></p>
    <p><input type="button" value="Submit Answer" id="submit" /></p>
    </form>
  <script type="text/javascript" src="quiz.js"></script>
  </body>
</html>
```

This HTML file includes the following elements:

▶ The `<script>` tag in the `<head>` section includes the AJAX library you created in the previous section from the `ajax.js` file.

▶ The `<script>` tag in the `<body>` section includes the `quiz.js` file, which will contain the quiz script (you'll create this in a moment).

▶ The `<span id="question">` tag sets up a place for the question to be inserted by the script.

▶ The text field with the `id` value `"answer"` is where the user will answer the question.

▶ The button with the `id` value `"submit"` will submit an answer.

▶ The button with the `id` value `"startq"` will start the quiz.

You can test the HTML document at this time by placing the file on your web server and accessing it via the URL, but the buttons won't work until you add the XML and JavaScript files, as you'll learn about in the next two sections.

The XML File

The XML file for the quiz is shown in Listing 17.3. I've filled it with a few JavaScript questions, but it could easily be adapted for another purpose.

LISTING 17.3   The XML file containing the quiz questions and answers

```
<?xml version="1.0" ?>
<questions>
    <q>What DOM object contains URL information for the window?</q>
    <a>location</a>
    <q>Which method of the document object finds the
        object for an element?</q>
    <a>getElementById</a>
    <q>If you declare a variable outside a function,
        is it global or local?</q>
    <a>global</a>
    <q>What is the formal standard for the JavaScript language called?</q>
    <a>ECMAScript</a>
</questions>
```

The `<questions>` tag encloses the entire file and each question and answer are enclosed in `<q>` and `<a>` tags. Remember, this is XML, not HTML—these are not standard HTML tags, but tags that were created for this example. Because this file will be used only by your script, it does not need to follow a standard format.

To use this file, save it as `questions.xml` in the same folder as the HTML document. It will be loaded by the script you create in the next section.

Of course, with a quiz this small, you could have made things easier by storing the questions and answers in a JavaScript array. But imagine a much larger quiz, with thousands of questions, or a server-side program that pulls questions from a database, or even a hundred different files with different quizzes to choose from, and you can see the benefit of using a separate XML file.

The JavaScript File

Because you have a separate library to handle the complexities of making an AJAX request and receiving the response, the script for this example only needs to deal with the action for the quiz itself. Listing 17.4 shows the JavaScript file for this example.

LISTING 17.4   The JavaScript file for the quiz example

```
// global variable qn is the current question number
var qn=0;

// load the questions from the XML file
function getQuestions() {
   obj=document.getElementById("question");
   obj.firstChild.nodeValue="(please wait)";
   ajaxCallback = nextQuestion;
   ajaxRequest("questions.xml");
}

// display the next question
function nextQuestion() {
   questions = ajaxreq.responseXML.getElementsByTagName("q");
   obj=document.getElementById("question");
   if (qn < questions.length) {
      q = questions[qn].firstChild.nodeValue;
      obj.firstChild.nodeValue=q;
   } else {
      obj.firstChild.nodeValue="(no more questions)";
   }
}

// check the user's answer
function checkAnswer() {
   answers = ajaxreq.responseXML.getElementsByTagName("a");
   a = answers[qn].firstChild.nodeValue;
   answerfield = document.getElementById("answer");
   if (a == answerfield.value) {
      alert("Correct!");
   }
   else {
      alert("Incorrect. The correct answer is: " + a);
```

```
    }
    qn = qn + 1;
    answerfield.value="";
    nextQuestion();
}

// Set up the event handlers for the buttons
obj=document.getElementById("startq");
obj.onclick=getQuestions;
ans=document.getElementById("submit");
ans.onclick=checkAnswer;
```

This script consists of the following:

- ▶ The first `var` statement defines a global variable, `qn`, which will keep track of which question is currently displayed. It is initially set to zero for the first question.

- ▶ The `getQuestions()` function is called when the user clicks the Start Quiz button. This function uses the AJAX library to request the contents of the `questions.xml` file. It sets the `ajaxCallback` variable to the `nextQuestion()` function.

- ▶ The `nextQuestion()` function is called when the AJAX request is complete. This function uses the `getElementsByTagName()` method on the `responseXML` property to find all the questions (`<q>` tags) and store them in the `questions` array.

- ▶ The `checkAnswer()` function is called when the user submits an answer. It uses `getElementsByTagName()` to store the answers (`<a>` tags) in the `answers` array, and then compares the answer for the current question with the user's answer and displays an alert indicating whether they were right or wrong.

- ▶ The script commands after this function set up two event handlers. One attaches the `getQuestions()` function to the Start Quiz button to set up the quiz; the other attaches the `checkAnswer()` function to the Submit button.

Testing the Quiz

To try this example, you'll need all four files in the same folder: ajax.js (the AJAX library), quiz. js (the quiz functions), questions.xml (the questions), and the HTML document. All but the HTML document need to have the correct filenames so they will work correctly, since they are referred to by name within other files. Also remember that because it uses AJAX, this example requires a web server.

Figure 17.1 shows the quiz in action, after a question has been answered.

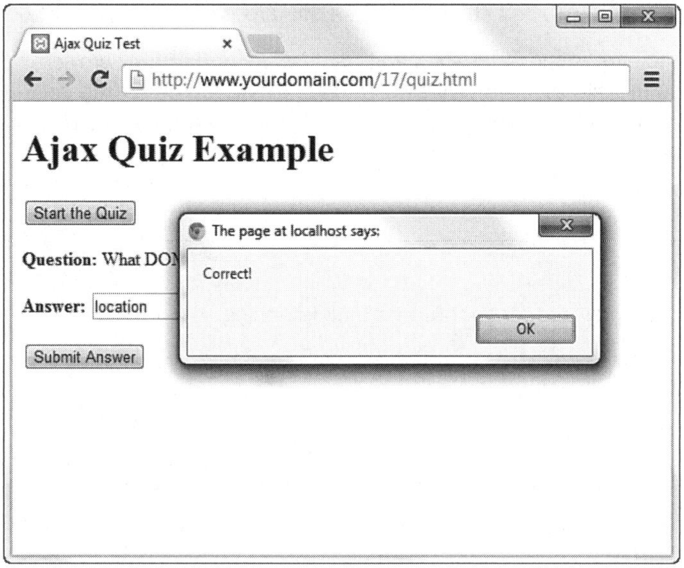

FIGURE 17.1
The quiz example loaded in a web browser.

Summary

In this hour, you've learned how AJAX, or remote scripting, allows JavaScript on the front end to communicate with scripts or data that live on a web server (the back end). You created a reusable AJAX library that can be used to create any number of AJAX applications, and you created an example quiz application based on questions and answers stored in an XML file.

Q&A

Q. What happens if the server is slow or never responds to the request?

A. This is another reason you should use AJAX as an *optional* feature—whether caused by the server or by the user's connection, there will be times when a request is slow to respond or never responds. In this case, the callback function will be called late or not at all. This can cause trouble with overlapping requests: For example, in the live search example, an erratic server might cause the responses for the first few characters typed to come in a few seconds apart, confusing the user. You can remedy this by checking the `readyState` property to make sure a request is not already in progress before you start another one.

Q. If I use a JavaScript or AJAX framework, do I still have to use the ajax.js library shown here?

A. Very likely not. One of the benefits of these libraries and frameworks is that they provide commonly used code for you in ways that are very easy to use. Be sure to check the documentation of the library or framework that you choose, so you know how to make AJAX requests within those frameworks.

Workshop

The quiz questions and exercises are provided for your further understanding.

Quiz

1. What does the acronym "AJAX" stand for?

2. What is the name of the built-in JavaScript object used to communicate with a web server?

3. Why is it important that connections are asynchronous?

4. What are two types of back-end data formats that often contain output results that are then used on the front-end?

5. True or false: To support Internet Explorer 5 and 6, you must create an ActiveX object rather than an `XMLHttpRequest` object when using AJAX.

6. Which JavaScript library currently has the greatest market share?

7. True or false: Requiring AJAX might compromise the accessibility of a site for disabled users.

8. Which method of the `XMLHttpRequest` object specifies the file to which data will be sent on the server?

9. Which `readyState` value indicates a request is complete?

10. Why was it important to create the basic ajax.js library file shown in Listing 17.1?

Answers

1. Asynchronous JavaScript and XML

2. `XMLHttpRequest`

3. Asynchronous connections provide a better user experience since the browser can continue to display information while waiting for the server to respond to other user interactions, including multiple requests at one time.

4. XML and JSON

5. True

6. jQuery

7. True

8. `open()`

9. 4

10. Since these basic functions are used every time you want to make an AJAX request and get a response, you would be typing them over and over again unless you created one file that you could just refer to each time.

Scripting with PHP

In 1995, a programmer named Rasmus Lerdorf created a set of scripts to help him manage some basic tasks within his own personal website, specifically around the use of HTML form data. He called this bundle of scripts "Personal Home Page/Forms Interpreter" or PHP/FI. Over the next few years, and with the help of some more developers—Zeev Suraski and Andi Gutmans—PHP/FI turned into the processing module we know today as PHP (which is now a recursive acronym that stands for "PHP: Hypertext Preprocessor"). From its humble beginnings as a server-side scripting language used for common tasks such as form handling and database interactions, PHP has grown in popularity such that more than 250 million websites use PHP in some way today.

Often working in conjunction with a web server, the PHP processing module interprets scripts when requested by the user and produces output that is returned to the user. For example, if a user requests a web page and that web page is actually a PHP script instead of pure HTML, the PHP processing module will process that script and produce output that in turn is sent back to the user as HTML and rendered in the browser.

The simplicity of the language itself makes it a popular language to learn, and especially a *first* scripting language to learn, but simple doesn't mean it isn't powerful and feature-rich. In this lesson, you'll get a whirlwind tour of the basics of the PHP language and its use.

The highlights of this hour include

- ▶ Understanding the basic structure of PHP scripts

- ▶ Learning about the variables, data types, and logical control structures used in PHP

- ▶ Using PHP's many built-in functions

- ▶ Creating functions of your own to perform tasks

- ▶ Creating and using objects in PHP

- ▶ Discovering common uses for PHP scripts

What You Need for PHP Programming

Like HTML documents, PHP files are made up of plain text. You can create them with any text editor, and most popular HTML editors and programming IDEs (integrated development environments) provide support for PHP. When working with the PHP samples in this hour, you can use the same text editor you have been using to create sample code from other lessons in this book.

Beyond a simple text editor used to create PHP source files, you will need access to a web server and the PHP processing module which will interpret your source files and produce output from them. Well over 90% of all web-hosting plans offer PHP support, so it is very likely that if you have a web-hosting account you have access to a web server and the PHP processing module.

If you do not have access to a web-hosting account, and if you simply want to practice on your own in a way that no one else can access your scripts, you might consider installing the Apache web server and PHP processing module on your own personal computer. While these technologies are available for Windows, Mac, and Linux, and you can download these technologies at http://httpd.apache.org and www.php.net, respectively, a third-party installation package might prove more efficient:

- ▶ **XAMPP**— Installation of Apache, MySQL, and PHP on Windows, Mac, or Linux. See www.apachefriends.org/ for more information.

- ▶ **WAMP**— Installation of Apache, MySQL, and PHP on Windows. See www.wampserver.com/ for more information.

- ▶ **MAMP**— Installation of Apache, MySQL, and PHP on Mac. See www.mamp.info/ for more information.

While these third-party installation packages install everything you need (and some things you didn't even know you needed, like the MySQL database server), one potential drawback to using third-party installation packages is that the version of the core technologies that are bundled together will always be a few revision versions behind. This happens because of the work that goes into creating and testing the bundle itself, to ensure that no conflicts exist between the latest versions of the technologies; it also has to go through a quality-assurance process. The upside of this process, however, is that when you install these technologies using a bundled installer, the upgrade process requires nothing more than running the new installer—it takes care of removing and updating all the files for you.

From this point forward in the hour, if you want to follow along with the source code, then you will need access to a PHP-enabled web server either through your hosting provider or through the installation of the core technologies. If you are unsure if your web-hosting provider is PHP-enabled, or if you want to test the packaged installation, you can create a small test script like the one shown in Listing 18.1.

LISTING 18.1   A simple PHP script

```php
<?php
    echo "<h1>Hello World!</h1>";
?>
```

Type in the example in Listing 18.1 and save the file to the document root of your web server, using a name something like `helloworld.php`.

If you are not working directly on the machine that will be serving your PHP script, you need to use a File Transfer Protocol (FTP) or Secure Copy (SCP) client to upload your saved document to the server. When the document is in place on the server, you should be able to access it using your browser. If all has gone well, you should see the script's output. Figure 18.1 shows the output from the `helloworld.php` script.

FIGURE 18.1
Success: the output from `helloworld.php`.

If you do not see a similar output, and instead see a replica of the code that you typed into the text file, then your web-hosting solution is not PHP-enabled.

Basic Structures in PHP Scripts

When writing PHP, you need to inform the PHP-processing module that you want it to execute your commands. If you don't do this, the code you write will be mistaken for HTML and will be output directly into the browser. You can designate your code as PHP with special tags that mark the beginning and end of PHP code blocks. The most common—and standard—tag pair is `<?php` and `?>`, which is what you will see used throughout this hour.

The `echo` and `print()` Statements

Simply put, you can use the `echo` statement to output data. In most cases, anything output by `echo` ends up viewable in the browser. Alternatively, you could have used the `print()` statement in place of the `echo` statement. Using `echo` or `print()` is a matter of taste; when you look at other people's scripts, you might see either used, which is why both are included here.

Referring back to the code you have seen so far, note the only line of code in Listing 18.1 ended with a semicolon. The semicolon informs the PHP engine that you have completed a statement, and is probably the most important bit of PHP syntax you could learn at this stage.

A *statement* represents an instruction to the PHP engine. Broadly, it is to PHP what a sentence is to written or spoken English. A sentence should usually end with a period; a statement should usually end with a semicolon. Exceptions to this rule include statements that enclose other statements and statements that end a block of code. In most cases, however, failure to end a statement with a semicolon will confuse the PHP engine and result in an error.

Combining HTML and PHP

The script in Listing 18.1 is pure PHP. You can incorporate this into an HTML document by simply adding HTML around the PHP start and end tags, as shown in Listing 18.2.

LISTING 18.2   A PHP script incorporated into HTML

```
<!DOCTYPE html>
<html>
<head>
   <title>A PHP script including HTML</title>
</head>
<body>
   <h1><?php echo "Hello World!"; ?></h1>
</body>
</html>
```

As you can see, incorporating PHP code into a predominantly HTML document is simply a matter of typing in that code. The PHP engine ignores everything outside the PHP open and close tags. If you were to save the contents of Listing 18.2 as `helloworldagain.php`, place it in your document root, and then view it with a browser, it would appear exactly as did Figure 18.1. If you were to view the document source, as shown in Figure 18.2, the listing would look just like a normal HTML document, because that's all the output actually is—the PHP processor has simply placed some text within an `<h1>` element before it got to your web browser.

FIGURE 18.2
The output of `helloworldagain.php` as HTML source code.

You can include as many blocks of PHP code as you need in a single document, interspersing them with HTML as required. Although you can have multiple blocks of code in a single document, they combine to form a single script. Any variables defined in the first block will usually be available to subsequent blocks.

Adding Comments to PHP Code

A *comment* is text in a script that is ignored by the PHP engine. Comments can make code more readable or annotate a script. Single-line comments begin with two forward slashes (//)—the preferred style—or a single hash or pound sign (#). The PHP engine ignores all text between these marks and either the end of the line or the PHP close tag:

```
// this is a comment
#  this is another comment
```

Multiline comments begin with a forward slash followed by an asterisk (/*) and end with an asterisk followed by a forward slash (*/):

```
/*
this is a comment
none of this will
be parsed by the
PHP engine
*/
```

Flow Control Functions

It is common for scripts to evaluate conditions and change their behavior accordingly. These decisions are what make your PHP pages dynamic—that is, able to change output according to circumstances. Like most programming languages, PHP enables you to control the logical flow with statements such as the `if` statement, among others that you'll learn about in a moment.

The `if` statement evaluates an expression found between parentheses. If this expression results in a `true` value, the statement is executed. Otherwise, the statement is skipped entirely. This functionality enables scripts to make decisions based on any number of factors:

```
if (expression) {
    // code to execute if the expression evaluates to true
}
```

When working with an `if` statement, you might want to define an alternative block of code that should be executed if the expression you are testing evaluates to `false`. You can do this by adding `else` to the `if` statement followed by a further block of code:

```
if (expression) {
    // code to execute if the expression evaluates to true
} else {
    // code to execute in all other cases
}
```

Using an `else` clause in conjunction with an `if` statement allows scripts to make decisions about code execution. However, your options are limited to an either-or branch: either the code block following the `if` statement or the code block following the `else` statement.

You can use an `if...elseif...else` clause to test multiple expressions (the `if...else` portion) before offering a default block of code (the `elseif` portion):

```
if (expression) {
    // code to execute if the expression evaluates to true
} elseif (another expression) {
    // code to execute if the previous expression failed
    // and this one evaluates to true
} else {
    // code to execute in all other cases
}
```

If the initial `if` expression does not evaluate to `true`, the first block of code is ignored. The `elseif` clause presents another expression for evaluation. If it evaluates to `true`, its corresponding block of code is executed. Otherwise, the block of code associated with the `else` clause is executed. You can include as many `elseif` clauses as you want; and if you don't need a default action, you can omit the `else` clause.

The `switch` statement is an alternative way of changing flow, based on the evaluation of an expression. Using the `if` statement in conjunction with `elseif`, you can evaluate multiple expressions, as you've just seen. However, a `switch` statement evaluates only one expression in a list of expressions, selecting the correct one based on a specific bit of matching code. Whereas the result of an expression evaluated as part of an `if` statement is interpreted as either `true` or `false`, the expression portion of a `switch` statement is subsequently tested against any number of values, in hopes of finding a match:

```
switch (expression) {
     case result1:
         // execute this if expression results in result1
         break;
     case result2:
         // execute this if expression results in result2
         break;
     default:
         // execute this if no break statement
         // has been encountered hitherto
}
```

The expression used in a `switch` statement is often just a variable. Within the `switch` statement, you find a number of `case` statements. Each of these cases tests a value against the value of the `switch` expression. If the case value is equivalent to the expression value, the code within the `case` statement is executed. The `break` statement ends the execution of the `switch` statement altogether.

If the `break` statement is omitted, the next `case` statement is executed, regardless of whether a previous match has been found. If the optional `default` statement is reached without a previous matching value having been found, its code is executed.

CAUTION

It is important to include a `break` statement at the end of any code that will be executed as part of a `case` statement. Without a `break` statement, the program flow continues to the next `case` statement and ultimately to the `default` statement. In most cases, this results in unexpected behavior, likely incorrect!

Finally, the `?:` or *ternary* operator is similar to the `if` statement, except that it returns a value derived from one of two expressions separated by a colon. This construct provides you with three parts of the whole, hence, the name *ternary*. The expression used to generate the returned value depends on the result of a test expression:

```
(expression) ? returned_if_expression_is_true : returned_if_expression_is_false;
```

If the test expression evaluates to true, the result of the second expression is returned; otherwise, the value of the third expression is returned.

Looping

So far, you've looked at decisions that a script can make about what code to execute. Scripts can also decide how many times to execute a block of code. Loop statements are specifically designed to enable you to perform repetitive tasks because they continue to operate until a specified condition is achieved or until you explicitly choose to exit the loop.

The while statement looks similar in structure to a basic if statement, but has the ability to loop:

```
while (expression) {
    // do something
}
```

Unlike an if statement, a while statement executes for as long as the expression evaluates to true, over and over again if need be. Each execution of a code block within a loop is called an *iteration*. Within the block, you usually change something that affects the while statement's expression; otherwise, your loop continues indefinitely. For example, you might use a variable to count the number of iterations and act accordingly. Listing 18.3 creates a while loop that calculates and prints multiples of 2 up to 24.

LISTING 18.3 A while statement

```php
<?php
$counter = 1;
while ($counter <= 12) {
    echo $counter." times 2 is ".($counter * 2)."<br />";
    $counter++;
}
?>
```

This example initializes the variable $counter in line 2 with a value of 1. The while statement in line 3 tests the $counter variable so that as long as the value of $counter is less than or equal to 12, the loop continues to run. Within the while statement's code block, the value of $counter is multiplied by 2, and the result is printed to the browser. In line 5, the value of $counter is incremented by 1. This step is extremely important because if you did not increment the value of the $counter variable, the while expression would never resolve to false and the loop would never end.

If you put these lines of code into a text file called `while.php` and place this file in your web server document root, then access the script through your web browser, it produces the following output:

```
1 times 2 is 2
2 times 2 is 4
3 times 2 is 6
4 times 2 is 8
5 times 2 is 10
6 times 2 is 12
7 times 2 is 14
8 times 2 is 16
9 times 2 is 18
10 times 2 is 20
11 times 2 is 22
12 times 2 is 24
```

A do...while statement looks a little like a `while` statement turned on its head. The essential difference between the two is that the code block is executed *before* the truth test and not after it:

```
do {
    // code to be executed
} while (expression);
```

This type of statement is useful when you want the code block to be executed at least once, even if the `while` expression evaluates to `false`.

The `while` statement is useful, but a `for` statement is often a more efficient method of achieving the same effect. In Listing 18.3, you saw how a variable was initialized outside the `while` statement and then tested within its expression and incremented within the code block. With a `for` statement, you can achieve this same series of events, but in a single line of code:

```
for (initialization expression; test expression; modification expression) {
    // code to be executed
}
```

This structure allows for more compact code and makes it less likely that you might forget to increment a counter variable, thereby creating an infinite loop.

NOTE

Infinite loops are, as the name suggests, loops that run without bounds. If your loop is running infinitely, your script is running for an infinite amount of time. This behavior is very stressful on your web server and renders the web page unusable.

The expressions within the parentheses of the `for` statement are separated by semicolons. Usually, the first expression initializes a counter variable, the second expression is the test condition for the loop, and the third expression increments the counter. Listing 18.4 shows a `for` statement that re-creates the example in Listing 18.3, which multiplies 12 numbers by 2.

LISTING 18.4   Using the `for` statement

```php
<?php
for ($counter=1; $counter<=12; $counter++) {
    echo $counter." times 2 is ".($counter * 2)."<br />";
}
?>
```

The results of Listings 18.3 and 18.4 are the same, but the `for` statement makes the code in Listing 18.4 more compact. Because the `$counter` variable is initialized and incremented at the beginning of the statement, the logic of the loop is clear at a glance.

TIP

Loops can contain other loop statements, thus creating nested loops, as long as the logic is valid and the loops are tidy.

The Building Blocks of PHP: Variables, Data Types, and Operators

Having learned of the basic structures you will encounter in PHP scripts, this section introduces you to more of the building blocks you'll use in those scripts. Many of these basic concepts are similar to other programming languages you might already have encountered, or will encounter, later in this book.

Variable Naming and Scope

In PHP, a variable consists of a name of your choosing, preceded by a dollar sign ($). Variable names can include letters, numbers, and the underscore character (_), but they cannot include spaces. Names must begin with a letter or an underscore. The following list shows some legal variables:

```php
$a;
$a_longish_variable_name;
$2453;
$sleepyZZZZ;
```

A semicolon (;)—also known as the *instruction terminator*—is used to end a PHP statement. The semicolons in the previous fragment of code are not part of the variable names, but are used to end the statement that declares the variable as "alive and kicking," if you will. To declare a variable, you need only include it in your script. When you declare a variable, you usually assign a value to it in the same statement, as shown here:

```
$num1 = 8;
```

```
$num2 = 23;
```

The preceding lines declare two variables and use the assignment operator (=) to assign values to them. After you assign values to your variables, you can treat them exactly as if they were the values themselves. In other words

```
echo $num1;
```

is equivalent to

```
echo 8;
```

as long as $num1 is assigned a value of 8.

In addition to the rules for naming variables, there are rules regarding the availability of variables. In general, the assigned value of a variable is present only within the function or script where it resides. For example, if you have scriptA.php that holds a variable called $name with a value of joe, and you want to create scriptB.php that also uses a $name variable, you can assign to that second $name variable a value of jane without affecting the variable in scriptA.php. The value of the $name variable is *local* to each script, and the assigned values are independent of each other.

However, you can also define the $name variable as *global* within a script or function. If the $name variable is defined as a global variable in both scriptA.php and scriptB.php, and these scripts are connected to each other (that is, one script calls the other or includes the other), there will be just one value for the now-shared $name variable.

In addition to global variables of your own creation, PHP has several predefined variables called *superglobals*. These variables are always present, and their values are available to all your scripts. Each of the following superglobals is actually an array of other variables:

- ▶ $_GET contains any variables provided to a script through the GET method.
- ▶ $_POST contains any variables provided to a script through the POST method.
- ▶ $_COOKIE contains any variables provided to a script through a cookie.

- ▶ $_FILES contains any variables provided to a script through file uploads.

- ▶ $_SERVER contains information such as headers, file paths, and script locations.

- ▶ $_ENV contains any variables provided to a script as part of the server environment.

- ▶ $_REQUEST contains any variables provided to a script via GET, POST, or COOKIE input mechanisms.

- ▶ $_SESSION contains any variables that are currently registered in a session.

Using superglobals is crucial in creating secure applications because they reduce the likelihood of user-injected input to your scripts. By coding your scripts to accept only what you want, in the manner defined by you (from a form using the POST method, or from a session, for example), you can eliminate some of the problems created by loosely written scripts.

Data Types

Different types of data take up different amounts of memory and may be treated differently when they are manipulated by a script. Some programming languages therefore demand that the programmer declare in advance which type of data a variable will contain. By contrast, PHP is *loosely typed*, meaning that it automatically determines the data type at the time data is assigned to each variable.

Table 18.1 shows the eight standard data types available in PHP.

TABLE 18.1 Standard data types

Type	Example	Description
Boolean	true	One of the special values true or false
Integer	5	A whole number
Float or double	3.234	A floating-point number
String	"hello"	A collection of characters
Object		An instance of a class
Array		An ordered set of keys and values
Resource		Reference to a third-party resource (a database, for example)
NULL		An uninitialized variable

TIP

PHP provides the function `settype()`, which is used to change the type of a variable. To use `settype()`, you place the variable to change and the type to change it to between the parentheses and separate the elements with a comma, like so:

```
settype($variabletochange, 'new type');
```

PHP also allows you to change the type of an existing variable by *casting*; this produces a copy, leaving the original variable untouched. To change type through casting, you indicate the name of a data type, in parentheses, in front of the variable you are copying:

```
$newvar = (integer) $originalvar
```

Operators and Expressions

With what you have learned so far, you can assign data to variables, and you can even investigate and change the data type of a variable. A programming language isn't very useful, though, unless you can manipulate the data you have stored. *Operators* are symbols used to manipulate data stored in variables, to make it possible to use one or more values to produce a new value, or to check the validity of data to determine the next step in a condition, and so forth.

The following sections describe the operators commonly used in PHP programming.

The Assignment Operator

You have seen the assignment operator in use each time a variable was declared in an example; the assignment operator consists of the single character: =. The assignment operator takes the value of the right-side operand and assigns it to the left-side operand:

```
$name = "John";
```

The variable $name now contains the string "John".

Arithmetic Operators

The *arithmetic operators* do exactly what you would expect—they perform arithmetic operations. Table 18.2 lists these operators along with examples of their usage and results.

TABLE 18.2 Arithmetic Operators

Operator	Name	Example	Sample Result
+	Addition	10+3	13
-	Subtraction	10-3	7
/	Division	10/3	3.3333333333333
*	Multiplication	10*3	30
%	Modulus	10%3	1

The addition operator adds the right-side operand to the left-side operand. The subtraction operator subtracts the right-side operand from the left-side operand. The division operator divides the left-side operand by the right-side operand. The multiplication operator multiplies the left-side operand by the right-side operand. The modulus operator returns the remainder of the left-side operand divided by the right-side operand.

The Concatenation Operator

The concatenation operator is represented by a single period (.). Treating both operands as strings, this operator appends the right-side operand to the left-side operand. So

```
"hello"." world"
```

returns

```
"hello world"
```

Note that the resulting space between the words occurs because there is a leading space in the second operand (" world" rather than "world"). The concatenation operator literally smashes together two strings without adding any padding. So, if you try to concatenate two strings without leading or trailing spaces, such as

```
"hello"."world"
```

you will get this as your result:

```
"helloworld"
```

Regardless of the data types of the operands used with the concatenation operator, they are treated as strings, and the result is always of the string type.

Combined Assignment Operators

Although there is only one true assignment operator, PHP provides a number of combination operators that transform the left-side operand and return a result while also modifying the original value of the variable. As a rule, operators use operands but do not change their original values, but combined assignment operators break this rule.

A combined assignment operator consists of a standard operator symbol followed by an equal sign. Combination assignment operators save you the trouble of using two operators in two different steps within your script. For example, if you have a variable with a value of 4, and you want to increase this value to 4 more, you might see this:

```
$x = 4;
$x = $x + 4; // $x now equals 8
```

However , you can also use a combination assignment operator (+=) to add and return the new value, as shown here:

```
$x = 4;
$x += 4; // $x now equals 8
```

Each arithmetic operator, as well as the concatenation operator, also has a corresponding combination assignment operator. Table 18.3 lists these new operators and shows an example of their usage.

TABLE 18.3 Some combined assignment operators

Operator	Example	Equivalent To
+=	$x += 5	$x = $x + 5
-=	$x -= 5	$x = $x - 5
/=	$x /= 5	$x = $x / 5
*=	$x *= 5	$x = $x * 5
%=	$x %= 5	$x = $x % 5
.=	$x .= " test"	$x = $x." test"

Automatically Incrementing and Decrementing an Integer Variable

When coding in PHP, you will often find it necessary to increment or decrement a variable that is an integer type. You usually need to do this when you are counting the iterations of a loop. You have already learned two ways of doing this—either by incrementing the value of $x using the addition operator

```
$x = $x + 1; // $x is incremented by 1
```

or by using a combined assignment operator

```
$x += 1; // $x is incremented by 1
```

In both cases, the new value is assigned to $x. Because expressions of this kind are common, PHP provides some special operators that allow you to add or subtract the integer constant 1 from an integer variable, assigning the result to the variable itself. These are known as the *post-increment* and *post-decrement* operators. The post-increment operator consists of two plus symbols appended to a variable name:

```
$x++; // $x is incremented by 1
```

This expression increments the value represented by the variable $x by 1. Using two minus symbols in the same way decrements the variable:

```
$x--; // $x is decremented by 1
```

If you use the post-increment or post-decrement operators in conjunction with a conditional operator, the operand is modified only after the first operation has finished:

```
$x = 3;
$y = $x++ + 3;
```

In this instance, $y first becomes 6 (the result of 3 + 3), and then $x is incremented.

In some circumstances, you might want to increment or decrement a variable in a test expression before the test is carried out. PHP provides the pre-increment and pre-decrement operators for this purpose. These operators behave in the same way as the post-increment and post-decrement operators, but they are written with the plus or minus symbols preceding the variable:

```
++$x; // $x is incremented by 1
--$x; // $x is decremented by 1
```

If these operators are used as part of a test expression, incrementing occurs before the test is carried out. For example, in the next fragment, $x is incremented before it is tested against 4:

```
$x = 3;
++$x < 4; // false
```

The test expression returns `false` because 4 is not smaller than 4.

Comparison Operators

Comparison operators perform comparative tests using their operands and return the Boolean value `true` if the test is successful or `false` if the test fails. This type of expression is useful when using control structures in your scripts, such as `if` and `while` statements.

Table 18.4 lists the comparison operators.

TABLE 18.4 Comparison operators

Operator	Name	Returns True If...	Example ($x Is 4)	Result
==	Equivalence	Left is equivalent to right.	$x == 5	false
!=	Nonequivalence	Left is not equivalent to right.	$x != 5	true
===	Identical	Left is equivalent to right, and they are the same type.	$x === 4	true

Operator	Name	Returns True If...	Example ($x Is 4)	Result
===	Non-equivalence	Left is equivalent to right, but they are not the same type.	`$x === "4"`	`false`
>	Greater than	Left is greater than right.	`$x > 4`	`false`
>=	Greater than or equal to	Left is greater than or equal to right.	`$x >= 4`	`true`
<	Less than	Left is less than right.	`$x < 4`	`false`
<=	Less than or equal to	Left is less than or equal to right.	`$x <= 4`	`true`

These operators are most commonly used with integers or doubles, although the equivalence operator is also used to compare strings. Be very sure to understand the difference between the `==` and `=` operators. The `==` operator tests equivalence, whereas the `=` operator assigns value. Also, remember that `===` tests equivalence with regard to both value and type.

Creating Complex Test Expressions with the Logical Operators

Logical operators test combinations of Boolean values. For example, the `or` operator, which is indicated by two pipe characters (| |) or simply the word `or`, returns the Boolean value `true` if either the left or the right operand is true:

```
true || false
```

This expression returns `true`.

The `and` operator, which is indicated by two ampersand characters (`&&`) or simply the word `and`, returns the Boolean value `true` only if both the left and right operands are true:

```
true && false
```

This expression returns the Boolean value `false`. It's unlikely that you will use a logical operator to test Boolean constants because it makes more sense to test two or more expressions that resolve to a Boolean. For example

```
($x > 2) && ($x < 15)
```

returns the Boolean value `true` if $x contains a value that is greater than 2 and smaller than 15. Parentheses are used when comparing expressions to make the code easier to read and to indicate the precedence of expression evaluation. Table 18.5 lists the logical operators.

TABLE 18.5 Logical operators

Operator	Name	Returns True If...	Example	Result
`||`	Or	Left or right is true.	`true || false`	`true`
`or`	Or	Left or right is true.	`true or false`	`true`
`xor`	Xor	Left or right is true, but not both.	`true xor true`	`false`
`&&`	And	Left and right are true.	`true && false`	`false`
`and`	And	Left and right are true.	`true and false`	`false`
`!`	Not	The single operand is not true.	`! true`	`false`

You might wonder why are there two versions of both the or and the and operators, and that's a good question. The answer lies in operator precedence, which we examine next.

Operator Precedence

When you use an operator within an expression, the PHP engine usually reads your expression from left to right. For complex expressions that use more than one operator, though, the PHP engine could be led astray without some guidance. First, consider a simple case:

`1 | 5`

There's no room for confusion here; PHP simply adds 4 to 5. But what about the following fragment, with two operators:

`4 + 5 * 2`

This presents a problem. Should PHP find the sum of 4 and 5, and then multiply it by 2, providing the result 18? Or does it mean 4 plus the result of 5 multiplied by 2, resolving to 14? If you were simply to read from left to right, the former would be true. However, PHP attaches different precedence to different operators, and because the multiplication operator has higher precedence than the addition operator, the second solution to the problem is the correct one: 4 plus the result of 5 multiplied by 2.

However, you can override operator precedence by putting parentheses around your expressions. In the following fragment, the addition expression is evaluated before the multiplication expression:

`(4 + 5) * 2`

Whatever the precedence of the operators in a complex expression, it is a good idea to use parentheses to make your code clearer and to save you from bugs such as applying sales tax to the wrong subtotal in a shopping cart situation. The following is a list of the operators covered in this section, in precedence order (those with the highest precedence listed first):

```
++,  --, (cast)
/, *, %
+, -
<, <=, =>, >
==, ===, !=
&&
||
=, +=, -=, /=, *=, %=, .=
and
xor
or
```

As you can see, `or` has a lower precedence than `||`, and `and` has a lower precedence than `&&`, so you can use the lower-precedence logical operators to change the way a complex test expression is read.

The order of precedence is the only reason that both `&&` and `and` are available in PHP. The same is true of `||` and `or`. In most circumstances, the use of parentheses makes for clearer code and fewer bugs than code that takes advantage of the difference in precedence of these operators.

Constants

Variables offer a flexible way of storing data because you can change their values and the type of data they store at any time during the execution of your scripts. However, if you want to work with a value that must remain unchanged throughout your script's execution, you can define and use a *constant*. You must use PHP's built-in `define()` function to create a constant, which subsequently cannot be changed unless you specifically `define()` it again. To use the `define()` function, place the name of the constant and the value you want to give it within parentheses and separated by a comma:

```
define("YOUR_CONSTANT_NAME", 42);
```

The value you want to set can be a number, a string, or a Boolean. By convention, the name of the constant should be in capital letters. Constants are accessed with the constant name only; no dollar symbol is required.

PHP automatically provides some built-in constants for you. For example, the constant __FILE__ returns the name of the file that the PHP engine is currently reading. The constant __LINE__ returns the current line number of the file. These are but two examples of what are called "magic constants," because they are not statically predefined and instead change depending on the context in which they are used. For a complete list, see www.php.net/manual/en/language.constants.predefined.php.

Using and Creating Functions in PHP

A *function* is a self-contained block of code that can be called by your scripts. When called, the function's code is executed and performs a particular task. You can pass values to a function, which then uses the values appropriately—storing them, transforming them, displaying them, whatever the function is told to do. When finished, a function can also pass a value back to the original code that called it into action.

Functions come in two flavors: those built in to the language and those you define yourself.

Using Built-in Functions

PHP has hundreds of built-in functions, ranging from simple string manipulation to mathematical operations to database interactions, and many, many things in between. To get a feel for the functions that PHP includes, browse the list in the online function reference at www.php.net/manual/en/funcref.php.

Using built-in functions in your scripts is often as simple as typing the function name and passing an argument to it. For example, take a look at the following snippet:

```
strtoupper("Hello Web!");
```

This example calls the built-in strtoupper() function, passing it the string "Hello Web!". The function then goes about its business of changing the contents of the string to uppercase letters.

A function call consists of the function name (strtoupper in this case) followed by parentheses. If you want to pass information to the function, you place it between these parentheses. A piece of information passed to a function in this way is called an *argument*. Some functions require that more than one argument be passed to them, separated by commas:

```
some_function($an_argument, $another_argument);
```

strtoupper() is typical for a PHP function in that it returns a value. Most functions return some information back after they've completed their task; they usually at least tell whether their mission was successful. strtoupper() returns a string value, so its usage requires the presence of a variable to accept the new string, such as the following:

```
$new_string = strtoupper("Hello Web!");
```

You may now use $new_string in your code, such as to print it to the screen:

```
echo $new_string;
```

This code results in the following text on the screen:

```
HELLO WEB!
```

You can call user-defined functions in exactly the same way that we have been calling built-in functions.

Defining a Function

You can define your own functions using the `function` statement:

```
function some_function($argument1, $argument2)
{
    //function code here
}
```

The name of the function follows the `function` statement and precedes a set of parentheses. If your function requires arguments, you must place comma-separated variable names within the parentheses. These variables are filled by the values passed to your function. Even if your function doesn't require arguments, you must nevertheless supply the parentheses.

NOTE

The naming rules for functions are similar to the naming rules for variables earlier in this hour. Names cannot include spaces, and they must begin with a letter or an underscore. As with variables, your function names should be meaningful and consistent in style. The capitalization of function names is one such stylistic touch you can add to your code; using mixed case in names, such as `MyFunction()` or `handleSomeDifficultTask()`, makes your code much easier to read. You may hear this naming convention referred to as CamelCase or lower CamelCase, depending on whether the first character is capitalized.

Listing 18.5 declares and calls a function of your own making.

LISTING 18.5   Declaring and calling a function

```php
<?php
function bighello()
{
    echo "<h1>HELLO!</h1>";
}
bighello();
?>
```

The script in Listing 18.5 simply outputs the string `"HELLO!"` wrapped in an HTML `<h1>` element.

Listing 18.5 declares a function, `bighello()`, that requires no arguments. Because of this, the parentheses are left empty. Although `bighello()` is a working function, it is not terribly useful. Listing 18.6 creates a function that requires an argument and actually does something with it.

LISTING 18.6   Declaring a function that requires an argument

```php
<?php
function printBR($txt)
{
    echo $txt."<br/>";
}
printBR("This is a line.");
printBR("This is a new line.");
printBR("This is yet another line.");
?>
```

NOTE

Unlike variable names, function names are not case sensitive. In Listing 18.6, the `printBR()` function could have been called as `printbr()`, `PRINTBR()`, or any combination thereof, with success.

The output of this script is three lines of text with HTML linebreaks after each line, which would not automatically be there otherwise.

Returning Values from User-Defined Functions

The previous example output an amended string to the browser through the use of the `printBR()` function. Sometimes, however, you will want a function to provide a value that you can work with yourself. If your function has transformed a string that you have provided, you might want to get the amended string back so that you can pass it to other functions. A function can return a value using the `return` statement in conjunction with a value. The `return` statement stops the execution of the function and sends the value back to the calling code.

Listing 18.7 creates a function that returns the sum of two numbers.

LISTING 18.7   A function that returns a value

```php
<?php
function addNums($firstnum, $secondnum)
{
    $result = $firstnum + $secondnum;
    return $result;
}
echo addNums(3,5);
//will print "8"
?>
```

The `return` statement can return a value or nothing at all. How you arrive at a value passed by `return` can vary. The value can be hard-coded:

```
return 4;
```

It can be the result of an expression:

```
return $a/$b;
```

It can be the value returned by yet another function call:

```
return another_function($an_argument);
```

Variable Scope in Functions

A variable declared within a function remains local to that function. In other words, it is not available outside the function or within other functions. In larger projects, this can save you from accidentally overwriting the contents of a variable when you declare two variables with the same name in separate functions.

From within one function, you cannot (by default) access a variable defined in another function or elsewhere in the script. Within a function, if you attempt to use a variable with the same name, you will only set or access a local variable. Let's put this to the test in Listing 18.8.

LISTING 18.8   Variables defined outside functions are inaccessible from within a function by default.

```
<?php
$life = 42;
function meaningOfLife()
{
    echo "The meaning of life is ".$life;
}
meaningOfLife();
?>
```

If you run this script, the output will be:

```
The meaning of life is
```

As you might expect, the `meaningOfLife()` function does not have access to the `$life` variable in line 2; `$life` is empty when the function attempts to print it. On the whole, this is a good thing because it saves you from potential clashes between identically named variables, and a function can always demand an argument if it needs information about the outside world.

Occasionally, you might want to access an important variable from within a function without passing it in as an argument. This is where the `global` statement comes into play. Listing 18.9 uses `global` to restore order to the universe.

LISTING 18.9   Accessing global variables with the `global` statement

```php
<?php
$life=42;
function meaningOfLife()
{
   global $life;
   echo "The meaning of life is ".$life;
}
meaningOfLife();
?>
```

If you run this script now, the output will be:

```
The meaning of life is 42
```

When you place the `global` statement in front of the `$life` variable when it is declared in the `meaningOfLife()` function (line 5), it refers to the `$life` variable declared outside the function (line 2).

You need to use the `global` statement within every function that needs to access a particular named global variable. Be careful, though: If you manipulate the contents of the variable within the function, the value of the variable changes for the script as a whole.

You can declare more than one variable at a time with the `global` statement by simply separating each of the variables you want to access with commas:

```
global $var1, $var2, $var3;
```

CAUTION

Usually, an argument is a copy of whatever value is passed by the calling code; changing it in a function has no effect beyond the function block. Changing a global variable within a function, however, changes the original and not a copy. Use the `global` statement carefully.

Working with Objects in PHP

Programmers use objects to store and organize data. Object-oriented programming (OOP) is a type of programming in which the structure of the program (or application) is designed around these objects and their relationships and interactions. OOP structures are found in many programming languages, and are also evident in PHP. In fact, many PHP programmers—especially those coming from a highly OOP background—choose to develop PHP applications in an object-oriented way.

However, in PHP, it is not required that you write your scripts in an object-oriented manner. Many PHP scripts are procedural and functional rather than object-oriented. That is to say, the emphasis is on stepping through the use of variables, data and control structures, and subroutines and functions in the course of creating a program. Regardless of which method you choose for writing your PHP scripts, it's important to understand a little bit about objects in PHP.

Creating an Object

Although it's easy to visualize a scalar variable, such as $color, with a value of red, some people have a difficult time visualizing objects. For now, try to think of an object as a little box with inputs and outputs on either side of it. The input mechanisms are *methods*, and methods have properties. Throughout this section, we look at how classes, methods, and properties work together to produce various outputs.

An object exists in a structure called a *class*. In each class, you define a set of characteristics. For example, suppose you have created an automobile class. In the automobile class, you might have color, make, and model characteristics. Each automobile object uses all the characteristics, but each object initializes the characteristics to different values, such as silver, Mazda, and Protege5, or red, Porsche, and Boxster.

The whole purpose of using objects is to create reusable code. Because classes are so tightly structured but self-contained and independent of one another, you can reuse them from one application to another. For example, suppose that you write a text-formatting class for one project and decide you can use that class in another project. Because a class is just a set of characteristics, you can pick up the code and use it in the second project, reaching into it with methods specific to the second application but using the inner workings of the existing code to achieve new results.

Creating an object is simple; you just declare it to be in existence:

```
class myClass {
    //code will go here
}
```

Now that you have a class, you can create a new instance of an object:

```
$object1 = new myClass();
```

In Listing 18.10, you have proof that your object exists, even though there's nothing in it—it's just been named.

LISTING 18.10   Proof that your object exists

```php
<?php
class myClass {
    //code will go here
}
$object1 = new myClass();
echo "\$object1 is an ".gettype($object1).".<br/>";

if (is_object($object1)) {
    echo "Really! I swear \$object1 is an object!";
}
?>
```

The output of this script is:

```
$object1 is an object.
Really! I swear $object1 is an object!
```

This is not a particularly useful class because it does absolutely nothing, but it is valid and shows you how the class template works in lines 2 to 5. Lines 8 to 10 use the is_object() function to test whether something is an object; in this case, the *something* is $object1. Because the test of is_object() evaluates to true, the string within the if statement is printed to the screen.

Properties of Objects

The variables declared inside an object are called *properties*. It is standard practice to declare your variables at the top of the class. These properties can be values, arrays, or even other objects. The following snippet uses simple scalar variables inside the class, prefaced with the public keyword:

```php
class myCar {
    public $color = "silver";
    public $make = "Mazda";
    public $model = "Protege5";
}
```

NOTE

If you use the keyword public, protected, or private before the variable name, you can indicate if the class member (the variable) can be accessed everywhere (public), within the class itself or a parent class or an inherited class (protected), or only by the class itself (private).

Now when you create a myCar object, it will always have those three properties. Listing 18.11 shows you how to access properties after they have been declared and values have been assigned to them.

LISTING 18.11   Showing object properties

```php
<?php
class myCar {
    public $color = "silver";
    public $make = "Mazda";
    public $model = "Protege5";
}
$car = new myCar();
echo "I drive a: ".$car -> color." ".$car -> make." ".$car -> model;
?>
```

The output of this script is:

```
I drive a: silver Mazda Protege5
```

Object Methods

Methods add functionality to your objects. No longer will your objects just sit there, holding on to their properties for dear life—they'll actually do something! Listing 18.12 shows just that.

LISTING 18.12   A class with a method

```php
<?php
class myClass {
   function sayHello() {
      echo "HELLO!";
   }
}
$object1 = new myClass();
$object1 -> sayHello();
?>
```

Running this code will produce the following:

```
HELLO!
```

A method looks and acts like a normal function but is defined within the framework of a class. The -> operator is used to call the object method in the context of your script. Had there been any variables stored in the object, the method would have been capable of accessing them for its own purposes, as illustrated in Listing 18.13.

LISTING 18.13   Accessing class properties within a method

```php
<?php
class myClass {
   public$name = "John";
```

```
    function sayHello() {
        echo "HELLO! My name is ".$this->name;
    }
}
$object1 = new myClass();
$object1 -> sayHello();
?>
```

Running this code will produce the following:

```
HELLO! My name is John
```

The special variable $this is used to refer to the currently instantiated object as you see on line 5. Anytime an object refers to itself, you must use the $this variable. Using the $this variable in conjunction with the -> operator enables you to access any property or method in a class, within the class itself.

Common Uses of PHP

Because PHP is relatively simple to work with and has a low barrier to entry—since the vast majority of web-hosting providers offer PHP support—you can imagine that web application developers use PHP in many different ways. That's one reason that PHP contains hundreds of built-in functions grouped together into many different categories (see www.php.net/manual/en/funcref.php): When it comes to working with strings, dates, files, images, databases, and everything in between, there aren't a lot of basic functions that are unique, so the language just includes a lot of these functions right out of the box.

What you *do* with these functions may be unique, but as a general purpose scripting language, PHP tries to cover all the bases so you can just get down to the business of scripting with built-in functions rather than reinventing the wheel. This feature of PHP is also one reason it has detractors—some people think the language contains too much built-in functionality and is too forgiving (for example, PHP allows developers to "get away with" too many imperfections in the code, where scripts in other languages would simply error and fail). While this and other points about the overall value of the language are debatable, that PHP is widely used *cannot* be debated. Following are some of the ways in which PHP is used by developers every day:

- ▶ **Processing form data**—As mentioned earlier in this lesson, PHP includes superglobal variables that hold all the values sent in an HTML form. Using either the $_POST or $_GET superglobal, you have at your fingertips all the information you need from a user to then manipulate it as necessary. That manipulation can come through text processing (see www.php.net/manual/en/book.strings.php), performing mathematical functions (see www.php.net/manual/en/book.math.php), or just sending an email (see www.php.net/manual/en/book.mail.php), among many, many other functions.

▶ **Setting and reading cookies and user sessions**—The primary way to track a user through your application is to set and maintain cookies that store pieces of data in the browser and are accessed and used by the application. PHP has built-in functions for handling both cookies (see www.php.net/manual/en/features.cookies.php) and user sessions (see www.php.net/manual/en/book.session.php).

▶ **Interacting with databases**—It would be difficult for you to come up with a database product that PHP cannot access. Whether through an abstraction layer or through vendor specific database functions, you can use PHP to put or retrieve data from your database and your application's custom database schema (see www.php.net/manual/en/refs.database.php).

If you look at these three points, you might think "that's all?" But think for a moment about how web applications are put together. Typically, you perform one of four operations when interacting with a web application and its underlying data: creating, reading, updating, and deleting (commonly referred to as CRUD operations). When creating, updating, and deleting data, you typically interact with a database through some sort of form action, which may or may not include custom string input. When reading information, you are also interacting with a database to retrieve that information, and thus the strings likely have some sort of manipulation happening between their raw state in the database and what you see on your screen.

PHP is a powerful general purpose scripting language that contains multitudes of useful functions. Some may argue that the most complicated aspect of using PHP is not the tactical application of the language itself, but instead it is in deciding which of the many approaches and functions are best suited to solving any given problem.

Summary

This brief lesson has not made you an expert in PHP—like anything, that takes thousands of hours of practice. But what you should now have is a solid understanding of the fundamentals of the PHP language and how it could be used to solve basic programming problems, especially in web application development.

Continue to practice with the variables, data types, logical structures, and built-in functions that PHP offers you, and create functions of your own that provide unique solutions. To learn a *lot* more about the PHP language and how to develop PHP-based applications using the MySQL database, take a look at *Sams Teach Yourself PHP, MySQL, and Apache All-in-One, 5th edition*.

Q&A

Q. **What editors should I avoid when creating PHP code?**

A. Any plaintext editor will do. Do not use word processors that format text for printing (Microsoft Word, for example). Even if you save files created using this type of editor in plain-text format, hidden characters are likely to creep into your code.

Q. **Should I learn the operator precedence table, or memorize *any* of the intricate details of the PHP language?**

A. There is no reason you shouldn't memorize the operator precedence table, but I would save the effort for more useful tasks. By using parentheses in your expressions, you can make your code easy to read while defining your own order of precedence. As for memorizing *any* of the details of the PHP language, I would recommend knowing the basics about variables, data types, operators, and logical structures, and over time you will begin to remember the syntax of the functions you use frequently. As with all new languages (programming or otherwise), repetition and practice will make the knowledge stick, but you always have the PHP Manual online at www.php.net should you need to refer to it.

Workshop

The quiz questions and exercises are provided for your further understanding.

Quiz

1. What are the standard opening and closing tags used in PHP scripts?

2. Which of the following statements contains an operator?

```
4;
is_int(44);
5/12;
```

3. Which of the following variable names are not valid and why?

```
$a_value_submitted_by_a_user
$666666xyz
$xyz666666
$_____counter_____
$the first
$file-name
```

4. True or false: If a function doesn't require an argument, you can omit the parentheses in the function call.

5. What is output of the following PHP code?

```
<?php
$number = 50;

function tenTimes() {
    global $number;
    $number = $number * 10;
}
tenTimes();
echo $number;
?>
```

6. Create a `while` statement that increments through and prints every odd number between 1 and 49 with an HTML line break after each.

7. Convert the answer from question 5 into a `for` statement that does the same.

8. When creating a function of your own design, what is the limit to the number of arguments you can pass?

9. How can you ensure that a variable is accessible by multiple functions?

10. Which PHP superglobal variable would you use to extract form values sent via the `POST` method?

Answers

1. `<?php` and `?>`

2. The statement `5/12;` contains a division operator.

3. The variable name `$666666xyz` is not valid because it does not begin with a letter or an underscore character. The variable name `$the first` is not valid because it contains a space. `$file-name` is also invalid because it contains a nonalphanumeric character (`-`).

4. False. You must always include the parentheses in your function calls, whether or not you are passing arguments to the function.

5. 500

6.
```
$num = 1;
while ($num <= 49) {
    echo $num."<br />";
    $num += 2;
}
```

7.
```
for ($num = 1; $num <= 49; $num += 2) {
    echo $num."<br />";
}
```

8. There is no limit to the number of arguments you can pass, but you might want to limit the number to a handful, for your own sanity and ease of maintenance.

9. Declare it as a global variable.

10. `$_POST`

Programming with C and C++

C is one of those programming languages that most programmers never predicted would take off. Designed as a highly efficient, somewhat cryptic language used to write an operating system named *UNIX*, C is a language designed by systems programmers. In the late 1980s, the same decade after its primary release, virtually every program on the store shelves was written in C. C, followed by its successor C++, quickly replaced the popular Pascal language in the 1980s and despite a much broader set of programming languages available today for different development jobs, C and C++ still remain viable programming choices. C's impact on the programming world cannot be stressed enough.

C++ is considered by many to be a better language than C. C++ offers full support for object-oriented programming (OOP). Whereas you work with objects in Visual Basic, the Visual Basic language is not a true OOP language. You'll learn in this hour how and why C++ provides strong OOP support and how the mechanics of C++ provide for more flexible, maintainable, and efficient programming than its predecessor, C.

The highlights of this hour include

- ▶ Understanding why C is so efficient
- ▶ Recognizing C commands and operators
- ▶ Outputting with C's printf() function
- ▶ Using C++ to build on C programming skills
- ▶ Using C++ classes
- ▶ Using inheritance to decrease programming time

Introducing C

C is highly efficient and C's developers required that efficiency because until C, programmers used *assembly language*, a language just above the machine language level, to write operating systems. Only assembly language had the efficiency needed for systems programs. C brought the advantage of a higher level language to the table when developers used C for operating systems. Along with the efficiency of a low-level language, C has the high-level-language advantage of being more maintainable and programmers were more easily able to update the operating system and produce accurate code. Assembly language doesn't lend itself very well to proper program maintenance.

To achieve its efficiency, C does have one drawback that other high-level languages don't: C is more cryptic than most other programming languages. Its cryptic nature comes in the form of a huge collection of operators and a small number of keywords. Table 19.1 lists C's keywords. In the standard C language, there are only 32 keywords, which is an extremely small number compared to other languages, such as Java and PHP.

TABLE 19.1   32 supported C command keywords

auto	double	int	struct
break	else	long	switch
case	enum	register	typedef
char	extern	return	union
const	float	short	unsigned
continue	for	signed	void
default	goto	sizeof	volatile
do	if	static	while

CAUTION

Notice that C's keywords all appear in lowercase. C's built-in functions also require lowercase names. C is *case sensitive* so if you use an uppercase letter anywhere inside a keyword or function, your program will not compile properly.

You should recognize some of C's commands because the JavaScript language that you learned about at the beginning of this tutorial borrows heavily from C and C++.

C has more operators than any other programming language, with the exception of the scientific APL language that is rarely, if ever, used anymore. Of course, languages derived from C, such as Java and C++, often have as many or more operators than C. Because you have already studied Java, you understand many of C's operators.

What You Need for C and C++ Programming

To program in C, you need a C compiler. Almost any C compiler you use today is a C++ compiler as well. Therefore, you get two languages for one, although C++ is really just an extension of the C language. In the early days, you often needed to purchase a compiler, usually from Borland or Microsoft. Now, there are a number of options available for free download. These are powerful packages that include an integrated development environment (IDE), compiler, debugger, and other helpful development tools.

If you plan on developing in multiple languages, including C (or C++), Microsoft's development tools can be an excellent choice, as the IDE for C/C++ is similar to the one for Visual Basic and other .NET languages. Remember that developers created Visual Basic from the beginning to be a Windows programming system. C, on the other hand, began in the world of text-based computers. Therefore, nothing is embedded in the C or C++ programming languages to support a graphical interface.

Looking at C

TRY IT YOURSELF ▼

Listing 19.1 contains a short but complete C program.

LISTING 19.1   C is cryptic and requires several elements that other languages do not.

```
/* Prints a message on the screen */
#include <stdio.h>
main()
{
   printf("C is efficient.\n");
   return 0;
}
```

If you were to enter the program in Listing 19.1 in your C compiler's editor, compile the program, and run it, you would see this message on the screen:

```
C is efficient.
```

You can test this program using Visual C++ or any of the many C and C++ compilers available from the Internet.

The program required seven lines to output one simple sentence—and they say C is a more efficient language! Actually, C is an efficient language, but it will take you getting into C and writing more complex programs to really take advantage of the power of C; the language was written by programmers for programmers. With C's compiled efficiency and power comes the responsibility to master the language and all its nuances.

Listing 19.1 contains three sets of grouping symbols: angled brackets, <>, braces, {}, and parentheses, (). Be extremely careful when typing a C program because the correct and exact symbol is important. C doesn't handle ambiguity very well, so if you type the wrong symbol, C won't work properly.

Using the `main()` Function's Format

The cornerstone of every C program is the `main()` function. Because `main()` is a function and not a command, the parentheses after are required. A C function, just like a JavaScript function, is a section of code that does something. The `main()` function is required because execution of a C program always begins in its `main()` function. Programmers use `main()` to control the rest of the program. The `main()` function often includes a series of procedure calls.

The actual code for `main()`, as with all C functions (except the built-in functions whose code you never see), begins after the opening brace, {, and `main()` continues until the closing brace, }, where `main()` terminates and other functions often begin. Other sets of braces, always in pairs, may appear within a function such as `main()` as well.

As in JavaScript, many of C's (and C++'s) statements end with a semicolon (;). The more you work with C, the better you'll learn which statements require the semicolon and which don't. Full statements require the semicolon. In Listing 19.1, the line with `main()` doesn't require a semicolon because `main()` doesn't terminate until the final closing brace in the last line. The brace requires no semicolon because it is a grouping character and does nothing on its own.

NOTE

The next few sections concentrate on the fundamental C language but the material is applicable to C++ also. C++'s strength over C is its ability for OOP as you'll see later in this hour.

Using the `#include` Statement

You'll never see `#include` in a list of C commands because `#include` is not a C command. Statements in a C program that begin with the pound sign are called *preprocessor directives*. The compiler analyzes the directive and, instead of compiling the statement, acts upon the statement immediately during compilation.

The #include preprocessor directive tells the compiler to insert another file that resides in source code form at the location in the program where the directive resides. Therefore, before the program is actually compiled, more code is inserted, at the programmer's request, at the place where #include occurs. That code is compiled along with the programmer's code.

The stdio.h file is a source code auxiliary file that helps a C program perform input/output (I/O) properly. C files that end with the .H extension are called *header files* as opposed to C program source code files that end with the .C filename extension. All C programs perform some kind of I/O, and the most common header file used to help C with its I/O is stdio.h. As you learn more about C, you'll learn additional header files that can be helpful, such as the time.h header file that includes definitions that help with time and date conversions.

C Data

C supports data formats that work much like Java's data formats. For example, C supports the following kinds of data:

- ▶ Character

- ▶ Integer

- ▶ Floating point (decimal numbers)

C supports several types of integers and floating-point data such as long and short integers as well as single-precision and double-precision floating-point decimal data.

Unlike Java, C does *not* support a string data type. Although C has some built-in functionality to handle strings in some situations, generally the C language leaves it to the programmer and functions to handle strings. C doesn't support an intrinsic string data type. Therefore, the only text-based data type that C supports is a single character.

NOTE
_____

The fact that C doesn't include support for a built-in string data type isn't a huge problem because ample built-in functions are available in the language to work with string data. Also, C does allow for string *literals*, such as strings that you type directly in the code, just not string variables. Unlike Java, however, string data is not inherently supported in the fundamental language, which sometimes makes for some interesting programming.
_____

Listing 19.1 included a string literal as well. String literals (remember there is no string variable) are always enclosed in quotation marks. Therefore, the following are string literals:

```
"C is efficient"

"3"

"443-55-9999"
```

TIP

> **TIP**
>
> Given the cryptic nature of C, you should add comments to your code as much as possible. You will need the comments when you later make changes to the program. You'll be happy to know that the style of comments used in C is exactly the same as in JavaScript—enclose comments between /* and */ or preceded by // as shown in the statements below:
>
> ```
>     /* Ask how old the user is */
>     printf("How old are you? "); // Ask for the age
>     scanf(" %d", &age);    /* Ampersand required */
> ```

When you declare variables in C, you need to be more specific of the type of variable you need than in JavaScript. Consider the following section of a `main()` function:

```
main()
{
   char initial;
   int age;
   float amount;
...// more code here

}
```

This code declares three variables, `initial`, `age`, and `amount`. They hold three different types of data: a character, an integer, and a floating-point value. These variables are local to the function and cannot be used outside `main()`. (You can declare variables before `main()` and those variables would be global to the whole program, but global variables are not recommended, as you already know.)

The assignment statement works just as it does in JavaScript. You can initialize variables like this:

```
initial = 'G';
age = 21;
amount = 6.75;
```

C Functions

C is built on a foundation of functions—both those functions that you write and the functions supplied by C. The next two sections should help you understand the nature of C functions.

Using Built-In Functions

Unlike just about every other programming language in the world, C has *no* input or output statements. Look through Table 19.1 once more. You don't see a print statement or anything else that might be considered an I/O statement.

C performs all its I/O through functions that your C compiler provides. By letting the compiler makers implement I/O in functions, the C language is highly *portable*, meaning that a C program that runs on one kind of computer should run on any other computer that is capable of running C programs. A C program written for a Macintosh will work on a PC without change, assuming that you compile the program using each computer's own C compiler.

The printf() Output Function

The most common I/O function is the printf() function. printf() outputs data to the screen in most cases (although the programmer can route the output to other devices, if needed, through operating system options). Here is the format for printf():

```
printf(controlString [, data]);
```

The controlString determines how the output will look. The controlString will format any data values that you specify (separated by commas if more than one value is output) in the data area. Consider the following printf():

```
printf("Read a lot");
```

This printf() doesn't include a data list of any kind. The controlString is the only argument to this printf(). When you use a string of text for the controlString value, C outputs the text directly to the screen. Therefore, the printf() produces this onscreen when the user runs the program:

```
Read a lot
```

CAUTION

Just like JavaScript, remember to use the \n character if you want output to force the cursor to the next line. If the previous printf() was followed by this printf():

```
    printf("Keep learning");
```

the output would look like this:

```
    Read a lotKeep learning
```

Obviously, the second printf() should have used the \n character like this:

```
    printf("Keep learning\n");
```

With \n, subsequent printf() output would appear on the next line.

When you print numbers and characters, you must tell C exactly how to print them. You indicate the format of numbers with *conversion characters* that format data. The conversion characters format data in functions such as printf() (see Table 19.2).

TABLE 19.2   C's most-used conversion characters

Control Character	Description
%d	Integer
%f	Floating point
%c	Character
%s	String

When you want to print a value inside a string, insert the appropriate conversion characters in the *controlstring*. Then, to the right of the *controlstring*, list the value you want printed. Figure 19.1 shows how a printf() can print three numbers—an integer, a floating-point value, and another integer.

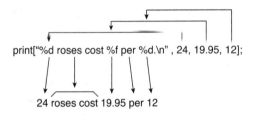

print["%d roses cost %f per %d.\n" , 24, 19.95, 12];

24 roses cost 19.95 per 12

FIGURE 19.1
Conversion characters determine how and where the output appears.

Strings and characters have their own conversion characters as well. You don't need %s to print strings by themselves because strings included inside the *controlstring* that don't have the formatting percent sign before them print exactly as you type them. Nevertheless, you might need to use %s when combining strings with other data.

The next printf() prints a different type of data value using each of the conversion characters from Table 19.2:

```
print("%s %d %f %c\n", "Sams", 14, -8.76, 'X');
```

This printf() produces this:

```
Sams 14 -8.760000 X
```

The string Sams needs quotation marks, as do all string literals, and the character X needs single quote marks, as do all characters. C formats the floating-point numbers with full precision, hence the four zeros at the end of the value. You can limit the number of places printed by using format specifiers. If the printf()'s conversion characters for the floating-point number had been %5.2, the -8.76 would have been output in five spaces, with two of those five spaces used for the decimal portion. Therefore, the following printf()

```
printf("%s %d %f %c\n", "Sams", 14, -8.76, 'X');
```

would yield this output:

```
Sams 14 -8.76 X
```

Working with Strings

Although C doesn't support string variables, there is a way to store strings. C represents all strings with a null zero character at the end of the string. This null zero has an ASCII value of zero. When C encounters the null zero, the end of the string is reached. You never see this null zero on a string, but it is there, internally, at the closing quotation mark. You never add the null zero; C adds it.

If a string includes a 0 as part of its text, such as the following address: "190 S. Oak Road", the embedded zero is not the null zero because the embedded zero is a regular ASCII character for zero (ASCII number 48).

Figure 19.2 shows how the string "Sams" is stored in memory as a string. The \0 character is C's representation for the null string. The length of a string includes the characters within the string but never includes the null zero.

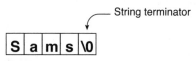

Memory

FIGURE 19.2
Strings always terminate with a null zero character.

C uses a character array to hold strings, including the string's null zero. All of C's data types can appear in their own arrays, but when a character array appears and a null zero is included at the end of the data, C treats that character array just like a string. C uses brackets instead of parentheses for array subscripts. To define a character array that will hold a ten-character string, you could declare the following array:

```
char month[10];   /* Defines a character array */
```

The month array can hold ten individual characters or a string if the string includes the null zero. Always leave room for the null zero in the array. C uses zero-based arrays, so month can hold a ten-character string in elements 0 through 9 and the null zero in element 10. You can initialize a string when you define the array like this:

```
char month[10] = "September"; /* Declare and initialize the string */
```

You can also assign the array at runtime using a special `strcpy()` function like this:

```
strcpy(month, "September");  /* Assigns September to the month array */
```

To use `strcpy()`, you must include the header file named string.h in the same area of the program where you include stdio.h.

CAUTION

The only data `printf()` doesn't format is string data. Therefore, if you use `printf()` to print anything other than a single string, you must supply a conversion code.

The `scanf()` Input Function

Getting keyboard input is much more difficult than producing output on the screen. Use `scanf()` to accept keyboard input. `scanf()` is fairly simple now that you understand `printf()` but `scanf()` does behave strangely at times. Here is the format for `scanf()`:

```
scanf(controlString [, data]);
```

Understand the following rule and `scanf()` should work for you every time:

> Prefix each variable inside the `scanf()` with an ampersand unless that variable is an array.

Therefore, the following `scanf()` gets an age value entered by the user:

```
scanf(" %d", &Age);
```

CAUTION

Do you see the blank before the `%d` in `scanf()`'s *controlString*? Always include the blank because the input of values works better with the blank.

The following `scanf()` gets the user's first name into a character array as a result of the user following the prompting `printf()`:

```
printf("What is your first name? ");
scanf(" %s", name);  /* Get the name */
```

The `scanf()` function is a mirror-image function to `printf()`. Often, you will write programs that ask the user for values with a `printf()` and get those values with `scanf()`. When your program gets to `scanf()`, C stops and waits for the user to type values. The variables listed inside `scanf()` (following the *controlString* argument) will accept whatever the user types and `scanf()` quits receiving input when the user presses Enter.

CAUTION

When the user types a space, `scanf()` also stops getting input! Therefore, `scanf()` is good for getting only one word at a time in a string.

Despite its problems, `scanf()` is useful to learn early in your C tutorial so you can practice getting user input. There are many other ways to get user input in C and C++, and often they work better than `scanf()`, but `scanf()`'s similarity to the simpler `printf()` makes `scanf()` an acceptable keyboard-input function for beginners.

TRY IT YOURSELF ▼

The program in Listing 19.2 shows a complete program that prompts for user input and gets output. You can study the program to gain a better understanding of the material you've covered so far in this lesson.

LISTING 19.2 Use `scanf()` and `printf()` for input and output.

```
#include <stdio.h>
main()
{
  int age;
  float weight;
  char first[15], last[15];  /* 2 char arrays */

  printf("\nWhat is your first name? ");
  scanf(" %s", first);  /* No ampersand on char arrays */
  printf("What is your last name? ");
  scanf(" %s", last);

  printf("How old are you? ");
  scanf(" %d", &age);     /* Ampersand required */
  printf("How much do you weigh? ");
  scanf(" %f", &weight); /* Ampersand required */

  printf("\nHere is the information you entered:\n");
  printf("Name: %s %s\n", first, last);
```

▼
```
printf("Weight: %3.0f\n", weight);
printf("Age: %d", age);
return 0;  /* Always best to do this */
}
```

Here is a sample execution of Listing 19.2:

```
What is your first name? Joe
What is your last name? Harrison
How old are you? 41
How much do you weigh? 205

Here is the information you entered:
Name: Joe Harrison
Weight: 205
Age: 41
```

Writing General Program Functions

As with a JavaScript program's collection of functions and event procedures, C programs are modular and are comprised of many functions. Although you *can* put all of a C program's code in the main() function, main() was intended to be used as a controlling function for the rest of the program. Listing 19.3 illustrates the outline of a C program that has proper form.

LISTING 19.3 Use main() to control the rest of the program.

```
#include <stdio.h>
main()
{
  getNums();   /* Get a list of numbers */
  sortNums();  /* Sort the numbers */
  printNums(); /* Print the list */
  return 0;    /* End the program */
}
getNums()
{
  /* Body of function goes here
     that gets a list of values
     from the user */
}
sortNums()
{
  /* Body of function goes here
     that sorts the values */
}
```

```
printNums()
{
  /* Body of function goes here
     that prints the values */
}
```

The `main()` function is composed of a series of function calls to three separate procedures. (The code bodies of the procedures are not included in this example.) The `main()` function, and hence the entire running program, terminates when the `return 0;` statement is reached. The `return` often appears at the end of a function when the function is returning a value to the calling function. The `main()` function is returning a 0 to the operating system. Zero is a standard return value that the operating system can check.

C Operators

C's collection of operators matches those you learned in JavaScript. For example, the plus sign works exactly as it does in JavaScript. In addition, C supports the increment and decrement operators, `++` and `--`, that add and subtract one from whatever variable you apply them to. The following statements each add one to the variables a, b, and c:

```
a++;
b++;
c++;
```

The following statements decrease a, b, and c by one:

```
a--;
b--;
c--;
```

C Control Statements Mimic JavaScript

Actually, C came first (just not in this book), so it's accurate to state that JavaScript's control statements mimic those of C (and C++). For example, C supports an `if...else` statement such as this:

```
if (age < 18)
  { printf("You cannot vote yet\n");
    yrs = 18 - age;
    printf("You can vote in %d years.\n", yrs);
  }
else
  {
    printf("You can vote.\n");
  }
```

C also supports several kinds of looping statements that use the relational operators. For example, the following code shows a `while` loop that continues as long as the relational expression evaluates to `true`:

```
while (amount < 25)
  {
    printf("Amount is too small.\n");
    wrongVal++;    /* Keep track of number of problems */
    printf("Try again... What is the new amount? ");
    scanf(" %d", &amount);
  }
```

Learning C++

Much of a C++ program looks like pure C code, which it is. The C++ language introduces some new language elements, but the keywords and structure are similar to C. Most of C++'s change over C is a result of injecting OOP technology into C. The primary differences between C and C++ don't lie in commands and keyword differences but rather in how the language supports the use of objects.

C programs use the `.c` filename extension, and C++ programs use the `.cpp` filename extension. Not all C++ compilers support programming in the Windows environment, but most PC-based C++ compilers sold today do provide full Windows programming support, including the support for a visual interface such as a toolbox with controls, just as Visual Basic provides.

Object Terminology

You learned some about OOP in Part III, "Object-Oriented Programming with Java," earlier in this tutorial. OOP is laden with terminology that might seem daunting at first. The actual implementation of OOP is fairly easy to understand and with your quick introduction, you will already be somewhat acquainted with terms such as these:

- ▶ **Abstraction**—The internals of an object do not always have to be known by the programmer to use an object.

- ▶ **Class**—The definition of a related group of objects.

- ▶ **Inheritance**—The ability to create a new class of objects from an existing class. By inheriting a new class of objects, you can create new objects with new behaviors and characteristics based on existing objects and classes.

- ▶ **Message**—A command that acts on specific objects as opposed to the other language commands that are not tied to specific objects.

▶ **Object**—A collection of characteristics and behaviors, perhaps even two or more variables treated as a single unit, that appears in OOP programs.

▶ **Polymorphism**—A name given to the ability of different objects to respond differently to the same commands (called *messages*).

▶ **Reuse**—The ability of the language to utilize objects defined in other programs.

Fundamental Differences Between C and C++

Some of the new language features that C++ provides over C have nothing directly to do with OOP. The following sections preview some of the non-OOP language differences that you'll find between C and C++.

Name Differences

Some differences between C and C++ are simple changes. For example, instead of C's `#include <stdio.h>` directive, C++ programs almost always include the following directive:

```
#include <iostream>
```

As with the C header files, C++ programmers will include many other header files in addition to iostream.h, but iostream.h is the most commonly included file. iostream.h is the header file that defines basic input and output.

I/O Differences

C++ includes several new operators. The two most common C++ operators are >> for output (the *insertion* operator) and << (the *extraction* operator). These operators are usually combined with the two *stream objects* `cout` and `cin`. `cout` always represents an output device and defaults to the screen. `cin` always represents an input device and defaults to the keyboard. You can redirect `cout` and `cin` to other devices through the operating system and through compilers such as Visual C++ if you ever have the need. Your program considers these stream objects to be nothing more than a series of data values that are being input or output.

A few examples will quickly show you how to combine the insertion and the extraction operators with stream objects. The following statement sends a string and a number to the screen (typically the output stream goes to the screen although you can change that destination to a different device):

```
cout << "Here is the total: " << 1000.00;
```

If you want to write several lines of output, you can by embedding the newline character in the output stream. The following line

```
cout << "Line 1" << '\n' << "Line 2" << '\n' << "Line 3" << '\n';
```

produces this output:

```
Line 1
Line 2
Line 3
```

TIP

Generally, C++ programmers don't use the newline character, \n, at the end of a statement with cout. They use a special object called endl, which not only produces a newline character but also empties the output buffer if you send data to a device that buffers output, such as a printer. Therefore, the following statement would be more likely than the one shown before this tip:

```
cout << "Line 1" << '\n' << "Line 2" << '\n' << "Line 3" << endl;
```

C++ combines the cin input stream with the >> extraction object to support keyboard input. As with scanf(), keyboard-based input with C++ is fairly simple to understand and implement, but C++'s input capabilities are limited when you use cin >> just to start with a way to get keyboard input quickly. However, keep in mind that more advanced and better input methods exist that you will master if you pursue the C++ language.

To get a keyboard value into an integer variable named intAge, you could use the following:

```
cin >> intAge;
```

Of course, you would probably prompt the user first with a cout so the I/O would more likely look like this:

```
cout << "How old are you? ";
cin >> intAge;     // Get the age
```

Introducing C++ Objects

To declare a C++ object you first must declare a class. A class is not an object but rather a description of an object. The C++ language includes the class keyword that you use to define a class.

Consider the following class declaration:

```
class Person {
  char strLastName[25];
  int  intAge;
  float flSalary;
};
```

The class name is `Person`. The class is said to have three *members*. The member names are `strLastName`, `intAge`, and `flSalary`. This class, therefore, describes objects that contain three members. Individually, each member could be considered a separate variable, but taken together (and C++ will *always* consider the members to be part of the class) the members form the class. The members are not objects but parts of objects that you can define with this class.

CAUTION

Remember, a class is a description of an object but not the object itself. In a way, `int` is a keyword that defines a class; `int` is a data type that describes a type of numeric value or variable. Only after you define integer variables do you have an integer object.

Declaring Object Variables

C++, without your help, would have no idea what the `Person` class would be because `Person` is not some internal class native to C++. Therefore, the multilined `class` statement shown earlier tells C++ exactly what the class's characteristics are like. After you define the class, you then can declare variables, or, more accurately, objects of the class. The following statement declares a `Person` object called `Mike`:

```
Person Mike;    // Declares an instance of the Person class
```

Figure 19.3 shows what the object (or variable or instance of the class) looks like. The object named `Mike` is a three-part object. The characteristics are as follows: `Mike` is an object that begins with a 25-character array, followed by an integer, followed by a floating-point value.

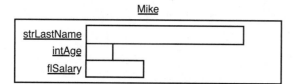

FIGURE 19.3
The object named `Mike` internally contains three members.

All `Person` objects that you declare from the `Person` class will look like `Mike`, but they will have different names just as integer variables in a program have different names. In addition, the objects will have local or global scope depending on where you declare them.

Generally, programmers place the `class` definition globally or even stored in a header file that they include in subsequent programs. After the `class` definition appears globally (such as before the `main()` procedure), any place in the rest of the program can declare object variables from the class. The variables might be global, but they will probably be local if the programmer follows the suggested standards and maintains only local variables to a procedure. As with any variables, you can pass object variables between procedures as needed.

Any place in the program can declare additional object variables. The following statement would declare three additional objects that take on the characteristics of the `Person` class:

```
Person Judy, Paul, Terry;
```

Accessing Members

You'll use the dot operator (a period) to access members in an object. For example, the following assignment stores a value in the `Mike` object's `intAge` member:

```
Mike.intAge = 32;   // Initialize the member named age
```

As long as you qualify the member name with the object name, C++ knows which object to assign to. Therefore, if several `Person` objects are declared in the program, the object name before the member informs the program exactly which object member you want to initialize. Anywhere you can use a variable, you can use a member name as long as you qualify the name with the object. For example, you cannot directly assign a string literal to a character array in C++ (or in C), but you can use the `strcpy()` function like this:

```
strcpy(Mike.strLastName, "Johnson");   // Assign the name
```

You could print one of the members like this:

```
cout << Mike.intAge;   // Display the age
```

If you wanted to print the three members, you might do so like this:

```
cout << Mike.strLastName << ", " << Mike.intAge << ", " << Mike.flSalary << endl;
```

Adding Behavior to Objects

Until now, you've only seen how to add characteristics to a class by defining the class members. You can also define the class behaviors. The behaviors describe what objects in the class can do. Adding behaviors to a class requires much more time to cover than the rest of this hour will allow. Nevertheless, by seeing an example or two of a class with defined behavior, you will begin to see how objects begin to take on a life of their own, something that simple variables cannot do.

The following `Person` class definition is more complete than the previous one because it defines not only the characteristics (the members and their data types) but also the behaviors (called *member functions*):

```
class Person {
  char strLastName[25];
  int   intAge;
  float flSalary;
  // Member functions appear next
  void dispName( void )
    { cout << "The last name is ";
      cout << strLastName << endl;
    }
  void compTaxes(float taxRate)
    { float taxes;
      taxes = taxRate * flSalary;
      cout << "The taxes are ";
      cout << taxes << endl;
    }
  char * getName( void )
    { return strLastName; }
  int getAge ( void )
    { return intAge; }
  float getSalary ( void )
    { return flSalary; }
};
```

Just as a member can be an instance of a variable, a member can also be a function. The embedded function, the member function, applies only to objects declared from this class. In other words, only `Person` objects behave exactly this way but those `Person` objects can perform the operations defined by the member functions. In a way, the objects are smart; they know how to behave, and the more member functions you supply, the more the objects know how to do.

Many programmers elect to use function declarations (the declaration, or first line of a function, is called the function's *prototype*) in the `class` statement, but then define the actual function code later. By placing function prototypes after the `class` itself, you keep the class cleaner like this:

```
class Person {
  char strLastName[25];
  int   intAge;
  float flSalary;
  // Member functions appear next
  void dispName( void );
  void compTaxes(float taxRate);
  char [] getName( void );
```

```
  int getAge ( void );
  float getSalary ( void );
};

void Person::dispName( void )
  { cout << "The last name is ";
    cout << strLastName << endl;
  }
void Person::compTaxes(float taxRate)
  {  float taxes;
     taxes = taxRate * flSalary;
     cout << "The taxes are ";
     cout << taxes << endl;
  }
char [] Person::getName( void )
  { return strLastName; }
int Person::getAge ( void )
  { return intAge; }
float Person::getSalary ( void )
  { return flSalary; }
```

The `class` statement is more compact because only prototypes appear in the definition and not member function code. The member function code could appear elsewhere in the program or, more likely, would be included from a file you or another programmer created that contains the member functions you need to call. Notice that if you place the function's definition later in the program, you must preface the definition with the class name followed by the `::` operator. The class name qualifies the function because different classes may have member functions with the same name as other classes in the program.

Before explaining how to apply the member functions to objects, you need to understand how scope affects objects and their member functions.

Working with Class Scope

As you know, the `class` statement defines a class and its members and member functions. However, special consideration must be given to the scope of individual data and function members. In the previous class definition, all members were *private*, meaning no code outside the class could access the data members. You can override the default privatization of members by using special `public` and `private` qualifiers to make the class available to code.

Consider this modified `Person` class definition (the member function code is omitted for brevity):

```
class Person {
  char strLastName[25];
  int  intAge;
  float flSalary;
```

```
  // Member functions appear next
public:
  void dispName( void );
  void compTaxes(float taxRate);
  char [] getName( void );
  int getAge ( void );
  float getSalary ( void );
};
```

All members are considered to be private unless you precede them with the `public` keyword. All members before `public` are private but you can optionally place `private:` before the first member so other programmers know your intention is that the class members up to the next `public` keyword remain private. All members (both data members and function members) that follow `public:` are public.

Being private means that any program that uses the class can *never access private members*. This is critical for data protection that the class provides. Earlier in this hour you saw the following statement:

```
cout << Mike.intAge;   // Display the age
```

Actually, this statement will not work in the program because the program does *not* have access to the `intAge` data member. The `intAge` data member is private so no code outside the class can access `intAge`. By protecting the data members, you keep the object intact and ensure that only predefined functions available in the class can access the age. That's why you often see member functions that begin with `get` as in the `getAge()` function shown previously. Because `getAge()` is in the public section of the class, any program that defines `Person` objects *can* use the `getAge()` function. Therefore, you cannot display `intAge` directly, but you can call the `getAge()` function like this:

```
cout << Mike.getAge();   // Display the age
```

Notice that when you apply the member function to the object, you use the dot operator just as you do for data members. Other class objects may be defined and also have functions named `getAge()`, so you must qualify the member function by letting the program know you want the `getAge()` function applied to one specific object variable in the program named `Mike`.

Keep in mind that complete college courses and huge texts exist that teach OOP in C++. You're getting only an overview here, although the overview is actually rather complete. After mastering this introductory hour, you should be able to understand the early portions of a course or text on C++ much more easily.

Things to Come

Given the introduction to C++ that you've now had, you can better understand the advantages that C++ provides over more traditional, non-OOP languages. One of the benefits of OOP is that you can create your own operators. More accurately, you can change the way an operator works when the program uses that operator with one of your objects.

By writing special *operator overloading* member functions, you can make any C++ operator work on your own objects. For example, a plus sign is the addition operator that automatically works on all numeric values. The plus sign, however, cannot work on a Person object such as Mike. Therefore, if you wanted to add two Person objects together to get a total of the salaries, you could write a function that added the salaries of two or more flSalary data members. When you apply the totaling function members to objects, you can produce the total of the salaries, but you can also overload the plus sign operator so that plus works not only for two numbers but also for two Person objects like this:

```
totalSals = Mike + Terry;   // Possible by overloading the +
```

You could never ordinarily use a plus sign between two Person objects such as Mike and Terry because they are objects you created and they contain three data members of different data types. But once you overload the plus operator to add the appropriate values inside Person objects, you can add their values easily.

NOTE
_____

You saw an example of operator overloading when you learned JavaScript earlier in this tutorial. When the plus sign (+) is used with two numbers in JavaScript, it adds the values, but when it is used with two strings, it concatenates them into one larger string. It's one operator, but it can perform different jobs.
_____

Such operator overloading means that you can simplify a program's code. Instead of using a function to simulate a common operation, you can actually use the operator itself, applied to your own objects. The member function that describes the operator overloading determines exactly which data members are affected and used by the operation.

NOTE
_____

The overloading of operators is how you can use the << and >> to input and output complete classes of objects with multiple members and even use Windows-based controls such as text boxes to receive or initiate the special I/O.
_____

The concept of polymorphism makes the overloading of operators possible. For example, the same operator applied to an integer variable behaves much differently if you apply that operator to a class object that you define.

In addition to overloading operators, you can create your own data types. Keep in mind that a class simply defines a collection of data that is composed of data members that conform to an ordinary data type. You could, for example, create a `String` class whose only data member is a character array. By overloading the appropriate operators, you can make C++ behave like Java and support string-like variables.

The `String` class is just one example of the many classes you and others can write to support object reuse later down the road. Over time, you will build a large library of classes that you can use for future programs. As you build classes, the amount of code that you have to write should lessen and you should complete applications more quickly. In addition, as you build and debug object class libraries, your programs should become more maintainable. Using operator overloading and other OOP advantages means that your code will be less bulky. When you need an object, you will simply create one from one of your class libraries just as you add new stereo components when you want to expand your music system.

One of C++'s most productive features is inheritance. When you or someone else writes a class that you use, you are not limited to objects of that class. The C++ language supports inheritance so that you can derive new classes and create new objects that have all the benefits and features of their parent classes but with additional features as well.

Summary

Are you a C or C++ expert after one hour's lesson? No way. Do you understand the fundamentals of C and C++? You'd be surprised at how well you now already understand the language, especially with your Java introduction earlier. You could not master OOP with C++ in one hour either, but you've already learned the fundamentals of how C++ works. At its most basic level, the C++ language offers language improvements over C even if you don't use OOP. Nevertheless, when you begin to use OOP, you will learn to create classes that define objects that seem to take on a life of their own. The objects understand how to perform some duties based on their member functions and you can extend the objects through inheritance to derive new classes that you can use later.

Q&A

Q. Why is #include not a C command?

A. #include is a preprocessor directive and is not part of the C language. #include, and all other lines that begin with #, such as #define, control how C compiles a program instead of controlling the way that the C program executes.

Q. Can the programmer extend the class by adding functionality if a class does not quite contain enough power?

A. Certainly. That's where the power of class inheritance comes into play. The programmer can include the class and then inherit a new class from the existing class. The inherited class contains all the data members and member functions of the parent class without the programmer doing anything special. Then, the programmer can add additional data members and member functions (both private and public) to the class to make the class operate as needed. Such inheritance makes the reuse and extension of objects extremely easy and should improve the efficiency of programmers as more object libraries are written and distributed.

Workshop

The quiz questions and exercises are provided for your further understanding.

Quiz

1. How is C more efficient than JavaScript?

2. What is a header file?

3. What function do all C programs begin with?

4. True or false: C supports string literals.

5. What is wrong with the following statement?

```
if (sales < 2500.00);
   {
     printf("You need to work harder.\n");
   }
```

6. What included header file defines I/O in most C++ programs?

7. Where do you define an object's data members and member functions?

8. What two operators and system objects do C++ programmers often use for input and output?

9. What OOP term allows for operator overloading?

10. How does inheritance improve a C++ programmer's efficiency?

Answers

1. C compiles into a more efficient language than JavaScript, often because of its heavy use of operators instead of commands.

2. A header file brings in extra routines and library definitions and is brought in with the `#include` statement, not unlike the Java `import` command.

3. All C programs start with `main()`.

4. True.

5. The semicolon should not appear after the `if`'s closing parentheses.

6. `<iostream>` defines the I/O routines for most C++ programs.

7. Define an object's data members and member functions inside the object's class definition.

8. C++ programmers often use `cin>>` and `cout<<` for input and output.

9. Polymorphism allows for operator overloading.

10. Programmers do not have to repeat all the code when defining inherited objects; programmers only have to write code that adds or changes functionality.

HOUR 20

Programming with Visual Basic 2012

Unlike many programming languages, much of the work of a Visual Basic programmer doesn't lie in code but in the design of the application's visual elements, such as the controls that the programmer places on forms at design time. These controls allow interaction to and from the user. The code that the programmer places behind the controls handles the events as well as data calculations and manipulations that produce the information required by the program.

This chapter is intended to introduce you to Visual Basic and Microsoft's Visual Studio Environment. Like other chapters in this section, you will only be getting a taste of the language, but if you like it, you can dive deeper into Visual Basic 2012 with a tutorial book such as *Sams Teach Yourself Visual Basic 2012 in 24 Hours.*

The highlights of this hour include

- ▶ How to set control property values
- ▶ How to embed code within a Visual Basic application
- ▶ How to place and size controls so they look correct on the form
- ▶ What kind of code appears in a Visual Basic application

Reviewing the Visual Basic Screen

Unlike most programming languages, Visual Basic is and always has been a Windows programming language. Whevn you learn to write programs with Visual Basic, you learn not only the language but also its environment. With its most recent release, Visual Basic is part of Microsoft's Visual Studio, a shared Integrated Development Environment (IDE) where you can develop in Visual C++, Visual C#, SQL Server, and F#. The advantage to a shared IDE like this is that once you learn the ins and outs using the editor and tools of one programming language, you've got a head start on your next language. Before you can do anything in Visual Basic you must understand the Visual Basic screen.

NOTE

This hour will assume that you've installed the Visual Studio environment and instead focus on using Visual Basic 2012. If you need help installing Visual Studio, there are many online resources to help.

Figure 20.1 shows the New Project selection screen with Visual Basic 2012 Windows options selected. You can see there's a rich variety of options, and on the left side, there are more template choices depending on the languages and the submenu (Windows, Web, Office, for example). You can always select an Empty Project and build your offering from scratch, but picking a template gets things started for you. Much of what you do with Visual Basic is Windows-based, so Windows Form Application will be a common starting point.

FIGURE 20.1
When you start a new Visual Basic project, you have a rich variety of options to choose.

A Windows application is often comprised of several files, including the following:

▶ Form files that contain the form and its description, controls, and related event procedure code

▶ Code modules that hold general-purpose code

▶ Other files that contain elements needed by the application

The Project window keeps track of all items within an application.

The term *project* is used to describe the collection of all files that compose a single Windows application. (The Project window is often called the Project Explorer window because of its tree-structured nature that mimics the Windows Explorer program.) The Form Layout window lets you determine, by dragging with your mouse, the location of the current form on the user's screen when the user runs the program.

CAUTION

Depending on the version of Visual Studio you have, you may see slightly different screens than the ones presented here. Figure 20.1 shows the project options in Visual Studio 2012 Professional. Other versions of Visual Studio will have fewer options to select. Don't worry though, Windows Form Application, covered in this hour is a universal option to all Visual Studio installations.

The latest versions of Visual Basic include tools that go far beyond those found in most other languages. However, creating a Visual Basic application from scratch involves little more than these steps:

1. Design the application by stating its goals and detailing its requirements.

2. Place graphics controls on the application's Form window (this is the output definition design stage). As you place the controls, you'll assign many of the initial properties to the controls.

3. Add event procedures that handle control events.

4. Add any other code needed to tie the controls together and process data as required by the application.

5. Test and distribute the application to users.

As you'll see in the next section, Visual Basic can greatly help reduce the time it takes between steps 1 and 5.

Creating a Simple Application from Scratch

With just a single lesson on Visual Basic, you might as well take the plunge into the creation of a program from scratch. However, if you don't have access to a Visual Basic programming environment, reading through this section still has some value. You can follow along the task list to get an idea of what Visual Basic requires when you create applications.

This first application displays a picture and a command button. The program will change the picture when you click the command button. You would follow these steps to create this simple application:

1. After starting Visual Studio, select File, New Project to display the New Project list.

2. Make sure Windows Form Application is highlighted and type your project name in the space at the bottom. This project is being named `TyBegin24App`, but feel free to name yours something better.

3. Click OK to create your project. Visual Basic will add a single form (currently named `Form1`) for you to start building your project.

NOTE

The small white squares that appear on the right side, bottom, and bottom right corner of the form are sizing handles that you can use to change the width or length of your form. Notice that the Properties window in the bottom right displays properties about the form.

4. Drag the form's lower right sizing handle down and to the right. As you drag the form, notice the width and height measurements at the right of the toolbar as they change. Size the form so that it measures about 740 by 520 pixels. If you want to be exact in the size of the form and you are finding that stretching the form with the sizing handles is too difficult, click the plus sign next to the Size information in the Properties window. This will make two lines, Width and Height, appear. You can then type the specific data you want and the window will instantly resize to your new numbers. Figure 20.2 shows your screen.

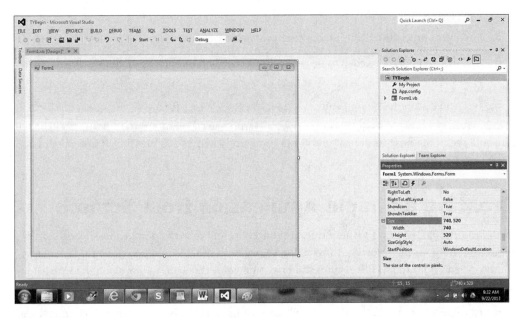

FIGURE 20.2
When you resize the Form window, you are resizing your application's program window.

NOTE

The size of the window is measured in pixels, a refreshing change from previous Visual Basic versions that used twips. Twips were screen units used commonly during programming screen controls. The number of twips was somewhat dependent on hardware, however, the general calculation of a twip was approximately 1/1,440th of an inch. That is, there were 1,440 twips to an inch. Switching to pixels made so much more sense as it is a more universal measurement to computers in general.

caused the box to lose its centering, feel free to go back and tweak the positioning of the label.

4. Click the Toolbox button on the upper left corner to bring back the choices, and double-click the toolbox's Button control to place a button in the center of your form. The icon on each choice in the toolbox should illustrate the purpose of the button. You can also point to any button to see a ToolTip pop up at the mouse pointer that shows the name of the button. Use the other properties to alter the size of the button and the style and size of the font for the button's text label that you can change from Button1 by typing in the words in the Text Property.

5. Locate the toolbox's PictureBox control. Instead of double-clicking to place the control as you did with the label, click the control's icon once. Move your mouse to the Form window and draw the Image control, trying to first anchor the image at 260 pixels from the form's left edge and 210 from the form's top edge. Size the image at approximately 220 pixels wide and 190 pixels high. Again, you can do this by meticulously dragging the handles so that Visual Basic's ScreenTips pop up showing you the coordinates of the image. When the coordinates appear at their proper size, release your mouse button to place the image at that size. Or you can type the information into the Location and Size property boxes. I find the latter so much easier. Figure 20.3 shows your screen at this point. The PictureBox control displays a graphics image when you run the program.

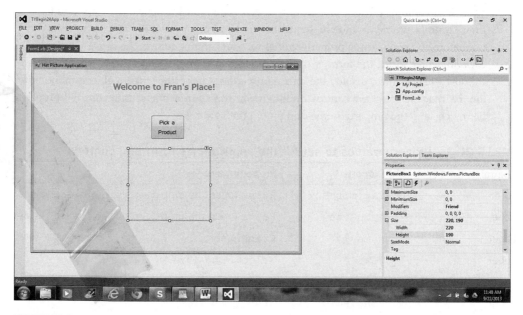

FIGURE 20.3
Your application is taking shape.

TIP

The sample application is not exactly centered at this point. You can use some simple math to center align your controls if you wish. Simply divide the size of the form in two. (Our form is 740, so half would be 370.) Then take the size of your controls, divide them in half, subtract that number from our form half number, and that should be the first number of the location of your form. This sounds complicated, but once you do one or two it gets easy. So if the label is 300 pixels wide, it should start at 220 pixels in order to center it.

NOTE

Location pixel coordinates and size pixel coordinates are always specified in pairs. Often, you'll see such coordinate pairs specified inside parentheses, as in a location value of (250, 280). For the coordinates, such a pair of values would signify that the width is 250 pixels and the height is 280 pixels.

6. Now that you're more familiar with setting property values for controls, even though you may not understand many of the properties yet, you are now equipped to set additional properties for the form and controls to finalize the look of the application. After you set appropriate property values, you will then add code to connect the controls and make them work together.

Table 20.1 contains a list of properties that you would need to set for the form and the three controls in order to match. Remember that you must select the form or specific control before you can change property values for that form or control. To select the form, click anywhere inside the form or title bar but not over any of the controls. The Properties window will change to display the form's properties. Click either the label, command button, or image to select the control, and then you can change one of that control's properties by clicking the property name and typing the new value.

TABLE 20.1   Property values to set for the application's form and controls

Control	Property	Property Value
Form	MaximizeBox	False (open the drop-down list box to see values)
Label	AutoSize	False (open the drop-down list box to see values)
Label	Name	FranPlace
Label	Text	Welcome to Fran's Place
Label	Font	Meiryo
Label	Font.Bold	True
Label	Font.Size	15.75

Control	Property	Property Value
Label	Location	220,30
Label	Size	300,30
Image	Name	ProductPicture
Image	Location	260,210
Image	Size	220,190
Command Button	Name	FranPic
Command Button	Text	Pick a Product

Finalizing with Code

Adding Visual Basic programming statements will turn your creation into a working, although simple, application. Visual Basic automatically adds the opening and closing statements needed when you write a subroutine as you'll see in the following steps:

1. Double-click the command button to open the Code window. A set of beginning and ending statements will appear for a new procedure related to the command button that looks like this:

```
Private Sub FranPic_Click() Handles FranPic.Click
End Sub
```

These lines are two of the three lines needed for code required by the command button. The Code window works like a miniature text editor in which you can add, delete, and change statements that appear in your program code.

NOTE

All code appears in procedures and every procedure requires beginning and ending lines of code that define the procedure's start and stop locations. Visual Basic automatically adds the first and final line of many procedures.

2. Press the spacebar three times and type the following line between the two that are there:

```
ProductPicture.Image = Image.FromFile("C:\Users\DeanWork\Documents\TY Begin
24\product1.jpg")
```

As soon as you type the `Image.FromFile`, Visual Basic offers pop-up help with the statement's format. Some Visual Basic statements, especially those with parentheses, such as the ones you see in this statement, require that you type one or more values. Visual Basic pops up the format of these required values, so you'll know how many to enter. You'll learn more about why these values are required if you decide to pursue the language in more depth. Visual Basic is a large language, so this help comes in handy. By the way, depending on the location where you installed Visual Basic, your pathname to the graphics file will differ from the pathname specified here.

3. Run your program and click the command button. A figure appears as shown in Figure 20.4. You have successfully completed your first Visual Basic application. You've created an application that displays a picture when you click the command button. The application contains code, and its controls all have property values that you've set.

4. Click the Close window button to terminate the program. Be sure to save your project before you exit Visual Studio.

FIGURE 20.4
Your application produces a graphics image from the click of your mouse.

Other Visual Basic Programming Considerations

This hour approaches the Visual Basic language differently from most other languages discussed in these 24 hours. Instead of walking you through specific programming language commands, this hour walked you through the steps required to create a sample application from start to finish. If you look back through the previous sections, you'll notice that very little of the discussion included actual programming language statements. Visual Basic does so much just from its visual environment that adding code sometimes seems like an afterthought.

Even adding menus to the Visual Basic applications that you create from scratch is relatively simple because of another tool called the MenuStrip control (see Figure 20.5). The *MenuStrip* lets you build a menu bar and the pull-down options from that menu bar by selecting and specifying options inside the MenuStrip. No code is required as you add the menu options to your application but once you use the MenuStrip to add the options, you'll have to specify event code procedures for each menu option. When the user selects a menu option, a `Click` event for that menu option occurs and each event procedure that you write will tell Visual Basic how to respond to that event.

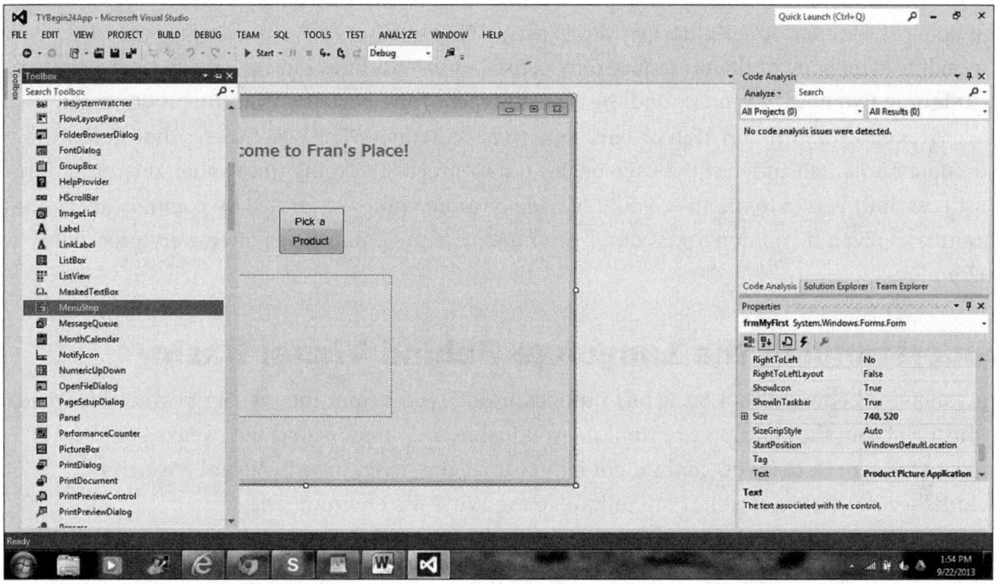

FIGURE 20.5
Use the MenuStrip control in the Toolbox to add menu options to your Visual Basic application.

Understanding Procedures

Consider the following event procedure for the File, Exit menu option:

```
Private Sub ExitToolStripMenuItem_Click(sender As Object, e As EventArgs) Handles
ExitToolStripMenuItem.Click
        ' Terminates The Program
        End
    End Sub
```

By studying this simple procedure, you can learn quite a bit about all event procedures. The Private keyword indicates that the procedure is *local* to the current form and cannot be called by other form modules. Therefore, if several forms exist in the current Windows application, selecting File, Exit from this form will execute this specific event procedure and not one outside the scope of this form. The opposite of Private is Public and public procedures are available to any code in the entire application. Such public procedures are known as *global* procedures because any procedure in the application can call them.

The keyword Sub or Function always follows the Private (or Public) keyword and indicates the type of the procedure. A subroutine is a procedure that always performs work and then returns control to whatever code was executing before the event took place. A function is a procedure that always performs its job when the event takes place and then returns a value to another place in the program that might need that value.

The name of the event procedure specifies exactly which control and event this procedure responds to. The body of the procedure may consist of several lines but this one happens to include only two lines, a remark and the End statement that stops the running program. All procedures end with an End Sub or End Function statement. The parentheses that follow the procedure name indicate that the code begins a new procedure; sometimes, when one procedure must pass data values to another, you'll list one or more values separated by commas inside the parentheses. Even if you don't pass data, you must type the parentheses after every procedure declaration.

Understanding the Language Behind Visual Basic

The language behind Visual Basic has significant differences from the JavaScript you've learned to this point, but the concepts are similar—you just need to understand the tweaks you must make to the syntax of loops, conditional expressions, and assignments. Visual Basic also includes several statements that are unique to the Windows environment.

One of the ways that Visual Basic is unique, however, is in its distribution of procedures across different areas of an application. You now know that several small event procedures reside in a form's Code window to handle any events that occur on that form. Other forms can exist as well and code appears in them to handle events that occur there. In addition, other files might be part of a complex application. A *code module* is a file, separate from any form and the form's associated code, which holds code that you might use in more than one application. Suppose that you write a procedure that prints your company logo at the top of a page. Such a logo would appear before any report that you produce, before any accounting statement, and before anything you print. Therefore, you'll use this procedure in many different applications.

Instead of typing the procedure in every application that needs it, you can put the code in a general-purpose code module that you then can copy into a new code module for all applications that need to produce the logo. You can, from anywhere else in the application, call a `Public` general procedure with a `Call` statement such as this:

```
Call logoPrint    ' Detour to the procedure
```

When the `Call` finishes, execution returns to the statement that follows the `Call`.

Your Next Step

This hour offers only a walkthrough of the steps that you take to create a Visual Basic application and it provides some insight into the nature of Visual Basic programming. Although Visual Basic is probably the easiest programming tool available for creating Windows applications, Visual Basic is vast compared to a simpler language such as JavaScript. Therefore, an hour's lesson could not hope to cover more than what is included here. Nevertheless, you now have a firm grasp of what it takes to write Windows applications in Visual Basic.

TIP

If you want more in-depth Visual Basic programming coverage, pick up a copy of *Sams Teach Yourself Visual Basic 2012 in 24 Hours*, from Sams Publishing, a tutorial that explores Visual Basic programming and takes the beginning Visual Basic programmer to advanced levels in 24 lessons.

Summary

Visual Basic is more than a language; it is part of a complete Microsoft programming environment called Visual Studio. Other languages are available for Visual Studio, such as Visual C#. Visual Basic was the first language to use the Visual Studio environment. When you create a Visual Basic application, you first create the visual elements of the program by placing the controls from the Toolbox window onto the form. As you place the controls, you set the properties and then write event procedure code to activate the controls when certain events take place.

The next hour describes another language within Visual Studio, C#, as well as Microsoft's overall .NET strategy.

Q&A

Q. Could I allow the user to pick an image instead of displaying a specific image when they click a button?

A. Absolutely. With Visual Basic you can use most controls you see in windows-based programs, so you can trigger a dialog box that lets users browse their hard drive and select an image of their choice instead of a predetermined file.

Q. **Do all Visual Basic applications contain code in addition to event procedures?**

A. Some Visual Basic applications contain code that forms event procedures only but most other Visual Basic applications contain other kinds of code. More goes on in most applications than events. Data must be processed, calculations must be performed, reports must be printed, and files must be read and written. The code behind these specific tasks often appears in a code module separate from the form module.

Workshop

The quiz questions and exercises are provided for your further understanding.

Quiz

1. How much code do you have to write to add Internet access to a Visual Basic application?

2. What toolbox control would you use to add menus to a form?

3. Why is it a good practice to change the names of controls from their default names that Visual Basic assigns?

4. What happens when you double-click a Toolbox control?

5. What tool do you use to help you create menus for Visual Basic applications?

6. How does Visual Basic determine which control properties appear in the Properties window?

7. Name one advantage to running a Visual Basic application inside of Visual Basic's environment as opposed to running a compiled application from Windows.

8. Which runs faster: a Visual Basic application running inside Visual Basic's environment or a compiled Visual Basic application running outside Visual Basic's environment?

9. What information can you gather from the following Visual Basic procedure's declaration line?

```
Private Sub scrMeter_Change()
```

10. True or false: All Visual Basic procedures reside in the application's form module.

Answers

1. You don't have to write any extra code to add Internet access to a Visual Basic application.

2. You would use the `MenuStrip` control.

3. The default names are not meaningful, and when your application uses several controls, you should name those controls with names that you will recognize when maintaining the program so you modify correct controls when needed.

4. The Toolbox control appears in the center of your Form window.

5. The Menu Editor helps you build and test menus.

6. The control you place on the form determines which properties appear in the Properties window.

7. You can debug the application inside the Visual Basic environment.

8. A compiled Visual Basic application is faster than one run inside the Visual Basic environment.

9. The procedure is private, which means only the enclosing program can access the procedure, the procedure is a subroutine so it does not return any values, and no arguments are passed to the procedure.

10. False. Some procedure code can appear in Code modules.

C# and the .NET Framework

One of the most important technologies for developing applications and web services is Microsoft's .NET framework. Now close to 15 years old, .NET continues to evolve, incorporating new standards that allow developers to create full-featured windows applications. .NET is not new technology, but a way to approach new technology. .NET consists of today's software and hardware tools as well as tomorrow's more advanced ones. Microsoft's .NET development environment, Visual Studio, was introduced in the last hour. With it, you can create programs in a variety of languages, including C#, which will be touched upon in this hour.

The concepts behind the .NET Framework are complicated, so don't be discouraged if the material in this hour doesn't make immediate sense. But if you wish to take your rudimentary knowledge gained throughout this book to the next level, .NET is an excellent place to go.

The highlights of this hour include

- ▶ Understanding why developers use the .NET Framework
- ▶ Breaking down the elements of the .NET Framework
- ▶ Defining the C# language
- ▶ Writing your first C# program
- ▶ Creating a C# windows application

Understanding the Purpose of .NET

Throughout the earlier hours, you have seen ways to tackle online programming, including JavaScript, Java, HTML, CSS, and PHP. Microsoft's .NET is a centralized approach to online and networked technology. For the past decade and a half, Microsoft has developed an approach to online programming and encapsulated that approach into an umbrella of multiple technologies called .NET.

Microsoft's goal is for .NET to address the needs of users who will live in an always on and connected online world. Developers that use .NET are looking to build next-generation, platform-independent products. With the significant changes to the computing space, being platform-independent has become more crucial than ever—since the introduction of .NET, programmers now need to worry about multiple operating systems, a host of mobile environments and devices, and cloud-based services as well. Code written for the .NET Framework is called managed code (which can easily be shared thanks to the Common Intermediate Language (CIL), covered later in this hour). Code written in languages such as C and C++, is compiled into machine code tied specifically to the computer on which it was compiled, and is known as unmanaged code.

TIP

If you are looking to create managed code in C or C++, that option is available when you use Visual C++ in Visual Studio.

The .NET Framework creates simplified software deployment agnostic of platform thanks to the common language runtime (CLR), the framework class library (FCL), parallel computer platform, and the dynamic language runtime (DLR).

The Common Language Runtime

The heart of the .NET Framework is the common language runtime (CLR). The CLR allows multiple languages to share objects and methods and cuts down on memory leak problems thanks to garbage collection.

CLR might sound difficult to understand at first, but it's simple. A .NET-compatible language such as Visual Basic, Visual C++, or C# will not compile to a specific machine, as is historically the case for computer languages, but rather will compile to a common machine language. Every .NET-based operating system will emulate this common language. So, in theory, a single program written in C++ could run, unaltered, on a PC, a Windows phone, and as a web service.

TIP

If a programmer learns a language that compiles to a CLR, that program runs on any device that supports .NET. A different compiler and a different language no longer have to be developed for each kind of computing device.

The key components of the CLR include

▶ **The Common Type System**—As you have probably noticed during your survey of languages throughout this book, while most programming concepts and syntaxes are fairly universal, there are subtle differences (like dialects within a shared language) that can cause problems if you attempt to integrate multiple languages. The common type system (CTS) allows all languages within the .NET framework to share type definitions, preventing problems that could arise if an incompatible piece of data is assigned to a type. The CTS also sets rules that allow types written in different programming languages to interact with each other. These rules are enforced by the CLR.

▶ **The Common Intermediate Language**—As discussed in earlier lessons, other languages covered in this book like C and C++ compile their code into machine language that is unreadable and also specific to the platform and machine on which it was compiled. Not a great start to creating platform-independent applications and services. The CIL creates a middle step of low-level instructions called an assembly, which when combined with the metadata that describes the types, members, and references in the code, allows your code to run on a variety of platforms—it just needs to be put through a just-in-time compiler (JIT) to run on your specific hardware platform.

▶ **Garbage Collection**—Although it was not covered in great detail in the hour on C and C++, effective programming practice is to declare only the memory you need for your programs, and then release the memory back to the system when you are done with it. Inefficient memory use can slow both your program and your entire system. The .NET Framework introduced garbage collection, an automatic memory management feature which makes you not have to worry about these issues. This isn't to say you are completely free from any involvement in memory management—in fact, if you pursue development in .NET, you should learn how garbage collection works.

TIP

If you want to know more about .NET, its strengths, and the C# language, I'd recommend picking up *Sams Teach Yourself C# 5.0 in 24 Hours*. It covers in excellent detail the subjects touched upon in this hour.

The Framework Class Library

There is little sense in reinventing the wheel. While writing your own code from scratch is always a bit gratifying, taking existing code and using it as a foundation helps you to build more robust code. The .NET Framework's FCL includes a number of reusable classes, interfaces, and types. There are thousands of classes in the FCL and you can find detailed information on some of the most commonly used classes at msdn.microsoft.com/en-us/library/gg145045.aspx.

Some of the lowest-level FCL offerings are the base class libraries (BCL), which you use for string manipulation, working with streams, file input and output, and more.

With these thousands of classes, .NET uses namespaces to avoid ambiguity between type names and to clarify hierarchal groupings. The website listed earlier in this section has a robust table that lists several dozen of the most common namespaces, many of which fall in the system grouping. Specific namespaces use the dot operator to clarify each level of the hierarchy, that is, `system.collections`. If you click on the `system.collections` element in the table on Microsoft's website, you will get a listing of the base namespaces and four others within the collections hierarchy. Clicking on any of them gives you their classes, interfaces, structures, and more. Effective use of the elements in the FCL will save you considerable development time and add impressive power to your programming abilities.

Parallel Computing Platform

Developers looking to speed up the execution of their programs have turned to multithreaded and asynchronous applications. While these methodologies can greatly increase the speed of programs, they also can lead to problematic, error-filled programs. The .NET Framework simplifies creating these apps with the parallel computing platform, which allows developers to write code that can take advantage of multiple processors. This is a topic far beyond your knowledge and experience at this point, but it is a key feature of the .NET Framework that you should know about in case you want to head in that direction.

Dynamic Language Runtime

JavaScript, covered in the first half of the book, is considered a dynamic language, as are many other scripting languages you may have heard of, like Python and Ruby. These languages have subtle differences from languages like C and Visual Basic. One example you may remember is that you don't have to specify a type for your variables. You can declare a variable culture and have it first hold a floating point number like 14.3 and then assign it a string like "breakfast cereal". Other languages don't allow this in order to make sure variables aren't used improperly. This is known as *type safety*. Obviously, you don't want any interactivity problems to arise when a statically typed language like Visual Basic or C# interact with dynamic languages, and the DLR covers these potential problems, allowing you as the developer to choose whatever language you feel suits your development purposes best.

The C# Language

C# was developed specifically for .NET, to act as a scripting language for applications and web pages. C#, like Java, is based on the C and C++ programming languages. C# is an object-oriented language (also like Java and C++) and supports classes, inheritance, polymorphism, encapsulation, and abstraction.

If you installed Visual Studio in order to follow along with the Visual Basic examples in the previous lesson, you already have your C# Integrated Development Environment (IDE) ready to go. To build a C# (also called Visual C#) program, you would select New Project, just like you did in the last hour. This time though, you would click on one of the Visual C# choices on the list on the left side (they are a subhead under Other Languages), so if nothing is below Other Languages, click the arrow to its left and choices for Visual C#, Visual C++, and Visual F# should appear, as in Figure 21.1.

NOTE

As mentioned in the last hour (but worth repeating), your dialog boxes and choices may look a bit different than what you see here depending on what version of Visual Studio you have installed.

FIGURE 21.1
Much like with Visual Basic, the project choices for Visual C++ are quite diverse.

TRY IT YOURSELF ▼

If you remember with Visual Basic, you selected a Windows Form Application. While you could do the same here, and get the same setup of a form on which you could drag and drop controls and then add lines of underlying code to activate them, select instead Console Application so we can create a simple program to display the area of a circle. After you've selected Console Application, you should get the screen seen in Figure 21.2.

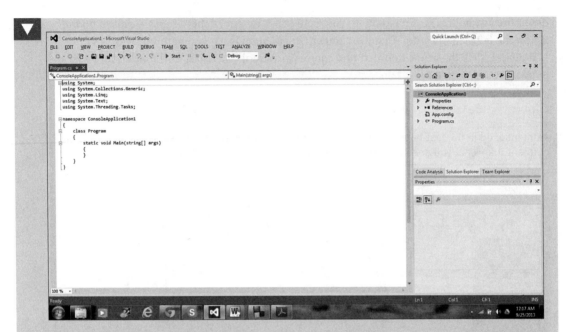

FIGURE 21.2
When you create a new application, Visual C# creates much of the baseline code your application will need.

You have yet to write a line of code, but you are already seeing the power of the .NET framework. Several of the namespaces from the FCL are listed in the first five lines of your program. This is a signal to your compiler that you can use the classes and other objects of these namespaces in your program. If you found yourself wanting to use others, you would just need to add a using line at the top of the code listing.

Type the code in Listing 21.1 into your Visual C# window.

LISTING 21.1   A simple C# program to calculate the area of a circle when given the radius

```
using System;
using System.Collections.Generic;
using System.Linq;
using System.Text;
using System.Threading.Tasks;
```

```
namespace ConsoleApplication1
{
    class Program
    {
        static void Main(string[] args)
        {
            string enteredRadius;
            double radius, area;

            //Get the number from the user
            Console.WriteLine("Enter the radius of the circle: ");
            enteredRadius = Console.ReadLine();

            // The entered value, currently a string, must be turned into a number
            radius = double.Parse(enteredRadius);

            // Once you have the radius, mutiply it by itself and PI (3.14)
            // to get the area of the circle
            area = 3.14 * radius * radius;

            //Now output the answer
            Console.WriteLine("The area of a circle with a radius of "+ radius );
            Console.WriteLine("is " + area);

            //Your code window will just disappear if you don't add these lines
            Console.WriteLine("Press any key to continue");
            Console.ReadKey();


        }
    }
}
```

When you run this program, you will get the results pictured in Figure 21.3.

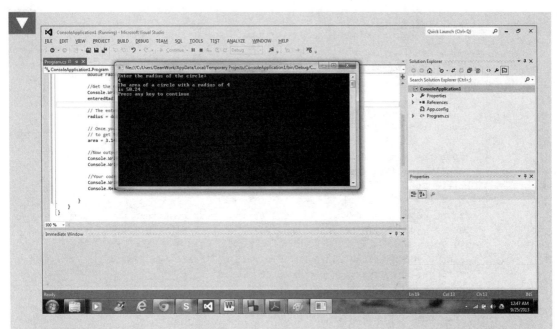

FIGURE 21.3
Your first C# accomplishes the same goal as one of your first JavaScript programs (remember way back then?).

This should be a fairly easy program to follow by this time in the book. Actually, first programs are "Hello World" examples, but giving you a little credit, working on a program with not just output but input and variables can be a bit more instructive.

The most confusing part of the program is probably the first few lines. As mentioned earlier, these using lines instruct the compiler to let you use the classes and objects associated with the namespaces that follow. Frankly, you don't really need any of them except System and if you comment out the next four (adding the double slashes // at the beginning of the lines) and re-build the project, it will work just fine. Remember that these were generated automatically when you selected your project.

The previous paragraph should point out a similarity that C# has with C, C++, and JavaScript. You use // to create comments, telling the compiler to ignore anything that comes to the right of the slashes. As emphasized throughout the book, it is good programming practice to use comments frequently. Some would argue this listing has too many comments, and that's a fair point—you don't want to overdo things and state the obvious. But undercommenting is far worse, particularly if you have to return to a piece of code you wrote months, or even years, earlier and have to waste time piecing together what the code is accomplishing.

Input and output are the staples to any programming language and for C#, Console.Readline and Console.Writeline are great starting points. A secondary input function, Console.Readkey, is also being used, although its value is not being assigned to a variable. This is just a way to keep the output window from disappearing once it calculates the area and presents the result onscreen. Without that line waiting for you to input any single character (hence, press any key), the program will output the value of the area, and then end the program, making the window go away before you have time to read it properly. To see what I mean, comment out those last two lines and rebuild and rerun the program.

Taking Advantage of the Visual Nature of Visual C#

That example is easy to follow and demonstrates the use of C# code in an old-school way, but one of the advantages of Visual Studio is creating Windows applications. So let's see how easy it is to make a windows form that does this same calculation. So save your previous project and select a new C# project, this time a Windows Form Application. Once it sets things up for you, you will get the work area you see in Figure 21.4.

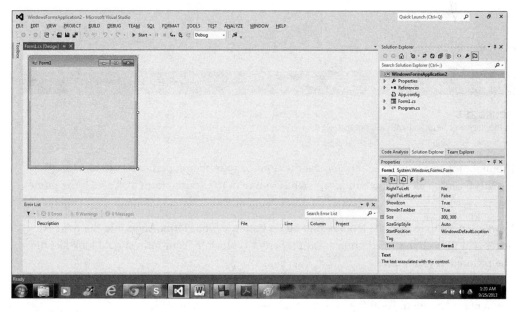

FIGURE 21.4
Visual C# Windows-based applications will be easy to understand if you've read through the introduction to Visual Basic in the previous lesson.

This should look familiar to you, as it is virtually identical to the Windows Form Application you saw for Visual Basic. The controls in the toolbox will also be similar—the underlying code you write for the application will be where Visual Basic and Visual C# truly diverge.

Open your toolbox and place two labels and two text boxes on your form. It's easy to align them, as once you start dragging a text box under the other, a blue guideline will appear to ensure you place one under the other. These guidelines appear both vertically and horizontally, as shown in Figure 21.5.

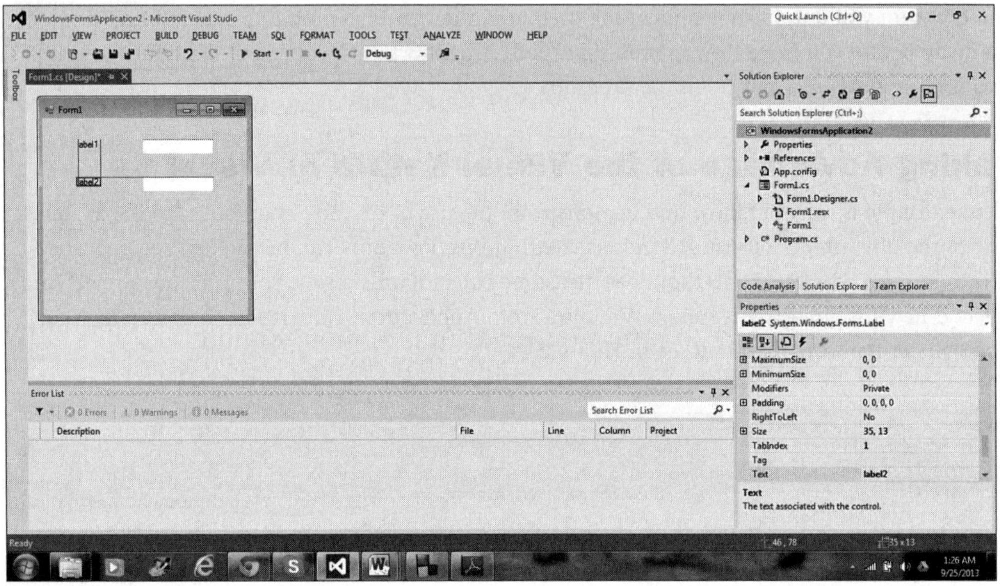

FIGURE 21.5
Guidelines will help you with alignment.

Highlight the two labels and rename their text property in the properties box to Radius (the top label) and Area (the bottom label). While you're at it, click the form and give it the name "Radius to Area Calculator".

Now you need to reopen the toolbox and add a button to your form. Align it to the two text boxes and then change the button's text property to calculate. Your form should look like the one pictured in Figure 21.6.

Next you need to highlight the text box to the right of Radius and name the textbox for when we do our calculation. For this example, it is named enteredRadius.

TIP

When you have a variable name made up of multiple words, capitalizing the first letter of the second word (and all following words) is common practice and is known as camel notation—because it is like you are creating little camel humps within your word.

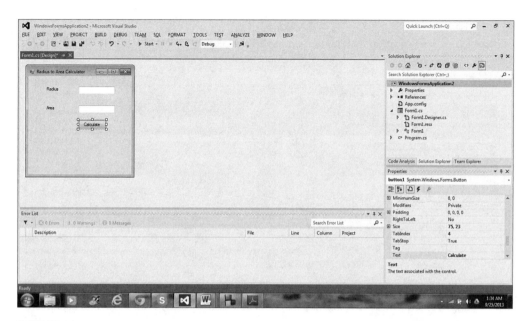

FIGURE 21.6
Your area calculator should be coming along nicely.

You then need to do the same for the area text box. It is named `enteredArea`. (I understand that the area is being calculated, not entered, but consistency of names can be a good thing.)

Now all that is left is to put some code behind the calculate button. If you double-click on the button, you will bring up the code section. Between the two braces following `private void calculate_Click`, enter the following code:

```
double radius, area;

radius = double.Parse(enteredRadius.Text);
area = 3.14 * radius * radius;

enteredArea.Text = area.ToString();
```

It should look like Figure 21.7.

The first three lines of code are similar to your console version. You declare two variables named `radius` and `area`. The information entered by the user into the `enteredRadius` text box is considered a string, so you need to parse it into a number before you do math with it. Then you use the radius of the circle to calculate the area. But before you can display the calculated area in its text box, you must turn the number back into a string, which is easy enough with the `ToString` method. Now your control is ready to go. Build it and run it. If you enter the same radius as you did in the console example, you should get the same area, as displayed in Figure 21.8.

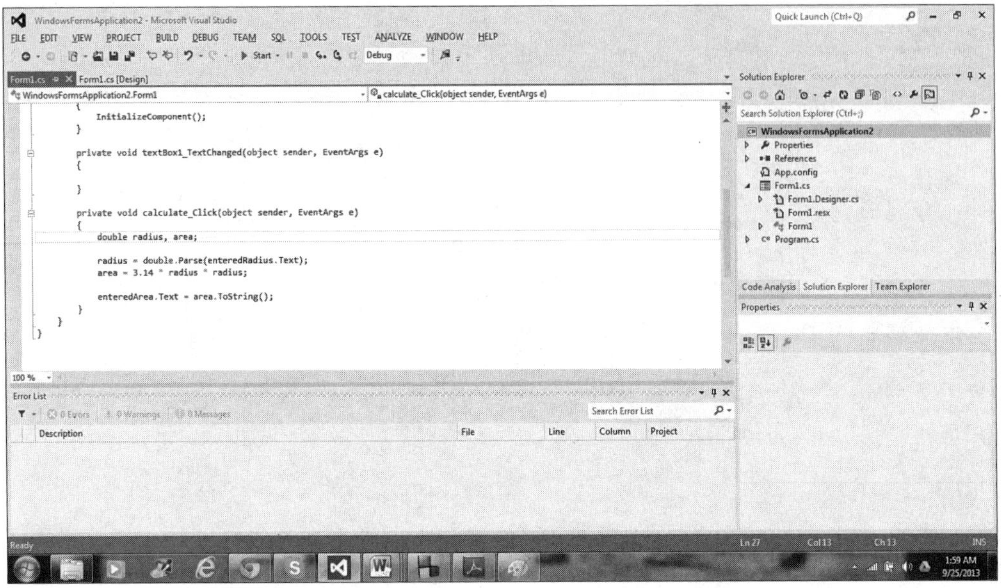

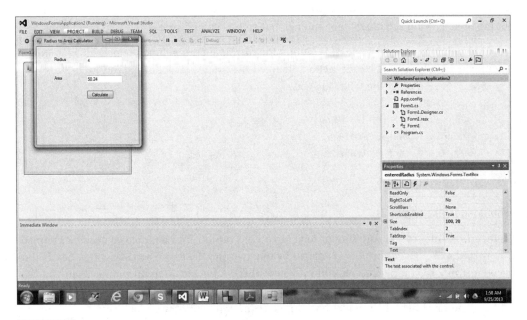

FIGURE 21.7
Just like with Visual Basic, once you set your controls, you then enter code to get the controls to do what you want.

FIGURE 21.8
Now you can calculate circle areas whenever you want!

Not the sexiest example, but it is nice to see the text-based and windows-based versions of the same program. This obviously is just scratching the surface of what you can do with C#—like the other languages you've learned, you can do loops, conditional statements, object-oriented programming (OOP), and so much more. There's almost no limits to the power of C#, particularly when you learn to use it in conjunction with the other tools of Visual Studio.

Summary

The 30,000 foot view of Microsoft's .NET Framework terrain should give you some idea of where you can take your programming knowledge next. The world of application and web service development continues to splinter into different devices and platforms, so the ability to create solutions that work regardless of platform is crucial. In addition, it makes little to no sense to learn multiple development environments as well as languages, so the commonality of tools and editor in Visual Studio can save you time and effort and allow you to focus on solving the business issues at hand.

This completes the survey of other languages and environments. The next part (Part V) begins a three-hour look at the business of programming, giving you some understanding of where the skills you are acquiring can be used in the corporate world.

Q&A

Q. Is .NET the only way to develop platform-independent applications and services?

A. Not at all. Some people initially thought that .NET and C# were going to replace Java, but as you've seen in Part III of this book, Java is still going strong. In addition, new cloud-based programming methods like Infrastructure as a Service (IaaS) and Software as a Service (SaaS) can also deliver applications largely platform-independent. Microsoft's size and marketing muscle will always keep .NET in the game, but there are other options as well.

Q. Is it best to use a particular programming language with .NET?

A. While Visual Studio offers a suite of programming languages and tools, there are certain advantages to using C#. It was developed specifically for the .NET Framework. Its similarities to C, C++, and Java make it easy to pick up for anyone that has any experience with those other languages, and it incorporates both the strength of an object-oriented language and a component-oriented language. However, if you prefer VB or C/C++, you have those options in Visual Studio as well.

Workshop

The quiz questions are provided for your further understanding.

Quiz

1. What is the IDE developers use to create .NET applications?

2. What are the components of the .NET framework?

3. What does CIL stand for?

4. True or false: The power of the FCL is that it has just a few dozen classes, so they are easy to memorize.

5. What is garbage collection in .NET?

6. What language is an example of a dynamic language?

7. C# is similar to what other languages?

8. Why is it not wise to immediately do math with numbers entered by users in C#?

9. How do you add comments to your code in C#?

10. What is the purpose for the CLR?

Answers

1. Visual Studio.

2. The components of the .NET Framework are the CLR, the FCL, the parallel computing platform, and the DLR.

3. CIL stands for the common intermediate language.

4. False. The power of the FCL is that it has hundreds of classes that cover a number of programming needs.

5. Garbage collection is automatic memory management.

6. JavaScript is an example of a dynamic language.

7. C# is similar to C and C++ (as well as Java).

8. You should parse entered values into numbers before doing math or C# may assume the value is a string, and you won't get the value you expect.

9. You can either create single-line comments with the double slash (//) or multi-line comments enclosed in (/* and */) just as you do in JavaScript, C, and C++.

10. The CLR allows all computers with a CLR compiler to be .NET compatible.

How Companies Program

This hour attempts to give you an idea of how companies program computers. While the focus here is on larger companies working on data processing or enterprise application development, you will also learn about some of the differences working with smaller companies and even technology startups.

Regardless of size, companies must coordinate their programming efforts to make the best use of their resources. This doesn't always mean that every program wanted by every person gets written. Actually, the allocation of programming talents is one of the primary tasks of a software development manager (or other similar supervisory position). You will learn about some of the different types of available jobs and their common titles and how those people interface with one another. After this hour, you will better understand the wording of the employment ads for computer professionals, and you will get an idea of the experience needed to obtain the different jobs in the computer industry.

Highlights of this hour include:

- ▶ Learning about typical computer-related departments in large companies
- ▶ Schooling behind programming: which programming degree may give you a boost on the job market
- ▶ Getting computer experience without a degree or training
- ▶ Understanding programming-related jobs
- ▶ How programming teams perform structured walkthroughs of their work

Data Processing and Information Technology Departments

In large companies, core aspects of computer programming might not happen in a department labeled as such. This is especially true in companies that do not actually develop commercial software products. Instead, a large company might have a sort of data processing department known as *Data Processing, Information Services, Information Systems, or Management Information*

Systems (MIS). Or, this function could be subsumed within a greater Information Technology (IT) department, which would also include desktop hardware, communications, servers, and networking (among other things).

No matter what the company's employees call this sort of department, it is commonly in the center of almost every major new project the company takes on. When a company expansion, acquisition, or merger is about to take place, this department must prepare for the additional computing resources needed. When an internal engineering project begins, this department supplies engineers and analysts to perform tasks.

As Figure 22.1 shows, a data processing or internal software development department writes programs for every other department in the company. Unless the company itself is a software-writing company (such as Microsoft), the company's main focus is not going to be software development. The company has other objectives, but there is a data processing and IT department that supplies the computer systems and programming resources needed to keep the other departments working as effectively as they can.

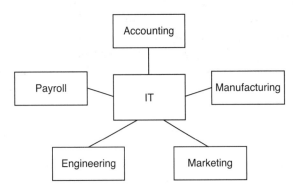

FIGURE 22.1
An IT department writes programs for the rest of the company.

Such a corporate setup is natural. In the early years of business computing, the computer department was placed in the accounting department and governed by the accounting staff. The problem with putting the computer department under direct control of accounting is that accounting will tend to write computer systems it needs and the engineering, marketing, and upper management departments might take a back seat. This doesn't mean that the accounting department would selfishly hoard the computer resources, but the accounting bias would be natural because part of the accounting department's own budget was set aside for the computers and their people.

It was realized in the late 1960s that the data processing department was not directly tied to any one department such as accounting, but, instead, computer people worked for the entire company because they developed programs that the entire company used. Therefore, standalone computer departments started appearing on companies' organizational charts. Organizations began viewing their computer departments as individual cost centers that required their own budget and autonomy. Figure 22.2 shows how the typical data processing or IT department fits into today's organizational charts. As you can see, the data processing department is located on the same level as accounting, payroll, engineering, and the rest of the departments.

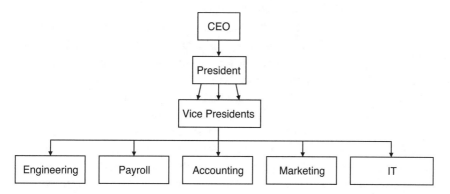

FIGURE 22.2
The IT department is evenly ranked with the company's other departments.

Despite the fact that the data processing or IT department is now autonomous in most companies, that autonomy still doesn't ensure proper allocation of computer resources. A data processing department's resources consist of the hardware, peripheral material, such as paper and tapes, and people. The people are the most expensive resource in a data processing department. Their office spaces, desks, supplies, personal computer equipment, telephones, benefits, and payroll costs all add up to a tidy sum.

CAUTION

No matter how much money a company makes, it cannot allow unlimited spending for the computer resources just described. There must be some checks and balances applied to the money spent in data processing. Unlike other departments, whose worth is measured in dollars received by outside customers, the company itself is the only customer of its data processing department. (Many of the accounting-related departments, such as payroll, often have a similar setup where they work for the rest of the company and produce no outside income of their own.) That is, each department's budget includes a little extra for overhead expenses (lights, desks, paper, telephones, faxes, copying, secretarial, and data processing usage). By collecting some of each department's overhead budget, the company can pay for the data processing resources.

This overhead method of paying for data processing costs doesn't always work well. Overhead is fine for departments such as the accounting department's general ledger group, but the data processing department's skills are more in demand than are other departments'. Without checks and balances of some kind, all the other departments will want programs written with little regard to cost (after all, they've already paid their share of the overhead expense). The information technology or internal software development department can't hire an unlimited supply of programmers just because it receives endless requests for programs.

Not all computer programmers work at the company's location. This is increasingly true for companies that are wholly focused on creating and distributing software as a product or service, where programmers and analysts make up the bulk of the employee roster. As technology improves, companies are learning that some jobs, such as programming, can be performed from any location, including the employee's own home. For some companies—even large companies—partial-week telecommuting is available to staff members who want to work from home. These employees must still come into the office for meetings and team evaluation and review but the bulk of their work can be done from a PC with an Internet connection. Other companies allow full telecommuting, using video conferences to substitute for meetings, such that remote employees might work for a company several timezones away from their home location. Telecommuters can save money for the company because the company no longer has the expense of the office space and other support services for each employee. Telecommuting can make for happier employees, especially those who thrive in their own environment (as opposed to going in to a sterile office environment every day).

Understanding the Chargeback Approach

Companies have been turning away from the overhead approach to another approach called *chargeback*. With chargeback, the data processing center or IT department is given no funds from the overhead account (which immediately lowers the overhead expenses for all the other departments). When a department needs a program written, that department requests the program from the internal group, which estimates the cost of writing the program and sends that estimate back to the original department.

It is then up to the requesting department to accept or reject the charge for the programming resources. If the department wants the program badly enough, and it has the funds in its budget, that department's management can then transfer those funds to the data processing department's budget, and work begins.

One of the biggest advantages of the chargeback method is that a department cannot ask for the world unless it is willing to pay for it. A department's own limited resources keep it from requesting more than it really needs.

NOTE

The money being transferred is sometimes referred to as *funny money*. It is made up of internal funds that already belong to the company that are being passed from department to department. The company is still out the cost of the computing resources, but when it comes directly from the requesting department's budget, that department puts its own check-and-balance system in place to determine whether its data processing requests are reasonable.

The nice thing about chargeback is that one department works like a miniature company within the parent company, supplying services as long as those services are paid for. The company doesn't have to worry about skyrocketing costs; after all, if the money is already in a department's budget and that department wants to spend it on internal computer programming projects, there is nothing wrong with that. The department will not have those funds to spend on other things, and departments have the right to determine how they spend their own budgets.

Often, the computer programming or IT department hires contract programmers, analysts, and systems administrators when the company's requests grow. If the department predicts that its workload will increase for a short time, such as when another company is bought by the parent company, or a specific project needs to be completed on an aggressive deadline, *contract programmers* are hired to program for a fixed time period. Whether the time is six months, a year, or longer is negotiable.

Generally, contract programmers are paid a large salary because the company doesn't have to pay for the contract programmer's benefits and retirement. There are software companies that hire programmers full-time, giving them benefits and insurance, and then those companies do nothing but hire out their programmers to other companies who need contract programming. Don't rule out an opportunity for contract programming if you are looking for a job. The pay is good, the experience is often better (or at least more varied), and often a company eventually hires contract programmers full time as permanent employees if they turn out to be productive workers.

Computer-Related Jobs

Several times a year, media outlets list the job outlook for the coming year, five years, and ten years. For the last twenty years, computer-related jobs have been high on the lists for the best job environments, highest pay, long-term stability, and so forth. That trend will continue for many years. Despite advancements, computer technology is still in its infancy because there are a lot more programs to write than those that have been written in the past.

Companies, especially startups and small to mid-size companies, often allow computer programmers and managers to work in more relaxed conditions than other departments. Whereas a company's accounting department reports in at 8:00 a.m., clocks out for exactly 60 minutes for lunch, and leaves at 5:00 p.m. on the dot, the software development staff might not all arrive and leave at a uniform time, if they even work on-site at all.

The reason working conditions can be more relaxed is that programmers and analysts often need to pursue a problem or programming task until its conclusion, even if that means staying awake in the computer room for 20 hours straight. Many programmers love to burn the midnight oil. As you now know, programming is not a science yet, and it might never be one. A large part of programming reflects a person's style and involves a personal commitment to a project. There is a creative side to programming that programmers often find addictive. A programmer who drags in at 11:00 a.m. might be doing so because he stayed up until 4:30 a.m. trying to debug some code for the company.

Managers understand that the creative spirit that programming brings often comes in spurts. When a programmer gets involved on a programming project, she spends more voluntary overtime than any other type of worker would consider. The trade-off seems to be worth the relaxed attitude in many programming organizations.

NOTE

Another primary advantage of the programming field over many others is its equal opportunity. Because the business computer industry didn't really begin until the mid-1960s—when the idea of equal pay for equal work was coming into acceptance—equal opportunity was already a part of the computer industry. There are many female, minority, and physically disabled employees in technical fields, and the norm has always been for their jobs and salaries to be equal to those of others among them.

Job Titles

You should understand the kinds of jobs that are out there for programmers. Then when you look at the employment ads in newspapers, you'll have an idea of the qualifications and experience needed for the different jobs that are advertised.

CAUTION

The titles described in this section are common in the computer industry, but they are by no means universal. Whereas the title for a job in one company might be *Programmer Analyst*, another company might give the same duties a title of *Senior Programmer*. The specific titles mentioned here, although open to change and interpretation, are common enough to describe most of the responsibilities and titles you will see in larger companies.

Degrees and Certificates

Most jobs in technical fields require some kind of degree or certification; whether or not this degree or certification is *useful* is a common topic for debate. There is also a debate as to whether a two-year associate degree or a four-year bachelor's degree is best. The four-year degree is always better in one respect: You are more grounded in the theory behind how computers work and will be able to learn new computer skills faster because of it. However, a four-year degree keeps you out of the work force two years longer than a two-year degree, and two years is a long time in the rapidly changing field of computers.

However, a two-year programming degree simply doesn't give you enough time to learn much about foundational computing theory. In two years, a college will teach you as many hands-on skills as possible. You'll become familiar with one or two programming languages but likely not have extended time to hone your skills by doing group projects or advanced work. While you may find you can enter the programming marketplace at the same job rank and get paid just as much as someone with a four-year degree (that is to say, at the entry level), a two-year degree in many companies will be a limiting factor to progression in your job.

Perhaps the best of both worlds is possible. You can get a two-year degree, go to work for a company in an entry-level programming job, and go the last two years part-time to finish a four-year degree (most four-year colleges give credit for classes taken for a two-year degree with only a few exceptions here and there). Often a company will pay for, or at least supplement, its employees' continuing education.

TIP

If you have time and money to spare, and who doesn't (seriously, though, there are always scholarships, grants, and loans), consider getting a second degree, either an additional two-year degree or a master's in a field other than programming. A second degree will augment your programming skills. In addition to understanding programming, you will be able to apply those programming skills more readily to an area such as accounting or engineering.

Certification

Another kind of "degree" in the computing scene is not a degree at all. Instead of a degree, a technical certificate shows that you are well skilled in a specific area of computing. Microsoft, Cisco, Oracle, and several other companies offer certification training classes and certifications for their product offerings. After you pass the certification test for a specific area, you are then certified by the corporation offering the certificate. In some fields, job applicants in the computing industry are in much greater demand if they are certified. Unlike a college degree, the certificate demonstrates a specific, measurable ability in a high-demand area of computing such as networking or operating systems.

CAUTION

The certification tests are rigid and difficult. That's a good thing (if you pass one) because it demonstrates true proficiency in a subject matter. With a certificate, your minimum skill level is known in advance by those hiring.

Data Entry

Some computer-related jobs don't require any programming skills. On the low end of the computer ranks are the *Data Entry Clerks* (often called *Data Entry Operators*). Data Entry Clerks typically need only a high school diploma or its equivalent and some keyboarding skills. Data Entry Clerks, except for the ones who have been with a company for a long time and have often received pay raises, make the lowest salaries of any of the computer jobs in the company.

The life of a Data Entry Clerk is simple; he sits in front of a computer screen typing data into the computer. Typically, as Figure 22.3 shows, all the Data Entry Clerks type on terminals (keyboard and screen combinations) attached to a central computer, usually a mainframe. Eight hours a day, five days a week, the data entry department enters data.

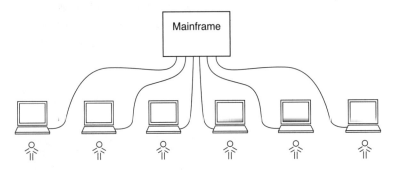

FIGURE 22.3
Data Entry Clerks normally enter data into the same computer.

A company's data-entry requirements are massive. Payroll figures, sales figures, government figures, competing statistics, market trends, industry trends, projections, and so forth all must be factored into the company's working atmosphere. The computer programs that process a large amount of data need it to be entered somehow. The larger the organization, the larger the data needs: Some companies have hundreds of full-time Data Entry Clerks.

At first glance, you might want to stay away from such a job. The data-entry position, however, can be a powerful first step into a computing career for some people. People with little or no computer training who need experience can begin as a Data Entry Operator. While with the company, they can show a positive attitude, meet others within the company, and receive the typical company insurance and benefits. If the clerk pursues the proper training, she can move into higher programming positions, such as data analyst or database administrator.

TIP

As mentioned earlier, a company will often pay for some or all of an employee's part-time education. Therefore, a Data Entry Clerk, with no programming background at all, can take night classes to begin training in programming skills. After he finishes a degree, or is trained adequately enough, the company can move him into one of the entry-level programming jobs. Such a person might never have been able to get a programming job if he had not started out in data entry.

Programming

A person with knowledge of programming, either a self-taught programmer who has a degree in another area, a person who received programming training in a two-year or four-year institution, or a certified programmer, will bypass the data-entry job and move straight into a job actually related to programming. The first job title given to a new programmer hired fresh out of college (or one with little professional programming experience) is usually *Junior Programmer* (also known as *Junior Software Developer* or *Programmer I*). Junior Programmer is generally considered the entry-level job for anyone without experience as a programmer in another company.

A person typically doesn't remain a Junior Programmer for more than a year or two. Often, a Junior Programmer does not create new code, but instead focuses entirely on programs others have written, often doing routine program maintenance. During this initial period, a Junior Programmer learns how the company operates, gets acquainted with other team members and the team's coding styles, and generally "learns the ropes" of the company's working environment.

After a person stays in the Junior Programmer role for a while, he is usually promoted to *Programmer*, along with a small raise and a pat on the back. The Programmer title means that the company expects good things in the coming years and has trust in the person. It is rare for a person to hold a Junior Programmer title for several years and still be with the same company.

The Programmer's primary job is to collaborate on new features as well as work on programs written by others, both maintaining them and modifying them when the need arises. The Programmer's supervisor will begin to have the Programmer write programs from scratch. Of course, the specifications of the program (the flowchart, output definition, and possibly pseudo-code) will already be done and the Programmer has to implement only those specifications into a new program. After a while, the Programmer's attitude and on-the-job learning can justify moving into a more advanced job with the title *Senior Programmer*.

The Senior Programmer is primarily responsible for writing new programs after being given specifications to follow, and sometimes advises other teams during the creation of specifications. In some companies, the Senior Programmer doesn't have to worry much about maintaining older code because the new Junior Programmers and mid-level Programmers take care of that, but many times the Senior Programmer will also act as a team lead and mentor to less experienced colleagues, and naturally will revisit old code with them.

The Senior Programmer title usually commands a pay raise and maybe an office of his own instead of sharing an office with other Programmers. A person is a Senior Programmer for a few years, writing code and getting to know the workings of the company, its users' needs, and the base of programs already in existence. Senior Programmers may eventually move into managerial roles, or they may remain as Senior Programmers for as long as the work remains interesting to them. Another option for experienced programmers is to move laterally into systems analysis and design.

Analysis and Design Staff

In many companies, *Systems Analysts* never write programs, but they will have done so in the past. These skills help them efficiently and thoroughly analyze and design programs that others will write.

NOTE

Isn't it strange that you train for a long time to be a computer programmer and work hard at programming for several years, just so you don't have to program anymore? Actually, the programming experience is a must for the high-level Systems Analyst. Without the understanding that programming brings, one cannot design systems for others to program.

The Systems Analyst is often a liaison between the users and the other departments who need data processing work performed. As Figure 22.4 shows, the Systems Analyst talks to both the users and the programming staff. The users don't understand computer requirements; they only know what they want (or what they think they want). The users must work with the Systems Analyst to design the needed computer system. The Systems Analyst has worked in the company for many years. The Systems Analyst understands the needs of the programmers and the needs of the users in the company. The programmers might appear too technically oriented to the users; sometimes the users themselves don't even know what they want. The Systems Analyst must be able to produce the output definition and logic design through numerous conversations with the users.

Some companies reward years of excellent performance by promoting a Systems Analyst to *Senior Systems Analyst*. The Senior Systems Analyst often participates in higher-profile projects and works on many projects at once. Additionally, there may be managerial aspects to the position.

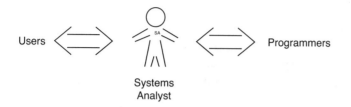

Users ⟨⟩ Systems Analyst ⟨⟩ Programmers

FIGURE 22.4
The Systems Analyst is the go-between for the users and the programmers.

NOTE

In smaller programming departments (or companies), one person might wear lots of hats, but that person's job title doesn't accurately reflect the range of jobs performed. For example, some companies have only two or three people in the entire software development or IT department. All of them might program and also perform systems analysis and design duties. Smaller companies give you the opportunity to perform a wider range of programming tasks, improve your skills, and gain an understanding of the responsibilities of lots of job titles. Larger companies, however, usually offer better benefits, pay, and job security, but it will take you longer to broaden your skills.

Internet and Network-Related Jobs

The online world has created its own set of job positions, many of which overlap those you've read about in this hour. "Programmers" for web development agencies, companies that produce web applications, and even mobile application developers might make a distinction between "front end" and "back end" programming, specializing in one or the other. You might also hear the term "full stack" developer, which indicates that a company is hiring programmers who have skills and ability to program both the user (UI) of a software application as well as the underlying logic and systems interactions. You may see the same Junior/Senior distinction in job titles that you do with traditional programmers, or you may see the distinction only in the specialization, such as *Front End* or *UI Developer, Back End Developer, Mobile Developer,* and so on.

The huge collection of networked computers generates its own set of jobs as well. You will see jobs with titles such as LAN Designer and WAN Specialist as well as managers of these positions and technologies, including security officers who patrol the network for unauthorized access. *LAN* is an acronym for *Local Area Network,* a network that links two or more computers located in the same area, floor, or building, usually by direct wiring or wireless technology. *WAN* is an acronym for *Wide Area Network,* which is a network that spans more territory than the usual one-building network.

Demand plays a big role in the pay scales and corporate level of all computer-related jobs. For example, in the last half of the 1990s when the Internet was still gaining popularity and use by leaps and bounds, people with Internet-related skills received a bonus that boosted their pay levels higher than they would have traditionally earned based on seniority. This was due to the demand for workers with those types of skills. While there is still a demand for workers in the programming and technology fields in general, to some extent, salaries have leveled because there is now a different baseline for technological competency in a position. That is to say, basic familiarity with computer technology is no longer a differentiating factor between applicants.

The higher salaries offered in the computer field can be a mixed blessing. When you've been in data processing for a few years, your salary becomes much higher than that of others who have been with other departments for the same amount of time. A person who becomes a Systems Analyst and then decides that computers are no longer a challenge often finds it difficult to move to another position within that company. Companies rarely let people move to a position that requires a pay cut; such employees soon miss the money they were used to, and they start looking elsewhere for a job.

Often, upward moves for computing professionals include a move into management. One of the first management-level job titles is that of *Team Lead* or *Supervisor*. Leads and Supervisors manage a small group of programmers and analysts, directing projects from a management point of view (making sure their people have adequate resources to do their jobs, are properly evaluated for raises, and so forth). Companies normally prefer their Leads and Supervisors to have experience similar to those they are managing, which is why many managers are promoted from within.

From a supervisory position, you might next move into a position with *Director* in its title, and be responsible for several Supervisors and their projects. The Director may be even in rank with the Vice Presidents in other departments of the firm.

Structured Walkthroughs

Once you have a job as a programmer in a corporate environment, you should soon learn the norms adhered to by your colleagues. These norms and standards within the company are most often in focus during a walkthrough, which you may participate in on a regular basis. A structured walkthrough is a review of a newly written program by some of the programming staff.

A programmer may generally follow these steps after completing a programming task:

1. The programmer tests the program at her desk and tries to get as many bugs out as possible.

2. The programmer passes the program on to the user for testing (often, parallel tests are performed).

3. The user puts the program into use.

Now that you are more familiar with the roles of the programming staff, you might be interested to know about an extra step that often takes place between steps 1 and 2. When the programmer is satisfied that the program is as accurate as possible, he prepares for a structured walkthrough.

In the structured walkthrough, several other Programmers and Systems Analysts get together with the source code of the program, with the Programmer in the room, and they pick apart the program in detail, trying to find errors, weak spots, broken standards, and poor documentation. Along the way, they make suggestions on how to improve the code. You might also find this process is called a code review in some companies, and may occur frequently (even daily).

NOTE

A structured walkthrough often produces what is known in the industry as *egoless programmers*. Programmers are often known for their egos; a good structured walkthrough often shows that a program is not as well written as the original programmer might have first thought.

The structured walkthrough is not an attempt to point fingers. Its only purpose is to produce the best code possible. The other programmers are not going to be critical of the programmer personally; after all, they are going to be at the center of a future structured walkthrough themselves.

After a programmer implements many of the suggestions from the structured walkthrough, the programmer usually finds that he agrees that the program is better written than it was originally. After many such walkthroughs, the programmer develops better programming skills and the company acquires better programs.

Putting a Program into Production

Figure 22.5 shows one version of the steps needed to get a program into use by the user. When the user is finally convinced that the program works as well as originally asked for, and the user is convinced that the parallel testing went smoothly, the program is then moved into production.

When a program moves into production, it is considered complete. The user begins to use the program in a working, non-test environment. The program's results are considered reliable within reason. (Over time, a program's reliability improves as it is used and continues to work well.)

Being in production hardly implies that the program needs no changing and updating over the years. Nevertheless, a production program is one that is considered fixed and usable until a user makes a request to update the program or scrap it for a completely new one. If changes are made to a program that is in production, the Systems Analyst may go back to user interviews and determine what the user wants. The entire systems analysis and design stage is then repeated for the revised program.

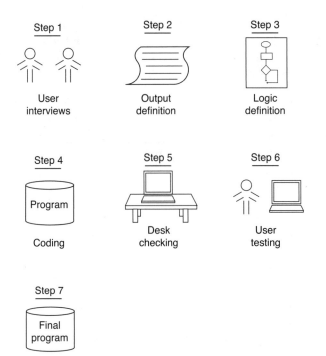

Step 1
User
interviews

Step 2
Output
definition

Step 3
Logic
definition

Step 4
Program
Coding

Step 5
Desk
checking

Step 6
User
testing

Step 7
Final
program
Move program
into production

FIGURE 22.5
Common steps for designing, writing, and installing programs.

Depending on the extent of the changes, a program's revision might take more or less development time that its ancestor program took to write. As you have read throughout this entire book, the maintenance of programs is critical in our ever-changing world. If you write your code better, by supplying more documentation and closely following your company's programming standards, then you will have a better chance at locking in your career in the computer field.

"I Want Job Security!"

Job security is an overused term. Often, you hear programmers jokingly talk about the cryptic code they write so that "only they will be able to understand it." Modern programmers are only too aware of the fact that the better employers seek programmers who write clear, clean code, are more concerned with proper programming, and follow as many of the company's programming standards as possible.

Some people can write programs very quickly, but the spaghetti code they produce is unreadable for future maintenance. Don't fall into the trap of thinking that speed is more important than clear programs.

Some systems don't enable programmers to change a program once the system is instructed to treat that source program as a production program. Programmers are able to make copies of the program's source code, but the program is read-only and cannot be changed. If an update has to be made, the programmer copies the source code and makes changes to the copy. After the updates are made and the new version is ready for production, the production records are changed to reflect the new source code. From that point, the production system treats the new version of the code as the production version, but the original remains in place as a backup.

This tight control over production source code enables a company to ensure that it always has an unmodified copy of every program used by every user in the company. Without such control, a programmer could write a program, compile and test it, and install it on the user's system. When installed, the programmer might inadvertently change the program. Because it is virtually impossible to reproduce source code from compiled code, the data processing department would have no way to generate the original source code if the users wanted a change made to the program they are using.

Consulting

Many programmers, systems analysts, and other IT professionals find enriching lives as computer consultants. Too many businesses and individuals buy a computer system or software package thinking all their problems will be solved, and they don't realize the amount of training that is often needed to use the computer effectively. There has been a growing niche for computer consultants over the last several years, and you might find success as a consultant yourself.

As a consultant, you can be a hero or a heroine to your clients. So many times, computer consultants rush to help someone with a problem getting a report completed, only to find that the client is inserting a disk upside-down or forgetting to press the online button on the printer. The computer is still a mystery to a vast number of people.

As a consultant, you can take on as much or as little work as you want. Many programmers moonlight as consultants, sometimes finding that their consulting business grows enough to do it full time. They might give up the benefits that a company can provide, but they like having full say over what they do.

Getting started as a consultant takes little more than word-of-mouth coverage. Offer to help your accountant, attorney, or anyone you know who uses a computer or needs a website with a little interactivity. Tell them that you'd like to start doing some consulting and that you'd be glad to give them an hour or two free of charge just to see how they like the work (and how you like the work). Often, these initial free calls turn into a long-term proposition that is good for both you and your clients.

Summary

You now have an understanding of some common types of computer departments and the people in them. There are many jobs in the computer industry, both for entry-level and advanced programmers and analysts. A computer job is a fun, well-respected, and needed occupation; you'll be glad you're a part of the computer industry.

Understanding the job levels and job promotions can be confusing, especially because many companies follow a unique promotion and title scheme. Nevertheless, the general order of jobs that a programmer follows from the beginning to the end of her career is similar across many companies. The online and networking worlds have increased the nature of jobs and improved demand to further complicate the industry and make the roles of programmers even more interesting.

Q&A

Q. Can I get a programming job without a college degree?

A. Many people will argue that one does not need a college degree to be a good programmer and a solid employee, as many programmers are in fact self-taught in their areas of expertise. However, it is often difficult to get through Human Resources screening without a college degree on your resume, regardless of what that degree is in. For example, you might find many holders of liberal arts degrees among a company's programmer ranks—it wasn't their degree that got them the job (or even their skillset), but it did get them in the door. Focus on honing your skills and producing programs that people can see and use when evaluating your candidacy for employment. Some companies, especially small companies and startups, are often more willing to look at programmers with nontraditional backgrounds who nevertheless have produced good work.

Workshop

The quiz questions and exercises are provided for your further understanding.

Quiz

1. What does MIS stand for?

2. Who do the data processing or IT department's programmers write programs for?

3. True or false: Computer programmers may find they have the luxury of flexible working hours and telecommute options.

4. What is one downside of a four-year college degree in a computing field?

5. What does a junior programmer typically do?

6. What does a systems analyst do?

7. What is a structured walkthrough?

8. How can computer-programming personnel ensure job security?

9. What is a contract programmer?

10. Is management always the next step for a senior programmer?

Answers

1. Management Information Systems

2. Any department in the company which requests (and potentially pays for) their assistance.

3. True

4. What you learn during the course of your degree may be obsolete by the time you begin working in the "real world."

5. Junior programmers often work only on code produced by others, and doing routine maintenance tasks.

6. A systems analyst acts as a go-between for users and programmers, and often designs the rules around the input, output, and logical features of programs.

7. A structured walkthrough, or code review, is a collaborative session to review a program for potential issues.

8. Follow good coding practices and internal coding guidelines, and always keep enhancing skills by learning on your own.

9. A contract programmer is one who is hired on a temporary basis to perform specific tasks over a period of time, often paid more to make up for the lack of benefits.

10. No. Some programmers do not see management as a step "up," but rather a completely different step altogether that holds no interest for them. Some senior programmers may become analysts, but that is also a lateral move.

Distributing Applications

After you write a program, test it, and debug it, you must get your program into the hands of those who will use it. If you are developing software for Windows, Mac, Linux/UNIX, mobile devices, or just deploying web applications, you'll have different processes and procedures for doing so from both a technical and commercial perspective.

This hour introduces you to some of the issues associated with software distribution. You want to be sure that your users have an easy time installing or accessing the programs you write. In addition, those programs have to work after they are installed.

The highlights of this hour include

- ▶ Learning why installation issues can be complex
- ▶ Using build tools to simplify the creation of installation routines
- ▶ Understanding why compiling the application is so critical to proper installation
- ▶ Using version control
- ▶ Distributing open-source software

Issues Surrounding Software Distribution

One of the easier aspects of software distribution is finding an outlet to sell the product. More computer-related online stores are open than ever before, and even discount stores and warehouse chains carry some commercial software products, since software has become a staple item in the daily lives of many people. All the time, software companies are looking for new titles to distribute and new programmers to write the code, and the business of computers today gives you many avenues in which to market your product.

Of course, you don't have to charge money for your software program. You could distribute freeware or shareware software via download links on your own website or on websites that aggregate such software for distribution rather than sale. *Freeware* is typically closed-source software that is distributed without a cost to the consumer, while *shareware* is also typically closed-source software distributed without a cost to the consumer, but is available only for a trial period or other limited basis. Additionally, you could also distribute open-source software, which may or may not be free (it typically is) but definitely provides all the source code so that it can be modified by the consumer.

Just because you wrote a program that works on your computer with your software settings certainly does not mean that the program will work on others' computers. For happy users, you must make sure that the program installs on the user's computer and that the program will run after it's installed. You may choose to provide cross-platform versions of software, only provide software for one operating system such as Windows or Mac, or some other option in between.

Application Compilation and Packaging

The process for compiling and packing applications for distribution depends entirely on the target installation platform. That is to say, compiling applications for Windows requires one set of tools, while compiling applications for Mac, Linux, mobile devices, or web applications require completely different tools. Additionally, the language that you develop in will require different tools for different platforms; that is to say, if you develop Java applications to distribute to Windows users, you will use a different set of tools than if you are developing Ruby applications to deploy to a web server. Because each combination provides a range of options, this section will describe the process in an abstract way.

All the resource files (source code, libraries, graphics, and so on) for your application will be maintained in a project or code repository with version control applied to it (you'll learn more about version control later in this hour). In addition to developing the source code that makes up the core of the program you are developing, you will likely also include an *installation script* that controls the full installation process initiated by the user (if it is a distributed application) or you (if you are deploying to a web server, for example).

In many instances of distributing applications, you will be distributing the compiled version of the source code; compiled code means you are creating a single executable file that, when run, extracts and installs individual files. Using Windows as an example, you probably have run into setup files with an .exe file extension—these are compiled executable files. In these files, all the related Windows application modules and forms work together to form this executable file.

NOTE

A compiled application is more secure than a distributed-source project. If you distribute the source code (the project and its related files), anyone with skills in the language can modify your work (which might be what you want in an open-source project, but not in a closed-source project). However, most people won't be able to do anything with the source code, and therefore, a compiled file is not only secure, but it is also necessary so that all can use your application.

CAUTION

Before you finish compiling your application for distribution, make sure that you've debugged the application as much as is feasible to eliminate as many bugs as possible.

Once you have a compiled a project for your platform of choice (or all the platforms), you can begin the manufacturing process if you wish to distribute it on CD-ROM, or you can place it online for sale or free distribution through one of the many software "stores" such as download.com.

Mobile Application Distribution

The process for distributing mobile applications is slightly different than for desktop applications, as typically software distribution goes through the specific store for the mobile operating system. For example, if you develop an application for iOS, that application is distributed through the Apple's App Store; if you develop an Android application, it is distributed through Google Play. The same concept holds true for developers of BlackBerry and Windows Phone applications, which go through BlackBerry World and Windows Phone Store, respectively, and the list goes on.

While it is not required that developers distribute applications through the respective stores, users *expect* to find new and updated applications for their devices in the stores for those devices, so it is in the developer's best interest to participate in the platform-specific programs. Each of these developer programs (one for iOS, one for Android, and so on) typically charge an annual fee for participation and provide access to additional documentation and development toolkits that are not otherwise available to the public. Each store also maintains guidelines for inclusion and reviews submissions to ensure that applications are not full of viruses or (in some cases) potentially objectionable content.

Distributing Open-Source Software

You might decide that you want to create and distribute applications under one of several different open-source licenses. These licenses allow for the entire source code, and not just a compiled executable file, to be shared under specific terms, including terms that limit reuse and what is to be done with modifications to the software. Open-source software is often free to consumers, but some developers will sell additional versions (such as customized compiled binaries) or support contracts to consumers in lieu of specifically charging money for the software itself.

One of the most important factors when distributing open-source software is determining which license to use. Some developers are concerned primarily with maintaining ownership in the case of patents, others want to ensure that any external modifications in the source code are shared with others, and some developers are not concerned with either (or any) of these issues. There are at least 10 different variations of open-source licenses in use today; you can learn more about licenses and how to choose one at the informative website choosealicense.com.

Using Version Control

During the course of your development, you will likely use version control to maintain your source code and other application resources. Although there are several different version control systems available for use—some free and open source and some proprietary—two of the most popular systems are Subversion (http://subversion.apache.org) and Git (http://git-scm.com). If you have a web hosting service that enables you to install Subversion, you can create your own repository and use a Subversion client to connect to it.

But an increasingly popular tool is Git, which is a decentralized approach to version control and also offers numerous tools and hosting options for users who want to get started with a repository but don't necessarily want/need/understand all the extra installation and maintenance overhead that goes with it. One such hosting option for Git repositories is GitHub (http://github.org), which allows users to create accounts and store and maintain as many code repositories for free as they would like (as long as they are open source), while also providing paid solutions for users who would like to maintain private code repositories.

Git and GitHub come highly recommended for users new to version control because of their relative ease of use and free, cross-platform tools for use. The GitHub Help site would be a great place to start: http://help.github.com/. An added benefit of the already-free GitHub account is the ability to use Gist (http://gist.github.com), which is a way to share code snippets (or whole pages) with others, while these snippets themselves are git repositories and thus versioned and forkable in their own right. GitHub repositories, including Gists, are both excellent ways to get started with version control of your work.

Summary

This hour's lesson provided a high-level overview of the process that developers go through to bundle and distribute applications to end users. You were also introduced to the nuances of mobile application distribution, as well as considerations for distributing your source code under an open-source license.

Q&A

Q. Using version control seems like a lot of overhead for a simple set of scripts I want to distribute for free. Do I have to use it?

A. No one requires developers to use version control or other backup systems, but it's a rare person who hasn't experienced some data loss or computer crash. Within a corporate environment, the loss of any work such that it would need to be recreated from scratch is equivalent to spending money twice, hence, the guidelines for maintaining work in a version control system.

Workshop

The quiz questions are provided for your further understanding.

Quiz

1. What is freeware?

2. What is the difference between freeware and shareware?

3. Why are compiled programs more secure than distributing the source code?

4. What is an installation script?

5. What filename extension do compiled Windows programs use?

6. Where do users of mobile devices primarily look for software applications to install?

7. What is one of the most important decisions to make when distributing open-source software?

8. What are two popular version control systems?

9. True or false: If you create an installation package for Windows users, Linux users can also double-click that .exe file and install your program.

10. True or false: You can bypass all stores, avoid manufacturing CD-ROMs and printed manuals, and simply put an executable installation file on your website for people to download for free.

Answers

1. Freeware is closed-source software that is distributed without a cost to the consumer.

2. Shareware is typically available only on a limited basis (for example, 30 days).

3. If you distribute the source code, anyone with skills in the language can modify your work. This works for an open-source project, but could have terrible financial consequences if your product is supposed to be closed-source.

4. A script that controls the full installation process necessary for the user.

5. An .exe extension.

6. In the operating system-specific store for their device, such as the App Store for iOS and Google Play for Android.

7. Which of the many open-source licenses to choose for your work.

8. Subversion and Git.

9. False.

10. True. There's nothing stopping you from doing this, but would a user trust you? For all they know, your file contains a horrible virus, so you would have marketing barriers to overcome before you began to earn revenue.

HOUR 24
The Future of Programming

What's in store for you as a programmer? One thing is certain and that's *change*. Change occurs rapidly in computing. The face of programming has dramatically changed since computers were first invented, and the rate of change is increasing. Today's programming tools were not even dreamed of 10 years ago, and now it seems that every day a new programming language, framework, database system, or utility pops up to help us innovate even more.

This final hour in Part V, "The Business of Programming," introduces you to some tools available to help you become a better programmer. More important than the tools, however, is understanding and maintaining a proper coding that is easily maintained by you and your future colleagues.

The highlights of this hour include

- ▶ Improving your programs with the proper tools
- ▶ Profiling for improving your program's efficiency
- ▶ Keeping efficiency and retaining maintainability
- ▶ Finding other resources available to improve your programming skills

Some Helpful Tools

As you develop more programming skills and work with more programming language environments, you will run across tools that you will want to add to your bag of coding tricks. The following sections briefly describe tools that you might run across as a programmer that you'll want to look into.

Profilers

Available for many different programming languages, a profiler analyzes parts of your program and determines exactly which parts are sluggish. It is thought that 90% of a program's execution time is spent in less than 10% of the code. Of course, this rule of thumb is probably not scientifically provable but its concept is understandable.

Perhaps a sorting algorithm is inefficient and needs looking into to speed it up. Perhaps you are performing a sequential search when a binary search might be faster. Perhaps a calculation is inefficient and you can combine operations to make the program compute results more quickly. A profiler can analyze the execution of your program and tell you where the time is being spent during the execution.

CAUTION

Speed and efficiency are great factors, but don't forsake proper programming techniques if doing so means eeking out a microsecond or two of machine time. Clear code should be paramount in your coding. Computers are getting faster, not slower, so you know that your program will never run *slower* than it runs today. Some scientific and financial calculations, for example, get extremely complex. To clarify your code, you could break such calculations into several statements, storing intermediate calculation results along the way. Although it might be more efficient and execute a few microseconds faster, if you combined all the calculations into one long expression, this expression would later be difficult to debug or change if a problem arises. Therefore, unless a system's speed is critical (as might be the case in some medical or space exploration programs), don't make your code too tricky to be maintained later.

Many of the major programming languages used both in large corporations and by smaller programming shops and web application development agencies have profilers available for them—Java, .NET, Python, and Ruby programs are all able to be profiled and improved through computerized review. With these tools, a balance can be met between efficient code and clear, maintainable code.

Resource Editors

A Windows programming language brings its own requirements to the table. Tools exist to help the Windows programmer that were not needed in the DOS environment and make no sense in the mainframe world.

One such tool is called a *resource editor*. A Windows resource is just about anything used in Windows. A resource might be an icon, a text string, a bitmap image, a menu, or a dialog box. As you work with programming languages, you will manipulate such resources.

Several ways exist for you to use resources in your Windows applications. You can, for example, designate an icon to use for the end user's installation of your application. The user can click that icon to start the application. You might want to create your own icon. A resource editor can help you create and edit icons and other Windows resources. Microsoft Visual Studio contains a resource editor, and there are several free and commercial programs that help you achieve the same goals (such as ResEdit, at www.resedit.net/).

Integrated Development Environments

You can think of *Integrated Development Environments*, or IDEs, as souped-up text editors that try to automate many common programming tasks. Within a unified graphical user interface (GUI), an IDE may offer a programmer a source code editor plus connections to a version control system, plus a build automation tools, plus debugging and code inspection tools. While a programmer may operate all of these types of tools independently, having installed several different applications to do so, one benefit of an IDE is that it simply allows the programmer to stay "in the flow" and not switch between applications to complete their tasks. Additionally, many IDEs have secondary features that are specific to the programmer's development language of choice. For example, if you are a PHP developer using an IDE that has been finely tuned for use with PHP, you may be able to take advantage of autocomplete functionality such that the IDE reduces your need to memorize specific built-in function names or even complete syntax.

IDEs are not new technology, and as such, have been refined over many years of use. A common design paradigm for IDEs is to have a strong base feature set but allow for developers to add custom functionality through the use of add-ons or plugins. Eclipse (www.eclipse.org/) is one such popular IDE that provides the programmer with hundreds of plugins that enhance functionality, from changing the GUI theme to integrating automated diagramming functionality, and a lot in between. Eclipse is a free and open-source IDE, as are many others; Microsoft Visual Studio is an example of a feature-rich commercial IDE. You can find a good list of IDEs and their feature sets at http://en.wikipedia.org/wiki/Comparison_of_integrated_development_environments.

Automated Testing

While software quality assurance (QA) testing is not a new concept, the handling of many types of tests through automated means has been on the rise in the last several years. This shift is due in some part to the availability of better tools for the programmer, and in another part to a shift in attitude toward a development process known as *test-driven development*. In test-driven development, the developer examines the use cases and requirements for a feature, and then writes the tests before actually writing any code. Code is then written until the automated tests pass, and the tests and the code both go through continual refinement throughout the development process.

Even if your programming group does not practice test-driven development, automated testing has a place in your work. There are automated testing frameworks and tools for many programming languages, such as Cucumber (http://cucumber.info) for Ruby and Selenium (http://seleniumhq.org/) for front-end testing of web applications, among many others. Once you begin to automate tests, you will likely find that your programs become more reliable and your process more efficient overall—after all, it is easier to fix something that is constantly being monitored than to have to continually (and manually) search through incrementally larger applications to find needle-in-a-haystack bugs.

Automated testing is *not* a replacement for a manual QA process or user acceptance testing—it is always important to have actual human eyes on programs and interfaces especially when the target user of these programs and interfaces is a human and not a machine. I have personally experienced web applications in which code has significant test coverage and all of these automated tests pass, but the application itself is completely unusable. Don't be that developer!

Continuous Integration and Deployment

Automated testing often goes hand in hand with the continuous integration and deployment of applications. *Continuous integration* (CI) is a process by which work by multiple developers is merged together as it is completed—or checked in to the code repository—and the automated tests are run at that time to detect any errors in the merged code. The idea here is that if multiple developers are working on different parts of an application at the same time, these different parts have dependencies on each other or are in some way affected by each other such that if changes in one part break functionality in another part, it's much more efficient to detect these issues and fix them sooner rather than later. When using CI, a little up-front effort in writing tests and often checking code into the repository saves development teams a lot of effort later in the process as there is less code to weed through to look for errors.

There are many CI systems available to developers, again ranging from free and open-source to proprietary and commercial. Some popular free and open-source CI software includes Jenkins (http://jenkins-ci.org/) and Travis (https://travis-ci.org/), while Microsoft Team Foundation Server is an example of a proprietary solution.

A natural extension of CI is continuous deployment (or continuous delivery), in which tools assist developers in performing the next logical steps after a codebase has been verified and all tests pass: the packaging and release of the software into a staging environment for manual testing, or into a final production environment for all to use.

Will Programming Go Away?

In the mid-1970s, *Management Information Systems* (*MIS*) were going to be the answer to all computing needs. Each company would have MIS in place and all data needed by the company would be at each computer user's fingertips. That kind of data filtering was to be so vast and efficient that ordinary and more specific programs would not be needed. Obviously, the promise of MIS was not only over-predicted, but also never materialized.

For some time in the last few decades, people have predicted the demise of programmers. However, as those predictions get older and more numerous, the demand for programmers has grown tremendously. The need for programming is increasing at a rapid pace, and at last count in North America, there were four job openings for every developer—the need is still there, and programmers haven't yet developed the tools that will replace their own jobs.

CASE Tools

In the late 1980s, *CASE (Computer-Aided Software Engineering)* was going to replace programmers. Instead of having coders who knew one or more programming languages, programming teams would master CASE tools. CASE is like a program generator, only instead of helping programmers write programs, CASE tools help the DP staff create programs starting at the initial design level. A Systems Analyst can use CASE from the inception of a program request to the program's movement into production.

CASE is a massive program on the computer that the Systems Analyst can use for the initial output design, data definitions, logic definition (some CASE programs even draw flowcharts from a flowchart description entered by the Systems Analyst), and program generation. CASE often produces code based on the Analyst's logic definition, but heavy programmer intervention is needed to implement any but the most general of programs and to ensure the project's overall success.

CASE's proponents promised that it would revolutionize the programming environment and decrease the time and resources needed to produce a finished program. (Most of the newer programming advances promote quicker development time and easier maintenance as their primary goals.) The promise of CASE, however, never materialized. Although CASE has achieved some success, it has yet to produce the advances in software development that were originally hoped.

NOTE

The CASE products of the 1980s were not bad tools. The problems that resulted from them were due to the fact that CASE helped Systems Analysts and programmers do faster what the Systems Analysts and programmers already did incorrectly. Pre–object-oriented programming (OOP) methods suffer from difficult maintenance and documentation problems that OOP does not introduce. CASE could not eliminate the inherent problems that non-OOP programming contains. (OOP has its own set of problems as well, however, but it is viewed as an improvement over other traditional methods.)

TIP

Think of CASE as a program that helps you and others design and write programs. CASE is good for handling the minute details throughout the system's development, so you and the other programmers and Systems Analysts can work on implementing all the user's requests.

In recent years, programmer's tools have certainly become sophisticated, as you've seen throughout this entire 24-hour tutorial. The reason that programmers are needed more than ever is that computer technology keeps changing along with the programming tools. The early PCs brought new challenges to programs because of their lack of speed and their high demand. As PCs got faster, people networked them together and to mainframes, so distributed client/server programs were needed. Windows required much more effort to program than the simpler, text-based DOS mode. The Internet brought a new set of requirements for programmers that was not dreamed of before.

As you can see, programming demand keeps increasing because the nature of computing keeps changing and becoming more complex. That's the trend that will probably continue for years to come. Programming language developers are recognizing that new tools are needed not to replace programmers but to help them perform their ever-complex jobs.

UML: Data Modeling

UML, or the *Unified Modeling Language*, provides a uniform definition of modeling a program. Therefore, a company that models one program can share that model with companies that are writing similar programs. The models are not code but are definitions of the applications.

The UML is extremely useful, initially, for database designers and database application writers to share the components of each database and to transfer those components between computers. The concepts in the UML, however, are also being applied to program designs.

UML benefits the following five areas of computing:

1. **Reuse**—After a company completes a design, that design can be reused.

2. **Tool interoperability**—The UML design uses different programming and database sys-
tems. Therefore, a UNIX-based Java programmer will be able to use the same UML model as a Microsoft Visual Basic programmer.

3. **Team development**—The UML tools are usable in a team-programming environment.

4. **Data resource management**—Resources that appear along with the required data in the UML design are tracked along with the UML's objects.

5. **Dependency tracking**—If files are required by other files in the design, the UML keeps track of those dependents.

As with the other design tools of the past, the UML will not replace programming, but should enhance programming and enable the design of a system to be used with other systems to improve programmer productivity.

Your Ongoing Training Needs

Only if you keep up with industry changes can you help ensure that computer problems do not occur in the future. Programmers continually hone their skills to keep up with the changing technology in languages, operating systems, software, and hardware. As you learn more about programming, you should consider sharing your knowledge with others through training, consulting, writing, mentoring, or contributing to open-source projects. You will likely find that your own programming skills improve the more you practice and collaborate.

The need for training is never as apparent as it is in virtually every programming department in the world. Programmers are often called to offer a training class for others who do not possess some needed skills. In-house training enables a company to keep a cap on its training costs and control the material being covered.

Your own computer training does not stop. The computer industry changes rapidly. The skills you have today can be obsolete in five years, so part of your job is to continue your own training. It is incumbent upon you to stay up with current trends if you want to secure your computer position in the future.

Industry Standards

Not every new breakthrough in computer hardware and software becomes an industry standard. You do not have to be on the *bleeding edge* of technology (a pun describing very new and unproved technology), learning everything there is to learn. You do not even have to be on the *leading edge* of computer programming innovations. For instance, OOP is considered by most to be the best way to program, yet many computer programmers haven't learned how to program with objects. They might or might not have to master OOP depending on where their jobs take them and the language they must master in their companies. While it is a good idea to stay on top of the latest trends, it isn't necessary to learn them all because today's breakthrough might be tomorrow's flop (OOP is not a flop).

You will find your own niche in the computer field, and specialization is often the way to go, since it is so very difficult to master everything. However, there are plenty of developers who are quite successful as generalists—people who know quite a bit, if not at an expert level, about many different aspects of development. As you learn more about programming, you will find the area that best fits your own interests and you will master that area.

Try to read one good computer book or online tutorial every month or two. Every few months, research a new topic of computer programming to improve your skill levels. Most computer people find that self-study is not a job they balk at; the field of programming is exciting. It never gets old. The new innovations everywhere you look are always exciting and hold the promise of powerful computing power in the future.

Now that you have a more solid foundation than almost any other beginning programmer has ever had, you are ready to direct your education toward more specific goals. You should now begin tackling a programming language in depth. Mastering a programming language takes a while, and people learn at different rates. Nevertheless, the biggest problem budding programmers face is that they jump in too fast. After reading *Sams Teach Yourself Beginning Programming in 24 Hours*, you will not have that problem; you will be surprised at how well this book's concepts prepare you for your programming future, whether that future is just for fun or for a career.

NOTE

Computer books are known for their series approach. As you already know, the *Sams Teach Yourself in 24 Hours* series is designed to teach you the basics of a subject in as little time as possible. In addition to the highly successful *Sams Teach Yourself* series, you'll want to use the *Unleashed* books to master the advanced aspects of a programming language.

The following Sams Publishing titles are a sampling of some books that you might want to look at to improve your skills as a programmer. These books were specifically chosen to get you up to speed in a specific area of programming:

▶ *Sams Teach Yourself HTML and CSS in 24 Hours; Sams Teach Yourself Visual Basic .NET in 24 Hours; Sams Teach Yourself Java in 24 Hours; Sams Teach Yourself JavaScript in 24 Hours;* and *Sams Teach Yourself C++ in 24 Hours*—These books are the perfect next step from this book to take you more deeply into the language of your choice.

▶ *Sams Teach Yourself Java in 21 Days; Sams Teach Yourself Web Publishing with HTML and CSS in One Hour a Day;* and *Sams Teach Yourself C++ in One Hour a Day*—These books take you far into the languages to prepare you for your career or hobby.

TIP

To keep up with the latest in programming titles, regularly check out Sams Publishing's website at www.informit.com/sams.

Summary

Programming tools go far beyond just the languages themselves. Throughout this 24-hour tutorial, you've seen examples of languages and programming tools that help you be a better programmer. This hour showed you additional tools that programmers can use to become more efficient and productive programmers. The most important part of programming is writing clear and concise code so that others can maintain your programs when needed.

After you've mastered programming, what's next? Keep mastering! Continuing education is almost as vital in the field of computers as it is in the medical profession. The rapidly changing computer technologies require that programmers stay on top of current trends by reading books and magazines and taking courses when possible. Share your knowledge with others to help improve the programming community and reduce the backlog that the computer industry faces. Knowledge shared is knowledge improved.

Q&A

Q. Is it important to know multiple programming languages?

A. Depending on your job or the company you work for (or want to work for), knowledge of several different programming languages might be overkill—if you work for a large corporation that develops software products, everyone in the company might use the same programming language for all time. But if you want to move to a different company, you've already pigeonholed yourself as a developer only in that language. If that language falls out of popularity, you will find yourself competing for only a handful of available jobs. Therefore, it's important to stay familiar with the concepts within different programming languages—many of these concepts are the same, if not the specific syntax of the languages—so you can ramp up your knowledge as needed.

Workshop

The quiz questions are provided for your further understanding.

Quiz

1. How can a profiler improve program efficiency?

2. What is an IDE?

3. True or false: Automated testing goes hand in hand with CI and delivery processes.

4. Should programmers and other computer professionals continually update their skillsets to keep up with changes in the industry?

5. True or false: Automated tools are a good replacement for manual testing and review.

6. What does a resource editor do?

7. Are you a bad computer professional if you don't learn about every single bleeding edge technology that is invented?

8. True or false: The computer industry changes often so you must continually hone your skills to maintain your competence and stay in demand.

9. What is CASE?

10. What is UML?

Answers

1. A profiler locates inefficiencies in code.

2. An Integrated Development Environment brings together tools for completing common programming tasks into a unified GUI.

3. True

4. Absolutely.

5. False

6. A resource editor is a program that helps you create and keep track of Windows resources.

7. No. Many technologies have come and gone; focus on knowing concepts and general information and be selective about what you learn (unless you have infinite time and brainpower).

8. True

9. CASE is a complex design technology to help organizations design, build, test, and implement complete computer systems.

10. Unified Modeling Language provides a uniform definition of modeling a program.

Index

drawString() function, 215-217

drawString() method, 257

dynamic language runtime (DLR), .NET Framework, 378

E

EBCDIC, tables, 78

echo statement, 304

elements, arrays, 87

Ember.js, 288

empty strings, 64

encryption, 211

environment, IDEs (Integrated Development Environments), 415

errors. See bugs

escape sequences, Java, 222-223

events, mouse, capturing, 66-71

executable content, Java, 204-206

expires property (cookies), 191

extraction operators, 347

F

Facebook, 287

FCL (framework class library), .NET Framework, 377-378

fields, 42

Firefox, debugging tools, 120

first program, typing, 16-18

Float data type (PHP), 312

floating-point numbers, 82

floating-point variables, 225

flow control functions, PHP, 306-308

flowcharts, 51, 97, 133

for loop, 101-105, 234-235

    controlling, 105-107

    printing, 102-105

form data, processing, PHP, 328

format, Java statements, 230

Forte for Java, 217

FORTRAN programming language, 34

framework class library (FCL), .NET Framework, 377-378

frameworks, AJAX (Asynchronous JavaScript and XML), 288

functions

    ajaxRequest, 292

    ajaxResponse, 292

    C programming language, 338

        built-in, 339-343

        main(), 336

        printf(), 339-341

        scanf(), 341-343

        writing general program, 343-345

    case sensitivity, 322

    collecting into .js file, 140

    creating, 137-139

    drawString(), 215-217

    JavaScript code, packaging into, 137-139

    versus methods, 216

    optimizing, 165-169

    PHP, 320

        built-in, 320-321

        calling, 321

        declaring, 321-322

        defining, 321-323

        returning values from user-defined, 322-323

        variable scope, 323-324

    printBR(), 322

    user-defined, 321

        returning values from, 322-323

G

garbage collection, CLR (common language runtime), 377

Git, 410

GitHub, 410

global variables, 224

Gmail (Google), 287

goto statement, 133

graphical user interface (GUI)

    Java programs, 244-245

graphics. See images

GUI (graphical user interface)

    Java programs, 244-245

Gutmans, Andi, 301

H

<h> tag, 278

hiding data, 211

Hopper, Grace, 114

horizontal scrolling, websites, 437

Hörnell, Karl, 212

versus C++, 202

development of, 202

example program, 213-214

interface, 209-211

literals, 222-223

multi-platform executable content, 206-208

NetBeans, 217

OOP (object-oriented programming), 245-246, 248-249

operators, 227-230

seamless execution, 206

security issues, 211

standalone, 209-210

usage, 208-209

variables, 223-226

JavaScript, 10-13, 34, 285

writing code, 13

PHP, 34, 301, 329

requirements, 302-303

Visual Basic, 333, 359, 370-371

programs, 95. *See also* **applets (Java); applications; code**

branching, 133

comparing data with if statement, 95-98

controlling, 109-111

looping statements, 96-109

debugging, 126-129

designing, 39, 41-42

benefits, 39-40

bottom-up design, 48

defining output and data flows, 43-50

logic, 51-53

OOD (object-oriented design), 44

prototyping, 45-47

RAD (rapid application development), 47

top-down, 48-50

user-program agreements, 40-41

existing, 9

fields, 42

first, typing, 16-18

instructions, 25-34

JavaScript, 27-28

Java

case sensitivity, 214

running with NetBeans, 239-244

maintaining, 19

need for, 21-24

obtaining, 22

output, 42

obtaining keyboard data, 62-71

printing, 57-58

sorting data, 59-61

ownership, 10

parameters, 42

putting into production, 401-403

relational tests, writing, 96-100

saved instructions, 29-31

setting breakpoints, 127

software licenses, 10

source code, 12-13

tasks, 6

testing, 139-142

beta, 141

desk checking, 141

parallel, 141-142

ubiquity, 24-25

value, 9-10

writing, 119-120

prompt method, keyboard data, obtaining, 62-71

properties

cookies, 190-191

PHP objects, 326-327

Prototype JavaScript library, 288

prototyping, 45-47

pseudocode, 51-52, 133

public class, 215-216

purchasing programs, 22

Python, 378

Q-R

QA (quality assurance) testing, 415-416

RAD (rapid application development), 47

reading cookies, 192-193

relational operators, if statement, 99

relational tests, writing, 96-100

remarks. *See* **comments**

repeating news tickers, websites, adding to, 179-183

reserving space, arrays, 149-150

resize() method, 258

Resource data type (PHP), 312

informIT.com THE TRUSTED TECHNOLOGY LEARNING SOURCE

PEARSON

InformIT is a brand of Pearson and the online presence for the world's leading technology publishers. It's your source for reliable and qualified content and knowledge, providing access to the top brands, authors, and contributors from the tech community.

Addison-Wesley   **Cisco Press**   EXAM/**CRAM**   **IBM** Press.   QUE   **PRENTICE HALL**   **SAMS** | Safari Books Online

LearnIT at InformIT

Looking for a book, eBook, or training video on a new technology? Seeking timely and relevant information and tutorials? Looking for expert opinions, advice, and tips? **InformIT has the solution.**

- Learn about new releases and special promotions by subscribing to a wide variety of newsletters.
Visit **informit.com/newsletters**.

- Access FREE podcasts from experts at **informit.com/podcasts**.

- Read the latest author articles and sample chapters at **informit.com/articles**.

- Access thousands of books and videos in the Safari Books Online digital library at **safari.informit.com**.

- Get tips from expert blogs at **informit.com/blogs**

Visit **informit.com/learn** to discover all the ways you can access the hottest technology content.

Are You Part of the IT Crowd?

Connect with Pearson authors and editors via RSS feeds, Facebook, Twitter, YouTube, and more! Visit **informit.com/socialconnect**.

informIT.com THE TRUSTED TECHNOLOGY LEARNING SOURCE   PEARSON

Addison-Wesley   **Cisco Press**   EXAM/**CRAM**   **IBM** Press.   QUE   **PRENTICE HALL**   **SAMS** | Safari Books Online

THIRD EDITION
Learn computer programming in just 24 one-hour lessons

Greg Perry
Dean Miller

Sams **Teach Yourself**

Beginning Programming

in **24 Hours**

SAMS

Safari
Books Online

FREE
Online Edition

Your purchase of *Sams Teach Yourself Beginning Programming in 24 Hours* includes access to a free online edition for 45 days through the **Safari Books Online** subscription service. Nearly every Sams book is available online through **Safari Books Online**, along with thousands of books and videos from publishers such as Addison-Wesley Professional, Cisco Press, Exam Cram, IBM Press, O'Reilly Media, Prentice Hall, Que, and VMware Press.

Safari Books Online is a digital library providing searchable, on-demand access to thousands of technology, digital media, and professional development books and videos from leading publishers. With one monthly or yearly subscription price, you get unlimited access to learning tools and information on topics including mobile app and software development, tips and tricks on using your favorite gadgets, networking, project management, graphic design, and much more.

Activate your FREE Online Edition at
informit.com/safarifree

STEP 1:   Enter the coupon code: ALKQXAA.

STEP 2:   New Safari users, complete the brief registration form.
Safari subscribers, just log in.

If you have difficulty registering on Safari or accessing the online edition,
please e-mail customer-service@safaribooksonline.com

Addison Wesley   AdobePress   ALPHA   Cisco Press   FT Press   IBM Press   Microsoft Press   New Riders   O'REILLY

Peachpit Press   PRENTICE HALL   QUE   Redbooks   SAMS   SAS Publishing   vmware PRESS   WILEY   wrox